Secrets

of

Heaven

SECRETS

OF

HEAVEN

The Portable New Century Edition

EMANUEL SWEDENBORG

Volume 6

Translated from the Latin by Lisa Hyatt Cooper

SWEDENBORG FOUNDATION
West Chester, Pennsylvania

Originally published in Latin as *Arcana Coelestia*, London, 1749–1756. The volume contents of this and the original Latin edition, along with ISBNs of the annotated version, are as follows:

Volume number in this edition	Text treated	Volume number in the Latin first edition	Section numbers	ISBN (hardcover)
1	Genesis 1–8	1	§§1–946	978-0-87785-486-9
2	Genesis 9–15	1	§§947–1885	978-0-87785-487-6
3	Genesis 16–21	2 (in 6 fascicles)	§§1886–2759	978-0-87785-488-3
4	Genesis 22–26	3	§§2760–3485	978-0-87785-489-0
5	Genesis 27–30	3	§§3486–4055	978-0-87785-490-6
6	Genesis 31–35	4	§§4056–4634	978-0-87785-491-3
7	Genesis 36–40	4	§§4635–5190	978-0-87785-492-0
8	Genesis 41–44	5	§§5191–5866	978-0-87785-493-7
9	Genesis 45–50	5	§§5867–6626	978-0-87785-494-4
10	Exodus 1–8	6	§§6627–7487	978-0-87785-495-1
11	Exodus 9–15	6	§§7488–8386	978-0-87785-496-8
12	Exodus 16–21	7	§§8387–9111	978-0-87785-497-5
13	Exodus 22–24	7	§§9112–9442	978-0-87785-498-2
14	Exodus 25–29	8	§§9443–10166	978-0-87785-499-9
15	Exodus 30–40	8	§§10167–10837	978-0-87785-500-2

ISBN of e-book of library edition, vol. 6: 978-0-87785-731-0
ISBN of Portable Edition, vol. 6, containing translation only: 978-0-87785-422-7
ISBN of e-book of Portable Edition, vol. 6: 978-0-87785-728-0

(The ISBN in the Library of Congress data shown below is that of volume 1.)

Library of Congress Cataloging-in-Publication Data

Swedenborg, Emanuel, 1688–1772.
    [Arcana coelestia. English]
    Secrets of heaven / Emanuel Swedenborg ; translated from the Latin by
Lisa Hyatt Cooper. — Portable New Century ed.
    p. cm.
    Includes bibliographical references and indexes.
    ISBN 978-0-87785-408-1 (alk. paper)
    1. New Jerusalem Church—Doctrines. 2. Bible. O.T. Genesis—Commentaries—Early works to 1800. 3. Bible. O.T. Exodus—Commentaries—Early works to 1800. I. Title.
    BX8712.A8 2010
    230'.94—dc22

    2009054171

Ornaments from the first Latin edition, 1749–1756
Text designed by Joanna V. Hill
Senior copy editor, Alicia L. Dole
Typesetting by Mary M. Wachsmann and Sarah Dole
Cover design by Karen Connor
Cover photograph by Magda Indigo

For information about the New Century Edition of the Works of Emanuel Swedenborg, contact the Swedenborg Foundation, 320 North Church Street, West Chester, PA 19380 U.S.A.
Telephone: (610) 430-3222 • Web: www.swedenborg.com • E-mail: info@swedenborg.com

Contents

Genesis Chapter 34

Genesis Chapter 35

Conventions Used in This Work

MOST of the following conventions apply generally to the transla-
tions in the New Century Edition Portable series. For introductory
material on the content and history of *Secrets of Heaven*, and for annotations on the subject matter, including obscure or problematic content,
and extensive indexes, the reader is referred to the Deluxe New Century
Edition volumes.

Volume designation *Secrets of Heaven* was originally published in eight
volumes; in this edition all but the second original volume have been
divided into two. Thus Swedenborg's eight volumes now fill fifteen volumes, of which this is the sixth. It corresponds to approximately the first
half of Swedenborg's volume 4.

Section numbers Following a practice common in his time, Swedenborg
divided his published theological works into sections numbered in sequence
from beginning to end. His original section numbers have been preserved
in this edition; they appear in boxes in the outside margins. Traditionally,
these sections have been referred to as "numbers" and designated by the
abbreviation "n." In this edition, however, the more common section symbol (§) is used to designate the section numbers, and the sections are referred
to as such.

Subsection numbers Because many sections throughout Swedenborg's
works are too long for precise cross-referencing, Swedenborgian scholar
John Faulkner Potts (1838–1923) further divided them into subsections;
these have since become standard, though minor variations occur from
one edition to another. These subsections are indicated by bracketed numbers that appear in the text itself: [2], [3], and so on. Because the beginning of the first *subsection* always coincides with the beginning of the
section proper, it is not labeled in the text.

Citations of Swedenborg's text As is common in Swedenborgian studies, text citations of Swedenborg's works refer not to page numbers but to
section numbers, which unlike page numbers are uniform in most edi-
tions. In citations the section symbol (§) is generally omitted after the title
of a work by Swedenborg. Thus "*Secrets of Heaven* 29" refers to section 29
(§29) of Swedenborg's *Secrets of Heaven*, not to page 29 of any edition.

Subsection numbers are given after a colon; a reference such as "29:2" indicates subsection 2 of section 29. The reference "29:1" would indicate the first subsection of section 29, though that subsection is not in fact labeled in the text. Where section numbers stand alone without titles, their function is indicated by the prefixed section symbol; for example, "§29:2".

Citations of the Bible Biblical citations in this edition follow the accepted standard: a semicolon is used between book references and between chapter references, and a comma between verse references. Therefore "Matthew 5:11, 12; 6:1; 10:41, 42; Luke 6:23, 35" would refer to Matthew chapter 5, verses 11 and 12; Matthew chapter 6, verse 1; Matthew chapter 10, verses 41 and 42; and Luke chapter 6, verses 23 and 35. Swedenborg often incorporated the numbers of verses not actually represented in his text when listing verse numbers for a passage he quoted; these apparently constitute a kind of "see also" reference to other material he felt was relevant. This edition includes these extra verses and also follows Swedenborg where he cites contiguous verses individually (for example, John 14:8, 9, 10, 11), rather than as a range (John 14:8–11). Occasionally this edition supplies a full, conventional Bible reference where Swedenborg omits one after a quotation.

Quotations in Swedenborg's works Some features of the original Latin text of *Secrets of Heaven* have been modernized in this edition. For example, Swedenborg's first edition generally relies on context or italics rather than on quotation marks to indicate passages taken from the Bible or from other works. The manner in which these conventions are used in the original suggests that Swedenborg did not belabor the distinction between direct quotation and paraphrase; but in this edition, directly quoted material is indicated by either block quotations or quotation marks, and paraphrased material is usually presented without such indicators. In passages of dialog as well, quotation marks have been introduced that were not present as such in the original. Furthermore, Swedenborg did not mark his omissions from or changes to material he quoted, a practice in which this edition generally follows him. One exception consists of those instances in which Swedenborg did not include a complete sentence at the beginning or end of a Bible quotation. The omission in such cases has been marked in this edition with added points of ellipsis.

Grammatical anomalies Swedenborg sometimes uses a singular verb with certain dual subjects such as love and wisdom, goodness and truth, and love and charity. The wider context of his works indicates that his reason for doing so is that he understands the two given subjects as forming a unity. This translation generally preserves such singular verbs.

Italicized terms Any words in indented scriptural extracts that are here set in italics reflect a similar emphasis in the first edition.

Special use of vertical rule The opening passages of the early chapters of *Secrets of Heaven,* as well as the ends of all chapters, contain material that derives in some way from Swedenborg's experiences in the spiritual world. Swedenborg specified that the text of these and similar passages be set in continuous italics to distinguish it from exegetical and other material. For this edition, the heavy use of italic text was felt to be antithetical to modern tastes, as well as difficult to read, and so such passages are instead marked by a vertical rule in the margin.

Changes to and insertions in the text This translation is based on the first Latin edition, published by Swedenborg himself (1749–1756); it also reflects emendations in the third Latin edition, edited by P. H. Johnson, John E. Elliott, and others, and published by the Swedenborg Society (1949–1973). It incorporates the silent correction of minor errors, not only in the text proper but in Bible verse references. The text has also been changed without notice where the verse numbering of the Latin Bible cited by Swedenborg differs from that of modern English Bibles. Throughout the translation, references or cross-references that were implied but not stated have been inserted in brackets; for example, [John 3:27]. In many cases, it is very difficult to determine what Swedenborg had in mind when he referred to other passages giving evidence for a statement or providing further discussion on a topic. Because of this difficulty, the missing references that are occasionally supplied in this edition should not be considered definitive or exhaustive. In contrast to such references in square brackets, references that occur in parentheses are those that appear in the first edition; for example, (1 Samuel 30:16), (see §42 above). Occasionally square brackets signal an insertion of other material that was not present in the first edition. These insertions fall into two classes: words likely to have been deleted through a copying or typesetting error, and words supplied by the translator as necessary for the understanding of the English text, though they have no direct parallel in the Latin. The latter device has been used sparingly, however, even at the risk of some inconsistency in its application. Unfortunately, no annotations concerning these insertions can be supplied in this Portable edition.

Biblical titles Swedenborg refers to the Hebrew Scriptures as the Old Testament and to the Greek Scriptures as the New Testament; his terminology has been adopted in this edition. As was the custom in his day, he refers to the Pentateuch (Genesis, Exodus, Leviticus, Numbers, and

Deuteronomy) simply as "Moses"; for example, in §4444:4 he writes "as recorded in Moses" and then quotes a passage from Exodus. Similarly, in sentences or phrases introducing quotations he sometimes refers to the Psalms as "David," to Lamentations as "Jeremiah," and to the Gospel of John, the Epistles of John, and the Book of Revelation as simply "John." Conventional references supplied in parentheses after such quotations specify their sources more precisely.

Problematic content Occasionally Swedenborg makes statements that, although mild by the standards of eighteenth-century theological discourse, now read as harsh, dismissive, or insensitive. The most problematic are assertions about or criticisms of various religious traditions and their adherents—including Judaism, ancient or contemporary; Roman Catholicism; Islam; and the Protestantism in which Swedenborg himself grew up. These statements are far outweighed in size and importance by other passages in Swedenborg's works earnestly maintaining the value of every individual and of all religions. This wider context is discussed in the introductions and annotations of the Deluxe edition mentioned above. In the present format, however, problematic statements must be retained without comment. The other option—to omit them—would obscure some aspects of Swedenborg's presentation and in any case compromise its historicity.

SECRETS
OF
HEAVEN

Genesis 31

[Matthew 24:29–31]

I N the fourth and fifth volumes, chapters 26, 27, 28, 29, and 30 were 4056 introduced with an explanation of the Lord's words in Matthew 24:3–28 predicting the close of the age, or the Last Judgment. Now at the head of the current chapter comes an explanation of the words that follow there, starting with verses 29, 30, 31, which say:

> Immediately after the affliction of those days, though, the sun will go dark, and the moon will not shed its light, and the stars will fall down from the sky, and the powers of the heavens will be shaken. And then the sign of the Son of Humankind will appear in heaven, and then all the tribes of the earth will mourn. And they will see the Son of Humankind coming in the clouds of heaven with power and great glory. And he will send his angels out with a trumpet and a loud voice, and they will gather his chosen people from the four winds, from one end of the heavens right to the other end of them. (Matthew 24:29, 30, 31)

I have already explained that the close of the age, or the Last Judg- 4057 ment, means the church's final days, which are said to occur when there is no longer any neighborly love or faith in it; I have also shown that these closes or final periods have happened several times [§§931, 1850, 2118, 3353]. The close of the first church was depicted by the Flood; that of the second church, by the eradication of various nations in the land of Canaan, and by many other mentions in the Prophets of [the people] being uprooted and cut off. The Word does not describe but predicts the close of the third church, which was the destruction of Jerusalem and the worldwide scattering of the Jewish nation and its people (among whom that church existed). The fourth close is that of the modern Christian church, which is foretold by the Lord in the Gospels and John's Revelation and is currently at hand.

4058 The previous verses of this chapter in Matthew spoke of the growing devastation of the church: first, people would start to forget what was good and true and would quarrel over it; second, they would despise it; third, they would refuse to acknowledge it at heart; fourth, they would profane it. These stages were the theme in verses 3–22 of the chapter. Since religious truth and neighborly kindness would survive at the church's core, among the people referred to as the chosen, verses 23–28 describe what the state of religious truth will then be like, and the verses just quoted describe the state of charitable, loving goodness. They also tell about the start of a new church.

4059 Everything said in these verses makes it obvious that they have an inner meaning, and that if we do not understand that meaning, we cannot possibly know what is involved. What does it imply to say that the sun and moon will go dark, the stars will fall from the sky and the powers of the heavens will be shaken, the Lord will appear in the clouds of heaven, and angels will blow a trumpet to gather the chosen? If we do not know the inner meaning of these words we have to believe that such things will happen and in fact that the world will perish, along with every visible object in the universe. But the Last Judgment does not mean the end of the world, or some such thing; it means the culmination of the church, or the stripping away of its charity and faith. This can be seen in §3353 and is quite plain from the next sentences in Matthew 24, verses 40, 41: "Two will then be in the field; one will be taken, the other left. Two grinding; one will be taken, the other left."

4060 Accordingly, the symbolism of the words quoted above (the state of the church at that point in regard to goodness, or to charity for one's neighbor and love for the Lord) can be seen from their inner meaning, which is this:

Immediately after the affliction of those days, though symbolizes the condition of the church in respect to the religious truth discussed in the verses just preceding. In various places the Word refers to the ruination of truth as affliction; and days mean states (see §§23, 487, 488, 493, 893, 2788, 3462, 3785). Clearly, then, these words mean that after faith ceases, charity will cease. Faith leads to charity, because it teaches us what charity is, and charity takes its character from religious truth, but religious truth takes its essence and life from charity (as demonstrated many times in earlier volumes [§3986]).

[2] *The sun will go dark, and the moon will not shed its light* symbolizes love for the Lord (the sun) and charity for one's neighbor (the moon), and going dark and not shedding its light means that they will not be visible; they will disappear. To see that the sun means heavenly love and the moon means spiritual love—that is, that the sun means love for the Lord, and the moon means charity for one's neighbor growing out of faith—consult §§1053, 1529, 1530, 2120, 2441, 2495. The reason for this symbolism of sun and moon is that in the other world the Lord appears as a sun to the inhabitants of heaven who love him ("the heavenly") and as a moon to the inhabitants who treat their neighbor with charity ("the spiritual"). See §§1053, 1521, 1529, 1530, 1531, 3636, 3643.

[3] The sun and moon in the heavens—that is, the Lord—never go dark or lose their light but are always shining. Neither does love for him fade among the heavenly nor charity for one's neighbor among the spiritual in the heavens. On earth they do not fade among people who have heavenly and spiritual angels with them—in other words, among people who possess love and charity. No, they are extinguished among people devoid of love and charity who love themselves and their worldly advantages instead, and who therefore seethe with hatred and vengefulness. These people bring the darkness on themselves. The case resembles that of the earthly sun, which shines constantly, though it is not visible when clouds block it; see §2441.

[4] *And the stars will fall down from the sky* means that knowledge of goodness and truth will die. When the Word mentions stars, they actually symbolize such knowledge (§§1808, 2849).

And the powers of the heavens will be shaken symbolizes the foundations of the church. They are said to shake and tremble when that knowledge dies. The church on earth is the foundation of heaven, because the stream of goodness and truth flowing through the heavens from the Lord reaches its final destination in the good urges and true ideas of people in the church. So when the attitude of people in the church is so contrary that they refuse to let goodness and truth influence them anymore, the powers of the heavens are said to be shaken. The Lord as a result always provides that some trace of the church will remain and that a new church will be established when the old one dies.

[5] *And then the sign of the Son of Humankind will appear in heaven* means that divine truth will then appear. The sign means its emergence. The Son of Humankind means the Lord in regard to divine truth (see §§2803, 2813, 3704). This manifestation, or sign, is what the disciples

asked about in verse 3 of this chapter [Matthew 24] when they said to the Lord, "Tell us when these things will happen—especially what the sign of your coming and of the close of the age will be." They knew from the Word that the Lord would come when the era ended, and they knew from the Lord that he would come again. This they took to mean that he would come into the world once more, since they did not yet realize that he comes whenever a church has been spiritually devastated. He does not come in person, as he did when he clothed himself in humanity by being born and made his humanity divine. Rather, he comes by emerging either in visible ways, as when he appeared to Abraham in Mamre, to Moses in the bramble, to the Israelite people on Mount Sinai, and to Joshua when he entered the land of Canaan, or in less visible ways, as in the kind of inspiration that produced the Word. He also comes by means of the Word, in which he is present, since everything in the Word is from him and about him, as many previous discussions have already shown. What the sign of the Son of Humankind symbolizes and the verse here treats of is this manifestation.

[6] *And then all the tribes of the earth will mourn* means that everyone who possesses a loving goodness and religious truth will grieve. For this symbolism of mourning, see Zechariah 12:10, 11, 12, 13, 14. Tribes symbolize every facet of goodness and truth, or of love and faith (§§3858, 3926), so they symbolize people who possess those things. They are called tribes of the earth because they symbolize people in the church—the earth meaning the church (see §§662, 1066, 1068, 1262, 1733, 1850, 2117, 2928, 3355).

[7] *And they will see the Son of Humankind coming in the clouds of the heavens with power and great glory* means that the inner meaning of the Word, which contains the Lord, will then be revealed. The Son of Humankind means divine truth in the Word (§§2803, 2813, 3704). The cloud stands for the literal meaning. Power is an attribute of the goodness there, and glory, of the truth. For this symbolism of seeing the Son of Humankind coming in the clouds of the heavens, consult the preface to Genesis 18. The Lord's coming in this way is what is meant here, not a literal future appearance by him in the clouds. The subject addressed next is the establishment of a new church, which happens when the old one has been devastated and rejected.

[8] *He will send angels out with a trumpet and a loud voice* symbolizes being chosen—not by visible angels, let alone with trumpets and loud voices, but by sacred goodness and truth flowing in from the Lord through the angels. That is why angels in the Word symbolize something belonging to the Lord (§§1925, 2821, 3039). In this instance they

symbolize what comes from the Lord and tells about him. The trumpet and loud voice symbolize spreading the good news, as they do elsewhere in the Word.

[9] *And they will gather his chosen people from the four winds, from one end of the heavens right to the other end of them* symbolizes the establishment of a new church. The chosen people are those with the goodness that comes of love and faith (§§3755 at the end, 3900). The four winds from which they will be gathered mean all phases of goodness and truth (§3708). One end of the heavens to the other end of them means the inner and outer levels of the church.

This, now, is what the Lord's words here symbolize.

Genesis 31

1. And he heard the words of Laban's sons, saying, "Jacob took everything that belongs to our father, and from what belongs to our father he made all this wealth."

2. And Jacob saw the face of Laban, and here, [Laban] was by no means [the same] toward him as yesterday and the day before.

3. And Jehovah said to Jacob, "Return to your ancestors' land and to [the place of] your birth, and I will be with you."

4. And Jacob sent and called Rachel and Leah to the field, to his flock.

5. And he said to them, "I myself see the face of your father, that he is by no means toward me as yesterday and the day before; but the God of my father has been with me.

6. And you know that with all my strength I have served your father.

7. And your father has cheated me and changed my wage ten ways, but God has not allowed him to do me evil.

8. If he said this—'The speckled will be your wage'—then all the flocks bore speckled [offspring]; and if he said this—'The mottled will be your wage'—then all the flocks bore mottled [offspring].

9. And God has snatched your father's property and given it to me.

10. And it happened in the time of the flock's going into heat that I lifted my eyes and saw in a dream, and look! He-goats mounting on the flock of the mottled, the speckled, and the hail-spotted.

11. And God's angel said to me in the dream, 'Jacob!' And I said, 'Here I am.'

12. And he said, 'Please lift your eyes and see all the he-goats mounting on the flock—the mottled, the speckled, and the hail-spotted—because I have seen all that Laban is doing to you.

13. I am the God of Bethel, where you anointed a pillar, where you vowed me a vow; now get up, go from this land, and return to the land of your birth.'"

14. And Rachel and Leah answered and said to him, "Do we have an allotment and inheritance any longer in our father's house?

15. Aren't we deemed strangers to him? For he has sold us and most certainly eaten up our silver.

16. Because all the riches that God snatched from our father, to us they belong and to our children; and now all that God has said to you, do."

17. And Jacob got up and took up his sons and his women on camels.

18. And he took away all his property and all his substance that he had amassed, the property of his buying that he had amassed in Paddanaram, to come to Isaac his father, to the land of Canaan.

19. And Laban had gone to shear [his] flock; and Rachel stole the teraphim that belonged to her father.

20. And Jacob stole the heart of Laban the Aramean by not telling him that he was fleeing.

21. And he fled, and everything that was his; and he rose and crossed the river and turned his face toward Mount Gilead.

22. And it was told to Laban on the third day that Jacob had fled.

23. And he took his brothers with him and followed after [Jacob] a path of seven days and joined him on Mount Gilead.

24. And God came to Laban the Aramean in a dream by night and said to him, "Watch yourself, to keep from speaking anything with Jacob, whether good or evil."

25. And Laban overtook Jacob, and Jacob had pitched his tent on the mountain, and Laban pitched with his brothers on Mount Gilead.

26. And Laban said to Jacob, "What have you done? And you stole my heart and took away my daughters as if captured by a sword!

27. Why did you hide in fleeing and steal me and not tell me? And I would have sent you away with gladness and with songs, with a tambourine and with a harp.

28. And you did not let me kiss my sons and my daughters; now you have acted stupidly in doing this.

29. I wish my hand were as God to do you evil! But the God of your father last night said to me, saying, 'Keep yourself from speaking anything with Jacob, whether good or evil.'

30. And now you went completely away, because you longed so much for the house of your father. Why did you steal my gods?"

31. And Jacob answered and said to Laban, "Because I was afraid, because I said perhaps you will kidnap your daughters from me.

32. [The one] with whom you find your gods will not live before our brothers; examine for yourself what is with me and take it for yourself." And Jacob did not know that Rachel had stolen them.

33. And Laban came into Jacob's tent and into Leah's tent and into the two slaves' tent and did not find them; and he left Leah's tent and came into Rachel's tent.

34. And Rachel took the teraphim and put them in the camel's straw and sat on them, and Laban probed the whole tent and did not find them.

35. And she said to her father, "Do not let anger blaze in my lord's eyes, because I am unable to rise before you, because the way of women is on me"; and he searched and did not find the teraphim.

36. And anger blazed in Jacob, and he wrangled against Laban. And Jacob answered and said to Laban, "What is my transgression? What is my sin, that you pursued after me?

37. Because you have probed all my vessels; what have you found from all your household vessels? Put it here before my brothers and your brothers, and let them adjudicate between the two of us.

38. These twenty years I have been with you; your ewes and your she-goats have not miscarried, and the rams of your flock I have not eaten.

39. Torn flesh I have not brought to you. I have made up the loss of it; from my hand you have sought it, what was stolen by day and stolen by night.

40. [So] I was: in the day, heat devoured me, and cold in the night, and my sleep was driven from my eyes.

41. These twenty years of mine in your house I have served you—fourteen years for your two daughters, and six years for your flock—and you have changed my wage ten ways.

42. Had I not had the God of my father, the God of Abraham and the Dread of Isaac, you would have sent me away empty now; my misery and the wearying of the palms of my hands God has seen, and he adjudicated between [us] last night."

43. And Laban answered and said to Jacob, "The daughters are my daughters and the sons are my sons and the flock is my flock, and everything that you are seeing—it is mine. And to my daughters—what shall I do to them today, or to their sons whom they have borne?

44. And now, come, let us strike a pact, I and you, and let it be for a witness between me and you."

45. And Jacob took a stone and set it up as a pillar.

46. And Jacob said to his brothers, "Gather stones"; and they took stones and made a heap and ate there on the heap.

47. And Laban called it Jegar-sahadutha. And Jacob called it Galeed.

48. And Laban said, "This heap is a witness between me and you today"; so he called its name Galeed.

49. Also Mizpah, because he said, "Jehovah watch between me and you, because we will lie hidden, a man from his companion.

50. If you afflict my daughters, and if you take women in addition to my daughters, no man is with us [to witness it], [but] see! God is a witness between me and you."

51. And Laban said to Jacob, "Look: this heap; and look: the pillar that I have set up between me and you.

52. This heap will be a witness and the pillar will be a witness that I will not cross this heap to you and that you will not cross this heap or this pillar to me for evil.

53. Let the God of Abraham and the God of Nahor judge between us—the God of their father." And Jacob swore on the Dread of his father Isaac.

54. And Jacob offered a sacrifice on the mountain and called his brothers to eat bread, and they ate bread and spent the night on the mountain.

55. And Laban got up early in the morning and kissed his sons and his daughters and blessed them, and Laban went and returned to his place.

Summary

4061 THE inner meaning here describes how the goodness and truth represented by Jacob and his women separated from the goodness symbolized by Laban so as to unite with the divinity growing from the main divine branch. It also describes the condition of both parties at the time of separation.

Inner Meaning

G ENESIS 31:1, 2, 3. *And he heard the words of Laban's sons, saying,* 4062
*"Jacob took everything that belongs to our father, and from what belongs
to our father he made all this wealth." And Jacob saw the face of Laban, and
here, [Laban] was by no means [the same] toward him as yesterday and the
day before. And Jehovah said to Jacob, "Return to your ancestors' land and to
[the place of] your birth, and I will be with you."*

He heard the words of Laban's sons, saying, symbolizes the truth born
of the goodness symbolized by Laban, and its quality, compared to the
goodness the Lord acquired on the earthly level from the goodness symbolized by Laban. *Jacob took everything that belongs to our father* means
that the Lord received all the goodness now meant by Jacob from there.
And from what belongs to our father he made all this wealth means that he
gave it to himself. *And Jacob saw the face of Laban* symbolizes a change in
the state of that goodness when the goodness meant by Jacob withdrew.
*And here, he was by no means [the same] toward him as yesterday and the day
before* symbolizes a radically different attitude toward the goodness symbolized by Jacob, although nothing had been subtracted from [the goodness symbolized by Laban]; it still had everything it had before, except
for the state of union between them. *And Jehovah said to Jacob* symbolizes
what the Lord perceived from his divine side. *Return to your ancestors'
land* means that it was now to move closer to divine goodness. *And to [the
place of] your birth* means closer to the resulting truth. *And I will be with
you* means that it would then be divine.

He heard the words of Laban's sons, saying, symbolizes the truth born of 4063
the goodness symbolized by Laban, and its quality, compared to the goodness the Lord acquired on the earthly level from the goodness symbolized by
Laban, as the following shows: *Sons* symbolize truth, as discussed in §§489,
491, 533, 1147, 2623, 3373. And *Laban* represents a goodness branching off
from a shared stock, as discussed in §§3612, 3665, 3778, so he represents the
kind of goodness that would serve to introduce genuine goodness and truth
(§§3974, 3982, 3986 at the end). In this case the meaning is that it *did* serve,
because the theme is the process by which it was separated. Jacob *heard the
words* in an inner sense involves the quality [of the truth represented by

Laban's sons], compared to the goodness the Lord acquired on his earthly level. This can be seen from what follows next: They were outraged and said that Jacob had taken everything belonging to their father, and Jacob saw the face of Laban, that he was not as he had been yesterday and the day before. Jacob represents the Lord's earthly plane, and in the previous chapter he represented truth-based goodness on that plane; see §§3659, 3669, 3677, 3775, 3829, 4009.

[2] The character of the goodness symbolized by Laban compared to the truth-based goodness represented by Jacob is established by discussions and proofs in the previous chapter. Further light on the subject can come from the condition of human rebirth, which is also a focus here, on the representative level. When we are being reborn, the Lord maintains us in an intermediate kind of goodness. This kind serves to introduce genuine goodness and truth, but after they have been introduced, the intermediate kind is detached from them.

Anyone who knows something about regeneration and the new self can understand that the new self is entirely different from the old. After all, the new self feels drawn to spiritual and heavenly interests, which constitute its pleasure and bliss, but the old self feels drawn to worldly and earthly concerns, which constitute its pleasure and delight. The new self, then, looks toward goals in heaven, while the old self looks toward goals in the world, so the new self is clearly different and distinct from the old in every way.

[3] If we are to be brought from the condition of our old self into the condition of a new self, we have to strip ourselves of worldly cravings and clothe ourselves in heavenly desires. This is accomplished by countless means known to the Lord alone, some of which are also made known to angels by the Lord, but few if any of which are known to people on earth. Nonetheless, every single one of them is revealed in the Word's inner meaning. So when our old self becomes a new self—when we are being reborn—it does not happen instantly, as some believe. It spreads out over many years and in fact over our whole life right to the end of it. Our corrupt yearnings have to be rooted out, heavenly desires have to be instilled, and we have to receive a kind of life we never before possessed and hardly even knew anything about. Since the conditions of our life have to change so extensively, we inevitably have to stay a long time in an intermediate kind of goodness, or in a goodness marked by both worldly and heavenly desires. Unless we do, we can never accept heavenly goodness and truth.

[4] This intermediate goodness is what Laban and his flock symbolize, but we are kept in it only until it has served its purpose. When it has done its job, it is separated, and this separation is the subject of the current chapter.

The existence of this goodness and its removal after it has served its use can be illustrated by changes in state that we all undergo from infancy to old age. Everyone knows that we are in one state during early childhood, another during youth, another during early adulthood, another during full adulthood, and another during old age. People also recognize that we shed the state of childhood and its toys when we pass into the state of youth; that we shed the state of youth when we pass into the state of early adulthood; the same when we pass into the state of full adulthood; and the same when we pass into the state of old age. If we think about it, we can also see that each period has its pleasures, which gradually introduce us into the pleasures of the next stage and help us reach that stage. Eventually they help us attain the pleasures of understanding and wisdom in old age. [5] This makes it clear that we leave earlier pleasures behind whenever we adopt a new phase of life.

I bring this up only to show that pleasures are a means, and that we abandon the pleasures of one stage when we enter the next. When we are being reborn, though, our state is completely different from what it was before, and we are led to it not in a way dictated by nature but in a supernatural way by the Lord. No one reaches that state without the means of regeneration, provided by the Lord alone, and so except by way of the intermediate goodness just described. When we arrive at that state, and no longer have worldly, earthly, and bodily objectives but heavenly ones as our goal, the intermediate goodness is separated. To have something as a goal means to love it more than anything else.

Jacob took everything that belongs to our father means that the Lord received all the goodness meant by Jacob from there—from this intermediate goodness—as is self-evident. However, he did *not* receive it from there, as the following remarks will show. It was Laban's sons who said these words.   **4064**

And from what belongs to our father he made all this wealth means that he gave it to himself. This can be seen from the symbolism of *making wealth* as giving it to himself. In the highest sense, the statement has to do with the Lord, who never took anything good or true from anyone else, only from himself. Admittedly, another kind of goodness had served as an intermediate type for him—a kind that was related to his maternal   **4065** inheritance, since Laban (who symbolizes that goodness) was the brother of Rebekah, Jacob's mother. Through the intermediate goodness, though, he obtained for himself the means by which he made his earthly dimension divine under his own power. It is one thing to acquire something *from* intermediate goodness and another to acquire something *by* it. The Lord did acquire something for himself *by* intermediate goodness, because he was born as a human being and inherited from his mother a nature that needed to be cast off. He did not acquire anything *from* intermediate goodness, however, because he was conceived by Jehovah, who imparted divinity to him. So he gave himself everything good and true and made it all divine. Divinity itself never lacks for anything. He would not even have needed this intermediate goodness had he not wanted to accomplish everything in the ordinary way.

4066   *And Jacob saw the face of Laban* symbolizes a change in the state of that goodness when the goodness meant by Jacob withdrew, as can be seen from the following: *Jacob* represents goodness on the earthly plane, and *Laban* represents an intermediate goodness, as noted many times before. And a *face* symbolizes inner depths, as discussed in §§358, 1999, 2434, 3527, 3573. Here it symbolizes changes in the inner depths—in other words, changes of state—because the text says, "he saw his face, and here, he was by no means with him as yesterday and the day before." A face in the Word symbolizes inner depths because our inner reaches gleam from our face and reveal themselves in our face as in a mirror or an image. A face, or a facial expression, then, symbolizes the state of a person's thoughts and feelings.

4067   *And here, he was by no means [the same] toward him as yesterday and the day before* symbolizes a radically different attitude toward the goodness symbolized by Jacob, although nothing had been subtracted from [the goodness symbolized by Laban]; it still had everything it had before, except for the state of union between them. This stands to reason from the meaning of *he was by no means [the same] toward him as yesterday and the day before* as a radically different attitude toward Jacob—that is, toward the goodness symbolized by Jacob. It also stands to reason from the preceding story, because nothing had been subtracted from Laban (that is, from the goodness symbolized by Laban); he still had everything he had before.

[2] If the reader is to understand how matters stand with the goodness and truth in us, then information that scarcely anyone has known needs to be revealed. People realize and acknowledge that everything good and everything true comes from the Lord. Some also acknowledge the

existence of a spiritual inflow, but they do not know the nature of that inflow. Since they lack knowledge, or at least acknowledgment in their hearts, that we have spirits and angels around us, that our inner self lives among them, and that the Lord governs us through them, they say this is true but hardly believe it.

In the other world, there are myriad communities that the Lord arranges and organizes to match all the types of goodness and truth, and communities opposite them, to match all the types of evil and falsity. In fact, there is not one category of goodness and truth, or one subcategory, or even a single specific variety that does not have these angelic communities, or to which angelic communities do not correspond. Likewise there is not one category of evil and falsity, or one subcategory, or even a single specific variety to which devilish communities do not correspond. As to our inner levels, or as to our thoughts and feelings, we each exist in community with these beings, even though we are unaware of it. Everything we think and will comes from there—so much so that if the communities of spirits and angels in which we exist were taken away from us, we would instantly lose all thought and will. More than that, we would instantly fall down completely dead. Such is the state of the human being, although we consider ourselves self-sufficient and do not believe in hell or heaven, or else believe that hell and heaven are both far removed from us.

[3] Furthermore, the goodness in us appears to us to be an uncomplicated entity, a single whole, but it is so multifaceted and consists of so many different parts that we could never examine even its most general aspects. The same holds true for the evil in us.

Whatever the goodness in us is like, such is the community of angels with us; and whatever the evil in us is like, such is the community of evil spirits with us. We ourselves summon these communities to us, or place ourselves in the company of such beings, because like associates with like. If we are greedy, for instance, we invite communities of like-minded individuals with the same obsession. If we love ourselves more than others and view others with contempt, we invite like-minded individuals. If we take pleasure in revenge, we invite those who take the same pleasure. And so on. Those spirits communicate with hell, and we are in their midst, entirely under their control, to the point where we are not under our own jurisdiction, we are under theirs. They determine everything for us, even though the pleasure and therefore the freedom we enjoy convinces us that we are governing ourselves. On the other hand, if we are not greedy, do not love ourselves more than others and despise them, and do not enjoy revenge, we keep company with like-minded angels. Through these angels the Lord leads us in freedom to every kind of goodness and every truth to which we allow ourselves to be led. The deeper and more perfect the goodness we allow ourselves to be brought to, the deeper and more perfect the angelic communities we reach. Changes in state are nothing but changes of community.

Many years of constant experience by now have shown me that this is how matters stand. I have become so accustomed to the idea that it is as if I grew up with it.

[4] This discussion now clarifies how human regeneration works. It shows the part played by intermediate pleasures and goodness, through which the Lord leads us from the condition of our old self to that of a new self. To repeat, he uses angelic communities and our changing association with them. The intermediate goodness and pleasures quite simply *are* these communities, and the Lord brings them into contact with us so that by them he can introduce us to spiritual and heavenly goodness and truth. When we arrive at this goodness and truth, the former communities are separated, and deeper, more perfect ones are linked to us.

This alone is what is meant by the intermediate goodness that Laban symbolizes and by the separation of it depicted in the current chapter.

4068   *And Jehovah said to Jacob* symbolizes what the Lord perceived from his divine side. This is clear from the symbolism of *saying* in the Word's narratives as perceiving (discussed in §§1791, 1815, 1819, 1822, 1898, 1919, 2080, 2619, 2862, 3395, 3509). Jehovah is the Lord (see §§1343, 1736, 1793, 2921, 3023, 3035), so *Jehovah said* symbolizes what the Lord perceived from his divine side.

4069   *Return to your ancestors' land* means that [the goodness symbolized by Jacob] was now to move closer to divine goodness. This can be seen from the symbolism of *ancestors' land* in this case as divine goodness, since it applies to the Lord. The *land*, Canaan, symbolizes the Lord's kingdom (§§1607, 3481), and in the highest sense, the Lord's divine humanity, since this constitutes his kingdom when it flows into us (§§3038, 3705); and an *ancestor* [or father] means goodness (§3703). Since the Lord by now had acquired the goodness and truth through which he was to make his earthly part divine, and since they were represented by Jacob's stay with Laban and by Jacob's acquisitions there, it follows that *return to your ancestors' land* means moving closer to divine goodness.

4070   *And to [the place of] your birth* means closer to the resulting truth. This can be seen from the symbolism of *birth* as truth produced by goodness.

All truth is born of goodness; it has no other source. It is called truth because it relates to goodness and because it confirms its source—in other words, confirms what is good. Hence the symbolism of birth here. Birth has to do with faith (see §§1145, 1255), and giving birth means acknowledging something in faith and deed (§§3905, 3915).

And I will be with you means that it would then be divine, as can be seen from the fact that Jehovah said this, and Jehovah means the Lord (as above in §4068) and his divinity. *Being with* the one in whom it exists, or who is the same as it, stands for being divine. The highest meaning, which focuses on the Lord, appears on the literal plane as something divided up, but in the highest inner meaning it is a single entity.

4071

Genesis 31:4–13. *And Jacob sent and called Rachel and Leah to the field, to his flock. And he said to them, "I myself see the face of your father, that he is by no means toward me as yesterday and the day before; but the God of my father has been with me. And you know that with all my strength I have served your father. And your father has cheated me and changed my wage ten ways, but God has not allowed him to do me evil. If he said this—'The speckled will be your wage'—then all the flocks bore speckled [offspring]; and if he said this—'The mottled will be your wage'—then all the flocks bore mottled [offspring]. And God has snatched your father's property and given it to me. And it happened in the time of the flock's going into heat that I lifted my eyes and saw in a dream, and look! He-goats mounting on the flock of the mottled, the speckled, and the hail-spotted. And God's angel said to me in the dream, 'Jacob!' And I said, 'Here I am.' And he said, 'Please lift your eyes and see all the he-goats mounting on the flock—the mottled, the speckled, and the hail-spotted—because I have seen all that Laban is doing to you. I am the God of Bethel, where you anointed a pillar, where you vowed me a vow; now get up, go from this land, and return to the land of your birth.'"*

4072

Jacob sent and called Rachel and Leah to the field, to his flock, symbolizes a connection with the desire for truth formed by the goodness that Jacob now stands for, and attachment when it withdrew. *And he said to them, "I myself see the face of your father, that he is by no means toward me as yesterday and the day before,"* symbolizes a change in the state of the goodness symbolized by Laban. *But the God of my father has been with me* means that everything [the Lord] had came from his divine side. *And you know that with all my strength I have served your father* means he used his own power. *And your father has cheated me and changed my wage ten ways* symbolizes the attitude of that type of goodness toward the Lord when he adopted the benefits of such goodness on his own; and frequent change in that attitude. *But God has not allowed him to do me evil* means that even so it could not interfere. *If he said this—"The speckled will be your wage"—then all the flocks bore speckled [offspring]* means that it was free, and that without violating its freedom the Lord took the benefits—referring to evil connected with goodness. *And if he said this—"The mottled will be your wage"—then all the flocks bore mottled [offspring]* means the same—referring to falsity connected with [goodness]. *And God has snatched your father's property and given it to me* means that these came from the Divine. *And it happened in the time of the flock's going into heat* symbolizes a burning desire for them to unite. *That I lifted my eyes and saw in a dream* symbolizes what earthly goodness perceived in the dimness. *And look! He-goats mounting on the flock of the mottled, the speckled, and the hail-spotted* symbolizes the outcome: the earthly goodness meant by Jacob would be endowed with these benefits. *And God's angel said to me in the dream, "Jacob!" And I said, "Here I am,"* symbolizes perception from his divine side and its presence in that dim state. *And he said, "Please lift your eyes,"* means deliberately noticing. *And see all the he-goats mounting on the flock—the mottled, the speckled, and the hail-spotted* means that such things would be introduced. *Because I have seen all that Laban is doing to you* symbolizes the identity of the goodness symbolized by Laban, which is not the type to act on its own initiative. *I am the God of Bethel* symbolizes divinity on the earthly plane. *Where you anointed a pillar* means where there was goodness based on truth and a boundary. *Where you vowed me a vow* symbolizes what is holy. *Now get up* symbolizes an elevation. *Go from this land* symbolizes being separated from that kind of goodness. *And return to the land of your birth* symbolizes union with divine goodness that comes of truth.

4073   *And Jacob sent and called Rachel and Leah to the field, to his flock,* symbolizes a connection with the desire for truth formed by the goodness that Jacob now stands for, and attachment when it withdrew. This can be seen from the representation of *Jacob* as earthly goodness (discussed many times before) and from that of *Rachel and Leah* as a desire for truth, connected to that goodness, *Rachel* being a desire for inner truth, and *Leah,* a desire for outer truth (discussed in §§3758, 3782, 3793, 3819). *Sending* someone to them and *calling them to the field, to his flock* clearly means connecting them to itself. A *field* symbolizes different facets of goodness, and a place where goodness exists (§§2971, 3196, 3310, 3317), while a *flock* symbolizes the goodness and truth that [earthly goodness] had acquired by now, to which the desire for truth meant by Rachel and Leah would be attached when [that kind of goodness] withdrew.

In this chapter Jacob represents goodness on the earthly plane, which was to draw closer to union with the Divine (§4069) because it was ready to separate from the goodness symbolized by Laban and was actually doing so (see the remarks on Jacob in §3775). Representations vary with changes in the state of goodness and truth, and changes in state vary with changes in the spirits and angels who possess the particular kind of goodness and truth involved, as discussed above at §4067. [2] When groups of spirits and angels that have an intermediate kind of goodness pull back, new communities with a fuller kind of goodness come close. Our state is determined entirely by the communities of spirits and angels surrounding us. Our will and our thought match theirs. However, changes in our state are not at all the same when we ourselves summon those communities, or connect ourselves with them, as when the Lord connects them to us. When we connect ourselves with them, we are in trouble, but when the Lord connects them to us, we are doing well. When we are doing well, we receive through these communities the kind of goodness that helps us live a life of reformation.

Everything the inner meaning of this passage says about the goodness represented by Jacob, the desire for truth meant by Rachel and Leah, and the attachment of the latter when the former withdrew from the goodness symbolized by Laban, corresponds perfectly and vividly with these communities and our changing association with them. From the communities around us, angels perceive what states we are going through and therefore what our goodness and truth are like, so they perceive countless details that barely appear to us as even a general whole. As a result, angels are aware of actual causes, because they see and perceive these communities; but we are aware of effects and do not see the communities. We are capable only of dimly perceiving them by certain changes in state resulting from them, and not of perceiving any goodness or truth, unless the Lord enlightens us through the angels.

And he said to them, "I myself see the face of your father, that he is by no means toward me as yesterday and the day before," symbolizes a change in the state of the goodness symbolized by Laban. This is established by the remarks above at §4067, where the same words occur.

4074

4075   *But the God of my father has been with me* means that everything [the Lord] had came from his divine side. This can be seen from the fact that when *the God of my father* relates to the Lord, it means the divinity he had. And *has been with me* means that everything he had came from there.

When the Lord made the humanity in himself divine, he also had communities of spirits and angels around him, because he wanted everything to be done by the regular steps. But he invited to himself the kinds that could help him and changed them at will. Still, he took nothing good or true from them to apply to himself, only from his divine side. In this way he also reduced both heaven and hell to order, doing so gradually, until he had fully glorified himself.

Examples can clarify how groups of spirits and angels were able to serve a purpose even though the Lord took nothing from them. [2] Some communities by their nature see goodness as originating in themselves and consequently take credit for it. These communities enabled the Lord to introduce himself to a knowledge of such goodness. In the process he was able to develop a wisdom concerning the kind of goodness that lacks all sense of merit, as goodness that comes from the Lord does. The knowledge and the resulting wisdom did not come from those communities but through them.

To take another example, some communities consider themselves quite wise but argue about goodness and truth and challenge its validity at every turn. Most of these communities are populated by spiritual individuals. They enabled the Lord to introduce himself to a knowledge concerning them and the extent of relative shadow they live in, the fact that they would be undone if the Lord did not have mercy on them, and so on. This knowledge came from the Lord's divine side—not from the communities but through them.

[3] For yet another example, some communities love God and believe that if they fix their eyes on the Infinite and worship a hidden God they can love him. In reality, though, they do not love him unless they use their minds to make his infinity finite, or use the finite thinking of their intellect to present the hidden God to themselves as visible. To do otherwise would be to gaze on darkness and lovingly embrace what inhabits the shadows, which means embracing many other confused, incoherent concepts, as dictated by the individual mind. These communities also helped by enabling the Lord to introduce himself to knowledge about the nature of their inner depths and of their love, to compassion, and to the fact that they could not be saved unless his humanity became divine and

they could focus on it. Again, this wisdom did not come from the communities but through them from the Lord's divine side.

The same is true in all other cases.

This clarifies how it could be that nothing was taken from the goodness symbolized by Laban but that everything the Lord had came from his divine nature—in other words, from himself.

And you know that with all my strength I have served your father means he used his own power. This can be seen from the symbolism of *serving* as study (discussed in §§3824, 3846), though when it applies to the Lord, it symbolizes his own power (discussed in §§3975, 3977), especially when the text says *with all my strength.*

4076

And your father has cheated me and changed my wage ten ways symbolizes the attitude of that type of goodness toward the Lord when he adopted the benefits of such goodness on his own; and frequent change in that attitude. This symbolism can be seen from the following: The *father,* Laban, symbolizes intermediate goodness, as dealt with before. The *wage* means on his own, as discussed in §§3996, 3999. And *ten ways* means frequent change, *ten* meaning a large amount (§1988), and *ways* meaning changes. The implication is that the actual state of that goodness changed when the Lord adopted its benefits on his own.

4077

If you replace the idea of the goodness symbolized by Laban with the idea of a community of spirits and angels who have that goodness, the situation becomes clearer. Communities cannot easily leave the people they have accompanied; when the person they are with leaves them, they become upset and behave the way Laban did toward Jacob. If they sense that the person has accrued anything good through them, they claim she or he gained it *from* them. In their anger they say bad things.

[2] The same thing happens to all who are being reborn. The Lord sets them up with communities that help in the introduction of genuine goodness and truth, although these qualities do not come from those communities but through them. When the people being reborn transfer to other communities, the ones that used to surround them take offense. This is not apparent to the people, because they do not think they are in the company of spirits and angels, but angels see it clearly. So do those whom the Lord in his divine mercy allows to speak to angels and interact with them as one of them. That is how I was taught that the case is such.

Spirits complain vehemently about our ignorance, that we do not even know they are with us—not to mention that many of us deny not only their presence but also the existence of hell and heaven. But they chalk it up to human stupidity. The fact of the matter, they point out, is that we do not have a trace of thought or a trace of will that does not flow in through them from the Lord; they are the ones through whom the Lord indirectly governs the human race in general and each member of it in particular.

4078   *But God has not allowed him to do me evil* means that even so, [intermediate goodness] could not interfere. This can be seen from the symbolism of *not allowing someone to do evil*, in connection with the Lord, as not being able to interfere with him. Nothing can do evil to the Divine; it can only interfere with inflow from the Divine, as every evil thing does. This shows what doing evil means in the current verse.

4079   *If he said this—"The speckled will be your wage"—then all the flocks bore speckled [offspring]* means that it was free, and that without violating its freedom the Lord took the benefits—referring to evil connected with goodness. This can be seen from the state of affairs in the inner meaning, which is that [intermediate goodness] was free to change the wage, so without violating its freedom the Lord took the benefits. The reference to evil connected with goodness is evident from the symbolism of the *speckled* as goodness tinged with evil (discussed in §§3993, 3995, 4005).

4080   *And if he said this—"The mottled will be your wage"—then all the flocks bore mottled [offspring]* means the same—referring to falsity connected with [goodness]. This can be seen from the remarks just above and from the symbolism of the *mottled* as truth sprinkled and tinged with evil (discussed in §4005) and therefore as falsity.

4081   *And God has snatched your father's property and given it to me* means that these came from the Divine. This is established by the remarks and explanations above at §4065 and at §4075.

4082   *And it happened in the time of the flock's going into heat* symbolizes a burning desire for them to unite. This is established by the symbolism of *going into heat* as burning desire and its effect (treated of in §§4018, 4019) and so as the intent that they—goodness and truth—unite.

4083   *That I lifted my eyes and saw in a dream* symbolizes what earthly goodness perceived in the dimness. This can be seen from the symbolism of *lifting the eyes* as thinking and also focusing (discussed in §§2789, 2829, 3198) and therefore as perceiving; and from the meaning of *in a dream* as in the dimness (discussed in §§2514, 2528). The earthly goodness is Jacob.

4084   *And look! He-goats mounting on the flock of the mottled, the speckled, and the hail-spotted* symbolizes the outcome: the earthly goodness meant by Jacob would be endowed with these benefits. This can be seen from comments on the topic in the previous chapter, where Jacob acquired through Laban's flock the "mottled, speckled, and spotted," or the qualities symbolized by them.

And God's angel said to me in the dream, "Jacob!" And I said, "Here I am," symbolizes perception from his divine side and its presence in the dimness, as can be seen from the following: In scriptural narratives, *saying* means perceiving, as noted many times before. *God's angel* means that it comes from the Lord's divine side, because when the Word mentions an angel, it symbolizes something of the Lord's—that is, something belonging to the Divine (§§1925, 2319, 2821, 3039). The reason for this symbolism is that angels do not speak on their own behalf but on behalf of the Lord, especially when they say something in a dream, as one did to Jacob here. Angels naturally become indignant if you attribute anything good or true they say to them, and so far as they can, they remove any such thought in others, especially in people on earth. They know and perceive that they receive from the Lord—and so from his divinity—everything good and true that they think, will, or do. ■ 4085

This shows that in the Word angels symbolize something of the Lord's, or something divine. And *in the dream* means in the dimness, as discussed in §§2514, 2528. The presence [of his divinity] on the earthly level, in the dimness there, is what Jacob's answer symbolizes.

And he said, "Please lift your eyes," means deliberately noticing. This is established by the symbolism of *lifting the eyes* as thinking and focusing (discussed in §§2789, 2829) and therefore as noticing. The fact that he was to do it deliberately can be seen from the imperatives "*Lift* your eyes and *see*" and from the context. ■ 4086

And see all the he-goats mounting on the flock—the mottled, the speckled, and the hail-spotted means that such things would be introduced and consequently that they would be instilled in him. This is established by the discussion just above at §4084, where similar words occur. ■ 4087

Because I have seen all that Laban is doing to you symbolizes the identity of the goodness symbolized by Laban, which is not the type to act on its own initiative. This is established by the representation of *Laban* as intermediate goodness (discussed many times before). ■ 4088

The identity of this goodness is not the type to act on its own initiative, as *I have seen all that he is doing to you* symbolizes. The symbolism becomes clear when one looks into the ideas expressed in the inner meaning, and it becomes clear from communities that possess such goodness. The latter demonstrate clearly what that goodness is like, because they are groups of spirits serving as means of communication, as described in §4047. By nature they do little on their own or independently but rather allow themselves to be led by others—by the angels to what is good, and by evil spirits to what is bad. This fact also stands out plainly from Laban's current story, especially the parts that follow. From this you can see what is meant by the identity of the goodness symbolized by Laban, that it is not the type to act on its own initiative.

The inner-level contents of verses 6, 7, 8, 9, 10, 11, 12 are explained briefly because they are similar to those dealt with in the previous chapter, where they were explained more fully.

4089   *I am the God of Bethel* symbolizes divinity on the earthly plane. This can be seen from the symbolism of *Bethel* as goodness on the outermost level of the divine design (discussed in §3729) and accordingly on the earthly plane. The earthly plane is the outermost level of the design because heavenly and spiritual elements rest on it. Clearly, then, the *God of Bethel* means divinity on the earthly plane.

Because Bethel symbolizes goodness on the earthly plane, it also symbolizes heavenly knowledge on that plane, since knowledge of what is heavenly is a knowledge of goodness.

4090   *Where you anointed a pillar* means where there was goodness based on truth and a boundary, as can be seen from the following: A *pillar* symbolizes a sacred boundary, and therefore the outermost level of the divine design, and therefore truth, as discussed in §3727. And *anointing, or pouring oil over the top of the pillar* as Jacob did, means turning truth into goodness, as discussed in §3728.

4091   *Where you vowed me a vow* symbolizes what is holy. This can be seen from the symbolism of *vowing a vow* as wanting the Lord to provide, and in the highest sense, which has to do with the Lord, as his providing (discussed in §3732). Whatever the Lord provides comes from him, and whatever comes from him is holy, which is why this vowing of a vow symbolizes what is holy.

The idea that vowing a vow means something that comes from the Lord and therefore something holy seems rather outlandish at first glance. That is because we humans are the ones who vow a vow, committing ourselves to a course of action, or giving ourselves some obligation to the Divine, provided we obtain our wish. However, when the Divine itself, or the Lord, is the one said to vow, there is no vowing but willing and providing, or doing. Therefore what the Divine—in other words, the Lord— does comes from him, and whatever comes from him is holy.

Now get up symbolizes an elevation. This can be seen from the symbolism of *getting up* as involving elevation, in passages where the term is used (dealt with at §§2401, 2785, 2912, 2927; for a definition of elevation, see §3171).

4092

Go from this land symbolizes being separated from that kind of goodness, the goodness symbolized by Laban, as can be seen without explanation.

4093

And return to the land of your birth symbolizes union with divine goodness that comes of truth. This can be seen from the symbolism of *returning to the land* as moving closer to divine goodness (dealt with above in §4069) and from the symbolism of *birth* as truth (also dealt with above, in §4070). This makes it clear that returning to the land of his birth symbolizes union with divine goodness that comes of truth.

4094

Genesis 31:14, 15, 16. *And Rachel and Leah answered and said to him, "Do we have an allotment and inheritance any longer in our father's house? Aren't we deemed strangers to him? For he has sold us and most certainly eaten up our silver. Because all the riches that God snatched from our father, to us they belong and to our children. And now all that God has said to you, do."*

4095

Rachel and Leah answered and said to him symbolizes reciprocation by the [two kinds of] desire for truth. *Do we have an allotment and inheritance any longer in our father's house?* symbolizes the first stage of their separation from the goodness symbolized by Laban. *Aren't we deemed strangers to him? For he has sold us* means that it disowned them, ending their connection with it. *And most certainly eaten up our silver* symbolizes the truth associated with those desires, which [intermediate goodness] would consume if they were not separated from it. *Because all the riches that God snatched from our father, to us they belong and to our children* means that the Lord did everything by his own power and no one contributed anything, as his divine side flowed into the benefits he took from [intermediate goodness]. *And now all that God has said to you, do,* symbolizes the Lord's providence.

Rachel and Leah answered and said to him symbolizes reciprocation by the [two kinds of] desire for truth, as the following shows: *Answering,* when the answer is affirmative, symbolizes reciprocation (as noted in §2919) and acceptance (§§2941, 2957). And *Rachel* represents a desire for inner truth, while *Leah* represents a desire for outer truth (as discussed in §§3758, 3782, 3793, 3819).

4096

The inner meaning of the story so far has had to do with earthly goodness, symbolized by Jacob, when it separated from intermediate goodness, which is Laban, and the way this goodness connected to itself the desire for truth symbolized by Rachel and Leah. The new topic is the reciprocal attachment of that desire to goodness. Such an attachment is contained in the inner meaning of the words now spoken by Rachel and Leah.

[2] These concepts, though, are inaccessible by their very nature except to a well-informed intellect that enjoys learning such things and that consequently has spiritual knowledge as its goal. Other people do not care about the subject and cannot stretch their minds that far. Those whose goals are tied to the world and the earth cannot drag their senses away from there. If they did, they would not enjoy it, because they would be withdrawing and removing themselves from the concerns that they focus on as their goals—in other words, that they love. Let those who fit this description experiment on themselves to see whether they want to know how goodness connects itself to a desire for truth and how a desire for truth attaches itself to goodness, and whether the knowledge is annoying to them. They will say it does them no good and they do not understand a bit of it.

[3] If you talk to them about their business dealings in the world, no matter how abstruse the topic, they not only understand it but perceive its deeper implications. Likewise if you talk to them about the interests of another and how to use those interests to connect to that other, attaching themselves by an attitude and certain phrases. It is the same with those who devote themselves to investigating scientific mysteries because they want to; they love to probe into more intricate matters than these, and do probe into them. But when the subject is spiritual goodness and spiritual truth, they find it boring and even distasteful.

These comments are intended to show what people in the church are like today.

[4] The situation of goodness when it connects truth to itself through desire, and of truth when it attaches itself, is not very easy to see when focusing one's thoughts and ideas on goodness and on truth. It is better to focus on the communities of spirits and angels through which goodness and truth flow in. As noted at §4067, our willing and thinking comes from those communities, as an inflow, and appears to exist inside us.

To learn from these communities of spirits and [outer] angels how the case stands is to learn from the real causes. To learn from heaven and its [inner] angels is to learn from the purposes behind the causes. There are also stories that apply and shed light to make the matter plainer.

[5] The inner meaning deals with the connection of goodness to truth and truth's attachment on the earthly plane. Jacob means goodness on

that plane, as mentioned many times, and his women mean a desire for truth. Goodness, which is a matter of love and charity, flows in from the Lord through the angels with us, and the only thing it can flow into in us is the knowledge we possess. Since goodness fastens on to knowledge, our thoughts linger on the truth we know, which stirs up other related or pertinent ideas. This process continues until desire [for the truth] moves us to think, "That is so," and to will it because it is so. At that point, goodness unites with truth, and truth freely attaches itself, because desire always creates freedom (§§2870, 2875, 3158, 4031).

[6] When this happens, the spirits allied with us actually raise doubts and sometimes even denial, but so far as desire [for the truth] prevails, we are led to affirm the truth, and doubt and denial then only strengthen us in it.

When goodness flows into us this way, we do not perceive that it comes through angels, because it flows in deeply and lands in the shadows that worldly and bodily concerns cast in us.

It needs to be realized that goodness flows in not from angels but through angels from the Lord. All angels admit this, so they never claim any goodness as their own. In fact, they bristle when anyone attributes it to them.

These considerations—the real causes—now show how matters stand with the connection of goodness to truth and truth's attachment, the theme of the inner meaning here.

Do we have an allotment and inheritance any longer in our father's house? **4097** symbolizes the first stage of their separation from the goodness symbolized by Laban. This can be seen from the meaning of *do we have an allotment and inheritance any longer* as the question of whether there was any union anymore; and from the symbolism of *our father's house* as the goodness represented by Laban. These words, as a result, symbolize the first stage of the separation of [both kinds of desire] from the goodness symbolized by Laban.

In the first stage, the mind falls into doubt. In the second, reasoning puts the doubt to flight. The third stage is affirmation. The final is action. So goodness accompanied by truth makes its way from the intellectual side of the mind into the volitional side, and we adopt it as our own.

Aren't we deemed strangers to him? For he has sold us means that it dis- **4098** owned them, ending their connection with it. This can be seen from the symbolism of *deeming them strangers* as disowning them, and from that of *selling* as disowning them so completely as to end their connection with it.

4099   *And most certainly eaten up our silver* symbolizes the truth associated with those desires, which [intermediate goodness] would consume if they were not separated from it. This is established by the symbolism of *eating* as consuming, and from that of *silver* as truth (discussed in §§1551, 2954). *Our silver* plainly means the truth associated with those desires, since Rachel and Leah represent two kinds of desire for truth, as shown many times before.

What these concepts involve cannot be known unless one knows about the goodness and truth instilled by means of intermediate goodness, or about the groups of spirits that serve in the role of intermediate goodness. Groups of spirits that serve in the role of intermediate goodness concentrate on what is worldly, but groups of angels that serve to introduce a desire for truth concentrate on what is heavenly rather than what is worldly. These two kinds of communities act on a person who is being reborn. [2] The more the person is initiated into heavenly attributes by the angels, the more the spirits involved in worldly affairs are removed. If they are not removed, truth evaporates.

Worldly and heavenly qualities harmonize in us when heavenly qualities are more dominant than worldly ones. They clash when worldly qualities are more dominant than heavenly ones. When they harmonize, truth multiplies in our earthly level. When they clash, truth dwindles and is even consumed, because worldly elements cast darkness on heavenly ones and therefore place them in doubt; but when heavenly elements dominate, they cast light on worldly ones, clarify them, and remove doubt. The side that dominates is the side that we love more.

This shows what is meant by the claim that [intermediate goodness] would consume the truth associated with those desires if they were not separated from it, which is what "he has certainly eaten up our silver" means.

4100   *Because all the riches that God snatched from our father, to us they belong and to our children* means that the Lord did everything by his own power and no one contributed anything, as his divine side flowed into what he received from [intermediate goodness]. This can be seen from the discussions and explanations above at §§4065, 4075, 4081.

4101   *And now all that God has said to you, do,* symbolizes the Lord's providence. This can be seen from the symbolism of *doing all that God says* as obeying, but when spoken in reference to the Lord, as providing. He does not act from another but on his own. Nor does God tell him to act but he himself speaks—that is, he acts on his own.

Genesis 31:17, 18. *And Jacob got up and took up his sons and his women* [4102]
*on camels. And he took away all his property and all his substance that he had
amassed, the property of his buying that he had amassed in Paddan-aram, to
come to Isaac his father, to the land of Canaan.*
Jacob got up means elevating the goodness meant by Jacob. *And took
up his sons and his women on camels* means elevating both truth and a
desire for truth and organizing them at a general level. *And he took away
all his property and all his substance that he had amassed* symbolizes the
separation of truth and goodness from Laban's. *The property of his buying*
symbolizes [truth and goodness] taken from those elsewhere. *That he had
amassed in Paddan-aram* symbolizes knowledge of truth and goodness on
the earthly level. *To come to Isaac his father, to the land of Canaan,* means
in order to unite with divine goodness on the rational level, so that his
humanity would become divine.

Jacob got up means elevating the goodness meant by Jacob. This is [4103]
established by the symbolism of *getting up* as involving elevation (discussed in §§2401, 2785, 2912, 2927) and from the representation of *Jacob*
as earthly goodness (mentioned many times before). In this case he represents goodness that approaches nearer to divine goodness, because it was
to separate from intermediate goodness, or Laban (§4073).

The elevation symbolized by getting up means a closer approach to
divinity. We human beings are said to be elevated when we more closely
approach heavenly traits, because people think heaven exists on high.
The expression is based on an appearance, because heaven (and consequently what exists in heaven, or heavenly and spiritual qualities) is not
up high but deep within; see §§450, 1735, 2148. Our inner depths are in
heaven, then, when we have spiritual love and faith.

And took up his sons and his women on camels means elevating both [4104]
truth and a desire for truth and organizing them at a general level, as the
following shows: *Sons* symbolize truth, as noted in §§489, 491, 533, 1147,
2623. *Women*—in this instance Rachel, Leah, and their slaves—symbolize
desire for truth and for religious and secular knowledge, as mentioned
before. And *camels* symbolize general facts on the earthly level, as discussed in §§3048, 3071, 3143, 3145.

[2] People who do not know about representations and correspondences cannot believe that the current sentence, "He took up his sons and
his women on camels," has this symbolism. To such people the sentence
seems too remote from that spiritual message to enfold or contain it,
because they are thinking about sons, women, and camels. Angels, who

see and perceive everything of this kind in a spiritual way, do not think of sons when sons are mentioned but of truth. They do not think of women when women are mentioned but of a desire for truth and for religious and secular knowledge. They do not think of camels but of general categories [of knowledge] on the earthly plane. That is what such things correspond to, and that is how angels think. Surprising to say, that is also how the inner, spiritual self thinks while living inside the body, even though the outer self is wholly unaware of it. When people who have been reborn die, then, they take up the same kind of thoughts and can think and talk with angels without learning how, which could never happen if their deeper thinking had not run along these lines—which it does because of the correspondence between earthly and spiritual phenomena.

These considerations show that even though the Word's literal meaning is earthly it still holds spiritual content at every single point. That is, it holds the kinds of elements that belong to inner thought and therefore speech, or spiritual thought and speech, or the kind of thought and speech that angels engage in.

[3] How are truth and a desire for truth elevated, and how are they organized at a general level? Truth and desire are elevated when the concerns of eternal life and of the Lord's kingdom are placed before those of physical life and our worldly kingdom. When we acknowledge the former as principal and primary, and the latter as instrumental and secondary, truth and the desire for it are elevated in us. The more they are, the more we cross over into heaven's light, which holds understanding and wisdom, and the objects of worldly light become images and mirrors in which we can see them.

The opposite happens when we set the concerns of physical life and our worldly kingdom before those of eternal life and the Lord's kingdom. For instance, we might disbelieve in eternal life or the Lord's kingdom because we do not see them and no one has come from there to announce their existence. Or we might believe that if they do exist, it will turn out no worse for us there than for others. We might prove it to ourselves and live a worldly life, in utter contempt of charity and faith. If that is what we are like, truth and its desire are not lifted up in us but are choked, rejected, or twisted, because we see by an earthly light that has no heavenly light flowing into it. This description makes it clear what the elevation of truth and a desire for it means.

[4] The way they are organized at a general level follows as a consequence, because the more preference we give to heavenly qualities over worldly ones, the more the contents of our earthly dimension are arranged to match a state of heaven. As noted, our earthly elements resemble images and mirrors of heavenly ones because they represent and correspond to them.

Goals—or rather the Lord working through one's goals—are what organize anything. After all, there are three things that follow in order: goals, means, and results. Goals produce means, and through the means they produce results, so the nature of our goals determines what kind of means emerge and therefore what kind of results emerge. Goals exist at our core; means are in the middle and are called intermediate goals; while results come last and are called final goals. Results are also referred to as the general or comprehensive level. This discussion clarifies what organization at the general level is: when we make the concerns of eternal life and of the Lord's kingdom our goals, all intermediate goals (means) and final goals (results) are organized in accord with the true goal. This occurs on the earthly level because that is where results come about or, to put the same thing another way, that is the general or comprehensive level.

[5] Any adult with a modicum of judgment who is willing to consider the question can see that we live in two kingdoms, spiritual and earthly, the spiritual kingdom being inside and the earthly kingdom outside. We can put one of these before the other, or make one more our aim than the other, and the one that forms our goal or that we put first is the one that dominates in us. If our goal and main concern is the spiritual kingdom, or its qualities, what we acknowledge first and foremost is love for the Lord, charity for our neighbor, and any concept that strengthens either (which is called a tenet of faith). These are matters of the spiritual kingdom, and everything on our earthly level is then arranged and organized to accord with them, so as to serve them obediently.

When our goal and main concern is the earthly kingdom, or what exists there, we so resolutely block out anything related to love for the Lord, charity for our neighbor, or faith that we completely dismiss it; love for worldly advantages and for ourselves, and everything related to it is what we make our all-in-all. Under these circumstances, everything on our earthly level is organized to accord with these goals, so it is organized in direct opposition to the attributes of heaven. As a consequence, we create hell in ourselves.

To make something our aim is to love it. All purpose belongs to love, because what we love we take as our goal.

4105   *And he took away all his property and all his substance that he had amassed* symbolizes the separation of truth and goodness that come from Laban's. This can be seen from the symbolism of *taking away* as separating, from that of *property* as truth, and from that of *substance* as goodness. *That he had amassed* has to do with Laban and his flock, through which they were acquired.

Property means truth, and substance means goodness, because *property* in the original tongue is a word that also means livestock in general, which specifically symbolizes truth when flocks symbolize goodness. Substance symbolizes the resources from which they come. When the Word uses two terms of almost the same meaning, one relates to truth and the other to goodness. This is due to the heavenly marriage, which is the marriage of truth and goodness in every part of the Word; see §§683, 793, 801, 2173, 2516, 2712.

4106   *The property of his buying* symbolizes [truth and goodness] taken from those elsewhere. This can be seen from the symbolism of *property* as truth (discussed just above) and from that of *buying* as items acquired from elsewhere. The property Jacob bought came from elsewhere but at the same time from what he had acquired through Laban's flock.

4107   *That he had amassed in Paddan-aram* symbolizes knowledge of goodness and truth on the earthly level. This is established by the symbolism of *Paddan-aram* as knowledge of goodness and truth (discussed in §§3664, 3680).

4108   *To come to Isaac his father, to the land of Canaan,* means in order to unite with divine goodness on the rational level, so that his humanity would become divine, as the following shows: *Isaac* represents divine rationality, as mentioned in §§1893, 2066, 2083, 2630—specifically, divine goodness on the rational plane (§§3012, 3194, 3210). And the *land of Canaan* symbolizes the Lord's heavenly kingdom (as discussed in §§1607, 3481), and in the highest sense—when mentioned in connection with the Lord, that is—as his divine humanity (§§3038, 3705). These remarks make it clear that *to come to Isaac his father, to the land of Canaan,* means in order to unite with divine goodness on the rational level, so that his humanity would become divine.

[2] In respect to the union of the rational and earthly dimensions in us, it is important to see that the rational dimension belongs to our inner self, the earthly dimension to our outer self. Their union makes us human, the quality of our humanity depending on the nature of the union. The union occurs when they act in concert, and they act in concert when the earthly level assists and serves the rational level.

This cannot possibly be accomplished in us except by the Lord, but in the Lord it was accomplished by himself.

Genesis 31:19, 20, 21. *And Laban had gone to shear his flock. And Rachel stole the teraphim that belonged to her father. And Jacob stole the heart of Laban the Aramean by not telling him that he was fleeing. And he fled, and everything that was his; and he rose and crossed the river and turned his face toward Mount Gilead.*

4109

Laban had gone to shear his flock symbolizes a useful and purposeful state of the goodness meant by Laban's flock. *And Rachel stole the teraphim that belonged to her father* symbolizes a change in the attitude symbolized by Laban regarding truth. *And Jacob stole the heart of Laban the Aramean* symbolizes a change in the attitude symbolized by Laban regarding goodness— *Laban the Aramean* meaning a type of goodness that did not have divine truth and goodness in it, as it had before. *By not telling him that he was fleeing* means because of being separated. *And he fled, and everything that was his* symbolizes separation. *And he rose* symbolizes elevation. *And crossed the river* symbolizes a state in which there is union. *And turned his face toward Mount Gilead* symbolizes what is good about that state.

Laban had gone to shear his flock symbolizes a useful and purposeful state of the goodness meant by Laban's flock. This can be seen from the symbolism of *shearing* as usefulness and accordingly as purpose, since usefulness is purpose, as discussed below; and from that of a *flock* as goodness (discussed in §§343, 2566). Plainly, then, a useful and purposeful state is symbolized by *going to shear.*

4110

The theme now is the separation of intermediate goodness (Laban) from the goodness obtained through it (Jacob). The only way to understand the separation is to look at communities of spirits who have that kind of goodness, from whom it flows into humankind. Let me talk about it from experience.

[2] There are good spirits, spirits of an intermediate sort, and evil spirits connected to us while we are being reborn, so that we can be introduced by them into genuine goodness and truth through the agency of angels

from the Lord. However, they are the type of spirits (or of spirit communities) who harmonize only in the short term with the person being reborn. When they have performed their function, they are separated.

Their separation is achieved in different ways: one for good spirits, another for spirits of the intermediate sort, and another for evil spirits. Good spirits are separated from us when they are not aware of it, knowing that in the Lord's good pleasure things go well for them wherever they are, or wherever the Lord sends them. Spirits of the intermediate kind are separated through a variety of means, until eventually they leave willingly. You see, they are sent back into a state marked by their own kind of goodness, and so to a state of resulting usefulness and purpose, to enjoy their true pleasure and bliss. Since they drew a more sensual pleasure from their previous contact [with us], though, they return to it and are sent back by turns, until they finally find it unpleasant to delay any longer. Then they freely withdraw. As for evil spirits, they are also removed by their free choice, to be sure, but a free choice that only appears to them to be free. They are connected with us for the purpose of inflicting negative thoughts and feelings that we need to banish, so that we can strengthen ourselves all the more in what is true and good. When we start to confirm truth and goodness, the evil spirits sense discomfort. They find it a relief to detach and therefore do so with a freedom born of their relief.

That is how spirits are separated from us when we are being reborn, so it is how the state of goodness and truth changes in us.

[3] The meaning of *shearing a flock* as doing something useful becomes clear from the fact that in an inner sense the shearing of a flock actually means being useful, since wool is the result.

The meaning of shearing a flock as useful activity also becomes clear from the following passage in Moses:

> Every firstborn that is born in your herd and in your flock you shall consecrate to Jehovah your God. You shall not do work with the firstborn of your ox, and you *shall not shear the firstborn of your flock.* But you shall eat it before Jehovah your God yearly in the place that Jehovah chooses. (Deuteronomy 15:19, [20])

Not shearing the firstborn of the flock means not making it serve a domestic purpose.

Since the shearing of a flock symbolized useful activity, one of the most important functions and duties in those days was the shearing of the flock and attendance at the shearing. This can be seen from Judah's shearing of his flock in Genesis 38:12, 13, and from David's sons in 2 Samuel:

> It happened after two years of days that Absalom had *shearers* in Baalhazor, which is in Ephraim, and Absalom called all the sons of the king, and Absalom came to the king and said, *"Look, please: your servant's shearers;* let the king and your servants please go with your servant." (2 Samuel 13:23, 24)

And Rachel stole the teraphim that belonged to her father symbolizes a change in the attitude symbolized by Laban regarding truth, as can be seen from the following: *Stealing* here means taking away something dear and holy, changing the [owner's] attitude. The *teraphim* symbolize truth, as discussed below. And the *father*—Laban—symbolizes the goodness that Laban stands for, as discussed before. A father too symbolizes goodness (§3703). These considerations make it clear that *Rachel stole the teraphim that belonged to her father* symbolizes a change in the attitude meant by Laban regarding truth.

[2] The implications here can also be seen from the state of spirits when they are being separated. Their attitude toward goodness and truth matches that of the communities they are in, because all thought flows in through others, as shown before, and most immediately through those in whose company one is. When spirits are removed from one community and relegated to another, then, the state of their thoughts and feelings changes, so their stance regarding truth and goodness changes. If they are sent to communities they are not in tune with, they dislike it, and the unpleasantness of it puts them under pressure. As a result, they detach and move on to communities they are in tune with. That is why the evil cannot live and stay in communities of the good, and the good cannot do so in communities of the evil. It is why all spirits and angels are divided into groups according to their desires, which are part of love.

Every desire belonging to love contains many different aspects (§§3078, 3189, 4005), but one aspect is dominant. So we can each go to many different communities, but we still strive toward the one exhibiting our dominant desire, and that is where we end up.

[3] To comment further on the goodness symbolized by Laban and the change in its state: As long as it coexisted with the goodness represented by Jacob, it was closer to divinity, because Jacob means divine goodness on the earthly level. Since it was closer to divinity, it was also

in a more perfect state of truth and goodness. When it was separated from that goodness, it took another attitude toward truth and goodness. In the other world, changes in state in general are nothing but advances toward and retreats from divinity. These remarks now make it clear what is meant by a change of state when the goodness symbolized by Laban was separated.

[4] The reason Rachel's theft of the teraphim that belonged to her father symbolizes a change in state regarding truth is that *teraphim* refers to Laban's gods. (Later verses make this plain, because in verse 30 Laban says to Jacob, "Why did you steal *my gods?*" and in verse 32 Jacob answers, "[The one] with whom you find *your gods* will not live before our brothers.") And on an inner level, gods symbolize truth. That is why the name God is used in the Word when the subject is truth; see §§2586, 2769, 2807, 2822.

[5] Teraphim were idols people used when they consulted God or asked him questions, and since the answers they received were divine truth, as far as they were concerned, teraphim symbolize truth, as in Hosea:

> For many days the children of Israel sat: no monarch and no chieftain and no sacrifice, nor *ephod* and *teraphim*. (Hosea 3:4)

The ephod and teraphim stand for divine truth received in answer, because when they asked God a question, they put on the ephod (1 Samuel 23:9, 10, 11, 12). In Zechariah:

> The *teraphim speak wickedness,* and the diviners see falsehood, and dreams speak what is worthless. (Zechariah 10:2)

The teraphim again stand for answers—wicked ones, in that state.

[6] Since this was the symbolism of teraphim, some people had them even though they were outlawed, as Micah did in Judges:

> Micah had a house of God and made an *ephod* and *teraphim* and filled the hand of one of his sons to be priest to him. And certain Danites said to their brothers, "Do you know that in these houses there is an *ephod* and *teraphim,* and a carved image and a cast image?" And when they had entered Micah's house, they took the carved image, the *ephod* and the *teraphim,* and the cast image. And the heart of the priest felt good, and he took the *ephod* and the *teraphim,* and the carved image. And

Micah, pursuing the children of Dan, said, "You have taken my gods that I made, and the priest, and left; what more do I have?" (Judges 17:5; 18:14, 18, 20, 24)

Michal, David's wife, also had teraphim, as described in 1 Samuel:

Michal, David's wife, took the *teraphim* and put them on the bed and covered them with a garment. Saul's envoys came, but here, the *teraphim* were on the bed! (1 Samuel 19:13, 16)

Nevertheless they were idols, which were prohibited, as is evident from statements about them in 1 Samuel 15:23; 2 Kings 23:24; Ezekiel 21:21.

And Jacob stole the heart of Laban the Aramean symbolizes a change in the attitude symbolized by Laban regarding goodness, as the following indicates: *Stealing* means taking away something dear and holy, changing the [owner's] state, as just above in §4111. The *heart* symbolizes what comes out of the will, and since the will is composed of goodness, the heart symbolizes goodness, as discussed in §§2930, 3313, 3888, 3889. And *Laban* represents an intermediate goodness, which is now being separated. Since it is being separated, Laban is now called an Aramean, as he is again below, in verse 24, because *Laban the Aramean* means a type of goodness that did not have divine goodness and truth in it, as it did before.

4112

The reason for this last is that Aram, or Syria, was separated from the land of Canaan by the river Euphrates, so it was outside Canaan, which on an inner level symbolizes the Lord's kingdom, and on the highest level, the Lord's divine humanity (see above at §4108).

[2] In a specific sense Aram, or Syria, symbolizes knowledge of what is true and good (see §§1232, 1234, 3051, 3249, 3664, 3680), because the ancient church existed there as well. Traces of the ancient church remained there a long time, as can be seen from Balaam, a native who knew Jehovah and prophesied about the Lord. After idolatry spread in that land, though, and Abram was called away, and a representative religion was established in Canaan, Aram or Syria started to represent an area outside the church, isolated from it and therefore distant from attributes of the Lord's kingdom. However, it continued to symbolize a knowledge of goodness and truth.

Jacob is said to have stolen Laban's heart by not telling him that he was fleeing because the text just talked about a change in attitude toward truth, so now it is talking about a change in attitude toward goodness. Whenever the Word deals with truth, it also deals with goodness, on

account of the heavenly marriage, which is a marriage of truth and goodness in every detail of the Word (§§683, 793, 801, 2516, 2712).

4113 *By not telling him that he was fleeing* means because of being separated, as is self-evident.

On a narrative level, "Jacob stole the heart of Laban the Aramean by
not telling him that he was fleeing" means that Jacob spoiled any hope
Laban had of appropriating everything Jacob owned and caused Laban a
state of distress. Laban believed that since Jacob served him, everything of
Jacob's would become his. This included not only Jacob's women (Laban's
daughters) and their children but also his flocks, according to a rule then
known and accepted, and recorded by Moses:

> If you buy a Hebrew slave, for six years he shall serve and in the seventh
> go out free, for nothing. If his master has given him a woman, and she
> has borne him sons and daughters, the woman and her children shall be
> his master's, and he shall go out with his body. (Exodus 21:2, 4)

Jacob's words later in the current chapter show that Laban was thinking
this way:

> Had I not had the God of my father, the God of Abraham and the
> Dread of Isaac, you would have sent me away empty now. (verse 42)

So do Laban's own words:

> Laban answered and said to Jacob, "The daughters are my daughters
> and the sons are my sons and the flock is my flock, and everything that
> you are seeing—it is mine." (verse 43)

He did not think about the fact that Jacob had not been a purchased slave
or even a servant, that Jacob came from a more distinguished family than
his own, that Jacob had accepted both the women and the flock as his
wage, and consequently that the law did not apply to Jacob. Now since
Jacob in fleeing ruined Laban's hopes on this score, causing him a state of
distress, the text says that he stole the heart of Laban the Aramean by not
telling him that he was fleeing. On an inner level, though, these words
symbolize a change in the attitude symbolized by Laban regarding goodness because of being separated.

For information on a change in attitude or state on account of separation, see the discussion just above in §4111.

And he fled, and everything that was his symbolizes separation. This can be seen from the remarks just made and therefore needs no further explanation.   **4114**

And he rose symbolizes elevation. This can be seen from discussion above at §4103 concerning the symbolism of *rising* [or getting up].   **4115**

And crossed the river symbolizes a state in which there is union. This can be seen from the symbolism of the *river,* the Euphrates, as union—specifically union with the Divine. The reason the river has this symbolism is that it was the land of Canaan's border on that side. All of Canaan's borders represented and therefore symbolized what was last and what was first—what was last, because Canaan ended there, and what was first, because it started there. All borders by their very nature are last on the way out and first on the way in. Since Jacob was now entering, the river was an initial boundary and accordingly meant union—specifically, in the highest sense, union with the Divine. On an inner plane, the land of Canaan symbolizes the Lord's heavenly kingdom (§§1607, 3481), and on the highest plane it symbolizes the Lord's divine humanity (§§3038, 3705). From this it is evident what "he crossed the river" means in this passage.   **4116**

Everything in the land of Canaan had a representation that depended on distances, placement, and borders (see §§1585, 3686). So the rivers that formed its boundaries did too, and this included the river of Egypt, the Euphrates, and the Jordan (§1866).

And turned his face toward Mount Gilead symbolizes what is good about that state. This is established by the symbolism of a *mountain* as heavenly love, or goodness (discussed in §§795, 1430), with which there is union. *Gilead* symbolizes its quality.   **4117**

Because the river was the border, meaning the place where union starts (as noted), Mount Gilead, standing on the same side of the Jordan, symbolizes the element of goodness with which this union first takes place.

[2] The land of Gilead, in which the mountain stood, was within the limits of Canaan, broadly speaking. It was on the near [or east] side of the Jordan and fell as an inheritance to the Reubenites, the Gadites, and more particularly the half-tribe of Manasseh. The fact that the inherited regions extended that far explains why I say it was within the limits of Canaan broadly speaking. Moses makes it clear that these were the tribes that inherited it, in Numbers 32:1, 26–41; Deuteronomy 3:8, 10–16; Joshua 13:24–31.

For this reason, when an image of the land of Canaan was being presented in its entirety, the expression used was "from Gilead to Dan." (The expression "from Beer-sheba to Dan" also occurs, Dan too being a border: §§1710, 3923. Regarding "Beer-sheba to Dan," see §§2858, 2859.) The phrase "from Gilead to Dan" is used in Moses:

> Moses went up from the plains of Moab onto Mount Nebo, the head of Pisgah, which is toward Jericho, where Jehovah showed him the *land of Gilead all the way to Dan*. (Deuteronomy 34:1)

And in Judges:

> *Gilead* is living on the ford of the Jordan; and Dan—why must he be afraid of ships? (Judges 5:17)

[3] Since Gilead was a border, on a spiritual plane it symbolizes the first form of goodness, which belongs to physical sensation, because the goodness (that is, the pleasure) of physical sensation is the very first kind we are introduced to when we are being reborn. That is the sense in which Gilead is taken in the Prophets, such as Jeremiah 8:21, 22; 22:6; 46:11; 50:19; Ezekiel 47:18; Obadiah verse 19; Micah 7:14; Zechariah 10:10; Psalms 60:7; and in a negative sense, Hosea 6:8; 12:11.

4118   Genesis 31:22, 23, 24, 25. *And it was told to Laban on the third day that Jacob had fled. And he took his brothers with him and followed after [Jacob] a path of seven days and joined him on Mount Gilead. And God came to Laban the Aramean in a dream by night and said to him, "Watch yourself, to keep from speaking anything with Jacob, whether good or evil." And Laban overtook Jacob, and Jacob had pitched his tent on the mountain, and Laban pitched with his brothers on Mount Gilead.*

It was told to Laban on the third day symbolizes the end. *That Jacob had fled* symbolizes separation. *He took his brothers with him* symbolizes good qualities to replace those that were lost. *And followed after him* symbolizes a relentless passion for union. *A path of seven days* symbolizes sacred truth. *And joined him on Mount Gilead* means leading to a small amount of union. *And God came to Laban the Aramean in a dream by night* symbolizes a dim perception of that goodness on its own. *And said to him, "Watch yourself, to keep from speaking anything with Jacob, whether good or evil,"* means that there would no longer be any contact. *And Laban overtook Jacob* symbolizes limited union. *And Jacob had pitched his tent on the mountain* symbolizes a state of love characterizing the goodness now meant by Jacob. *And Laban pitched with his brothers on Mount Gilead* symbolizes a state of goodness present in that limited union.

It was told to Laban on the third day symbolizes the end—the end of 【4119】 union. This is established by the symbolism of a *third day* as a final stage, a completion, and therefore the end (discussed in §§1825, 2788), and also as a beginning (§2788). The end of a state of union is the start of the next state, which is one of separation, also symbolized by the third day here.

That Jacob had fled symbolizes separation. This can be seen from the 【4120】 symbolism of *fleeing* as separating (mentioned above at §§4113, 4114).

And he took his brothers with him symbolizes good qualities to replace 【4121】 those that were lost. This can be seen from the symbolism of *brothers* as goodness (discussed in §§2360, 3160, 3303, 3459, 3803, 3815). On an inner level brothers symbolize people who have the same goodness and truth, or who have the same desire for what is good and true. Everyone in the other world forms social ties on the basis of desires, and those who associate with each other form a brotherhood—not that they call each other sister and brother, but that the bonds they share make them so. Goodness and truth themselves in the other life create what we on earth call ties of blood and kinship, so they correspond to such ties.

Regarded in themselves, goodness and truth do not acknowledge any other father than the Lord, because they come from him alone. All people who have goodness and truth are brothers and sisters, then, but to different degrees, depending on the nature of the goodness and truth. In the Word the different degrees are symbolized by brothers, sisters, sons- and daughters-in-law, grandsons, granddaughters, and many other names for family members.

[2] On earth people receive these names by sharing ancestry, no matter how discordant their feelings are, but this kind of siblinghood and relationship dissolves in the next world. Everyone there develops new sisters and brothers, unless the family members had a similar kind of goodness on earth. They do usually come together at first but split up before long, because it is desires (as noted) rather than financial interest that bring people together there. What kinds of desires people have are then as plain as day, as are the feelings one person had toward another. Since these are visible, and desire draws us all to our own community, people whose dispositions clashed break apart. All sister- or brotherhood and friendship previously belonging to the outer self is obliterated on either side, while those belonging to the inner self remain.

The reason "he took his brothers with him" symbolizes good qualities to replace those that were lost is that when one community separates from another, as described above in §§4077, 4110, 4111, it moves on to a third one and consequently to other kinds of goodness that replace the earlier types.

4122   *And followed after him* symbolizes a relentless passion for union. This can be seen from the symbolism of *following*, in this case, as a relentless passion for union.

The inner meaning is dealing with the separation of intermediate goodness from real goodness after the former has served its purpose. The current passage depicts the process of separation in great detail, but it is a process whose existence we are not able even to sense, though angels see it clearly in all its permutations. In those of us who are being reborn, angels see and perceive all the changes of that state. They are present with us as helpers, using and conforming to those changes as they work for the Lord to lead us to what is good—so far as we allow ourselves to be led. It is because the process is such an important one in heaven that the current text has so much to say about it.

This discussion also reveals the nature of the inner meaning—that it is the angels' version of the Word.

4123   *A path of seven days* symbolizes sacred truth. This can be seen from the symbolism of a *path* or way as truth (discussed in §§627, 2333) and from that of *seven* as something holy (discussed in §§395, 433, 716, 881). In this case the meaning is that there was a passion for uniting with sacred truth.

4124   *And joined him on Mount Gilead* means leading to a small amount of union. This is established by the symbolism of *joining* as union, and from that of *Mount Gilead* as the goodness that is united first (discussed above in §4117). "He joined him on Mount Gilead," then, symbolizes a small amount of union.

4125   *And God came to Laban the Aramean in a dream by night* symbolizes a dim perception of that goodness on its own. This can be seen from the representation of *Laban* as intermediate goodness (mentioned before), who is called an *Aramean* when he has separated from the goodness represented by Jacob (§4112); and from the symbolism of *a dream by night* as dimness (dealt with in §§2514, 2528). Perception in that dimness is symbolized by *God's coming [to him]* in a dream by night.

4126   *And said to him, "Watch yourself, to keep from speaking anything with Jacob, whether good or evil,"* means that there would no longer be any contact. This can be seen from the symbolism of *speaking anything, whether* *good or evil,* as saying something good but thinking something evil and therefore eventually speaking and doing evil. People who think evil eventually speak and do it. Those who do so are no longer united to others, because thought and will rather than words are what unite. Words do bind people together in the world, but only when one believes that the person speaking is thinking and intending well too. In the next life, all thought lies open to view. Others share their thoughts with us through a kind of aura— a spiritual one—that emanates from them, revealing their character—in other words, their will and thoughts. So that is what unites us.

These remarks show that in an inner sense the clause *to keep from speaking anything, whether good or evil* means that there would no longer be any contact.

And Laban overtook Jacob symbolizes limited union, as stands to reason from the explanation above in §4124.

And Jacob had pitched his tent on the mountain symbolizes a state of love characterizing the goodness now meant by Jacob, as can be seen from the following: A *tent* symbolizes holy love, as explained in §§414, 1102, 2145, 2152, 3312; *pitching* a tent symbolizes the state of that love. And a *mountain* symbolizes goodness, as above in §4117—here, the goodness now meant by Jacob, which you may find discussed above in §4073.

And Laban pitched with his brothers on Mount Gilead symbolizes a state of goodness present in that limited union, as the following shows: *Laban* represents a goodness now separated from the goodness represented by Jacob. *Pitching* symbolizes the state of that goodness. The text does not speak of "pitching a tent" because there was no state of holy love except through that limited union. *Brothers* symbolize good qualities allied with the goodness symbolized by Laban, as discussed above in §4121. And *Mount Gilead* symbolizes a point where union starts and ends, as dealt with above in §4117. This discussion clarifies that *Laban pitched with his brothers on Mount Gilead* symbolizes a state of goodness present in that limited union.

[2] It is not possible to explain very intelligibly what more is involved in the concepts laid out here except by pointing to what happens in the other world when the Lord attaches groups of spirits and angels to us and detaches them. This process of attachment and detachment follows the established pattern there. The individual steps of the process are depicted in detail in the current passage, but since humankind is entirely ignorant of them, to explain them one by one would be to talk in mere riddles. A little information appeared above where I spoke about the communities

united with and separated from a person being reborn [§§4067, 4073, 4077, 4099, 4111].

It is enough to know that the secrets of this process are contained in the inner meaning—secrets so numerous and of such a kind that not a thousandth of them can be explained in a fully intelligible way.

4130   Genesis 31:26, 27, 28, 29, 30. *And Laban said to Jacob, "What have you done? And you stole my heart and took away my daughters as if captured by a sword! Why did you hide in fleeing and steal me and not tell me? And I would have sent you away with gladness and with songs, with a tambourine and with a harp. And you did not let me kiss my sons and my daughters; now you have acted stupidly in doing this. I wish my hand were as God to do you evil! But the God of your father last night said to me, saying, 'Keep yourself from speaking anything with Jacob, whether good or evil.' And now you went completely away, because you longed so much for the house of your father. Why did you steal my gods?"*

Laban said to Jacob symbolizes a state of communication. *What have you done?* symbolizes outrage. *And you stole my heart* means that it no longer had divine goodness, as it did before. *And took away my daughters* means it no longer had the desire for truth it had before. *As if captured by a sword* means that this had been taken from it. *Why did you hide in fleeing and steal me and not tell me?* symbolizes the state it would be in if it freely chose separation. *And I would have sent you away with gladness and with songs* symbolizes the attitude that self-interest led it to believe it would then have taken toward truth. *With a tambourine and with a harp* means toward spiritual goodness. *And you did not let me kiss my sons and my daughters* symbolizes being disconnected or cut off from a state of freedom, as that kind of goodness believed. *Now you have acted stupidly in doing this* symbolizes outrage. *I wish my hand were as God to do you evil!* symbolizes the state of rage it would achieve if it had the power. *But the God of your father last night said to me* means that the Divine did not allow it. *Saying, "Keep yourself from speaking anything with Jacob, whether good or evil,"* means that contact was forbidden. *And now you went completely away* means that it detached on its own. *Because you longed so much for the house of your father* symbolizes a longing for union with divine goodness that was flowing in directly. *Why did you steal my gods?* symbolizes resentment for a state of lost truth.

4131   *Laban said to Jacob* symbolizes a state of communication—between the goodness represented by Laban and the goodness now represented by Jacob. This can be seen from the symbolism of *saying* in this instance as communicating, as in §3060. Since limited union was established, as described just above in §§4124, 4127, 4129, and since the words *Laban said to Jacob* follow immediately, saying symbolizes communication.

What have you done? symbolizes outrage. This can be seen from the emotion in these words and the following ones spoken by Laban, which exhibit outrage.

4132

And you stole my heart means that it no longer had divine goodness, as it did before. This can be seen from the symbolism of *stealing the heart* as taking away what is dear and holy (discussed above in §4112) and therefore as its no longer having the divine goodness it had before, because it was separated.

4133

And took away my daughters means it no longer had the desire for truth it had before. This can be seen from the symbolism of the *daughters*, Rachel and Leah, as desire for truth (discussed in §§3758, 3782, 3793, 3819).

4134

As if captured by a sword means that this—the desire for truth—had been taken from it, as is evident without explanation. The phrase *captured by a sword* is used because *swords* are mentioned in connection with truth (§2799).

4135

The circumstances surrounding this subject have already been explained [§§4096–4099].

Why did you hide in fleeing and steal me and not tell me? symbolizes the state it would have been in if separation had been freely chosen, as the following indicates: *Hiding to flee* means separating even though it was unwilling. (For the symbolism of *fleeing* as separating, see §§4113, 4114, 4120.) *Stealing me* means taking away what is dear and holy, as mentioned in §§4112, 4133. And *not telling me* in this case means because of separation, as mentioned in §4113. The meaning of the clause therefore is that separation occurred despite unwillingness, when it ought to have resulted from free choice. The next few words—"I would have sent you away with gladness and with songs, with a tambourine and with a harp"—symbolize and depict a state of freedom, but they merely express what Laban then believed. See above at §§4110, 4111 for the way in which intermediate goodness separates from real goodness in people who are being reborn and the fact that it happens in freedom.

4136

[2] We humans do not see that this is the case because we do not know how the varieties of goodness in us differ, let alone how the state of each variety changes. We do not even know how childhood goodness alters and changes into adolescent goodness, or this into the next kind,

which is that of early adulthood, then into the goodness of full adulthood, and finally into the goodness of old age. In people who are not being reborn, it is not goodness that changes but different kinds of desire and their pleasures. In people who are being reborn, different kinds of goodness change state, starting in infancy and continuing right to the end of life. The Lord foresees what kind of life we will lead and how we will allow him to lead us, and since he foresees absolutely everything down to the smallest detail, he also provides for it. We know nothing about stages in the development of goodness, the main reason being that we have not learned anything about it. People today have no interest in learning such things, and since the Lord does not teach us by flowing directly into us, but indirectly, into the knowledge we possess, we cannot possibly know about the developing stages of goodness.

Because we are lacking in knowledge on the subject, and few people these days allow themselves to be reborn anyway, if the material were to be explained any more fully, it would not be comprehensible.

[3] Experience with people coming into the other life from the Christian world has revealed to me that few today know anything about spiritual goodness or about freedom. Let me cite just one example to illustrate. Once there was a prelate who considered himself better educated than others and whom others acknowledged as such when he was alive. Because he had lived an evil life, he was so stupid and ignorant about goodness and freedom and about the pleasures and bliss they produce that he could not see the least difference between hellish and heavenly pleasure and freedom. In fact, he denied there is any. Given that ignorance runs so deep even among those considered more learned than others, you can conclude for yourself what great shadow and in fact what great and terrible insanity would swallow up anything that could be said here about the goodness and freedom spoken of in the inner meaning.

In reality, Scripture contains not even one word that does not enfold a heavenly secret, even when it appears to humankind to have no importance. If it looks unimportant, that is because of modern people's lack of knowledge or ignorance—willful ignorance—on heavenly subjects.

4137   *And I would have sent you away with gladness and with songs* symbolizes the attitude that self-interest led it to believe it would then have taken toward truth. This can be seen from the fact that *I would have sent you away* means that [intermediate goodness] would have freely chosen to detach; but it would not have detached when it was in that state, as the discussion above at §4113 shows. From this it is clear that Laban spoke these words from the point of view that self-interest led him to believe he would then have taken. To be led by self-interest in one's beliefs is to be led by nontruth, but to be led by the Lord rather than self-interest is to be led by truth.

The fact that this state relates to truth is symbolized by *sending with gladness and with songs,* since *gladness* and *songs* are connected with truth.

[2] The Word mentions *gladness* and joy in various places, and sometimes both in the same place. It speaks of gladness when talking about truth and its effect on us, and of joy when talking about goodness and its effect on us. In Isaiah, for instance:

> Indeed, it is *joy* and *gladness* to kill an ox and slaughter a member of the flock, to eat meat and drink wine. (Isaiah 22:13)

The joy has to do with goodness, and the gladness, with truth. In the same author:

> A shouting over the wine in the streets! All *gladness* will be abandoned, and all *joy* will go into exile. (Isaiah 24:11)

In the same author:

> Those ransomed by Jehovah will return and come to Zion with *song,* and eternal *joy* will be on their head. *Joy* and *gladness* will overtake them, and sorrow and groaning will flee. (Isaiah 35:10; 51:11)

In the same author:

> Jehovah will comfort Zion. *Joy* and *gladness* will be found in it; acclamation and the *voice of song.* (Isaiah 51:3)

In Jeremiah:

> I will bring an end in the cities of Judah and in the streets of Jerusalem to the *voice of joy* and the *voice of gladness,* the voice of the bridegroom and the voice of the bride, because the earth will become a wasteland. (Jeremiah 7:34; 25:10)

In the same author:

> The *voice of joy* and the *voice of gladness,* and the voice of the bridegroom and the voice of the bride, the voice of those who say, "Acclaim Jehovah Sabaoth!" (Jeremiah 33:11)

In the same author:

> *Gladness* and *exultation* have disappeared from Carmel and from the land of Moab. (Jeremiah 48:33)

In Joel:

> Hasn't food been cut off before our eyes, *gladness* and *exultation* [cut off] from the house of our God? (Joel 1:16)

In Zechariah:

> To the house of Judah, the fast will serve for *joy* and for *gladness,* and for good feasts. (Zechariah 8:19)

[3] People who are unaware that everything in the Word contains a heavenly marriage—the marriage of goodness and truth—would consider joy and gladness one and the same. They would believe both are mentioned only for greater emphasis, so that one is superfluous, but this is not the case. Not the smallest part of a word has been used without a spiritual meaning. In the passages quoted, and others, joy has to do with goodness, and gladness, with truth (see also §3118).

Songs also have to do with truth, as can be seen from many passages in the Word mentioning them, such as Isaiah 5:1; 24:9; 26:1; 30:29; 42:10; Ezekiel 26:13; Amos 5:23; and others.

[4] It needs to be known that everything in the Lord's kingdom relates either to goodness or to truth—that is, to attributes of love or to attributes of a charitable faith. Anything that relates to goodness, or is an attribute of love, is called heavenly, while anything that relates to truth, or is an attribute of a charitable faith, is called spiritual. Every part of the Word focuses on the Lord's kingdom and in the highest sense on the Lord; the Lord's kingdom is the marriage of goodness and truth, which is to say that it is the heavenly marriage; and the Lord himself is the one who has the divine marriage within him and who is the source of the heavenly marriage. As a consequence, every part of the Word contains that marriage. This is especially easy to see in the Prophets, where a single concept may be repeated with only a change in vocabulary—but nowhere is the repetition pointless. One expression symbolizes something heavenly, or something connected with love or goodness. The other symbolizes something spiritual, or something connected with charitable faith or truth. This explanation makes it clear how every detail of the Word contains the heavenly

marriage (the Lord's kingdom), and on its highest level, the divine marriage itself (the Lord).

With a tambourine and with a harp means toward spiritual goodness. That is, it symbolizes the attitude that self-interest led [intermediate goodness] to believe it would then have taken toward spiritual goodness. This can be seen from the fact that a *tambourine* and *harp* are mentioned in connection with goodness, but goodness of a spiritual kind, as numerous passages in the Word can illustrate. Spiritual goodness is associated with faith and consists in charity. Heavenly goodness is associated with love and consists in love for the Lord.

4138

The Lord has two kingdoms in the heavens. One is called his heavenly kingdom, and its inhabitants are devoted to love for the Lord. The other is called his spiritual kingdom, and its inhabitants are devoted to charity for their neighbor. These kingdoms are utterly distinct from one another, but they still form a single whole in the heavens. To learn about the two different kingdoms, heavenly and spiritual, see the large number of previous discussions.

[2] Different religions in the past employed various kinds of musical instruments, such as tambourines, lutes, flutes, harps, ten-string lutes, and so on—some of them belonging to a heavenly category and some to a spiritual category. When they are mentioned in the Word, that is the kind of meaning they involve, so that in fact you can tell from them just what type of goodness is being talked about, whether it is spiritual or heavenly. Tambourines and harps belong to the spiritual category, which is why the explanation here says "in regard to spiritual goodness." Regarding the connection between a harp and spiritual qualities, the symbolism of string instruments as spiritual qualities, and the symbolism of wind instruments as heavenly qualities, see §§418, 419, 420.

And you did not let me kiss my sons and my daughters symbolizes being disconnected or cut off from a state of freedom, as that kind of goodness believed, which can be seen from the following: *Kissing* symbolizes union growing out of desire, as discussed in §§3573, 3574, 3800, so *not letting someone kiss* symbolizes disconnection. *Sons* symbolize truth, and *daughters* symbolize goodness, as mentioned several times before, and therefore the disconnection has to do with truth and goodness. The text implies that a state of freedom was what intermediate goodness was being cut off from, as it believed. For a discussion of this idea, see earlier at §§4136, 4137.

4139

4140   *Now you have acted stupidly in doing this* symbolizes outrage, as the emotion in the words reveals.

4141   *I wish my hand were as God to do you evil!* symbolizes the state of rage it would achieve if it had the power. This can be seen from the symbolism of the *hand* as power (discussed in §§878, 3387). Obviously the sentence was delivered in a state of rage, and that state is accordingly the one symbolized.

4142   *But the God of your father last night said to me* means that the Divine did not allow it, as stands to reason without explanation. After all, Laban was forbidden in his dream to speak anything to Jacob, whether good or evil, as the next part also says.

4143   *Saying, "Keep yourself from speaking anything with Jacob, whether good or evil,"* means that contact was forbidden. This can be seen from the symbolism of *speaking anything, whether good or evil,* as the end of contact (discussed above at §4126) and so as a ban on it.

4144   *And now you went completely away* means that it detached on its own. This can be seen from the symbolism of *going completely away* as detaching. Obviously it detached on its own.

4145   *Because you longed so much for the house of your father* symbolizes a longing for union with divine goodness that was flowing in directly. This can be seen from the symbolism of the *house of your father* (that is, of Isaac and Abraham) as goodness flowing in directly. A *house* means goodness (see §§2233, 3652, 3720). A *father* also means goodness (§3703), Isaac meaning goodness on the rational plane (§§3012, 3194, 3210). Abraham together with Isaac represents divine goodness that flows in directly, and Laban represents a side branch of goodness, or a kind of goodness that does not flow in directly (§§3665, 3778).

A side branch of goodness, or goodness that does not flow in directly, is the goodness that has been called an intermediate goodness, because for the most part it draws on worldly qualities that appear to be good but are not. Goodness that flows in directly is goodness that either comes straight from the Lord or comes from him by way of heaven. It is a divine goodness separated from the kind of worldly goodness just mentioned.

[2] Everyone who is being reborn first has an intermediate goodness whose purpose is to introduce real goodness and truth. After it has served this use, though, it is detached, and the person is led to goodness that flows in more directly. In this way, people who are being reborn are gradually perfected.

For example, people who are regenerating believe at first that the good they think and do comes from themselves and that they deserve credit for it. They do not yet know—or if they know they do not grasp—that it can flow in from elsewhere. They fail to see that they do not have to be repaid for it just because they do it on their own. If they did not believe in this misconception at first, they would never do any good. The belief initiates them into a desire to do good and into knowledge about goodness and merit. Once they have achieved the desire to do good, they start to think and believe a new way: that goodness flows in from the Lord and that they do not deserve any credit for the good they do on their own. Eventually, when they enjoy intending what is good as well as doing it, they flatly reject credit and even loathe it, being drawn to goodness by goodness. Under these circumstances, goodness flows in directly.

[3] Marriage love offers another example. The goodness that precedes it and ushers it in is physical attraction, personal compatibility, one partner's outward attachment to the other, social equality, or desired social status. These kinds of goodness are the intermediate goodness that marriage love starts with. Later comes a meeting of minds, in which each partner wills what the other does and enjoys doing what pleases the other. This is the second stage, and although the earlier kinds of goodness are still present, they are disregarded. Finally comes union in heavenly goodness and spiritual truth, in which each partner has the same kind of beliefs as the other and responds to the same kind of goodness. When this is the case, both partners are in the heavenly marriage, the marriage of goodness and truth, and therefore they have marriage love, because that is exactly what marriage love is. The Lord then flows into the desires of both as if he were flowing into a single heart. This goodness is the kind that flows in directly, while the previous kinds, which flowed in indirectly, served as means for introducing it.

Why did you steal my gods? symbolizes resentment for a state of lost truth. This can be seen from the remarks and illustrations above in §4111 regarding the teraphim Rachel stole. **4146**

Genesis 31:31, 32. *And Jacob answered and said to Laban, "Because I was afraid, because I said perhaps you will kidnap your daughters from me. [The one] with whom you find your gods will not live before our brothers. Examine for yourself what is with me and take it for yourself." And Jacob did not know that Rachel had stolen them.* **4147**

Jacob answered and said to Laban, "Because I was afraid, because I said perhaps you will kidnap your daughters from me," symbolizes a state in which the desire for truth would be hurt if that kind of goodness willingly detached. *[The one] with whom you find your gods will not live before our brothers* means that the truth did not belong to [intermediate goodness], but the truth it did possess would not remain in the context of the goodness belonging to [the earthly level]. *Examine for yourself what is with me and take it for yourself* means that every trace of intermediate goodness had been removed. *And Jacob did not know that Rachel had stolen them* means that it belonged to the desire for inner truth.

4148   *Jacob answered and said to Laban, "Because I was afraid, because I said perhaps you will kidnap your daughters from me,"* symbolizes a state in which the desire for truth would be hurt if that kind of goodness willingly detached. This can be seen from the discussion so far, dealing with willing separation on the part of the goodness symbolized by Laban, to which the current statement is a response. On an inner level the individual words embrace secrets of heaven, which cannot be revealed, for the reason given just above at §4136.

What is symbolized is plainly the state resulting if that kind of goodness willingly detached. The harm that would be done to the desire for truth is symbolized by *perhaps you will kidnap your daughters from me,* since the daughters, Rachel and Leah, symbolize a desire for truth, as shown many times before.

What now follows will explain more clearly what is going on here.

4149   *[The one] with whom you find your gods will not live before our brothers* means that the truth did not belong to [intermediate goodness], and the truth it did possess would not remain in the context of the goodness belonging to [the earthly level]. This can be seen from the symbolism of the *gods*—teraphim—as truth (dealt with in §4111), but truth belonging to the desire represented here by Rachel rather than to the goodness symbolized by Laban. Since the gods symbolize that truth, the text says that Rachel stole them, and continues to talk about them in later verses, which it would never do if the event did not involve secrets that are revealed only in the inner meaning. Because the truth being discussed here belonged to the desire for truth represented by Rachel rather than to the goodness symbolized by Laban, the words *[the one] with whom you find your gods will not live before our brothers* mean that the truth did not belong to that goodness, and the truth it did possess would not remain in the context of the goodness belonging to [the earthly level].

[2] To delve more deeply into this secret: All spiritual goodness has its truth, because where spiritual goodness exists, truth exists. Regarded in itself, goodness is uniform, but truth differentiates it. Truth can be compared to the fibers that go to make up a given organ in the body. The arrangement of the fibers determines what the organ is and consequently how it works. Life flowing in through the soul enables it to operate, and life comes from goodness, which comes from the Lord. That is why goodness, although it is uniform, varies in every individual, and varies so widely that it is never precisely the same in one person as in another. It is also why one person's truth can never survive in the context of another person's goodness. When we have goodness, all our truths communicate with each other and create a certain pattern, so one person's truth cannot be transferred into another person. If it is transferred, it takes on the pattern of the person receiving it and develops a new look (though this secret is too deep and challenging to explain in a few words). That is why one person's mind is never exactly the same as another's; no, there are as many different ways of feeling and thinking as there are people. It is also why the entire heaven consists of angelic forms in unending variety, which come together as one when arranged by the Lord into a heavenly form. No single whole ever consists of identical parts but of parts that vary in form and create a unity according to that form.

From this it is now clear what is meant by the statement that the truth it did possess would not remain in the context of the goodness belonging to [the earthly level].

Examine for yourself what is with me and take it for yourself means that every trace of intermediate goodness had been removed. This can be seen from the meaning of the sentence, which is "I don't have anything of yours." In other words, none of the goodness symbolized by Laban was present in the goodness that is Jacob, so every trace of it had been removed. **4150**

And Jacob did not know that Rachel had stolen them means that it belonged to the desire for inner truth. This is established by the representation of *Rachel* as a desire for inner truth (discussed in §§3758, 3782, 3793, 3819) and from the symbolism of *stealing* as taking away something dear and holy (discussed in §§4112, 4113, 4133). Earlier, Rachel's theft of Laban's teraphim, or gods, symbolized a change in the attitude represented by Laban regarding truth (see §4111), a change delineated further here and in what comes next. The change was due to the fact that after the goodness represented by Laban separated from the goodness that is Jacob, the separation brought it into another state. It felt as though **4151** it had been robbed of the truth that had appeared to be its own while the two kinds of goodness were still united. This is the reason Laban complained about the teraphim, searched for them in the tents, and did not find them. The truth symbolized in a good sense by the teraphim (§4111) did not belong to him but to the desire for truth that is Rachel.

[2] Again, the way these matters stand cannot be explained except in terms of processes occurring in the other world. Anything that happens near us in that world seems to us to be happening inside us, and much the same is true of spirits in the next life. When groups of spirits who have an intermediate kind of goodness are in company with angels, it appears entirely as though they possess the truth and goodness belonging to the angels. They cannot see it any other way. When they separate, though, they sense that the real case is quite different, and consequently they complain, believing that the angels they were associating with have taken their (the spirits') property. That is what the teraphim symbolize on an inner level here and in what follows just below.

[3] To look at the broad picture, no one ever has goodness and truth that is her or his own. Everything good and true flows into us from the Lord both directly and through communities of angels, but goodness and truth still seem to be ours. They appear to be ours so that we will adopt them as our own until we reach the stage where we know and then acknowledge and finally believe they are not ours but the Lord's. The Christian world has learned from the Word that everything good and true comes from the Lord and that nothing good comes from humankind. In fact, the church's teachings, which come from the Word, assert that on our own we cannot even *attempt* good, so we cannot will it, and therefore we cannot do it, since doing good results from wanting to. Belief comes entirely from the Lord, too, which means that we cannot have the least faith unless it flows in from the Lord. [4] That is what the teachings of the church declare and what the preachers preach. Few—very few—believe it, though, and the evidence for this is that people imagine life to be completely inherent; hardly anyone thinks it flows in. Every bit of our life consists in the ability to think and will. If the ability to think and will were taken away, no life would remain. The essence of life consists in thinking what is good and willing it, and in thinking truth and willing what we think is true. Since teachings drawn from the Word assert that these abilities are not ours but the Lord's, and that they flow in from the Lord through heaven, anyone with any judgment and a capacity for reflection could come to the conclusion that all life flows in.

[5] The same is true of evil and falsity. According to teachings taken from the Word, the Devil constantly tries to lead us astray and constantly inspires evil. That is why whenever people do a heinous deed, it is said that they let themselves be seduced by the Devil—which is true, but few if any believe it. Just as everything good and true comes from the Lord, everything evil and false comes from hell—in other words, from the Devil (since hell is the Devil). From this consideration it can also be seen that everything evil and false flows in (just as everything good and true flows in), so thinking and willing evil do, too. Since these also flow in, people with any power of judgment and capacity for reflection can draw the conclusion that all life flows in, even if it appears to be innate in us.

[6] Spirits recently arriving from the world in the other life have been shown many times that this is so. Some of them say that if all evil and falsity flows in as well, nothing bad or wrong can be attributed to them, that they bear no blame, because it comes from somewhere else. The answer they receive is this: They have made the evil and falsity their own by believing they think and will on their own. If their beliefs had matched the reality instead, they would not have made those things their own. After all, they would have believed that everything good and true comes from the Lord, and if they had believed this, they would have let the Lord lead them, and then they would have been in a different state. The evil that infiltrated their thoughts and intentions would not have touched them, since nothing that is bad but only what is good would have issued from them. After all, what enters does not affect us, only what goes out from us, as the Lord said in Mark 7:15.

[7] Many can see this but few can believe it. Even evil people can see it, but they do not believe it because they want autonomy. They love their independence so much that when you show them that everything flows in, they grow anxious and frantically demand to be allowed to live on their own, saying that if they are denied, they will not survive. Even people who know better think this way.

These remarks have been offered to show how matters stand with communities of spirits characterized by intermediate goodness when they are united to other communities and when they detach. When they are united, they have no idea that the goodness and truth are not their own, although they are not.

Genesis 31:33, 34, 35. *And Laban came into Jacob's tent and into Leah's tent and into the two slaves' tent and did not find them. And he left Leah's tent and came into Rachel's tent. And Rachel took the teraphim and put them in*   **4152** *the camel's straw and sat on them. And Laban probed the whole tent and did not find them. And she said to her father, "Do not let anger blaze in my lord's eyes, because I am unable to rise before you, because the way of women is on me"; and he searched and did not find the teraphim.*

Laban came into Jacob's tent and into Leah's tent and into the two slaves' tent and did not find them means that this truth did not exist in those holy entities. *And he left Leah's tent and came into Rachel's tent* symbolizes the holiness of that truth. *And Rachel took the teraphim* symbolizes inner earthly truth from the Divine. *And put them in the camel's straw* means within facts. *And sat on them* means that it was within. *And Laban probed the whole tent and did not find them* means that nothing belonging to [the goodness symbolized by Laban] was there. *And she said to her father* means addressing goodness. *Do not let anger blaze in my lord's eyes, because I am unable to rise before you* means that it could not be revealed. *Because the way of women is on me* means that it was still mixed with unclean things. *And he searched and did not find the teraphim* means that it did not belong to him.

4153   *Laban came into Jacob's tent and into Leah's tent and into the two slaves' tent and did not find them* means that this truth did not exist in those holy entities. This is established by the symbolism of a *tent* as something holy (discussed in §§414, 1102, 2145, 2152, 3210, 3312, 4128), and here as holy entities, since there were several tents: Jacob's, Leah's, and the slaves'. The fact that the teraphim were *not found* there means that this truth was not there, teraphim in a good sense meaning truth (see above at §4111). *Jacob* represents earthly goodness; *Leah,* the desire for outer truth; and the *slaves,* outer desires, as noted before. Since the truth being discussed here was not external but internal, it was not found in their tents, or in those holy entities. Rather it was in Rachel's tent, or in the holy attribute of a desire for inner truth, since Rachel represents that desire.

4154   *And he left Leah's tent and came into Rachel's tent* symbolizes the holiness of that truth, as can be seen from the discussion just above.

Truth resembles goodness in being both external and internal, because there is an inner and an outer self. The goodness and truth of the inner self are what are called inner goodness and truth, while the goodness and truth of the outer self are called outer goodness and truth. The goodness and truth of the inner self come on three levels, as in the three heavens. The goodness and truth of the outer self also come on three levels, corresponding to the inner levels. There are goodness and truth midway between the inner and outer self, or a go-between (no communication occurs without something in the middle, or a go-between); there are goodness and truth proper to the earthly self (called outer goodness and truth); and there are sensory goodness and truth, which belong to the body and therefore lie on the outermost level. These three types of goodness and truth belong to the outer self and correspond to the same number of types in the inner self, as noted. They will be described elsewhere, by the Lord's divine providence.

[2] The goodness and truth at each level are completely different from each other and not at all intermingled. The inner kinds are components making up the outer kinds. Although they are completely different, they do not appear different to us. People who rely on their senses cannot help seeing all inner goodness and truth—and in fact internal goodness and truth themselves—as merely sensory, because they observe everything from the viewpoint of the senses and therefore from the outermost level. (Inner entities are never visible from the outermost level, only the other way around.) People who are earthly, or who think in terms of facts, cannot help seeing the earthly basis of their thoughts as the inmost level, when it is actually external. Deeper people, who base their judgments and conclusions on discoveries resulting from analysis of earthly facts, likewise believe that those discoveries form humankind's inmost layer, because they appear profound to such people. Nonetheless they lie below the rational dimension, so compared to genuinely rational goodness and truth they are shallow, or inferior. Such is the condition of human comprehension. The goodness and truth just discussed belong to the three planes of the earthly or outer self, but those that belong to the inner self—again on three planes, as noted—are the kinds that exist in the three heavens.

[3] The current remarks show why it is that the truth symbolized by the teraphim were not found in the tents of Jacob, Leah, and the slaves but in Rachel's tent—that is, in the holy quality of desire for inner truth.

All truth received from the Divine is embedded in holiness; this is unavoidable, because truth from the Divine is holy. What qualifies it to be described as holy is the desire involved—in other words, love that flows in from the Lord and elicits a desire for truth.

And Rachel took the teraphim symbolizes inner earthly truth from the Divine. This can be seen from the representation of *Rachel* as the desire for inner truth (discussed before), and from the symbolism of the *teraphim* as truth from the Divine (§4111) and therefore as inner truth. Section 4154 just above says what that truth is like and where it resides.   **4155**

And put them in the camel's straw means within facts. This is established by the symbolism of the *camel's straw* as facts (§3114). Facts are called *straw* both because straw is camel's food and because it is relatively   **4156** coarse and untidy—which is why tangled branches and forest thickets also symbolize facts (§2831). *Camels* stand for general facts belonging to the earthly self (see §§3048, 3071, 3143, 3145).

[2] People wrapped up in bare facts who therefore have a reputation for scholarship do not view facts as relatively coarse and untidy and will not see how facts are accordingly symbolized by straw and by thickets, as claimed. Such people believe that the more we know, or the more secular knowledge we possess, the wiser we are. The reality is quite different, though, as I have been able to tell from people in the other life who during their life in the world focused exclusively on facts and consequently won a name and reputation as scholars. Sometimes they are far stupider than people who had no grasp of the arts and sciences. The reason was also disclosed to me: yes, facts are a means of growing wise but also of going insane. To people who live good lives, facts are a means of growing wise. To people who live evil lives, facts are a means of going insane, since they use them to justify not only their evil life but also their false premises—which they do with arrogance and feigned conviction, considering themselves wiser than others. As a result they destroy their rationality.

[3] Enjoying the use of rationality is not the same as being able to argue from facts, even when one seems to do so in a loftier way than others; mere swamp light, so to speak, produces this skill. To possess rationality is to be capable of discerning that goodness is good, truth is true, evil is therefore evil, and falsity is false. People who regard goodness as evil, evil as good, truth as wrong, and falsity as true simply cannot be called rational but rather irrational, however good they are at arguing. In people who see plainly that goodness is good, and truth is true, and on the other hand that evil is bad, and falsity is false, light flows in from heaven. It shines on their intellect, turning the lines of reasoning they see with their intellect into so many rays of that light. The same light also illuminates facts, making them supportive, organizing them, and arranging them into a heavenly pattern.

In contrast, people who oppose goodness and truth (as everyone who lives an evil life does) refuse to let this heavenly light in. Their swamp light is the only kind that gives them pleasure. The nature of this light is such that they resemble people seeing spots and streaks on the wall in the dark and fantasizing all kinds of images, when there really are no images, only spots and streaks that appear as such when daylight floods back in.

[4] These considerations show that facts are a means of growing wise and of going insane. In other words, they are both a means of perfecting

and a means of destroying the rational mind. Consequently, people who have destroyed their rationality through facts are much stupider in the other life than people who had no grasp of the arts and sciences.

The relatively coarse nature of facts is evident when one considers that they belong to the earthly or outer self, and that rationality, which we cultivate by means of facts, belongs to the spiritual or inner self. How much they differ, specifically in regard to their refinement, can be seen from the discussion and explanation of the two kinds of memory in §§2469–2494.

And sat on them means that [the truth] was within—under Rachel, in the camel's straw. The camel's straw, as noted just above, symbolizes facts. The truth symbolized by the teraphim did not consist of facts but lay within facts. The situation with the three levels of truth described just above in §4154 is that inner levels lie within outer levels, since they settle in this order. **4157**

And Laban probed the whole tent and did not find them means that nothing belonging to [the goodness symbolized by Laban] was there. This can be seen from the inner-level context without further explanation. **4158**

And she said to her father means addressing goodness. This can be seen from the symbolism of a *father* as goodness (discussed in §3703) and from the representation of Laban, the father here, as intermediate goodness (discussed before). **4159**

Do not let anger blaze in my lord's eyes, because I am unable to rise before you means that it could not be revealed. This can also be seen from the inner-level context without further explanation. After all, to *rise* would be to expose the teraphim and therefore to reveal the truth they symbolize, so *not being able to rise* means that it could not be revealed. **4160**

Because the way of women is on me means that it was still mixed with unclean things. This can be seen from the symbolism of the *way of women* as uncleanness and also therefore as the unclean things on which Rachel sat (Leviticus 15:19–31). So the clause means that it was mixed with unclean things. Inner truth is said to be mixed with unclean things when it lies among facts that do not yet correspond, or that clash. They are removed when a person is washed—that is, reborn. **4161**

And he searched and did not find the teraphim means that it did not belong to him—this truth did not belong to Laban—as can be seen from the symbolism of *searching and not finding*. Taken superficially, as narrative, these words imply that the item was indeed Laban's but was hidden; in an inner sense, though, they mean that it was not his. The *teraphim* mean truth from the Divine (see §4111). **4162**

An explanation of the situation here—that this truth did not belong to the goodness symbolized by Laban but to the desire for inner truth—may be found in the discussion above at §4151. These remarks now clarify the secret lying hidden in the current clause concerning the teraphim.

[2] The teraphim symbolize truth from the Divine because people in the ancient church used various names to identify the Divine, or the Lord, according to different traits they could see in outward effects. For instance, they called him God Shaddai for times of trial, in which the Lord fights for us and after which he blesses us (see §§1992, 3667). Guardian beings were their symbol for the work of his providence to prevent us from prying into religious mysteries by our own powers (§308). They used the name teraphim for divine truth received in answer to their questions. And they had separate names for all the other divine attributes.

[3] The wiser ones among them did not take all those names to mean anything more than the one only Lord, but the less sophisticated made themselves an image for each of the names, an image representing something divine. When worship of God started to turn into idolatry, they fashioned each into a god for themselves, which is how there came to be so many forms of idolatry, even among people outside the church, who added to the number of deities.

However, since these names stood for divine qualities in ancient times, some of them were kept, including Shaddai, guardian beings, and teraphim. In the Word, they symbolize the traits mentioned. The symbolism of teraphim as divine truth received in answer becomes clear in Hosea 3:4.

4163 Genesis 31:36, 37, 38, 39, 40, 41, 42. *And anger blazed in Jacob, and he wrangled against Laban. And Jacob answered and said to Laban, "What is my transgression? What is my sin, that you pursued after me? Because you have probed all my vessels; what have you found from all your household vessels? Put it here before my brothers and your brothers, and let them adjudicate between the two of us. These twenty years I have been with you. Your ewes and your she-goats have not miscarried. And the rams of your flock I have not eaten. Torn flesh I have not brought to you. I have made up the loss of it; from my hand you have sought it, what was stolen by day and stolen by night. [So] I was: in the day, heat devoured me, and cold in the night, and my sleep was driven from my eyes. These twenty years of mine in your house I have served you—fourteen years for your two daughters, and six years for your flock—and you have changed my wage ten ways. Had I not had the God of my father, the God of Abraham and the Dread of Isaac, you would have sent me away* *empty now; my misery and the wearying of the palms of my hands God has seen, and he adjudicated between [us] last night."*

Anger blazed in Jacob, and he wrangled against Laban symbolizes earthly zeal. *And Jacob answered and said to Laban, "What is my transgression? What is my sin, that you pursued after me?"* means that earthly goodness did not detach for a bad reason. *Because you have probed all my vessels; what have you found from all your household vessels?* means that none of the truth belonging to that goodness had been its own; all of it was a gift. *Put it here before my brothers and your brothers, and let them adjudicate between the two of us* means that judgment is a product of justice and fairness. *These twenty years I have been with you* symbolizes autonomy. *Your ewes and your she-goats have not miscarried* symbolizes the state of [intermediate goodness] in regard to goodness and truth-based goodness. *And the rams of your flock I have not eaten* symbolizes truth marked by goodness and the fact that [the Lord] did not take any of this truth from the supply of [intermediate goodness]. *Torn flesh I have not brought to you* means that this goodness had evils for which it was blameless. *I have made up the loss of it* means that good resulted. *From my hand you have sought it* means that it was from the Lord. *What was stolen by day and stolen by night* means likewise improper merit. *[So] I was: in the day, heat devoured me, and cold in the night, and my sleep was driven from my eyes* symbolizes times of trial. *These twenty years of mine in your house I have served you* symbolizes autonomy. *Fourteen years for your two daughters* symbolizes a first period of time for independently acquiring [the two] kinds of desire for truth. *And six years for your flock* means and then for acquiring goodness. *And you have changed my wage ten ways* symbolizes the attitude toward him when he attached that goodness to himself. *Had I not had the God of my father, the God of Abraham and the Dread of Isaac,* means if not for divinity and divine humanity. *You would have sent me away empty now* means it would have claimed everything for itself. *My misery and the wearying of the palms of my hands God has seen, and he adjudicated between [us] last night* means that the Lord did everything for himself by his own power.

Anger blazed in Jacob, and he wrangled against Laban symbolizes earthly zeal. This can be seen from the symbolism of *blazing with anger* and consequently *wrangling* as zeal, and from the representation of *Jacob* as earthly goodness (discussed before).

The reason *blazing with anger* and consequently *wrangling* means zeal is that anger does not exist in heaven, among the angels. Instead, they have zeal. Anger differs from zeal in that anger contains evil, while zeal contains goodness. People who are angry intend evil to the target of their anger, but

4164

people who are zealous intend good to the target of their zeal. People with zeal, then, can instantly turn kindhearted, and in what they actually do they can be good to others; but people with anger cannot. Although zeal looks the same as anger on the outside, it is completely different inside.

4165   *And Jacob answered and said to Laban, "What is my transgression? What is my sin, that you pursued after me?"* means that earthly goodness did not detach for a bad reason. This can be seen from the symbolism of *transgression* and *sin* as what is evil. The *pursuit,* of course, was taken up because earthly goodness had detached, so the meaning is that it did not detach for a bad reason.

4166   *Because you have probed all my vessels; what have you found from all your household vessels?* means that none of the truth belonging to [intermediate goodness] had been its own; all of it was a gift. This can be seen from the symbolism of *household vessels* as one's own truth. *Vessels* mean truth (see §§3068, 3079, 3316, 3318), so *household* vessels obviously mean one's own truth. *Probing* them and *not finding* means that none had belonged to [intermediate goodness] and accordingly that all of it was a gift.

For the facts of the matter, see §4151.

4167   *Put it here before my brothers and your brothers, and let them adjudicate between the two of us* means that judgment is a product of justice and fairness. This can be seen from the symbolism of *brothers* as good qualities (discussed in §§2360, 3803, 3815, 4121), from which it follows that *my brothers and your brothers* means justice and fairness. *Let them adjudicate between the two of us* obviously means judgment.

The reason *my brothers and your brothers* means justice and fairness is that the current theme is the earthly dimension. What is called goodness and truth on the spiritual level is properly called justice and fairness on the earthly level.

We have in us two planes that support the heavenly and spiritual attributes the Lord sends us. One is inner; the other, outer. The planes themselves are nothing other than conscience. Without these planes—without conscience—nothing heavenly or spiritual from the Lord can ever be firmly fixed in us but flows through like water in a sieve. People without the plane of conscience do not know what conscience is and do not believe in the existence of anything spiritual or heavenly.

[2] The inner plane, or inner conscience, is where real goodness and truth exist, because goodness and truth flowing in from the Lord stir this conscience. The outer plane is the outer conscience, where true justice and fairness are found, because private and public justice and fairness (which also flow in) stir this conscience. There is also an outermost plane

that looks like conscience but is not. It consists in doing what is just and
fair for the sake of oneself and the world (that is, for the sake of personal
position or reputation, and for the sake of worldly riches and possessions)
and for fear of the law.

It is these three planes that govern us, or rather by which the Lord
governs us. If we have been reborn, he governs us on the inner plane,
through a conscience for spiritual goodness and truth. If we have not
been reborn but can be or are being reborn (in the other life if not during bodily life), he governs us on the outer plane, through a conscience
for justice and fairness, or a conscience for what is morally and civically
good and true. All others, including the evil, he governs on the outermost
plane, which imitates conscience although it is not. If they were not controlled in this way, they would plunge into all kinds of wickedness and
insanity, which they actually do when unchecked by restraints on that
plane. People who do not submit to such controls either are insane or
incur punishment according to the law.

[3] In regenerate people these three planes form a single whole, because
one flows into another, and the inner is in charge of the outer. The first
plane, the conscience for spiritual goodness and truth, lies in the rational
self. The second, the conscience for moral and civic goodness and truth,
or justice and fairness, lies in the earthly self.

This discussion has now identified the justice and fairness symbolized
by the brothers—justice, by *my brothers,* and fairness, by *your brothers.*
I speak of justice and fairness because the theme is the earthly self, and
justice and fairness (strictly speaking) are attributes of that self.

These twenty years I have been with you symbolizes autonomy. This
can be seen from the symbolism of *twenty* as remaining traces of goodness
(§2280). When a remnant is attributed to the Lord, though, it is actually
his autonomy (§1906). Twenty *years* symbolize the state that autonomy
has reached, years meaning states (see §§487, 488, 493, 893).

On the highest level the content of Jacob's words to Laban has to do
with autonomy in the earthly dimension—which the Lord acquired for
himself by his own power—and with various states of that autonomy.

Your ewes and your she-goats have not miscarried symbolizes the state of
[intermediate goodness] in regard to goodness and truth-based goodness.
This can be seen from the symbolism of a *ewe* as goodness (discussed
below) and from that of a *she-goat* as truth-based goodness (discussed in
§§3995, 4006).

The word *goodness* by itself means goodness in the will, while *truth-
based goodness* means goodness in the intellect. Goodness in the will consists

4168

4169

in doing good at the inspiration of goodness. Goodness in the intellect consists in doing good at the inspiration of truth.

People who are moved by truth to do good see these as one and the same, but they are vastly different. To be moved by goodness to do good is to be moved by a perception of what is good. Only people who are heavenly perceive what is good. To be moved by truth to do good is to be motivated by knowledge and therefore by intellect, without a perception that a thing is right, only with a consciousness that we have been taught so by others or have come to that conclusion on our own by using our power of intellect. This kind of truth can be wrong, although if our intentions are good, any action we base on such truth becomes essentially good.

[2] The symbolism of *ewes* as goodness is visible in many scriptural passages, of which let me quote just the following. In Isaiah:

> He was afflicted and did not open his mouth; as a member of the flock is led to the slaughter, and as a *ewe* before the shearers, he did not open his mouth. (Isaiah 53:7)

This description of the Lord compares him to a ewe, not because of his truth but because of his goodness. In Matthew:

> Jesus said to the twelve whom he sent out, "Do not go in the way of the surrounding nations, and do not enter the city of the Samaritans; go rather to the *lost sheep of Israel's house.*" (Matthew 10:5, 6)

The surrounding nations to which they were not to go stand for people given to evil. (For the meaning of nations as evil, see §§1259, 1260, 1849.) The cities of the Samaritans stand for people given to falsity. Sheep stand for people devoted to goodness. [3] In John:

> After the Resurrection Jesus said to Peter, "Pasture my lambs." A second time he said, "Pasture *my sheep.*" A third time he said, "Pasture *my sheep.*" (John 21:15, 16, 17)

The lambs stand for people with innocence. The sheep mentioned in the second place stand for people with goodness inspired by goodness, and in the third place for people with goodness inspired by truth. In Matthew:

> When the Son of Humankind comes in his glory, he will set *the sheep on the right,* the goats on the left. And he will say to those on the right, "Come, you who are blessed by my Father! Inherit the kingdom prepared for you from the foundation of the world. For I was hungry and

you gave me something to eat. I was thirsty and you gave me a drink.
I was a foreigner and you gathered me in. I was naked and you dressed
me. I was sick and you visited me. I was in prison and you came to me.
So far as you did it for one of these least consequential brothers and
sisters of mine, you did it for me." (Matthew 25:31–40)

The sheep very plainly stand for goodness, or for people with goodness.
All categories of neighborly kindness are contained in the inner meaning
here, as will be discussed elsewhere [§§4956, 4958], with the Lord's divine
mercy. The goats specifically symbolize people who possess faith but not
neighborly love. [4] Likewise in Ezekiel:

"You, my flock," the Lord Jehovih has said: "here, I am judging between
flock member and flock member, between the *rams* and the *he-goats*."
(Ezekiel 34:17)

The specific meaning of the goats as people with a faith that is devoid of
neighborly love can be seen from the symbolism of he-goats. In a positive sense they symbolize people with religious truth and therefore with
some love for their neighbor. In a negative sense they symbolize people
with a faith devoid of love for others who argue about salvation from the
premise that faith saves. The same thing is apparent from what the Lord
says about the goats in that quotation from Matthew. On the other hand,
people completely lacking in both religious truth and neighborly kindness go to hell without this kind of judgment—that is, without being
convicted of subscribing to falsity.

And the rams of your flock I have not eaten symbolizes truth marked
by goodness and the fact that [the Lord] did not take any of this truth
from the supply of [intermediate goodness], as the following shows: *Rams*
symbolize truth marked by goodness. Sheep symbolize what is good, and
rams are sheep, so they symbolize truth marked by goodness. And *eating*
something means making it one's own (discussed in §§3168, 3513, 3596,
3832) and therefore taking it on, since anything from another person that
we make our own is something we take on from that person.

Torn flesh I have not brought to you means that this goodness had evils
for which it was blameless. This can be seen from the symbolism of *torn
flesh* as death inflicted by another and accordingly as evils for which one
is blameless.

Our evil has many origins. The first is our inheritance, passed down over
and over from our grandparents and great-grandparents to our parents—
the evils piling up as they go—and from our parents to us. The second is

our practice of those evils; we acquire our own vices by living wrongly. In part we select these vices from the ocean of evil we inherit and put them in play, and in part we add on more vices of our own. This is the source of the personal store we procure for ourselves.

But this actual evil that we make our own also has different sources, and two in general. One kind of evil we receive from others without blame to ourselves; the other kind we deliberately embrace and are consequently responsible for. The evil we receive from others without blame to ourselves is what torn flesh symbolizes in the Word. The evil we deliberately embrace and incur guilt for is symbolized in the Word by a carcass. [2] That is why it was forbidden in both the ancient church and the Jewish religion to eat either what died naturally (a carcass) or torn flesh. Moses deals with the subject this way:

> All souls among the native and the immigrant that eat a *carcass* and *torn flesh* shall wash their clothes and rinse themselves with water; they shall be unclean up till the evening and [then] be clean. And if they do not wash and do not rinse their flesh, they shall carry their wickedness. (Leviticus 17:15, 16)

In the same author:

> *Carcass* and *torn flesh* they shall not eat, or they will defile themselves with it; I am Jehovah. (Leviticus 22:8)

The torn flesh stands for evil that comes of falsity. The wild animals of the forest that tear flesh stand for the wicked spirits who inflict this evil, because the Word compares the hellish to wild animals. In the same author:

> Men of holiness you shall be to me. Therefore you shall not eat *flesh in the field, torn flesh;* you shall throw it to the dogs. (Exodus 22:31)

In Ezekiel:

> The prophet to Jehovah: "My soul has not been defiled, and a *carcass* and *torn flesh* I have not eaten from my youth up to now, and abominable flesh has not come into my mouth." (Ezekiel 4:14)

In the same author:

> No *carcass* or *torn flesh* of bird or of beast shall the priests eat. (Ezekiel 44:31)

This speaks of the Lord's kingdom and indicates that the new earth is being described there.

[3] These quotations show what torn flesh means in an inner sense, but to see the meaning even more clearly, take for example people who live a good life, or who do good to others because they wish them well. Suppose they allow a person dedicated to evil to persuade them that living a good life makes no difference to their salvation. "After all," that person might say, "everyone is born in sin and none of us can will what is good or therefore do what is good on our own. That is why we have been provided with a means of salvation, which is called faith. We can be saved by faith without living a good life, even if we wait till the last moment before death to believe." If people who have lived a good life let themselves be persuaded and stop caring how they live, or even feel contempt for a good life, they are described as torn flesh. The term is used for goodness that has been infused with falsity, so that the goodness is no longer alive.

[4] Take marriage as an example, too. Everyone views marriage as a gift from heaven at first, but some—and it could be one spouse or both—later permit themselves to be persuaded that the only reasons for marriage are an orderly world, the raising and individual care of children, and inheritance. They may become convinced that the bonds of marriage are merely those of a contract that can be broken or bent by either party, as long as the two agree. After they accept this kind of argument, they stop thinking of marriage as heavenly. If this leads to sexual affairs, the marriage becomes the kind of thing referred to as torn flesh. And so on.

[5] The following passages show that the evil are the ones who tear flesh, which they do by superficial reasoning, refusing to admit deeper reasoning because of the evil life they live. In Jeremiah:

> A lion from the forest has struck the great; a wolf of the wilds has laid them waste. A leopard is keeping watch over their cities; *everyone leaving them will be torn apart,* because their transgressions have multiplied, their rebellions have intensified. (Jeremiah 5:5, 6)

And in Amos:

> Edom pursued his brother with a sword and destroyed his compassion and *tore flesh forever* in his anger and kept his fury always. (Amos 1:11, 12)

I have made up the loss of it means that good resulted. This can be seen **4172** from the symbolism of *making up a loss* as making good for something, and in this case, as the good that resulted.

Here is the situation with the blameworthy and blameless evil symbolized by carcasses and torn flesh, discussed just above: Blameworthy evil is the evil we procure for ourselves by actually committing it, the evil for which we think up so many justifications that we develop faith and conviction in it. This evil cannot be cured but lasts forever. Blameless evil, on the other hand, is evil that we do not justify in our thoughts and do not inwardly convince ourselves of. This evil does last, but instead of penetrating deeply and corrupting our inner self, it merely clings to the outside. This evil can lead to good, because our inner self, which does not yet yearn for and consent to it, can see in our outer self that it is bad, so it can be removed. Because our inner self can see this, it can also more clearly see what is good (since an opposite illustrates what is good more clearly than a nonopposite does) and be more keenly affected by it. This now is what "the good that resulted" means.

4173   *From my hand you have sought it* means that it was from the Lord. This is established by the symbolism of a *hand* as power (discussed in §§878, 3387) and therefore as the fact that it was from the Lord. What he does by his own power is from him.

4174   *What was stolen by day and stolen by night* means likewise improper merit. This can be seen from the symbolism of *what was stolen,* or theft, as improper merit. Merit is wrong when we attribute goodness to ourselves, suppose that it originates with us, and seek to earn salvation on that account. This is the evil symbolized on an inner level by theft.

Here is the case with this evil: Those of us who reform always think at first that goodness originates in us, so we expect to earn salvation by the good we do. The supposition that the good we do earns salvation comes from the belief that goodness originates in us; the one is bound up with the other. People who allow themselves to be reborn, though, do not confirm this belief in their thoughts, or convince themselves it is true. Instead, it gradually dissolves. As long as we are absorbed by our outer self (as we all are when we start on reformation), we cannot help thinking this way; but we think this way only in our outer self. [2] When our outer self and its cravings are set aside, our inner self begins to function—or rather the Lord flows in through our inner self with the light that gives us understanding and illuminates our outer self. Then we start to view the situation differently and to attribute goodness not to ourselves but to the Lord.

This identifies the improper merit meant here. Through it good likewise comes about, as it does through evil for which one is blameless (discussed before).

However, if we confirm the idea in our thoughts when we grow to adulthood and firmly persuade ourselves that we earn salvation by the good we do, the evil clings tenaciously and cannot be healed. We claim for ourselves what belongs to the Lord and therefore cannot accept the goodness that constantly flows in from the Lord. As soon as it reaches us we draw it off for ourselves and claim it as our own, defiling it. These are the evils properly symbolized by theft; see §2609.

[So] I was: in the day, heat devoured me, and cold in the night, and my sleep was driven from my eyes symbolizes times of trial, as can be seen from the following: Heat and cold symbolize something marked by too much love and by no love at all—two extremes. The day symbolizes a state of faith, or truth, then at its peak, and the night symbolizes a state of no faith or truth (§§221, 935, 936). And sleep driven from the eyes means constantly, or without rest. These are symptoms of spiritual trial, so the clause symbolizes such trials in general.

4175

Heat symbolizes too much love because spiritual fire and warmth is love, while spiritual cold is lack of love. Our very life is nothing but love, because without love we have absolutely no life. In fact, if we reflect on it we can see that all the vital heat and fire in the body comes from love. Cold, though, does not symbolize the loss of all love, only the loss of spiritual and heavenly love. The absence of these is what is called spiritual death. When we are deprived of spiritual and heavenly love, we blaze with love for ourselves and our worldly advantages. This love is relatively cold and grows colder in us not only while we live in our body but also when we go to the other world. If the love we have for ourselves and for worldly gain is taken from us during physical life, we turn so cold that we have hardly any life, and the same if we are forced to think reverently about heavenly and divine subjects. In the other life, when we live among the hellish, the fiery heat of our cravings forms our environment, but if we go close to heaven, this fiery heat turns cold. The closer we go, the deeper the chill, and the more torture we suffer, too.

This chill is what is meant by the gnashing or chattering of teeth among hell's inhabitants in Matthew 8:12; 13:42, 50; 22:13; 24:51; 25:30; Luke 13:28.

These twenty years of mine in your house I have served you symbolizes autonomy, as the following shows: Twenty symbolizes the goodness that remains in us, as discussed in §2280, and when this goodness is an attribute of the Lord's, it means what he acquired for himself (§1906), so it is his autonomy. And serving, when it is an attribute of the Lord's, symbolizes his own power, as discussed in §§3975, 3977.

4176

Fourteen years for your two daughters symbolizes a first period of time for independently acquiring [the two] kinds of desire for truth, as can be seen from the following: Fourteen, or two "weeks," symbolizes a first

4177

period, because in the Word, weeks simply mean a whole time span, long or short (see §§2044, 3845). When two weeks are referred to as a single period, the meaning is the same, because doubling or squaring a number does not do away with its symbolism. This clarifies the meaning of fourteen, or two weeks, in the current context. And the *two daughters,* Rachel and Leah, symbolize [two] kinds of desire for truth, as discussed in §§3758, 3782, 3793, 3819. Besides, daughters symbolize desires (§2362).

4178   *And six years for your flock* means and then for acquiring goodness, as the following shows: *Six* symbolizes combat and hard work, as noted in §§720, 737, 900. In the current verse it symbolizes the rest of the combat and hard work, so it means "then," or "next." And the *flock* symbolizes goodness, as discussed in §§343, 2566, 3518.

4179   *And you have changed my wage ten ways* symbolizes the attitude toward him when he attached that goodness to himself, as the following shows: A *wage,* when it is said to be the Lord's, means something from himself (dealt with in §§3996, 3999), so it means when he attached goodness to himself. And *changing* it symbolizes the attitude of the goodness symbolized by Laban toward him. *Ten ways* means frequent change (§4077).

4180   *Had I not had the God of my father, the God of Abraham and the Dread of Isaac,* means if not for divinity and divine humanity, as the following shows: A *father's God,* when attributed to the Lord, symbolizes the goodness of his divine side, the Father meaning divine goodness, and the Son, divine truth (see §§2803, 3704). In this case it symbolizes the divine goodness of both natures. The *God of Abraham* symbolizes divinity itself, which is called the divine nature. (For the representation of Abraham as the Lord's divinity itself, see §§[2010,] 2011, 3439.) And the *Dread of Isaac* symbolizes his divine humanity. The word *dread* is used because divine truth is meant, and divine truth brings fear, dread, and terror to people lacking in goodness. (Divine goodness does not; it frightens no one.) The same is true later in the chapter, at verse 53: "Jacob swore on the Dread of his father Isaac." After all, since Laban was now separated from Jacob—in other words, since intermediate goodness was now separated from divine goodness—it was in a malevolent state, as the details concerning Laban make plain. Because this was now his mood, the text refers to the Dread of Isaac.

Anyone can see that "the Dread of Isaac" means Isaac's God and that [Laban was] in this state.

For the representation of *Isaac* as the Lord's divine humanity and specifically as his divine rationality, see §§1893, 2066, 2072, 2083, 2630, 3012, 3194, 3210, 3704 at the beginning.

[2] To expand on the idea that divine truth from the Lord inspires dread in people lacking goodness, while divine goodness does not: The Lord's holy influence comprises divine goodness and divine truth, which stream constantly from him. That is the source of the light in the heavens and of the light in human minds, so it is the source of wisdom and understanding, since these are contained in such light. However, the effect that the light of wisdom and understanding has on individual people depends on their reception of it. Those under the sway of evil do not accept divine goodness, because they have no love or charity, and all goodness is a matter of love and charity. Divine truth *can* be received, however—even by the evil, although only by their outer, not their inner, self.

[3] It is like warmth and light from the sun. Spiritual warmth is love and therefore goodness; spiritual light is faith and therefore truth. When trees and flowers receive warmth from the sun, they grow and produce leaves, flowers, and fruit or seeds. This happens in spring and summer. When warmth from the sun is not received—only light—nothing grows. All plant life languishes, as it does in fall and winter. The case is the same with spiritual warmth and light from the Lord: if we resemble spring or summer, we receive goodness that comes of love and charity, and produce fruit, but if we resemble fall and winter, we do not receive goodness that comes of love and charity, so we do not produce fruit. Nonetheless we are capable of receiving light—that is, of learning faith's tenets, or truth. Winter light works the same, because like summer light it brings out color and beauty with sharp clarity, but it differs in not penetrating deeply, because it contains no warmth. Consequently nothing grows.

[4] When goodness is not accepted, then, but only light, it is like [cold-blooded] creatures that do not receive warmth, only the visible shape and visual appeal provided by light. Inside there is cold, and where there is cold inside, everything is sluggish; and when light streams in, there is a kind of furrowing and bristling in response. It causes fear, dread, and terror in the living creatures.

From this comparison, one can understand to some extent how matters stand with the fear, dread, and terror an evil person feels. These emotions are triggered not by divine goodness but by divine truth, and they occur when people do not accept divine goodness but do receive divine truth. Divine truth devoid of goodness cannot penetrate deeply but only clings to the surface, or to the outer self, and usually to the sensory level of the outer self. Sometimes it enables people to appear quite attractive on the outside even when they are disgusting on the inside.

This discussion can also show what faith is like in many people, who say that it saves us without good deeds—in other words, without our willing and doing what is good.

[5] Since divine truth emanates from the divine humanity rather than from divinity itself, the Dread of Isaac symbolizes the divine humanity. As noted, divine truth is what terrifies people, not divine goodness.

The fact that divine truth emanates from the Lord's divine humanity rather than from divinity itself is a secret that has never been revealed before, and here is what can be told about it: Before the Lord came into the world, divinity itself flowed into the whole of heaven. Since heaven at the time was mostly made up of heavenly individuals, or those dedicated to the good that comes of love, that inflow was the means by which divine omnipotence produced the light in the heavens and consequently wisdom and understanding. However, once the human race backed away from the good that comes of love and charity, heaven could no longer be the medium for generating the kind of light—and accordingly the kind of wisdom and understanding—that could reach the human race. As a result the Lord came into the world (he had to, in order to save us) and made the human nature in himself divine. This enabled his divine humanity to become divine light, illuminating heaven in its entirety and the world in its entirety.

The light itself had existed from eternity, because it came from divinity itself by way of heaven, and divinity itself was what adopted a human nature and made it divine. When this nature had become divine, the Lord could use it to enlighten not only the heavenlike heaven itself but also the spiritual heaven and even the human race. The receptacle of divine truth in humankind has been and is goodness—in other words, love for the Lord and charity for one's neighbor—as is plain in John:

> As many as did accept him, to them he gave the power to be God's children, to those believing in his name, who had their birth not from blood or from the will of the flesh or from a man's will but from God. (John 1:12, 13)

[6] The discussion here shows what is meant by the following words in John:

> In the beginning there was the Word. And the Word was with God, and the Word was God. This was with God in the beginning. Everything was made by him, and nothing that was made was made without him. In him was life, and the life was the light of humankind. It was the true

light that shines on every person coming into the world. (John 1:1, 2, 3, 4, 9, and following verses)

The Word here means divine truth.

Both natures in the Lord consist of divine goodness, but divine truth is what issues from him (see §3704). Divine goodness cannot be received by a human, not even by an angel, but only by the Lord's divine humanity. That is what the following words in John mean:

God has never been seen by anyone; the only-born Son, who is in the Father's embrace, is the one who has revealed him. (John 1:18)

Divine truth *can* be received, but only in a form capable of existing in the person who receives it. This truth is able to harbor divine goodness, with differences, depending on how it is received.

[7] These are the kinds of secrets that occur to angels when people on earth read the words *Had I not had the God of my father, the God of Abraham and the Dread of Isaac.* They demonstrate how much heavenly material there is in Scripture and in every single word of it, even though none of that material appears in the literal meaning. They also show how much better angelic wisdom is than human wisdom, and that angels are awake to the deepest secrets when we are not even aware that a secret is present.

The secrets mentioned here are few, though, because angels see and perceive in them countless other secrets—in fact, a relatively boundless number—that can never be enumerated. Human speech is just not suited to expressing these secrets, nor is the human mind capable of receiving them.

You would have sent me away empty now means it would have claimed everything for itself. This can be seen from the symbolism of *sending away empty* as taking everything from the owner and therefore claiming everything for itself.
4181

My misery and the wearying of the palms of my hands God has seen, and he adjudicated between [us] last night means that the Lord did everything for himself by his own power. This can be seen from the symbolism of *misery and the wearying of one's palms* as spiritual trials. Through his trials and victories the Lord united his divinity with his humanity and made his humanity divine, using his own power, so the same words also symbolize this. On the point that by his own power, through his trials and victories, the Lord united his divinity with his humanity and made his humanity divine, see §§1616, 1737, 1813, 1921, 2776, 3318 at the end.
4182

The *palm,* or hand, means power (§§878, 3387), so *my palms,* or my hands, mean one's own power.

God has seen and adjudicated symbolizes the Lord's divinity; that is, it was accomplished by the divinity that was in him and that was his.

4183   Genesis 31:43. *And Laban answered and said to Jacob, "The daughters are my daughters and the sons are my sons and the flock is my flock, and everything that you are seeing—it is mine. And to my daughters—what shall I do to them today, or to their sons whom they have borne?"*

Laban answered and said to Jacob symbolizes a state of dim perception. *The daughters are my daughters and the sons are my sons and the flock is my flock* means that all desire for truth, all truth, and all goodness belonged to [intermediate goodness]. *And everything that you are seeing—it is mine* means all perception and understanding. *And to my daughters—what shall I do to them today, or to their sons whom they have borne?* means that it did not dare to claim them as its own.

4184   *Laban answered and said to Jacob* symbolizes a state of dim perception. This is established by the symbolism of *answering and saying* as perception. In the Word's narratives, *saying* means perceiving (see §§1898, 1919, 2080, 2862, 3395, 3509). The dimness of the state and its perception can be seen from what Laban says in this verse, that the daughters, sons, and flock were his, when they were not; and, in an inner sense, that intermediate goodness claimed all goodness and truth for itself. See what was said before at §§3974, 4113 about this statement of Laban's.

4185   *The daughters are my daughters and the sons are my sons and the flock is my flock* means that all desire for truth, all truth, and all goodness belonged to [intermediate goodness], as the following indicates: The *daughters,* Rachel and Leah, symbolize desire for truth, as discussed in §§3758, 3782, 3793, 3819. The *sons* symbolize truth, as discussed in §§489, 491, 533, 1147, 3373. And the *flock* symbolizes goodness, as discussed in §§343, 1565, 2566. Obviously Laban claimed them for himself, as if they were his, because he said, "The daughters are my daughters and the sons are my sons and the flock is my flock."

4186   *And everything that you are seeing—it is mine* symbolizes all perception and understanding. This can be seen from the symbolism of *seeing* as perceiving and understanding (discussed in §§2150, 3863). So the clause means that all perception and understanding of truth and goodness belonged to [intermediate goodness].

The situation in all this has already been explained, and it has been illustrated by common occurrences in the other world [§§4075, 4077,

4151]. That is to say, when spirits (especially of an intermediate sort) are in an angelic community, they have no idea that the desire for goodness and truth flowing in from that community is not theirs. Such is the sharing of feelings and thoughts in the other world; and the more closely bound the spirits are to that community, the more convinced they are. When they are removed from it, they resent the fact, and when they come into a resentful state, they also come into a dim state, which is described above in §4184. Because their perception is not very deep in this state, they claim as their own the goodness and truth that belong to the angelic community, which they received through the sharing just mentioned. This is the state depicted in the current verse.

[2] In addition, a great deal of experience has taught me how a desire for goodness and truth is communicated to others. I have had spirits of the same sort with me a number of times, and when some trace of desire bound them to me, they had no idea that what was mine was not theirs.

I have been told that the same thing happens to everybody. We each have spirits with us who, as soon as they arrive and enter our emotions, are completely convinced that everything of ours—every feeling and thought we have—is theirs. This is how the spirits through whom the Lord governs us (§2488) are united to us. Later, at the ends of certain chapters [§§5846–5866, 5976–5993], I will address the subject from actual experience.

And to my daughters—what shall I do to them today, or to their sons whom they have borne? means that [intermediate goodness] did not dare to claim them as its own. This can be seen from the symbolism of *daughters* as desire for truth and of *sons* as truth (discussed just above at §4185). The fact that it did not dare to claim them as its own is symbolized by *what shall I do to them today?* and is evident from what comes before in verse 24, where God said to Laban in a dream, "Watch yourself, to keep from speaking anything with Jacob, whether good or evil."

Genesis 31:44, 45, 46. *"And now, come, let us strike a pact, I and you, and let it be for a witness between me and you." And Jacob took a stone and set it up as a pillar. And Jacob said to his brothers, "Gather stones"; and they took stones and made a heap and ate there on the heap.*

Now, come, let us strike a pact, I and you, and let it be for a witness between me and you symbolizes the union of earthly divinity with the good deeds performed by people who are off to the side, or non-Christians. *And Jacob took a stone and set it up as a pillar* symbolizes this kind of truth and the worship it leads to. *And Jacob said to his brothers* symbolizes people

> 4187

> 4188

who do good deeds. *"Gather stones"; and they took stones and made a heap* symbolizes truth that comes of goodness. *And ate there on the heap* means adoption at the urging of divine goodness.

4189   *Now, come, let us strike a pact, I and you,* symbolizes the union of earthly divinity with the good deeds performed by people who are off to the side, or non-Christians. This can be seen from the symbolism of a *pact* as union (discussed in §§665, 666, 1023, 1038, 1864, 1996, 2003, 2021); from the current representation of Laban *(I)* as good deeds (discussed below); and from the representation of Jacob *(you)* as earthly divinity.

[2] Laban currently symbolizes the good deeds done by people who are off to the side, or non-Christians, because now that he has separated from Jacob—now that intermediate goodness has separated from divine goodness on the earthly level—Laban can no longer represent intermediate goodness. Because it served as a means, though, he represents a kind of goodness, and specifically goodness that is off to the side, or a side branch of goodness. Before Laban joined forces with Jacob, he represented a side branch of goodness (see §§3612, 3665, 3778) and consequently goodness off to the side. The nature of that goodness will be described later on [§4197].

Laban's position is like that of Lot and Ishmael. Lot represented the Lord's outer, sensory self as long as he was with Abraham (§§1428, 1434, 1547, 1597, 1598, 1698). Once he separated from Abraham, he represented people whose worship is superficial but who still love their neighbor (2312, 2324, 2371, 2399), and he represented many later stages of the church in turn (2422, 2459). [3] Ishmael likewise represented the Lord's early rationality as long as he was with Abraham (1893, 1949, 1950, 1951), but later, when they separated, he represented spiritual people (2078, 2691, 2699, 3263, 3268).

It is the same with Laban. The reason for the change in meaning is that even when a separation takes place, a bond remains, although it is not the same as before. That is why Laban here and in the next verses represents good actions, as performed by people who are off to the side, or non-Christians. Non-Christians are said to be off to the side, or to have a side branch of goodness, because they are outside the church. People in the church have goodness and truth descending in a direct line rather than by a parallel branch, because they have the Word. Through the Word they have direct contact with heaven, and through heaven, with the Lord. Non-Christians do not, because they do not have the Word or know the Lord. That is why they are said to be off to the side. The non-Christians meant are the ones who do good actions—in other words, who focus on outward acts that are infused with neighborly kindness. These are what are being called good actions—but not good deeds. Good deeds are not always infused with goodness, but good actions are.

And Jacob took a stone and set it up as a pillar symbolizes this kind of truth and the worship it leads to. This is established by the symbolism of a *stone* as truth (dealt with in §§643, 1298, 3720) and from that of a *pillar* as the worship it leads to, or worship growing out of truth (dealt with in §3727). Clearly, then, the clause symbolizes this kind of truth and the worship it leads to. "This kind of truth" means the kind non-Christians have. Although they do not know the Word and therefore the Lord, they still have the same outer truth Christians do. For instance, they know they should reverently worship the Deity, keep their holy days, honor their parents, not steal, not commit adultery, not kill, and not envy another's possessions. In other words, they know the kind of truth embodied in the Ten Commandments, which also serve as standards of behavior within the church. The wise among them observe rules of this kind not only in outward form but also at a deeper level. Their thinking is that such misdeeds go against not only their religious tradition but also the common good, their inner duty toward others, and love for their neighbor—even though they know little about the true faith. In their darkness they have a semblance of conscience, which they do not want to violate; in fact, some are incapable of violating it. From this it can be seen that the Lord governs them from within, although they lack clarity there, and imparts to them an ability to accept inner truth, which they welcome in the other life. See what was shown about non-Christians in §§2589–2604.

[2] Several times I have been permitted to talk with Christians in the other world concerning the condition and lot of nations outside the church. "They accept religious truth and goodness more readily than Christians who failed to live by the Lord's commandments," I have said. "The way Christians think about them is cruel. They say everyone outside the church is damned, because of the widely accepted principle that there is no salvation without the Lord. That is true, but there are non-Christians who have lived lives of neighborly love for each other and been spurred by a kind of conscience to act justly and fairly, and in the other life they receive faith and acknowledge the Lord more readily than people inside the church who *haven't* lived this kind of charitable life. Christians are wrong to believe that heaven is all theirs because they have

4190

the Bible—written on paper but not on their hearts. They know about the Lord but don't believe that his humanity is divine. In fact, they don't acknowledge that he is different from an ordinary person in regard to his secondary nature, which they call his human nature. As a result, left to themselves and their own thoughts they don't even revere him. So they are the ones without the Lord and without salvation."

4191   *And Jacob said to his brothers* symbolizes people who do good deeds. This can be seen from the representation of *Jacob* as the Lord's earthly divinity (noted before) and from the symbolism of *brothers* as good qualities, or goodness (discussed in §§3815, 4121). In this verse brothers symbolize people who do good actions, which means non-Christians, as shown above in §4189. Everyone possessing goodness is united with the Lord in his divinity, and because of the close connection, the Lord calls such people brothers, as in Mark:

> Jesus, looking all around [at those] who were sitting about him, said, "Look: my mother and *my brothers*. For whoever does the will of God is *my brother* and my sister and my mother." (Mark 3:31, 34, 35)

All union comes by way of love and charity, as anyone can see, because spiritual union is simply love and charity. Love for the Lord is obviously union with him, and charity toward our neighbor is too, as can be seen from the Lord's words in Matthew:

> So far as you did it for one of these least consequential brothers and sisters of mine, you did it for me. (Matthew 25:40)

This passage is talking about deeds of charity.

4192   *"Gather stones"; and they took stones and made a heap* symbolizes truth that comes of goodness. This can be seen from the symbolism of *stones* as truth (discussed just above at §4190) and from that of a *heap* as goodness. The reason a heap symbolizes goodness is that long ago, before people built altars, they made heaps and ate on them, to testify to the love that united them. Later, when people came to view the representative objects of the ancients as sacred, they built altars instead of heaps, still using stones but arranging them more neatly (Joshua 22:28, 34). So a heap has the same symbolism as an altar, which is the good that comes of love; and its stones symbolize the truth that leads to faith.

4193   *And ate there on the heap* means adoption at the urging of divine goodness. This can be seen from the symbolism of *eating* as communication, union, and adoption (discussed in §§2187, 2343, 3168, 3513 at the end, 3596, 3832) and from that of a *heap* as goodness (discussed just above in §4192). In this instance it symbolizes divine goodness.

Genesis 31:47, 48, 49, 50. *And Laban called it Jegar-sahadutha. And Jacob called it Galeed. And Laban said, "This heap is a witness between me and you today"; so he called its name Galeed. Also Mizpah, because he said, "Jehovah watch between me and you, because we will lie hidden, a man from his companion. If you afflict my daughters, and if you take women in addition to my daughters, no man is with us [to witness it], [but] see! God is a witness between me and you."*

4194

Laban called it Jegar-sahadutha symbolizes its nature so far as it involves the goodness represented by Laban. *And Jacob called it Galeed* symbolizes its nature so far as it involves divine goodness on the earthly plane. *And Laban said, "This heap is a witness between me and you today"; so he called its name Galeed* means that it will be such forever, so again it means the quality. *Also Mizpah, because he said, "Jehovah watch between me and you,"* symbolizes the presence of the Lord's earthly divinity. *Because we will lie hidden, a man from his companion* symbolizes divergence in regard to the church's attributes. *If you afflict my daughters and take women in addition to my daughters, no man is with us [to witness it]* means that the desire for truth will remain within the church. *See! God is a witness between me and you* symbolizes confirmation.

Laban called it Jegar-sahadutha symbolizes its nature so far as it involves the goodness represented by Laban. This can be seen from the symbolism of *calling* something, or calling its *name*, as its quality (discussed in §§144, 145, 1754, 2009, 2724, 3421). *Jegar-sahadutha* in the dialect of Syria, Laban's native land, means "testimonial heap."

4195

In ancient times, such heaps served as a sign or a witness. Later on they were also used for worship. This particular heap served as a sign and a witness: as a sign that this was the border, and as a witness that a pact had been struck there preventing either party from crossing it to harm the other. Laban's words in verse 52 make the intent clear: "This heap will be a witness and the pillar will be a witness that I will not cross this heap to you and that you will not cross this heap or this pillar to me for evil." These considerations clarify what Jegar-sahadutha, "testimonial heap," involves. On an inner level, though, it symbolizes the nature of truth-based goodness on Laban's part—that is, on the part of people devoted to good actions—in other words, on the part of non-Christians.

4196   *And Jacob called it Galeed* symbolizes its nature so far as it involves
divine goodness on the earthly plane, which can be seen from the representation of *Jacob* as the Lord's earthly divinity, mentioned many times
before. In the Hebrew dialect, or the dialect of Canaan, Jacob's native
land, *Galeed* means "heap" and "witness," or "witness heap." The inner
meaning of "witness heap" now follows.

4197   *And Laban said, "This heap is a witness between me and you today";*
so he called its name Galeed means that it will be such forever, so again
it means the quality, as the following shows: A *heap* symbolizes goodness, as discussed above in §4192, and a *witness* symbolizes truth's confirmation of goodness and goodness's confirmation of truth, as discussed
below. *Today* means eternity, as noted in §§2838, 3998. And *calling some-*
thing's name symbolizes its quality, as discussed in §§144, 145, 1754, 2009,
2724, 3421. The quality itself is embraced in the name *Galeed,* because in
ancient times the names given contained a quality (§§340, 1946, 2643,
3422). These meanings make plain the symbolism of *Laban said, "This*
heap is a witness between me and you today"; so he called its name Galeed. It
symbolizes testimony to the union between the goodness now symbolized
by Laban and divine goodness on the Lord's earthly plane. So it symbolizes the Lord's union with non-Christians through goodness, because their
goodness is what Laban now represents (§4189).
    The truth belonging to that goodness is what bears witness to the
union, but the goodness of non-Christians lies off to the side as long as
they are living in the world, because they do not have divine truth. People
with that goodness, who live lives of shared neighborly kindness, do not
receive divine truth straight from the Word, the divine source, and yet
their goodness is not closed off. It is capable of opening up, and does
open up in the other life when they learn religious truth and are taught
about the Lord.
    Not so for Christians. The ones who show neighborly kindness toward
each other (especially those who love the Lord) receive goodness straight
from the source while living in the world, because they have divine truth.
They enter heaven without such instruction, unless the truth they knew
contained falsity that first needs to be banished. However, Christians who
did not live lives of neighborly love have shut heaven to themselves, and
many of them have shut it so tight that it cannot be opened. After all,
they know what is true and deny it and also harden themselves against
it—if not with their lips, with their heart nonetheless.

[2] The purpose behind Laban's first referring to the heap in his own dialect, as Jegar-sahadutha, and then in the Canaanite dialect, as Galeed (although the two have almost the same meaning), is inclination and then union. To speak in the Canaanite dialect, or the tongue of Canaan, is to incline toward what is divine, because Canaan symbolizes the Lord's kingdom, and in the highest sense, the Lord (§§1607, 3038, 3705). This is evident in Isaiah:

> On that day there will be five cities in the land of Egypt *speaking the tongues of Canaan* and swearing to Jehovah Sabaoth. On that day there will be an altar to Jehovah in the middle of the land of Egypt and a pillar to Jehovah by its border; and it will serve *as a sign* and *as a witness* to Jehovah Sabaoth in the land of Egypt. (Isaiah 19:18, 19, 20)

[3] Other places in the Word can demonstrate that a *witness* means truth's confirmation of goodness and goodness's confirmation of truth, and that testimony therefore means goodness that produces truth, and truth that comes from goodness. The following passages show that a witness means truth's confirmation of goodness and goodness's confirmation of truth. In Joshua:

> Joshua said to the people, "*You are witnesses against yourselves* that you have chosen Jehovah, to serve him." And they said, "*We are witnesses.*" "And now take away the foreign gods that are in your midst and incline your heart toward Jehovah, Israel's God." And the people said to Joshua, "Jehovah our God we will serve, and his voice we will obey." And Joshua cut a pact with the people on that day and set them a statute and judgment in Shechem, and Joshua wrote these words in the book of God's law and took a big *stone* and set it up there beneath the oak that was in Jehovah's sanctuary. And Joshua said to all the people, "*Look: this stone will serve as a witness to us,* because it has heard all Jehovah's sayings that he spoke with us, and it will *serve as a witness to you* to prevent you from denying your God." (Joshua 24:22, 23, 24, 25, 26, 27)

"Witness" in this passage obviously means confirmation—confirmation of the pact and accordingly of union, since a pact symbolizes union (§§665, 666, 1023, 1038, 1864, 1996, 2003, 2021). Union with Jehovah (the Lord) is possible only through what is good, and the only goodness that unites is goodness that receives its quality from truth, so it follows that a witness means truth's confirmation of goodness. The goodness here is that of being united with Jehovah (the Lord) by choosing him, to serve him. Stone meant truth that confirms. (For the meaning of a stone as truth, see §§643, 1298, 3720.) In the highest sense a stone means the Lord himself, because all truth comes from him. That is why he is also called the Stone of Israel (Genesis 49:24) and why the text above says, "Look: this stone will serve as a witness to us, because it has heard all Jehovah's sayings that he spoke with us." [4] In John:

> "*I will give my two witnesses* [the task] to prophesy for a thousand two hundred sixty days dressed in sackcloth garments. These are the two olive trees and the two lampstands that are standing before the God of the earth. And if anyone wants to hurt them, fire will issue from their mouth and consume their foes. They have the authority to close heaven. But when they have finished their *testimony,* the beast that comes up out of the abyss will make war with them and conquer them and kill them." But after three and a half days the spirit of life from God entered them, so that they could stand on their feet. (Revelation 11:3, 4, 5, 6, 7, 11)

The two witnesses are goodness and truth—goodness that holds truth, and truth that comes from goodness, both of them confirmed in people's hearts. This meaning is clear from the statement that the two witnesses are two olive trees and two lampstands. An olive tree means this kind of goodness (see §886), and the two olive trees stand for heavenly goodness and spiritual goodness. Heavenly goodness is goodness that comes of love for the Lord, while spiritual goodness is goodness that comes of charity for one's neighbor. Lampstands mean the truth that develops out of both kinds of goodness, as will become clear at the point where lampstands are to be discussed [§9548], the Lord in his divine mercy willing. Goodness and truth have the authority to close heaven and open it, as may be seen in the preface to Genesis 22. "The beast from the abyss will kill them" (the abyss being hell) symbolizes devastation of goodness and truth within the church. "The spirit of life from God entered them, so that they could stand on their feet," symbolizes a new religion.

[5] The fact that altars were set up as witnesses—just as heaps had been set up earlier by the ancients—can be seen in Joshua:

> The Reubenites and Gadites said, "See the form of Jehovah's altar, which our ancestors made not for burnt offering and not for sacrifice; no, *it*

is a witness between us and you." And the children of Reuben and the children of Gad called the *altar "it is a witness among us* that Jehovah is God." (Joshua 22:28, 34)

An altar means a loving goodness and in the highest sense the Lord himself (§§921, 2777, 2811). A witness stands for confirmation, and in an inner sense for truth's confirmation that something is good.

[6] Since a witness symbolizes truth's confirmation of goodness and goodness's confirmation of truth, in the highest sense it symbolizes the Lord, because he is the divine truth that confirms. In Isaiah, for instance:

I will strike with you an eternal pact—the reliable mercies [that I showed] to David. Here, now, *I have made him a witness to the peoples,* a chieftain and command-giver for the peoples. (Isaiah 55:3, 4)

In John:

. . . and from Jesus Christ, who is the *faithful witness,* the firstborn of the dead, and chief of the earth's monarchs. (Revelation 1:5)

In the same author:

These things says the *faithful and true witness,* the beginning of God's creation. (Revelation 3:14)

[7] In the representative religion it was commanded that all truth had to stand on the word of two or three witnesses, not on that of one (Numbers 35:30; Deuteronomy 17:6, 7; 19:15; Matthew 18:16). This precept was founded on a divine law that one truth does not confirm what is good, but many truths do. A single true concept unconnected with others offers no support, but when there are many, [they supply confirmation,] because one concept makes another visible. A single truth generates no form and therefore no quality; only many of them connected in a series do. Just as a solitary musical note creates no unison, much less harmony, neither does a solitary truth. These are the premises on which the law is founded. On the surface it appears to have been founded on societal conditions, but the one consideration is not in conflict with the other. The same holds true for the Ten Commandments, as noted in §2609.

[8] It follows, then, that *testimony* means goodness that produces truth, and truth that comes from goodness. Further evidence is provided by the

fact that the Ten Commandments written on stone tablets are referred to by the single word *testimony,* as in Moses:

> Jehovah gave Moses—when he had finished speaking with him on Mount Sinai—the *two tablets of the testimony,* tablets of stone written by God's finger. (Exodus 31:18)

In the same author:

> Moses came down out of the mountain, and the *two tablets of the testimony* were in his hand, tablets inscribed on their two sides. (Exodus 32:15)

And since the tablets were placed in the ark, it is called the ark of the testimony. Moses speaks of this event:

> Jehovah to Moses: *"You shall put into the ark the testimony* that I give you." (Exodus 25:16, 21)

> Moses took and *put the testimony into the ark.* (Exodus 40:20)

In the same author:

> I will meet you and speak with you from above the appeasement cover, from between the two guardian beings that are *on the ark of the testimony.* (Exodus 25:22)

In the same author:

> A cloud of incense shall cover the appeasement cover that is *over the testimony.* (Leviticus 16:13)

In the same author:

> The staffs of the twelve tribes were left in the meeting tent *in front of the testimony.* (Numbers 17:4)

For evidence that the ark is sometimes called the ark of the testimony, see Exodus 31:7, Revelation 15:5, in addition to the passage quoted from Exodus 25:22. [9] The Ten Commandments were called the testimony because they had to do with the compact and therefore the union between the Lord and humankind. This union cannot occur unless humankind keeps the Commandments not only in their outward but also in their inward form. (For the inward form of the Commandments, see §2609.) So goodness confirmed by truth, and truth derived from goodness, is what testimony symbolizes. Consequently the tablets were sometimes called the tablets of the covenant, and the ark was sometimes called the ark of the covenant.

This discussion now shows what testimony symbolizes in a positive sense in such Scripture passages as Deuteronomy 4:45; 6:17, 20; Isaiah 8:16; 2 Kings 17:15; Psalms 19:7; 25:10; 78:5, 6; 93:5; 119:1, 2, 22, 23, 24, 59, 79, 88, 138, 167; 122:4; Revelation 6:9; 12:17; 19:10.

Also Mizpah, because he said, "Jehovah watch between me and you," symbolizes the presence of the Lord's earthly divinity—that is, its presence in the goodness now represented by Laban. This can be seen from the symbolism of *watching* as presence, since one person who watches another or sees another from a tall watchtower is visually present with that person. What is more, the "seeing" that the Lord is said to do means foresight and providence (§§2837, 2839, 3686, 3854, 3863), so it also means presence, but presence through foresight and providence.

To take up the topic of the Lord's presence: The Lord is present with all of us, depending on the way we receive him. After all, the life in every one of us comes only from the Lord. When we receive his presence in goodness and truth, we live a life of understanding and wisdom. If we receive his presence in evil and falsity rather than goodness and truth, we live a life of insanity and folly, though we retain a capacity for understanding and wisdom. The survival of this capacity can be seen from the fact that we still know how to feign and imitate goodness and truth in outward appearances and how to win over those around us by doing so, which we could never do if we did not keep the ability.

Mizpah symbolizes the nature of that presence. In this verse it symbolizes the nature of that presence among people who do good actions, or non-Christians, whom Laban now represents. The word *Mizpah* in the original language comes from [a word for] watching.

Because we will lie hidden, a man from his companion symbolizes divergence in regard to the church's attributes. This can be seen from the current symbolism of *lying hidden* as diverging, and from that of *a man from his companion* as people in the church and people outside. They are said to lie hidden from each other because they diverge in goodness and truth and so in regard to the church's attributes.

If you afflict my daughters and take women in addition to my daughters, no man is with us [to witness it] means that the desire for truth will remain within the church, as the following shows. The *daughters,* Rachel and Leah, symbolize desire for truth, as discussed in §§3758, 3782, 3793,

4198

4199

4200

3819. The *women* symbolize desire for nongenuine truth and therefore symbolize a desire that is not part of the church. The desire for truth makes the church, so [the warning about] taking women in addition to Laban's daughters means not accepting any other desire than a desire for genuine truth. *No man is with us* means when "a man lies hidden from his companion," or when they diverge, as discussed just above at §4199. Plainly, then, the clause means that the desire for truth will remain within the church and is not to be defiled with nongenuine truth.

4201   *See! God is a witness between me and you* symbolizes confirmation—here, confirmation by the Divine. This is established by the symbolism of a *witness* as confirmation (discussed just above in §4197).

4202   Genesis 31:51, 52, 53. *And Laban said to Jacob, "Look: this heap; and look: the pillar that I have set up between me and you. This heap will be a witness and the pillar will be a witness that I will not cross this heap to you and that you will not cross this heap or this pillar to me for evil. Let the God of Abraham and the God of Nahor judge between us—the God of their father." And Jacob swore on the Dread of his father Isaac.*

Laban said to Jacob, "Look: this heap; and look: the pillar that I have set up between me and you," symbolizes union. *This heap will be a witness and the pillar will be a witness* symbolizes confirmation. *That I will not cross this heap to you and that you will not cross this heap or this pillar to me for evil* symbolizes a limit on the amount of good that can flow in. *Let the God of Abraham and the God of Nahor judge between us* symbolizes divinity as it affects both. *The God of their father* means from the highest level of divinity. *And Jacob swore on the Dread of his father Isaac* symbolizes confirmation by the divine humanity, which is called *dread* in that state.

4203   *Laban said to Jacob, "Look: this heap; and look: the pillar that I have set up between me and you,"* symbolizes union, as can be seen from the remarks above. The heap and pillar served as a sign and witness that a pact had been struck—in other words, that the parties were allies, and so in an inner sense that there was union.

4204   *This heap will be a witness and the pillar will be a witness* symbolizes confirmation. This is evident from the symbolism of a *witness* as confirmation—confirmation of goodness by the truth meant by the *pillar,* and confirmation of truth by the goodness meant by the *heap*—noted above in §4197.

4205   *That I will not cross this heap to you and that you will not cross this heap or this pillar to me for evil* symbolizes a limit on the amount of good that can flow in. This can be seen from the current symbolism of *crossing* as flowing in, from that of a *heap* as something good (discussed in §4192), and from that of a *pillar* as truth (discussed in §§3727, 3728, 4090). Both the heap and the pillar served as a sign and witness (see the same sections), and here as the sign of a limit. Since the theme is union, it follows from the progression of ideas that in an inner sense it is a limit on the amount of good that can flow in.

Union is achieved through goodness, which flows in to the extent that we receive it, as noted earlier [§§4197–4198]. However, we can receive goodness only in the measure that we know truth, because truth is what goodness flows into. Goodness acts, and truth receives the action, so all truth is a receiving vessel (§4166). Since truth is what goodness flows into, it limits the inflow of goodness. This is what is meant here by a limit on the amount of good that can flow in.

[2] I need to say a few words describing the situation. The truth we learn, whatever its amount or quality, enters our memory by way of desire—in other words, by way of some pleasure we love. Without desire, or some beloved pleasure, nothing can penetrate, because our life lies in our desire and pleasure. The concepts that do enter are brought back out when the same pleasure returns, together with many other ideas that have become associated or united with them. Moreover, when the same true thought is brought up again by ourselves or someone else, the desire, or the pleasure we loved when it entered, is also stirred, because the two cling together.

You can see how matters stand with the desire for truth, then. Truth that has entered in the company of some desire for goodness returns when the same desire comes back, as does the desire when the same truth comes up again.

You can also see that nothing true can ever have real desire planted and rooted deeply in it unless a person is governed by goodness, because a real desire for truth comes from the goodness belonging to love for the Lord and charity for one's neighbor.

This goodness flows in from the Lord, but it requires truth to fix it in place. Truth provides a lodging place for goodness, because they harmonize. So of course the nature of the truth determines how the goodness is welcomed. Goodness flowing in from the Lord can make a home in the truth known by non-Christians who live lives of mutual charity. But as long as they live in the world, it cannot make the same kind of home as it can in Christians who take truth from the Word and develop it into a life of spiritual charity. (See §§2589–2604.)

4206   *Let the God of Abraham and the God of Nahor judge between us* symbolizes divinity as it affects both—both the goodness of people in the
church and the goodness of people outside the church. This can be seen
from the symbolism of the *God of Abraham* as the Lord's divinity pertaining to people in the church, and from that of the *God of Nahor* as the
Lord's divinity pertaining to people outside the church. The clause, then,
plainly symbolizes divinity as it affects both.

The *God of Abraham* means the Lord's divinity pertaining to people in
the church because Abraham represents the Lord's divinity, so he represents
what comes directly from the Lord (§§3245, 3778). As a result, the children
of Abraham (John 8:39) specifically mean people in the church. The *God of
Nahor* means the Lord's divinity pertaining to people outside the church
because Nahor represents the church among non-Christians, and his children represent people in that church who are part of the fellowship (§§2863,
2866, 2868, 3052, 3778). In this verse, by the same token, Nahor's son Laban
represents a goodness lying off to the side—the goodness non-Christians
receive from the Lord.

[2] The reason so many different aspects of the Lord are represented
is not that various traits exist in the Lord but that we receive his divine
nature in various ways. It is like the life we have in us. It flows in and acts
on all the body's different sense organs and motor organs, on all the different limbs and viscera, creating variety everywhere. The eye sees in one way,
the ear hears in another, the tongue tastes in another; the arms and hands
move in one way, the hips and legs in another; the lungs act in one way,
the heart in another, then the liver in another, and the stomach in another,
and so on; but there is a single life force that activates all of them in such
different ways. It is not that the force itself acts in different ways but that
its action is received in different ways. The form of each organ is what
determines the form of its action.

4207   *The God of their father* means from the highest level of divinity. This
can be seen from the symbolism of a *father's God* as the highest level of
divinity. When Scripture uses the word *father*, on an inner level it symbolizes goodness (see §3703). The Lord's father, or the Father of whom
the Lord speaks, is the divine goodness in him (§3704). Divine goodness is the highest level of divinity, while divine truth comes from divine
goodness and is called the Son.

The father meant here is Terah, the father of both Abraham and Nahor,
and he represents the shared main stem of the churches (see §3778). In a
secondary sense, then, Abraham represents the church itself, and Nahor
represents the church among non-Christians, as noted just above at §4206.

And Jacob swore on the Dread of his father Isaac symbolizes confirma- **4208**
tion by the divine humanity, which is called *dread* in that state. This
is established by the symbolism of *swearing* as confirmation (discussed
in §§2842, 3375) and by that of the *Dread of Isaac* as the Lord's divine
humanity (discussed in §4180). The Lord's divine humanity is what oaths
were sworn on (§2842).

[2] The text mentions Abraham's God, Nahor's God, the God of their
father Terah, and the Dread of Jacob's father Isaac because Terah's descendants, being idolaters (§§1353, 1356, 1992, 3667), acknowledged this number of gods. It was a distinctive trait of this house that each clan worshiped
its own deity, which is why Abraham's God, Nahor's God, the God of
their father, and the Dread of Isaac are all mentioned here.

The members of Abraham's clan were ordered to acknowledge Jehovah
as their God, but they offered Jehovah no more recognition than they offered
any other god who distinguished them from the surrounding nations. In
other words, they acknowledged him only in name. This explains why they
so often defected to other gods, as the Word's narratives show.

The reason for this behavior was that they focused exclusively on the
surface. They had absolutely no idea what lay deeper and did not want to
learn. [3] Even the rituals of their church were nothing more than acts of
idolatry, so far as the people themselves were concerned, because those acts
were divorced from any inward significance. Any religious ritual isolated
from its inner content is idolatrous. Still, these people were able to represent a genuine church, because representation has nothing to do with per-
sonality, only with the quality being represented (§§665, 1097 at the end,
1361, 3147). However, in order for a representative church to come into
being, enabling the Lord to make some contact with humankind through
heaven, its people had to be held first and foremost to an acknowledgment of Jehovah. If they did not acknowledge him at heart, they at least
had to do so with their lips. With them, representative acts came not from
something inside but from something on the outside, through which contact was established. (It is different in a genuine church, where communication comes by an inner way.) Their worship of God did not touch their
souls, then; it did not bring them blessings in the next life, only good
fortune in the world.

[4] Therefore, in order to maintain superficial appearances among
them, they were exposed to a large number of miracles, which never would
have taken place if those people had possessed any depth. It was for the
same reason that they were so often forced into homage by punishment,
captivity, and threats. In reality, though, the Lord never forces anyone to

inward worship; it is implanted in the person's freedom (§§1937, 1947, 2874, 2875, 2876–2881, 3145, 3146, 3158, 4031). The main external requirement was that the people proclaim belief in Jehovah, because Jehovah was the Lord, who was represented in every facet of that religion. On the point that Jehovah was the Lord, see §§1343, 1736, 2921, 3035.

4209   Genesis 31:54, 55. *And Jacob offered a sacrifice on the mountain and called his brothers to eat bread, and they ate bread and spent the night on the mountain. And Laban got up early in the morning and kissed his sons and his daughters and blessed them, and Laban went and returned to his place.*

Jacob offered a sacrifice on the mountain symbolizes worship motivated by a loving goodness. *And called his brothers to eat bread* symbolizes adoption of goodness from the Lord's earthly divinity. *And they ate bread* symbolizes the outcome. *And spent the night on the mountain* symbolizes calm. *And Laban got up early in the morning* symbolizes the enlightenment of that goodness by the Lord's earthly divinity. *And kissed his sons and his daughters* symbolizes acknowledgment of that truth and of the desire for it. *And blessed them* symbolizes joy on that account. *And Laban went and returned to his place* symbolizes the end of Laban's representation.

4210   *Jacob offered a sacrifice on the mountain* symbolizes worship motivated by a loving goodness. This can be seen from the symbolism of *sacrifice* as worship (discussed at §§922, 923, 2180) and from that of a *mountain* as a loving goodness (discussed at §§795, 796, 1430).

Sacrifice symbolizes worship because sacrifices and burnt offerings were the main elements in all worship in the later representative church, or the Hebrew church.

The people of that church also sacrificed on mountains (as the Word reveals in various places) because *mountains* on account of their height symbolized what stood high above, like that which exists in heaven and is called heavenly. So in the highest sense mountains symbolized the Lord, whom people called the Highest One. Appearances caused them to think this way, because things that are inward seem to be lofty. Take heaven's presence in us: it exists inside us, but we assume it lies high above. When the Word mentions height, then, on an inner level it symbolizes what is within. In the world we cannot help thinking heaven is high up, for three reasons. One is that we use the same word for the visible dome above and all around us. Another is that we are immersed in time and space, so our thoughts are made up of ideas based on time and space. The last is that few people know what the inner dimension is, and still fewer that there is no space or time in that dimension. That is why the Word speaks in accord with human thought patterns. If it did not speak in those terms, but in terms of the angelic viewpoint, people would not have understood a bit of it. Everyone would have come to a halt, wondering, "What is this? Is it anything?" So all would have rejected it as a text with no semblance of meaning to it.

And called his brothers to eat bread symbolizes adoption of goodness from the Lord's earthly divinity, as the following indicates: *Brothers* mean people now united in a pact, or alliance, and on an inner level they symbolize people devoted to goodness and truth. For such people being called brothers, see §§367, 2360, 3303, 3459, 3803, 3815, 4121, 4191. *Eating* symbolizes adopting something as one's own, as discussed in §§3168, 3513 at the end, 3832. Among the ancients, meals and banquets symbolized adoption and union through love and charity (§3596). *Bread* symbolizes a loving goodness, as discussed in §§276, 680, 1798, 3478, 3735, and at the highest level it symbolizes the Lord, §§2165, 2177, 3478, 3813.

4211

Since at the highest level bread symbolizes the Lord, it symbolizes everything holy that comes from him—in other words, everything good and true. Goodness that actually is good results only from love and charity, so bread also symbolizes love and charity. Long ago, sacrifices also meant nothing else, which is why they were referred to by the single term "bread" (see §2165). People ate the meat of the sacrifices to represent a heavenly feast—in other words, to represent union through the goodness that springs from love and charity.

This, then, is what is symbolized by the Holy Supper, which took the place of sacrifices and of the feasting on consecrated meat. It is an outward religious observance with inner significance, through which it unites us with heaven (if we have love and charity) and through heaven with the Lord. In the Holy Supper, you see, eating symbolizes adoption, the bread symbolizes heavenly love, and the wine symbolizes spiritual love. In fact, if we are in a reverent frame of mind when we eat it, that is exactly what is perceived in heaven.

[2] The goodness is said to be adopted from the Lord's earthly divinity because the theme is non-Christian goodness, this being what Laban now represents (§4189). When we are united with the Lord, we unite not with his supreme divinity itself but with his divine humanity. We cannot form any idea at all of the Lord's most sublime divinity, which soars so far

above our thoughts that the idea dies out completely and disappears; but of his divine humanity we are able to form a picture. Our thoughts and feelings bind us to something we have some notion of, not to something we cannot have any notion of. If when we think about the Lord's human nature our mental image contains the idea of holiness, we also think of the holiness from the Lord that fills heaven. So we also think of heaven, because heaven in its entirety resembles a single human being, in imitation of the Lord (§§684, 1276, 2996, 2998, 3624–3649). Therefore direct unity with the highest level of the Lord's divinity is not possible, only unity with his divine humanity and through this with the highest level of his divinity. That is why it says in John that God has never been seen by anyone except the only-born Son (John 1:18) and that there is no access to the Father except through the Son [John 14:6]. It is also why the Lord is called a mediator [1 Timothy 2:5; Hebrews 8:6; 9:15; 12:24]. The truth of this notion can be seen plainly from the fact that people in the church who do not believe in anything (not even in the existence of heaven and hell) and who worship nature are the same ones who claim to believe in a supreme being but despise the Lord. [Anyone] willing to learn from experience will find that evil people—even the worst of them—make the same claim.

[3] People think of the Lord's humanity in various ways, one individual viewing it differently from another, one with more reverence than another. People in the church are capable of thinking that his humanity is divine and that he is one with the Father, as he himself says ("The Father is in me and I am in the Father"). People outside the church cannot, though—both because they know nothing of the Lord and because the only notion they have of divinity comes from images they see with their eyes and idols they can touch with their hands. Even so, the Lord unites with them in their coarse way of thinking through the good they do out of charity and obedience. That is the reason for saying here that they adopt goodness from the Lord's earthly divinity.

The Lord's bond with people conforms to the state of their thoughts and resulting feelings. Those who view the Lord with utmost reverence and who know and desire goodness and truth—as is possible for people in the church—connect with the Lord's divine rationality. Those who have less reverence, who think and feel less deeply and yet show kindness to their neighbor, connect with the Lord's earthly divinity. Those whose veneration is still coarser connect with the Lord's divinity on a sensory level. This last bond is represented by the bronze snake, the sight of which revived people from their snakebites (Numbers 21:9). The people with this connection to the Lord are non-Christians who worship idols but live lives of neighborly love in accord with their religious tradition.

This discussion now explains the meaning of the adoption of goodness from the Lord's earthly divinity, symbolized by Jacob's calling his brothers to eat bread.

And they ate bread symbolizes the outcome—in a superficial sense, friendship; in the highest sense, union through goodness and truth on the earthly plane.

    4212

And spent the night on the mountain symbolizes calm. This can be seen from the symbolism of *spending the night* as having peace (discussed in §3170) and so as having calm. It was also a tradition for the parties to a treaty to spend the night in the same place, because doing so meant they were no longer hostile. In an inner sense it means calm and peace, because people bound together in goodness and truth are tranquil and at peace. That is the reason for the phrase *on the mountain:* a mountain symbolizes a loving, charitable goodness (§4210), because this kind of goodness brings peace. For what peace and calm are, see §§92, 93, 1726, 2780, 3170, 3696, 3780.

    4213

And Laban got up early in the morning symbolizes the enlightenment of that goodness by the Lord's earthly divinity. This can be seen from the symbolism of *rising early in the morning* as enlightenment (discussed at §§3458, 3723) and from the representation of *Laban* as the kind of goodness that characterizes non-Christians (discussed in §4189). Context shows that the enlightenment of this goodness (the enlightenment meant here) comes from the Lord's earthly divinity.

    4214

In regard to enlightenment, all enlightenment comes from the Lord by way of the goodness in a person, and the nature of the goodness determines the quality of the light.

[2] Most people consider someone who can argue about goodness and truth, evil and falsity, to be enlightened. They believe one's state of enlightenment improves with one's ability to discuss such topics subtly and shrewdly, to confirm them with an abundance of facts, and to make one's claims sound likely—mainly through comparison with empirical evidence but also through other methods of persuasion. Such a person might be devoid of enlightenment, though, despite having the ability to imagine and perceive.

This ability comes in two forms, one provided by heaven's light, and the other by false light. On the outside the two look the same, but on the inside they are totally different. What comes from heaven's light resides in goodness; that is, it is found in people who have goodness. From goodness they are able to see truth and to tell as clear as day whether something is so or not. By contrast, what comes from false light resides in evil; that is, it is found in people who have evil. They can philosophize about these subjects, because they have some capacity for learning about them, but they have no desire to put their knowledge into practice. This is not the same as being enlightened, as anyone can see.

[3] Here is what happens with false light in the other life: People who enjoyed that light while they lived in the world enjoy the same kind in the other life. There too they argue about goodness and truth, evil and falsity, only much more perfectly and skillfully than during physical life. Their reasoning improves because their thoughts are not held back or hindered by bodily and worldly cares and are not as narrowly bounded by those concerns as when they lived in their body in the world. Yet it is immediately apparent to good spirits and angels (though not to these people themselves) that their reasoning is the product of false light. The light flowing into them from heaven changes into false light instantly. In them heaven's light meets one of three fates: It can be smothered, as sunlight is when it falls on something dark and turns black. It can be rejected, as it is in people whose assumptions are wrongheaded. Or it can be corrupted, as sunlight is when it shines on foul, disgusting objects, creating horrible colors and smells. That is what happens with people who enjoy false light and consider themselves more enlightened than others because they can reason intelligently and wisely even though they live evil lives.

[4] The identity and nature of these people is apparent in everything they say, provided they do not try to trick others by pretending to be good. They include the following kinds:

> those who deny or belittle the Lord and privately sneer at anyone who acknowledges him;
> those who love adultery and deride anyone who considers marriage holy and inviolable;
> those who view religious precepts and doctrines as useful for keeping the lower classes in check, but worthless for themselves;
> those who attribute everything to nature and consider others naive dupes if they claim it all for the Divine;

those who ascribe absolutely everything to their own good judgment,
saying that the Supreme Being rules some things on the large or
universal scale but nothing on the small or particular scale, and confirming this opinion in themselves.

And so on. [5] People like this see by a false light, even in the other life,
and they argue dexterously with others like them, but when they near any
heavenly community their light goes out and becomes dark. Their minds
are so clouded that they cannot even think, because they find heaven's
light painful, and in them it is smothered, rejected, or corrupted, as was
noted. So they hurry away and throw themselves into hell, where the
light is false.

This discussion shows that goodness from the Lord sheds true enlightenment and that wickedness from hell sheds false enlightenment.

And kissed his sons and his daughters symbolizes acknowledgment of **4215**
that truth and of the desire for it, as the following shows: *Kissing* symbolizes union motivated by desire, as discussed in §§3573, 3574, so it symbolizes acknowledgment, since when goodness and truth create a bond,
they are acknowledged. *Sons* symbolize truth, as discussed in §§489, 491,
533, 1147, 2623, 3773. And the *daughters,* Rachel and Leah, symbolize
desire for truth, as discussed in §§3758, 3782, 3793, 3819.

[2] Correspondence is the reason why *kissing* symbolizes union motivated by desire. All the organs and limbs of the body correspond to heaven,
you see (as is being discussed at the ends of the chapters). A correspondence exists between a person's inner reaches and all the facial features,
so that the lower mind gleams from the expression there, and the higher
or inner mind shines in the eyes. A correspondence also exists between a
person's thoughts and feelings on one hand and physical acts and gestures
on the other. People recognize this as true in regard to all voluntary action,
but it is true of involuntary action as well. Heartfelt humility makes us
kneel, and kneeling is an outward act of the body. An even stronger, deeper
sense of humility makes us throw ourselves to the ground. Gladness of the
lower mind and joy of the higher mind make us sing and rejoice. Sadness
and deep grief make us cry and lament. But uniting with someone out of
desire makes us kiss.

[3] Clearly, then, these outward actions are signs of something deeper,
since they correspond to something deeper, and as signs, they have something inside that gives them their character. Even if we are trying to use
outward acts to fake something deeper, such acts serve as signs, but as

signs of pretense, hypocrisy, and deceit. Take kisses as an example. We intend our kisses to signify that we love someone from the heart, because we know that is where kisses come from. We know they are signs of unity based on inclination, and by kissing our acquaintances, we hope to persuade them that we love them for something good in them, when what we really love them for is ourselves and our own status and wealth. So we love them for a bad rather than a good reason. People who take their own interests as their goal (and not as a goal halfway to something good) and who want to unite with someone else in pursuit of that goal are under the sway of evil.

4216   *And blessed them* symbolizes joy on that account. This is established by the symbolism of *blessing* someone as wishing that person all the best (discussed in §3185) and therefore as testifying, during a parting of the ways, to the joy that was shared.

4217   *And Laban went and returned to his place* symbolizes the end of Laban's representation. This can be seen from the symbolism of *returning to his place* as going back to an earlier condition. For the meaning of a *place* as a state, see §§2625, 2837, 3356, 3387, 3404. That is why this clause symbolizes the end of Laban's representation.

The explanations that have been given show that everything in the Word without exception contains something deeper, and that the deeper contents are the kind suited to the perception of the angels with us. When the Word mentions bread, for instance, angels do not know what bread made out of matter is but what spiritual bread is. In place of the bread they picture the Lord, who is the bread of life, as he teaches in John 6:33, 35. Since they picture him, they picture what comes from him, so they picture his love for the entire human race. At the same time they picture the love we return to him, because thought and feeling combine the two into a single concept. [2] Our own way of thinking is not very different when we receive the bread of the Holy Supper in a reverent frame of mind, because our thoughts are not on the bread then but on the Lord and his mercy. We are thinking about what is involved in love for him and charity for our neighbor, because we are thinking about repentance and the improvement of our life, each in our own way, depending on the reverence not only of our thoughts but also of our feelings. This information makes it clear that bread in the Word does not present angels with any image of bread but with the thought of love in all its countless facets.

The same applies to the wine mentioned in the Word and received in the Holy Supper. In neither case do angels think of wine but of charity for their neighbor. Since they do, and since this provides us with a connection to heaven and through heaven to the Lord, bread and wine became symbols, uniting people whose lives are holy with heaven and through heaven with the Lord.

[3] The same holds true for everything in the Word, which makes the Word a middle ground uniting us with the Lord. If it were not a middle ground, heaven would not be able to flow into us (since without a middle ground there is no oneness) but would distance itself from us. If it did, none of us could be led to goodness any longer, not even to bodily and worldly goodness. All restraints would burst, even the outermost ones. When we are involved in goodness, the Lord governs us through inner restraints, which are those of conscience; but when we are involved in evil, he can govern us only through outward restraints. If they were to shatter, we would all go crazy the way people do when they lack any fear of the law, any fear for their life, and any fear of losing status, wealth, and the resulting prestige, since these are outward restraints. Under those circumstances the human race would perish.

This shows why the Word exists and what it is like.

The part of the Lord's church where the Word exists resembles the heart and lungs, while the part where the Word does not exist resembles the other organs, whose life depends on the heart and lungs; see §§637, 931, 2054, 2853.

The Universal Human
and Correspondence (Continued)

AT the ends of chapters in earlier volumes, I mentioned what I had had the opportunity to see and perceive in the world of spirits and the heavens of the angels. Later I dealt with the universal human and correspondence. 4218

In the current volume, let me continue dealing with the subject undertaken at the ends of the last few chapters: our correspondence with the universal human. This will enable me to reveal fully what the human condition is. I will show that we are connected with heaven, not only in regard to our thoughts and feelings but also in regard to both our inner and our outer organic forms, and that without this connection we could not last even a moment.

4219   To see how matters in general stand with the universal human, it is important to grasp that heaven as a whole is a universal human. Heaven is called a universal human because it corresponds to the Lord's divine humanity. He alone is human, and the more that angels, spirits, and people on earth take from him, the more they too are human.

No one should think that we are human because we have a human face and a human body, and because we have a brain and organs and limbs; these are attributes we share with brute animals, so they are things that die and get put in the grave. No, what makes a person human is the ability to think and will as a human and therefore to receive attributes that are divine, or the Lord's. This is what distinguishes us from animals tame and wild. The way we have received those attributes and made them our own during bodily life determines the kind of human being we become in the other world.

4220   During physical life, some people accept the Lord's divine gifts: his love for the entire human race and consequently charity toward their neighbor, along with the love they return to him. In the other life they receive understanding, wisdom, and indescribable happiness, because they become angels and therefore truly human. Others, though, do not accept the Lord's divine gifts during physical life—no love for the human race, let alone any love they return to the Lord. Instead, they love and even worship themselves alone, so they make personal and worldly advantages their goal. In the other world, after spending a brief span of time living there, they are deprived of all intelligence, become utterly witless, and live among hellish morons.

4221   The way I learned this was by being allowed to talk with people who had lived such a life, including one person I had known during his physical life. Any good he had done his neighbor during that life, he had done for his own sake, to increase his status and wealth. Everyone else he had treated with contempt and even hatred. He *had* proclaimed God with his lips but had failed to acknowledge him at heart.

When I was given the chance to talk with him, he was exuding a sort of physical aura. His speech was not like that of spirits but like that of a person still living. The speech of spirits differs from human speech in being full of thoughts, or containing a spiritual and therefore a living quality that cannot be put into words. Not so with human speech. Such an aura was wafting from him, and I sensed it in every word he said.

He appeared in the company of worthless types, and I heard that the thoughts and feelings of people like him gradually become so crude and idiotic that no one anywhere in the world is more idiotic.

[2] They have a home under the buttocks, where their hell is. Another individual from there had already appeared to me, looking not like a spirit but like a grossly physical person with so little of the intelligent life proper to a human being that you might say you were seeing a model of stupidity. This experience clarified for me what people come to be like when they have no love for their neighbor or the larger public, not to mention the Lord's kingdom, but only for themselves; when they focus only on themselves at every point; when they even worship themselves as gods and want others to do the same, making this their intent in everything they do.

The correspondence of the universal human with the parts of a human being applies to each and every thing in us—to the organs, limbs, and viscera. In fact, there is not a single organ or limb in the body, or a single part of an organ or limb, or even a single little piece of a part that does not have something corresponding to it. People recognize that every organ and limb of the body is made up of components and subcomponents. Take the brain. Overall it consists of the cerebrum, cerebellum, medulla oblongata, and spinal cord (which is an extension of the brain, or an appendage of it, so to speak). The cerebrum consists of many component parts: the membranes called the dura mater and pia mater, the corpus callosum, corpora striata, ventricles and cavities, smaller glands, and walls. In general it is made up of gray matter and medullary substance, in addition to sinuses, blood vessels, and nerve plexuses. Something similar is true of the sense organs and motor organs of the body and the viscera, as the anatomists make fairly plain. **4222**

All these elements in general and particular correspond with minute precision to the universal human and to the heavens composing it, which are just as numerous. The Lord's heaven, you see, is likewise divided into smaller heavens, which are divided into still smaller ones. These are divided into the smallest and finally into angels, each of which is a miniature heaven corresponding to the largest-scale heaven.

All these heavens are perfectly distinct from each other, each belonging to its broader heaven, and the broader ones to the broadest of all, or the whole, which is the universal human.

One thing about correspondence: The heavens mentioned do correspond to the actual organic forms of the human body. That is why I have said that such and such a community or angel belongs to the region of the **4223** brain, the heart, the lungs, the eye, and so on. However, the correspondence is mainly with the functions of those viscera or organs. The case is like that of the organs or viscera themselves, in that the functions make a seamless whole with their organic forms. We cannot conceive of any function except from forms—in other words, from substances, because substances are what underlie the function. For example, sight cannot be conceived of without the eye, nor breathing without the lungs. The eye is the organic form from which and through which we see, and the lungs are the organic form from which and through which we breathe. The same applies in all other cases.

It is mainly the functions, then, to which heavenly communities correspond. Because they correspond to the functions, they also correspond to the organic forms, the one being indivisible and inseparable from the other—so much so that it is all the same whether you say the function or the organic form from and through which the function occurs. So there is a correspondence with the organs, limbs, and viscera because there is a correspondence with their functions. When the function is brought forward or proposed, the organ is stimulated. The same happens with all our activity. When we want to do this or that thing, or to do it in this or that way, and think to do it, our body parts move accordingly. They act in keeping with the job or task we intend. The function is what dictates the forms.

These considerations also show that before the organic forms of the body came into being, their purpose existed, and that this purpose brought those forms into being and adapted them to itself, rather than the other way around. Once the forms have been produced, or the organs have been adapted, useful activity comes out of them. From then on, it looks as though the forms or organs precede their purpose, but they do not. The purpose originates in the Lord and flows in through heaven. In doing so it adheres to the pattern and form in which the Lord organized heaven, so it adheres to correspondences. That is how we come into being and that is how we survive. Again you can see why it is that the human being corresponds to the heavens in each and every detail.

4224   Organic forms are not only those visible to the eye or detectable by microscope. There are also organic forms still more refined that could never be discovered by the naked or the aided eye. These forms are deeper. For instance, inner sight and ultimately the intellect has its forms, which are invisible but are still forms—in other words, substances. No type of vision, not even the intellectual kind, can exist without something to do

the seeing. The scholarly world knows this, too—that without some under-
lying substance there is no attribute or alteration or quality that manifests
itself in activity. These more refined or deeper forms, which are invisible,
are the ones that empower the inner senses and produce inward sensations.

The deeper heavens correspond to such forms, because they correspond to the senses and sensations connected with such forms.

[2] Since masses of information about these forms and their correspondence have been revealed to me, they cannot be explained clearly
unless the particulars are dealt with in detail. In what follows, then—by
the Lord's divine mercy—let me continue the discussion begun in the previous volume concerning the individual's correspondence with the universal human. The ultimate goal is for people to learn the following from
actual experience rather than from deduction, or even worse, conjecture:
how matters stand with them and their inner self, which is called their
soul; how they are united with heaven and through heaven with the Lord;
what makes them human and distinguishes them from animals; and how
they cut themselves off from that union and bind themselves to hell.

First it needs to be said who is in the universal human and who is
outside it. There are people who love the Lord, show charity to their
neighbor, benefit their neighbor from the heart according to the goodness in her or him, and possess a conscience for what is just and fair. They
are all in the universal human, because they are in the Lord and therefore in heaven. On the other hand there are people who love themselves
and their worldly advantages, are driven by cravings, and do good only
because of the law and for the sake of their position, worldly riches, and
the status these bring. Deep inside they are ruthless, cherish hatred and
vengefulness toward their neighbor out of arrogance and greed, and enjoy
seeing their neighbor hurt if he or she does not cater to them. They are
all outside the universal human, because they are in hell. They do not
correspond to any of the body's organs or limbs but to various defects
and diseases inflicted on the organs and limbs. They too will be described
from experience in what follows, by the Lord's divine mercy.

[2] Those who are outside the universal human—outside heaven—
cannot enter it, because their life opposes it. Occasionally a way in is
found by the types who used their bodily life to become skilled at imitat-
ing angels of light. When they arrive, though—as they are sometimes
permitted to do in order to learn what they are really like—they are let in
only to the first entry, or to join those who are still novices and not yet
fully instructed. If they do find a way in, the ones who enter as angels of

4225

light can barely stay even a few seconds, because the living energy of love for the Lord and love for one's neighbor is present. Since nothing there corresponds to their own life, they can hardly breathe. (On the point that spirits and angels also breathe, see §§3884–3893.) As a result they start to suffer, because one's breathing there reflects the freedom of one's life. What is amazing is that there they can scarcely move but become like people weighed down. Distress and torment seize their inward parts, so they throw themselves down headlong from there, all the way to hell, where they can breathe and move. That is why life is represented in the Word by the ability to move [Matthew 9:6–7; Mark 2:10–12; Luke 5:24–25].

[3] In contrast, those who are part of the universal human breathe freely when they are exercising a loving goodness, but they are still divided up according to the nature and amount of that goodness. That is the reason there are so many heavens, which the Word refers to as mansions (John 14:2). The individuals there are each in their element when they are in their heaven and have an inflow from heaven as a whole. Everyone there is a focal point for inflow from all others and is therefore in perfect balance. This balance reflects the miraculous form of heaven, produced by the Lord alone, so it comes in unending variety.

4226   Sometimes certain new spirits complain that they are not being allowed into heaven. These are people who had been evil on the inside during life in the world but had acquired a veneer of goodness by helping others for the sake of personal and worldly advantages. They complain because their only view of heaven had been that we gain entrance to it by grace. Sometimes the answer they receive is that heaven is not denied to anyone. If they want, they are to be admitted. Some actually are let into the heavenly communities closest to the entrance, but when they arrive, the fact that their life opposes and resists heaven leaves them with a sensation of respiratory stoppage, distress, and hellish torment, as already mentioned. They throw themselves down from there, saying afterward that heaven would be hell for them and that they never would have believed heaven could be like that.

4227   Many people of both genders were such during their physical life that they sought to manipulate others through trickery and deceit whenever they could. Their goal was to dominate people, especially the rich and powerful, so that they alone would actually rule while their victims were still nominally in charge. They worked in secret, and used various methods to remove others—particularly the honest. They did not denounce them openly, since honesty is its own defense, but found other means.

They would undermine such a person's advice, calling it simpleminded or bad. If any mishap occurred, they would lay it at such a person's door. And so on.

People who were like this during physical life are also like this in the other life, because our life always follows us. [2] This I found out by personal experience with such spirits when they were with me. They were still doing the same things, though even more skillfully and cleverly. Spirits act with greater subtlety than people on earth do, because they are free of their ties to the body and connection to the coarser types of sensation. They were so subtle that several times I did not perceive their aim or intention of taking control. When they talked to each other, they were careful not to let me hear or perceive it. Others who did hear them, though, told me that their plots were unspeakable and that they strove to achieve their goal through the use of magical arts—in other words, through the help of the Devil's crew. The death of good people meant nothing to them. The Lord—under whom they were saying they wanted to govern—they despised. They regarded him as an ordinary person who had a cult, as took place in other nations who made mortals into gods and worshiped them. They viewed it as a holdover from ancient times but would not dare to speak against it because they had been born into this cult and it would hurt their reputation.

I can say about them that they commandeer the thoughts and the will of people like themselves, worming their way into such people's feelings and intentions. Without the Lord's mercy, their victims could not possibly see that such spirits are present or that they themselves are in such company.

[3] These spirits correspond to disorders of the purer human blood, called the animal spirit. The disorders enter this blood in disarray, and wherever they run they are like poisons that chill and deaden the nerves and nerve fibers, causing severe and fatal illnesses to break out.

When spirits of this kind act as a group, they are identified by the fact that they go down on all fours, so to speak, and take possession of the back part of the head, under the cerebellum, on the left. Spirits who operate below the occiput work more secretively than others, and those who operate on the back part want to take control.

[4] They argued with me about the Lord. "It is surprising that he doesn't hear the prayers we pray, that he doesn't help his supplicants," they said.

"You cannot be heard," I was allowed to answer, "because what you are aiming for is contrary to the well-being of the human race. You are praying for yourselves at everyone's expense, and when you pray that way, heaven closes up, because in heaven they pay attention only to the goals of the people praying." The spirits did not want to acknowledge this but also could not come up with a response.

[5] There were some men of this type in company with some women, and they said they could learn more strategy from women because women are faster and cleverer at grasping such things. They greatly enjoy the company of those who had been prostitutes.

People like this usually apply themselves to secret magical arts in the other life, because in that realm are found many magical practices that are completely unknown in the world. As soon as these types reach the other world, they go to work learning to bewitch the people they are with, especially the ones whose rule they wish to coopt. They have no distaste for atrocity.

The nature of the hell of these spirits and where they live when they are not in the world of spirits will be discussed elsewhere.

These remarks show that our life awaits each of us after death.

4228 There is more on the universal human and correspondence at the end of the next chapter, where correspondence with the senses in general is discussed [§§4318–4331].

Genesis 32

[Matthew 24:32–35]

IN the fourth volume I started to explain the Lord's predictions concerning the Last Judgment in Matthew 24. The explanation came at the head of the later chapters in the volume and reached verse 31 of that Gospel chapter (see §§3353–3356, 3486–3489, 3650–3655, [3751–3757,] 3897–3901, 4056–4060).

The explanations there reveal the inner meaning of the whole. To sum up, the Lord predicted the growing devastation of the church and the eventual establishment of a new church, in the following order:

1. People would start to forget what was good and true and would quarrel over it.
2. They would despise it.
3. They would refuse to acknowledge it at heart.
4. They would profane it.
5. Since religious truth and neighborly kindness would survive among certain people referred to as the chosen, the text depicts the state of faith at that point
6. and afterward the state of neighborly love.
7. Finally it treats of the start of a new church.

The dawn of a new church is meant by the last sentence explained there: "And he will send his angels out with a trumpet and a loud voice, and they will gather his chosen people from the four winds, from one end of the heavens right to the other end of them" (verse 31). For these words meaning the beginning of a new church, see the end of §4060.

When the end of an old religion and the beginning of a new one is at hand, it is time for a final judgment. Such a time is meant in the Word by the Last Judgment (see §§2117–2133, 3353, 4057) and the Son of Humankind's arrival.

This arrival is the current topic and is what the disciples had asked the Lord about when they said, "Tell us when these things will happen—especially what the sign of your coming and of the close of the age will be" (Matthew 24:3). What now remains to be explained, therefore, are the Lord's predictions about the actual time of his Coming and of the close of the age (which is the Last Judgment). Here at the head of the current chapter the explanation will cover only the contents of verses 32, 33, 34, 35:

> From the fig tree, though, learn the parable: When its branch now becomes soft and the leaves come out, you know that the summer is near. So also when you see all these things, know for yourselves that [the time] is near—at the doors. Truly, I say to you: this generation will not pass away till all these things happen. Heaven and earth will pass away, but my words will not pass away. (Matthew 24:32, 33, 34, 35)

The inner meaning of these words follows.

4231 *From the fig tree, though, learn the parable: when its branch becomes soft and the leaves come out, you know that the summer is near* symbolizes the first stage of a new religion. The fig tree means earthly goodness, the branch means its desire, and the leaves mean true ideas. The parable they were to learn from means the existence of this symbolism.

Anyone who does not know the Word's inner meaning can never see what is involved in a comparison of the Lord's Coming with a fig tree and its branch and leaves. However, all comparisons in the Word are also symbolic (§3579), which means that we can learn their significance. Whenever the Word mentions a fig tree, on an inner level it symbolizes earthly goodness; see §217. A branch symbolizes its desire because desire stems from goodness as a branch forks from its trunk. For the meaning of leaves as truth, see §885.

These remarks now reveal the thrust of the parable: When the Lord creates a new religion, what appears first of all is earthly goodness, or a superficial form of goodness, with the desire and true ideas that accompany it. By earthly goodness I do not mean the goodness we are born with or inherit from our parents but goodness that has a spiritual origin. No one is born into this kind of goodness; no, the Lord introduces it into us through our knowledge of goodness and truth. Until we adopt this spiritual goodness, then, we do not belong to the church, no matter how much our inborn goodness makes it look as though we do.

[2] *So also when you see all these things, know for yourselves that [the time] is near—at the doors* means that when these effects appear—the effects symbolized on an inner level by the Lord's words just before this in verses

29, 30, 31 and his words here concerning the fig tree—the age will close (the Last Judgment will occur) and he will come. Consequently it means that the old religion will then be rejected and a new one established.

The text says "at the doors" because earthly goodness and its truth are the first traits instilled into a person who is being reborn and becoming an individual church.

Truly, I say to you: this generation will not pass away till all these things happen means that the Jewish nation will not be wiped out like other nations. For the reason, see §3479.

[3] *Heaven and earth will pass away, but my words will not pass away* means that the inner and outer levels of the previous religion will disappear but the Lord's Word will remain. Heaven means the inner level of a church, and the earth, its outer level; see §§82, 1411, 1733, 1850, 2117, 2118, 3355 at the end. "My words" obviously mean not only what the Lord says here about his Coming and the close of the age but everything in the Word.

This message comes right after the statement about the Jewish nation because the Jewish nation was preserved for the sake of the Word, as can be seen in the place cited, §3479.

This discussion now shows that the current passage foretells the beginnings of a new religion.

Genesis 32

1. And Jacob went on his way. And God's angels met him.

2. And Jacob said as he saw them, "This is the camp of God!" and called the name of that place Mahanaim.

3. And Jacob sent messengers before him to Esau his brother, to the land of Seir, to the field of Edom.

4. And he commanded them, saying, "This is what you will say to my lord Esau: 'This is what your servant Jacob says: With Laban I have resided and stayed till now.

5. And I have had ox and donkey, flock and male slave and female slave, and I am sending to tell my lord, to find favor in your eyes.'"

6. And the messengers returned to Jacob, saying, "We came to your brother, to Esau, and he is also coming to meet you, and four hundred men with him."

7. And Jacob was very frightened, and it was distressing for him; and he split the people who were with him and the flock and the herd and the camels into two camps.

8. And he said, "If Esau comes to one camp and strikes it, there will also be a camp left for escape."

9. And Jacob said, "God of my father Abraham, and God of my father Isaac, Jehovah, who said to me, 'Return to your land and to [the place of] your birth and I will deal well with you':

10. I am too small for all the mercies and for all the truth that you have done with your servant, because with my staff I crossed this Jordan, and now I have become two camps.

11. Rescue me, please, from the hand of my brother, from the hand of Esau, because I fear him; maybe he will come and strike me, mother upon children.

12. And you yourself said, 'I will do immense good to you and make your seed like the sand of the sea, which cannot be counted for abundance.'"

13. And he spent the night there that night and took a gift for Esau his brother from what came to his hand:

14. two hundred she-goats and twenty he-goats; two hundred ewes and twenty rams;

15. thirty nursing camels and their offspring; forty heifers and ten young bulls; twenty jennies and ten foals.

16. And he gave into the hand of his servants a drove, a drove, by itself. And he said to his servants, "Cross before me, and you are to put space between drove and drove."

17. And he commanded the first, saying, "Esau my brother might meet you and ask you, saying, 'Whose are you, and where are you going, and whose are these [animals] before you?'

18. And you will say, 'Your servant Jacob's; this is a gift sent to my lord Esau, and look: he is behind us, too.'"

19. And he commanded also the second, also the third, also all those going behind the droves, saying, "According to this word you will speak to Esau when you find him.

20. And you will also say, 'Look: your servant Jacob is behind us'"; because he said, "I will appease his [angry] face with the gift going before me, and afterward I will see his face; maybe he will lift my face."

21. And the gift crossed over before him, and he spent the night that night in the camp.

22. And he got up that night and took his two women and his two slave women and his eleven sons and crossed the crossing of the Jabbok.

23. And he took them and sent them across the river and sent across what he owned.

❋   ❋   ❋   ❋

24. And Jacob remained alone, and a man wrestled with him till the rising of dawn.

25. And [the man] saw that he did not prevail over [Jacob] and touched the hollow of his thigh, and the hollow of Jacob's thigh was dislocated in his wrestling with him.

26. And [the man] said, "Let me go, because dawn is rising." And he said, "I won't let you go unless you bless me."

27. And he said to him, "What is your name?" And he said, "Jacob."

28. And he said, "No longer will your name be called Jacob, but Israel, because you have competed nobly with God and with humans and prevailed."

29. And Jacob asked and said, "Tell me your name, please." And he said, "Why are you asking this, as to my name?" and blessed him there.

30. And Jacob called the name of the place Peniel "because I saw God face to face and my soul was delivered."

31. And the sun came up on him as he crossed Penuel, and he was limping on his thigh.

32. Therefore the children of Israel do not eat the displaced joint's tendon—which is in the hollow of the thigh—to this day, because he touched the displaced joint's tendon in the hollow of Jacob's thigh.

Summary

T HE theme of the inner meaning here is a reversal of state on the earthly level so that goodness comes first, and truth, second. The chapter tells about the implantation of truth in goodness (verses 1–23) and about the struggles of spiritual crisis that have to be endured in the process (verses 24–32). **4232**

A concurrent theme is the Jewish nation and the fact that it could not accept any religious values but still represented them.

Inner Meaning

4233 GENESIS 32:1, 2. *And Jacob went on his way. And God's angels met him. And Jacob said as he saw them, "This is the camp of God!" and called the name of that place Mahanaim.*

Jacob went on his way symbolizes the gradual development of truth so that it could unite with spiritual and heavenly goodness. *And God's angels met him* symbolizes the light provided by goodness. *And Jacob said as he saw them, "This is the camp of God!"* symbolizes heaven. *And called the name of that place Mahanaim* symbolizes the nature of the state.

4234 *Jacob went on his way* symbolizes the gradual development of truth so that it could unite with spiritual and heavenly goodness. This can be seen from the current representation of *Jacob* as earthly truth. It has already been noted that Jacob represented the Lord's earthly plane. When the story talks about Jacob, the inner meaning speaks of the Lord and the way he made his earthly plane divine. Consequently Jacob at first represented truth on that level and then truth connected with a side branch of goodness (meant by Laban). After the Lord connected these, Jacob represented that side branch of goodness. Such goodness does not consist in divine goodness on the earthly level but in an intermediate kind of goodness that enabled the Lord to receive divine goodness. Intermediate goodness is the kind Jacob represented when he left Laban, but such goodness is essentially truth, which therefore has the ability to unite with divine goodness on the earthly plane.

That is the type of truth Jacob now represents.

[2] The goodness with which this truth united is represented by Esau. (For the meaning of Esau as divine goodness in the Lord's earthly divinity, see §§3300, 3302, 3494, 3504, 3527, 3576, 3599, 3669, 3677.) That very union—the union between divine truth and divine goodness in the Lord's earthly divinity—is the current theme on its highest level. Once Jacob left Laban and arrived at the Jordan, or the first entry to Canaan, he started to represent such a union, because on an inner level Canaan symbolizes heaven, and on the highest level, the Lord's divine humanity (§§3038, 3705). That is why the clause *and Jacob went on his way* symbolizes the

gradual development of truth so that it could unite with spiritual and heavenly goodness.

[3] However, these concepts are of a kind that can never be explained in a fully intelligible way, because the broadest outlines of the subject are unknown to scholars, even in the Christian world. People barely know what the earthly and rational planes in a person are, or that these are completely separate from each other. They barely know what spiritual truth is, what the goodness that comes of it is, or that these two are utterly distinct. Still less do they realize that human rebirth involves a union of truth and goodness—a union on the earthly level and a separate union on the rational level—which is accomplished by numerous means. They do not even recognize that the Lord made his humanity divine by following the same series of steps he takes us through when regenerating us. [4] Since these broadest of concepts are unknown, anything said about them cannot help but seem obscure. Nevertheless it needs to be said, because there is no other way to explain the Word's inner meaning. At least the discussion can serve to identify and characterize angelic wisdom, since the Word's inner meaning is mainly for angels.

And God's angels met him symbolizes the light provided by goodness. This can be seen from the symbolism of *God's angels* as something of the Lord's. In this case they symbolize the divinity in him, because divinity itself (called the Father) existed in him. The actual essence of the Lord's life (which in us is called the soul) was from this divinity and was himself. The usual term for this divinity is the divine nature, or rather the divine essence, of the Lord. (To see that in the Word, God's angels symbolize something divine of the Lord's, consult §§1925, 2319, 2821, 3039, 4085.) *God's angels met him* in its first layer of meaning symbolizes inflow of the Divine into the earthly dimension and the resulting light, because all light results from an inflow of the Divine.

4235

The theme is the way the state of the Lord's earthly level turned around so that goodness came first, and truth, second; and this chapter tells about the implantation of truth in the goodness on that level (§4232). Without light from the Lord, truth could not have been implanted, so the chapter starts by talking about light provided by the goodness in which truth was planted.

And Jacob said, "This is the camp of God!" symbolizes heaven. The *camp of God* symbolizes heaven because an army symbolizes truth and

4236

goodness (§3448), and the Lord arranges truth and goodness in a heavenly pattern. So a camp here is something arranged into armies, and the actual heavenly pattern, or heaven, is the camp. By its very nature this camp or arrangement is completely incapable of being infiltrated by hell, despite hell's constant efforts. The arrangement of heaven is also *called* a camp, and the instances of truth and goodness—or angels—arranged in its pattern are called an army. These considerations now show why the camp of God symbolizes heaven.

The way the children of Israel camped in the wilderness represented this very pattern and therefore heaven itself. Their living together there by tribe is even called a camp. The tabernacle in the middle, around which they camped, represented the Lord himself.

For the fact that the children of Israel made such encampments, see Numbers 1:1–end and 33:2–56. They surrounded the tabernacle in their tribes: Judah, Issachar, and Zebulun to the east; Reuben, Simeon, and Gad to the south; Ephraim, Manasseh, and Benjamin to the west; Dan, Asher, and Naphtali to the north; and the Levites in the center, near the tabernacle (Numbers 2:2 and following verses). [2] The tribes symbolize everything good and true taken together; see §§3858, 3862, 3926, 3939, 4060. That is why, when Balaam saw Israel dwelling by tribes and the spirit of God then came over him, he uttered a pronouncement, saying:

How good are your tents, Jacob; your dwellings, Israel! They are planted as valleys are, as gardens beside the river. (Numbers 24:2, 3, 5, 6)

Obviously this prophecy did not mean the people called Jacob and Israel; it was rather the Lord's heaven that was being represented.

In other Scripture passages as well their arrangement or encampments by tribe in the wilderness are called a camp. On an inner level in those passages a camp symbolizes a heavenly pattern, and to camp means to be arranged in that pattern, which is the pattern displayed by goodness and truth in heaven. Such passages include Leviticus 4:12; 8:17; 13:46; 14:8; 16:26, 28; 24:14, 23; Numbers 3; 4:4 and following verses; 5:2–4; 9:17–end; 10:1–11, 28; 11:31, 32; 12:14, 15; 31:19–24; Deuteronomy 23:9, 10, 11, 12, 13, 14.

[3] The meaning of God's camp as heaven is also clear in Joel:

Before him the earth quaked, the heavens trembled, the sun and moon turned black, and the stars pulled in their rays; and Jehovah uttered his voice *before his army*, because *his camp* is very *abundant*, because those who do his word are numerous. (Joel 2:10, 11)

In Zechariah:

> I will *encamp some of the army* at my house because of the one passing through and because of the one leaving, to keep a despot from passing over them. (Zechariah 9:8)

In John:

> Gog and Magog went up over the plain of the earth and surrounded the *camp of the godly* and the well-loved city. But fire came down from God and consumed them. (Revelation 20:9)

Gog and Magog stand for people who engage in outward worship that has been cut off from anything inside and become idolatrous (§1151). The plain of the earth stands for the church's truth, a plain meaning doctrinal truth (§2450) and the earth meaning the church (§§566, 662, 1066, 1068, 1850, 2117, 2118, 3355). The camp of the godly stands for heaven or the Lord's kingdom on earth, which is the church.

[4] Most words in Scripture also have a negative meaning, and *camp* is one. When negative, it symbolizes evil and falsity and therefore hell, as in David:

> If the evil *pitch camp* against me, my heart will not be afraid. (Psalms 27:3)

In the same author:

> God scattered the *bones of those camping* against you; you humiliated them because God rejected them. (Psalms 53:5)

The *camp of Assyria* in which Jehovah's angel struck one hundred eighty-five thousand individuals (Isaiah 37:36) has the same meaning, as does the *camp of the Egyptians* (Exodus 14:19, 20).

And called the name of that place Mahanaim symbolizes the nature of the state. This is established by the symbolism of *calling something's name* as its quality (discussed in §§144, 145, 1754, 1896, 2009, 3421) and from that of a *place* as a state (discussed in §§2625, 2837, 3356, 3387). **4237**

In the original language, *Mahanaim* means a pair of camps, and a pair of camps symbolizes both heavens, or both kingdoms of the Lord—the heavenly one and the spiritual one. On the highest plane they symbolize the Lord's heavenly divinity and spiritual divinity. Mahanaim, then, symbolizes the character of the Lord's state when his earthly level was enlightened by spiritual and heavenly goodness.

The character of that state cannot be described, however, because the divine states the Lord experienced when he made the humanity in himself divine lie beyond the grasp of any human and even of angels. We can understand them only through appearances illuminated by heaven's light, which comes from the Lord, and through the states of human rebirth, since human rebirth is an image of the Lord's glorification (§§3138, 3212, 3296, 3490).

4238   Genesis 32:3, 4, 5. *And Jacob sent messengers before him to Esau his brother, to the land of Seir, to the field of Edom. And he commanded them, saying, "This is what you will say to my lord Esau: 'This is what your servant Jacob says: With Laban I have resided and stayed till now. And I have had ox and donkey, flock and male slave and female slave, and I am sending to tell my lord, to find favor in your eyes.'"*

Jacob sent messengers before him to Esau his brother symbolizes the first contact made with heavenly goodness. *To the land of Seir* symbolizes an earthly kind of heavenly goodness. *To the field of Edom* symbolizes the truth resulting. *And he commanded them, saying, "This is what you will say to my lord Esau,"* symbolizes a first acknowledgment of goodness and of its higher status. *With Laban I have resided and stayed till now* means that [the Lord] became steeped in the goodness symbolized by Laban. *And I have had ox and donkey, flock and male slave and female slave* symbolizes what he had acquired on that level, in sequence. *And I am sending to tell my lord, to find favor in your eyes* symbolizes instruction about his state, and truth's deference and humility in the face of goodness.

4239   *Jacob sent messengers before him to Esau his brother* symbolizes the first contact made with heavenly goodness. This can be seen from the symbolism of *sending messengers* as communicating, and from the representation of *Esau* as heavenly goodness on the earthly level (discussed in §§3300, 3302, 3494, 3504, 3527, 3576, 3599, 3669).

The focus currently is on the union between divine truth on the earthly plane (Jacob) and divine goodness there (Esau), as noted above at §4234. So the chapter initially dealt with the light shed by divinity on the earthly dimension (§4235) and now treats of the first contact made, as symbolized by *Jacob sent messengers to Esau his brother.* In the Word, goodness and truth are *brothers;* see §§367, 3303.

4240   *To the land of Seir* symbolizes an earthly kind of heavenly goodness. This can be seen from the symbolism of the *land of Seir,* which on the highest level is the Lord's heavenly goodness in its earthly form. The reason the land of Seir has this symbolism is that Mount Seir was Canaan's border on one side (Joshua 11:16, 17) and all bordering rivers, mountains, and lands represented the outermost attributes (§§1585, 1866, 4116). They took their representation from Canaan, the land they bounded, which represented the Lord's heavenly kingdom and, on the highest level, his divine humanity (see §§1607, 3038, 3481, 3705). The outermost attributes, which are the borders, are those referred to as earthly, because spiritual and heavenly attributes terminate in earthly ones. The situation is the same in the heavens. The inmost or third heaven is heavenly because it possesses love for the Lord; the intermediate or second heaven is spiritual because it possesses love for others; and the outermost or first heaven is heavenly and spiritual in an earthly way because it possesses a simple goodness, which finishes the sequence. It is the same in reborn individuals, because they are a miniature heaven.

These comments now show why the land of Seir symbolizes an earthly kind of heavenly goodness.

Esau, who lived in Seir, also represents that kind of goodness (as demonstrated above [§4234]), so the land in which he lived has the same symbolism. Different lands, you see, take on the representation of the people who inhabit them (§1675).

[2] From the discussion you can now see what Seir symbolizes in the Word, as in Moses:

Jehovah came from Sinai and *dawned from Seir on them;* he shone out from Mount Paran and came with the holy myriads. (Deuteronomy 33:2, 3)

In the song of Deborah and Barak in Judges:

Jehovah, when you *came out from Seir,* when you marched from the *field of Edom,* the earth trembled, the heavens also showered; yes, the clouds showered water, mountains streamed down. This is Sinai, in the presence of Jehovah, the God of Israel. (Judges 5:4, 5)

In Balaam's prophecy:

I see him, but not yet; I view him, but he is not near. A star will rise out of Jacob, and a scepter will spring up from Israel, and *Edom* will be *an inheritance,* and an *inheritance* will *Seir* be for its enemies, and Israel will do a powerful deed. (Numbers 24:17, 18)

Anyone can see that Seir symbolizes some aspect of the Lord in these passages, because they say that Jehovah dawned from Seir, that he came out from Seir and marched from the field of Edom, and that Edom and Seir would be an inheritance. No one can know what aspect of the Lord is symbolized by Seir, though, except from the Word's inner meaning. The remarks above show that it means his divine humanity, and specifically the goodness in the earthly divinity of his divine humanity. His rising and issuing from Seir means that he made even his earthly plane divine, so that it too would radiate the light of understanding and wisdom. In this way not only the rational but also the earthly level of his humanity would become Jehovah. That is why the passages say that Jehovah dawned from Seir and that Jehovah came out from Seir. On the point that the Lord is Jehovah, see §§1343, 1736, 2004, 2005, 2018, 2025, 2156, 2329, 2921, 3023, 3035. Isaiah's prophecy concerning Dumah involves something similar:

> One is *shouting* to me *from Seir*, "Guard, what is [left] of the night? Guard, what is [left] of the night?" The guard said, "Morning comes, and also night." (Isaiah 21:11, 12)

[3] In a secondary sense the land of Seir properly symbolizes the Lord's kingdom among people outside the church, or non-Christians, when the church is established among them, once the old or previous church falls away from charity and faith. At that point, light shines on people who have been in the dark, as shown by many passages in the Word. This is the particular symbolism of rising from Seir, of issuing from Seir and marching from the field of Edom, of Seir's becoming an inheritance, and of the quotation from Isaiah, "One is shouting to me from Seir, 'Guard, what is [left] of the night?' The guard said, 'Morning comes, and also night.'" "Morning comes" means the Lord's arrival (§§2405, 2780) and the light then shining on those who had been in nighttime, a light that is shed by the Lord's earthly divinity (§4211).

Since most words in Scripture also have a negative sense, Seir does too, as in Ezekiel 25:8, 9; 35:2–15; and several times in the Word's narrative parts.

4241   *To the field of Edom* symbolizes the truth resulting—that is, resulting from goodness. This is established by the symbolism of the *field of Edom* as goodness in the Lord's earthly divinity to which truth—doctrinal truth— is united (discussed in §§3302, 3322). Truth resulting from goodness is different from the truth that produces goodness. Truth that produces goodness is the truth we absorb before being reborn. Truth resulting from goodness is the truth we absorb after being reborn. After we are reborn, truth rises out of goodness, because goodness then enables us to perceive and recognize the validity of the truth. This truth, truth based on goodness, is what the field of Edom symbolizes. The same applies in the passage from Judges quoted above: "Jehovah, when you *came out from Seir,* when you *marched from the field of Edom . . ."* (Judges 5:4).

And he commanded them, saying, "This is what you will say to my lord Esau," symbolizes a first acknowledgment of goodness and of its higher status, as the following shows: In this instance, *commanding* the messengers *to say* symbolizes reflection leading to a perception that something is so (as discussed in §§3661, 3682) and consequently to an acknowledgment of it. *Esau* represents goodness, as noted above in §§4234, 4239. Its higher status is symbolized by Jacob's calling Esau his lord rather than his brother, and by his referring to himself as Esau's servant just afterward and further on as well. When we are being reborn, truth seems to hold first place, and goodness, second; but when we reach the end of the process, goodness comes first, and truth, second. (See §§1904, 2063, 2189, 2697, 2979, 3286, 3288, 3310 at the end, 3325, 3330, 3332, 3336, 3470, 3509, 3539, 3548, 3556, 3563, 3570, 3576, 3579, 3603, 3701.)

4242

The meaning is the same for the prophecy of Isaac the father to Esau his son: "By your sword you will live, and your brother you will serve; and it will happen *when you gain the dominance* that you will tear his yoke off your neck" (Genesis 27:40). The reversal in conditions that the prophecy predicted is the current subject.

With Laban I have resided and stayed till now means that [the Lord] became steeped in the goodness symbolized by Laban, as can be seen from the following: *Laban* represents an intermediate goodness, a goodness that is not genuine but nonetheless serves to introduce genuine truth and goodness, as mentioned in §§3974, 3982, 3986 at the end, 4063. *Residing* as an immigrant means being taught, as mentioned in §§1463, 2025. And *staying* somewhere has significance because the word is used to describe a life of truth accompanied by goodness, as mentioned in §3613. Here it means being steeped in something. This discussion shows, then, that the sentence *With Laban I have resided and stayed till now* means that [the Lord] became steeped in the goodness symbolized by Laban.

4243

[2] The fact of the matter is that truth cannot be implanted in goodness without the use of various means. The means were discussed in the previous chapters describing Jacob's residence and stay with Laban, and the flock he acquired there. The focus now becomes the process of union

and therefore the reversal of conditions, following a sequence of steps that takes place when truth yields control to goodness. Truth apparently takes priority when we are learning it with a will but are not yet living by it very fully; but goodness takes priority when we live by the truth we so eagerly learned. Truth then becomes goodness, because we then believe that goodness consists in acting on the truth. People who have been reborn possess this kind of goodness. So do people with conscience—in other words, people who no longer argue about the validity of truth but act on it because it is true. These are people who have steeped their faith and life in goodness.

4244   *And I have had ox and donkey, flock and male slave and female slave* symbolizes what he had acquired on that level, in sequence. This can be seen from the symbolism of *ox and donkey, flock and male slave and female slave* as subservient goodness and truth both outer and inner, and therefore as things he acquired, in sequence. An *ox* means outer earthly goodness, and a *donkey,* outer earthly truth (see §2781). A *flock* means inner earthly goodness; a *male slave,* the truth that goes with it; and a *female slave,* a desire for that truth. This can be seen from the symbolism of each, discussed several times before. These types of goodness and truth are the acquisitions being depicted. Plainly they are listed in sequence, the outer types being the ox and donkey, and the inner types, the flock, male slave, and female slave.

4245   *And I am sending to tell my lord, to find favor in your eyes* symbolizes instruction about his state, and truth's deference and humility in the face of goodness. This can be seen from the symbolism of *sending to tell* as instructing him about his state. It is clear that truth's subsequent deference and humility in the face of goodness is meant because Jacob calls Esau *his lord* and says *to find favor in your eyes,* which are words of deference and humility.

This verse tells what conditions are like when they are being turned around, or when truth is yielding control to goodness, or when people moved by truth start to be moved by goodness.

This reversal and yield of control, however, is apparent only to people who have been reborn, and then only to the ones who reflect on it. Few today regenerate, and even fewer reflect, so these assertions about truth and goodness cannot help seeming unclear to them and perhaps even the wrong kind of ideas to acknowledge. They will be particularly objectionable to people who put the truth that constitutes faith in first place and the goodness that constitutes charity in second, who accordingly think a lot about doctrine and not much about neighborly kindness and view eternal salvation in terms of doctrine rather than charity. People whose minds work this way cannot possibly see, let alone perceive, that the truth that composes faith is subordinate to the goodness that composes charity. The ideas we think and base our thinking on affect us. If we were to base our thoughts on neighborly kindness, we would see clearly that faith's truth comes second; and then we would see real truth in clear light. Charitable kindness is like a flame that radiates light, illuminating everything we had previously considered true. We would also discern the way in which falsity injected itself and took on the appearance of truth.

Genesis 32:6, 7, 8. *And the messengers returned to Jacob, saying, "We* **4246** *came to your brother, to Esau, and he is also coming to meet you, and four hundred men with him." And Jacob was very frightened, and it was distressing for him; and he split the people who were with him and the flock and the herd and the camels into two camps. And he said, "If Esau comes to one camp and strikes it, there will also be a camp left for escape."*

The messengers returned to Jacob, saying, "We came to your brother, to Esau, and he is also coming to meet you," means that goodness constantly flows in, seeking to take possession. *And four hundred men with him* symbolizes the state goodness is now in, as it takes the lead. *And Jacob was very frightened, and it was distressing for him* symbolizes that state in the process of change. *And he split the people who were with him and the flock and the herd and the camels into two camps* symbolizes preparing and arranging truth and goodness on the earthly level to receive the goodness represented by Esau. *And he said, "If Esau comes to one camp and strikes it, there will also be a camp left for escape,"* means taking all possible outcomes into account.

And the messengers returned to Jacob, saying, "We came to your brother, **4247** *to Esau, and he is also coming to meet you,"* means that goodness constantly flows in, seeking to take possession—possession of truth. This can be seen from the symbolism of the *brother,* Esau, as goodness, and specifically the goodness of the Lord's earthly divinity (dealt with above) and from that of *coming to meet* as flowing in (dealt with below). Since it means flowing in, it means taking possession.

[2] From several earlier, related discussions you can see what the case is with goodness and truth and with the way goodness flows into truth, adopting truth as its own. You can see that goodness constantly flows in and is received by truth, since truth is a vessel for goodness. The only vessels divine goodness can be put into are genuine truths, because divine goodness and genuine truth correspond to each other. When we have a

desire for truth, as we do at first, before being reborn, even then goodness is constantly flowing in, but it does not yet have vessels, or truth,
to which it can be added, or by which it can be adopted. When we are
starting to be reborn, we are not devoted to religious concepts yet. At that
stage, since goodness is always flowing in, it produces a desire for truth.
The source of such a desire is nothing but the constant effort of divine
goodness to flow in. So even then goodness comes first and does most of
the work, although it appears as though truth did. It is when we are being
reborn, as adults who possess knowledge, that goodness comes out into
the open. Then we want not so much to know truth as to act on it. Up
to that point, truth existed in the intellect, but afterward it exists in the
will, and when it exists in the will, it exists in the person—since the will
constitutes a person's real self.

Such is the ever-repeating cycle in a person: every form of secular and
religious knowledge enters through our eyes or ears into our thoughts,
from there into our will, and from there through our thoughts into act.
The starting point can also be the memory, which resembles inner sight,
or the inner eye. A similar cycle begins there, moving from the inner
eye through the thoughts into the will and from the will through the
thoughts into action. If anything blocks it, the cycle ends in the effort to
act, which proceeds to action as soon as the blockage is removed.

[3] These comments now show how matters stand with the inflow of
goodness and its adoption of truth: Faith's truth first of all enters through
the ears or eyes, is then stored in the memory, gradually rises from there
into thought, and finally moves to the will. From the will it proceeds
through thought into act or, if action is not possible, persists as an effort.
Effort itself is an inward act, because whenever opportunity arises, it turns
into outward activity.

This is how the cycle needs to be seen, but goodness is what produces
it. Life from the Lord flows only into goodness and therefore enters us
only through goodness, starting from our inmost depths. Anyone can see
that life flowing through our inmost depths produces the cycle, because
nothing happens without life. And since life from the Lord flows only
into goodness and only through goodness, it follows that goodness produces the cycle. Goodness flows into truth and adopts truth as its own,
so far as a person knows what is true and is willing to accept the inflow.

4248   *And four hundred men with him* symbolizes the state goodness is now
in, as it takes the lead. This is established by the specific symbolism of
four hundred as times of trial and the length of time they last (discussed
at §§2959, 2966). A state of trial is the state meant. What follows attests

to this meaning, because it says that Jacob was very frightened, that it was distressing for him, that he therefore divided his camp in two (verses 7, 8); that in his fear he prayed fervently to Jehovah (verses 9, 10, 11, 12); and that he wrestled an angel [verses 24, 25]. The wrestling symbolizes trials, as its explanation later in the chapter will show.

When our state is reversed as we are being reborn—when goodness takes the lead—trials come. Until then we cannot sustain them because as yet we do not possess the knowledge we need to defend ourselves and to resort to for comfort. So we also do not undergo such a test until we reach adulthood. Times of trial are what unite truth to goodness (§§2272, 3318, 3696, 3928).

Clearly, then, *four hundred men with him* symbolizes a state in which goodness takes the lead.

And Jacob was very frightened, and it was distressing for him symbolizes that state in the process of change. This can be seen from the consideration that fear and distress are the first stage of trial and that they come at the beginning of a reversal or change in state.   **4249**

It is not easy to disclose in an intelligible way the further secrets that lie hidden in these circumstances—that Esau went to meet Jacob with four hundred men, causing Jacob fear and distress—because the secrets are quite deep. Let me bring up just this one idea: When goodness takes the lead and subordinates truth to itself (as it does when we undergo spiritual trials), it flows from within, bringing with it many true ideas that lie stored up in our inner self. They cannot come to our attention or understanding until goodness takes charge, because not till then does the earthly level start to be illuminated by goodness. The light reveals both the harmonious and the discordant elements on that level; the discrepancies are the source of the fear and distress with which a spiritual crisis commences. What is being spiritually tested is our conscience, which belongs to our inner self, so when the crisis begins, we do not know where the fear and distress are coming from. The angels with us know precisely where they are coming from, though. The crisis results from the fact that they are holding us to a path of goodness and truth while evil spirits are holding us to a path of evil and falsity.

[2] Anything that exists with the spirits and angels who accompany us seems to us to be inside us; we cannot view it any other way. While living in our bodies we do not believe that everything comes to us from elsewhere, so we do not see events inside us as resulting from causes outside us. We imagine that all the causes are inside us and belong to us. Such is not the case. Everything we think and everything we intend—all our

thoughts and all our desires—come from either hell or heaven. When we think and intend evil and enjoy the false ideas that result, we can be sure our thoughts and desires come from hell. When we think and intend what is good and enjoy the true ideas that result, we can be sure our thoughts and desires come from heaven, or through heaven from the Lord. However, the thoughts and desires we have are usually disguised. When evil spirits fight angels over a regenerating person's thoughts and desires, for instance, the battles appear in the form of fear, distress, and trial.

[3] This information cannot help seeming strange, because people in the church today almost universally believe that the truth they think and the good they intend and do all comes from themselves (although that is not how they talk when they are speaking from religious doctrine). In fact, if you told them that spirits from hell are influencing their thoughts and their will when they think and intend evil, and that angels from heaven are influencing them when they think and intend something good, they would stand perplexed and amazed that anyone could make such an assertion. They would say that they can feel life inside themselves and that they think and form intentions on their own. They base their belief on this sensation rather than on doctrine, when the doctrine is true and the sensation is misleading.

Many years now of almost constant experience have enabled me to know this, and to know it so certainly that no doubt whatever remains.

4250 *And he split the people who were with him and the flock and the herd and the camels into two camps* symbolizes preparing and arranging truth and goodness on the earthly level to receive the goodness represented by Esau, as the following indicates: *People* symbolize truth, and falsity too, as discussed in §§1259, 1260, 3581. The *flock* symbolizes inner goodness, and inner nongoodness as well, and the *herd* symbolizes outer goodness, and outer nongoodness as well (discussed in §§2566, 4244). *Camels* symbolize outer or general truth, and nontruth too, as discussed in §§3048, 3071, 3143, 3145. And *camps* symbolize an orderly pattern—truly orderly, in a positive sense, and not truly orderly, in a negative sense—as discussed in §4236. *Splitting*, of course, means dividing in half and in this way preparing oneself to receive something.

The remarks just above tell what is going on here: When goodness flows in, as it does when the usual pattern is turned around and goodness takes the lead, light shines on the earthly plane. Then we see what is really true and good on that plane and what is not really true or good. We distinguish between them, keeping some and removing the rest. As a result, everything is arranged in a completely different pattern than before. This is a natural consequence when goodness takes control, because true concepts are then nothing more than attendants and servants. The more they fill up with goodness, the more nearly they are arranged in a heavenly pattern. The quality of the true concepts also affects the arrangement, since goodness takes its character from truth.

And he said, "If Esau comes to one camp and strikes it, there will also be **4251** *a camp left for escape,"* means taking all possible outcomes into account, as can be seen from the following: A *camp* symbolizes an orderly pattern, as noted just above. *Striking* means destroying. And *there will be a camp left for escape* symbolizes an intent to keep the orderly arrangement of the earthly dimension from dissolving completely, so that some part of it would survive. So the whole sentence symbolizes preparation and arrangements that take all possible outcomes into account.

As long as truth dominates the earthly dimension, that dimension cannot see what is really true and what is not, or what is really good and what is not. When the good resulting from love for the Lord and charity for one's neighbor dominates that dimension, it does see. In consequence, when the time or conditions arrive for goodness to take charge, we have little idea what is good and true, what has to be destroyed and what kept. This is plainly illustrated in times of trial. When we suffer this kind of confusion, it is not we but the Lord who does the preparing and arranging. In the current case, it was the Lord who did the preparing and arranging in himself. Everything in the Lord was arranged and reduced to divine order by him through his own power.

Genesis 32:9, 10, 11, 12. *And Jacob said, "God of my father Abraham, and* **4252a** *God of my father Isaac, Jehovah, who said to me, 'Return to your land and to [the place of] your birth and I will deal well with you': I am too small for all the mercies and for all the truth that you have done with your servant, because with my staff I crossed this Jordan, and now I have become two camps. Rescue me, please, from the hand of my brother, from the hand of Esau, because I fear him; maybe he will come and strike me, mother upon children. And you yourself said, 'I will do immense good to you and make your seed like the sand of the sea, which cannot be counted for abundance.'"*

Jacob said, "God of my father Abraham, and God of my father Isaac, Jehovah," symbolizes holy preparation and arrangement. *Who said to me, "Return to your land and to [the place of] your birth and I will deal well with you,"* means to union with divine goodness and truth. *I am too small for all the mercies and for all the truth that you have done with your servant* symbolizes humility in that state regarding goodness and truth. *Because with my staff I crossed this Jordan, and now I have become two camps* means from poverty to abundance. *Rescue me, please, from the hand of my brother, from the hand of Esau, because I fear him* symbolizes his comparative situation, since he had put himself first. *Maybe he will come and strike me, mother upon children* means that he would perish. *And you yourself said, "I will do immense good to you,"* means that even then it would come alive. *And make your seed like the sand of the sea, which cannot be counted for abundance,* symbolizes bearing fruit and multiplying at that point.

4252b *He said, "God of my father Abraham, and God of my father Isaac, Jehovah,"* symbolizes holy preparation and arrangement. This is established by the symbolism of the *God of his father Abraham* as the Lord's divinity itself (discussed in §3439) and from that of the *God of his father Isaac* as the Lord's divine humanity (discussed in §§3704, 4180). Since both are Jehovah, the text says *God of my father Abraham, and God of my father Isaac, Jehovah.* In this case, though, the names symbolize something holy that has its source in divinity, as everything holy does.

The reason it symbolizes something holy is that this was on the earthly level (represented by Jacob), where goodness (represented by Esau) was not yet united to truth. The current theme is a state in which goodness was received—at this point, a state in which preparations and arrangements were being made to receive it. Jacob's plea involves exactly this. The current clause, then, symbolizes holy preparation and arrangement.

4253 *Who said to me, "Return to your land and to [the place of] your birth and I will deal well with you,"* symbolizes union with divine goodness and truth. This can be seen from an earlier discussion at §§4069, 4070, where almost the same words occur.

4254 *I am too small for all the mercies and for all the truth that you have done with your servant* symbolizes humility in that state regarding goodness and truth. This can be seen from the use of *mercy,* which depicts a loving goodness, and from the use of *truth,* which depicts religious truth (see §3122). Obviously the words are an expression of humility. So the clause symbolizes humility in that state regarding goodness and truth.

4255 *Because with my staff I crossed this Jordan, and now I have become two camps* means from poverty to abundance, as the following shows: A *staff* [or rod] symbolizes power and is a word for describing truth, as noted in §§4013, 4015. The *Jordan* symbolizes a threshold to knowledge of what is good and true, as discussed below. And *two camps* symbolize what is good and true, as they did above in §4250. After all, the two camps consist of the people, flock, herd, and camels that Jacob split. This clarifies what the words symbolize in their first layer of meaning: the Lord had little truth when he crossed the threshold to knowledge but afterward had a wealth of truth and goodness. In other words, he went from poverty to abundance.

The explanations so far make it plain that the inner meaning has been about the Lord and the way he made the humanity in himself divine, step by step, in an orderly sequence. So it has dealt with his advance into understanding and wisdom, and finally into divine understanding and wisdom. This makes it clear what "from poverty to abundance" means.

[2] The *Jordan* means a threshold to knowledge of goodness and truth because it was a border to the land of Canaan. All the boundaries of that land symbolized what is first and last in the Lord's kingdom and in the church, so they symbolized the first and last heavenly and spiritual qualities that make up the Lord's kingdom and his church. (See §§1585, 1866, 4116, 4240.) The Jordan, being a boundary, symbolized a threshold to knowledge of goodness and truth. This knowledge comes first, but eventually, when we become an individual church, or a kingdom of the Lord, it comes last.

[3] Other passages in the Word can also demonstrate that the Jordan has this symbolism. In David, for instance:

My God, my soul is bowing down upon me. Therefore I will remember you *from the land of Jordan,* and [I will remember] the Hermons from the little mountain. (Psalms 42:6)

Remembering from the land of Jordan stands for remembering from last position and therefore from humility. In the same author:

Judah became [God's] sanctuary; Israel, his ruling power. The sea looked and fled; *the Jordan turned back.* (Psalms 114:2, 3, 5)

Judah stands for the goodness associated with heavenly love; Israel, for the goodness associated with spiritual love (§3654). The sea stands for knowledge of truth (§28). The Jordan stands for knowledge of goodness, which is said to turn back when goodness of a loving kind becomes dominant. At that stage we look at knowledge from the viewpoint of that goodness, rather than looking at goodness from the viewpoint of knowledge, as shown many times before. [4] In Judges:

> Gilead is living on the *ford of Jordan;* and Dan—why must he be afraid of ships? (Judges 5:17)

Gilead stands for the sensory goodness—the physical pleasure—that provides our first introduction to the process of rebirth (§§4117, 4124). Living on the ford of Jordan stands for living on the threshold and so for living among what is first and last in the Lord's church and kingdom.

The same things were represented by the Jordan when the children of Israel entered the land of Canaan (Joshua 3:14–end; 4:1–end). Canaan represented the Lord's kingdom (§§1413, 1437, 1607, 3038, 3481, 3686, 3705). The parting of the Jordan and the people's crossing on dry ground symbolized the removal of evil and falsity and the admittance of people with goodness and truth. So did the parting of the Jordan's water by Elijah when he was taken up to heaven (2 Kings 2:8) and by Elisha when he assumed the role of prophet in place of Elijah (2 Kings 2:14).

[5] Naaman was healed of leprosy by washing seven times in the Jordan, as Elisha had ordered (2 Kings 5:1–14). This event represented baptism, and baptism symbolizes initiation into the church and all that the church implies. So it symbolizes rebirth and all that rebirth implies—not that baptism regenerates anyone but that it is a sign reminding the person of regeneration. Since baptism symbolizes aspects of the church, and the Jordan does too (as noted just above), people were baptized by John in the Jordan (Matthew 3:6; Mark 1:5), and the Lord also chose to be baptized by John there (Matthew 3:13–17; Mark 1:9).

[6] Because the Jordan symbolizes what is first and last in the Lord's kingdom and church—as knowledge of what is good and true is, since it serves as an introduction—the Jordan is also mentioned as a border of the new holy land in Ezekiel 47:18. On the point that the new holy land or earth means the Lord's kingdom and a new church (the Lord's kingdom on earth), see §§1733, 1850, 2117, 2118 at the end, 3355 at the end.

4256   *Rescue me, please, from the hand of my brother, from the hand of Esau, because I fear him* symbolizes his comparative situation, since he had put himself first. This symbolism can be seen from discussions in various earlier sections, especially those dealing with the birthright Jacob acquired in exchange for his lentil soup, and with the blessing he took from Esau by trickery. See there the representation and symbolism involved: Truth apparently comes first when we are being reborn, and goodness, second;

but goodness is actually in first place, and truth, in second. This fact becomes clear once we have been reborn. On these subjects, see §§3539, 3548, 3556, 3563, 3570, 3576, 3603, 3701, 4243, 4245, 4247. When the pattern reverses, goodness openly takes its leading position—that is, it starts to exercise control over truth. Then our earthly self suffers fear and distress (§4249) and undergoes trial.

The reason for the fear, distress, and trial is that when truth led, or seemed to itself to be in control, falsity mingled with it. By itself truth cannot see whether a claim is true. It has to look at it from the standpoint of goodness, and where falsity exists, the approach of goodness causes fear. What is more, everyone moved by goodness starts to tremble when falsity becomes visible in the light cast by goodness, because such people are afraid of falsity. They want it rooted out, which is impossible if falsity is tenacious, unless divine means provided by the Lord come into play. That is why people being reborn who have gone through fear and distress come into trials as well: trials are the divine means for removing falsity. This is the deeply hidden reason that we undergo spiritual crises when we are being reborn. Such a reason is not at all visible to us, because it lies above the realm of our discernment. So does everything that provokes, vexes, and tortures our conscience.

Maybe he will come and strike me, mother upon children means that he would perish, as is self-evident.   **4257**

Striking mother upon children was a standard phrase among the ancients, who used representation and symbolism. The phrase symbolized the destruction of the church and everything having to do with the church, either in general or in an individual who *is* a church on a small scale. They took a *mother* to mean the church (§§289, 2691, 2717) and *children* to mean the church's truth (§§489, 491, 533, 1147, 2623, 3373). So striking mother upon children means being annihilated. We as individuals are annihilated when the church and its properties in us are destroyed, which is to say when our desire for truth is destroyed—a desire for truth being what a mother properly symbolizes and what constitutes the church in us.

And you yourself said, "I will do immense good to you," means that even   **4258**
then it would come alive. This can be seen from the symbolism of *doing good* as coming alive. Jacob represents truth, and truth has no life on its own. It receives life from the goodness that flows into it, as shown many times before. So *doing good* here means coming to life. Besides, the current topic of discussion is the life truth receives from goodness.

4259   *And make your seed like the sand of the sea, which cannot be counted for abundance,* symbolizes bearing fruit and multiplying at that point. This is established by the symbolism of *seed* as the faith that comes of charity, and as charity itself (discussed in §§1025, 1447, 1610, 2848, 3373). *Making* this faith *like the sand of the sea, which cannot be counted for abundance* obviously means multiplying it. "Bearing fruit" is used to describe goodness, which is a facet of charity, while "multiplying" is used to describe truth, which is a facet of faith (§§913, 983, 2846, 2847).

4260   Genesis 32:13, 14, 15. *And he spent the night there that night and took a gift for Esau his brother from what came to his hand: two hundred she-goats and twenty he-goats; two hundred ewes and twenty rams; thirty nursing camels and their offspring; forty heifers and ten young bulls; twenty jennies and ten foals.*

He spent the night that night means in that dim state. *And took a gift for Esau his brother from what came to his hand* symbolizes the divine qualities to be introduced into heavenly goodness of an earthly kind. *Two hundred she-goats and twenty he-goats; two hundred ewes and twenty rams* symbolize divine goodness and the resulting divine truth. *Thirty nursing camels and their offspring; forty heifers and ten young bulls; twenty jennies and ten foals* symbolize general and particular subservient attributes.

4261   *He spent the night that night* means in that dim state. This can be seen from the symbolism of *spending the night* and of *night* as a dim state (dealt with in §§1712, 3693).

4262   *And took a gift for Esau his brother from what came to his hand* symbolizes the divine qualities to be introduced into heavenly goodness of an earthly kind, as can be seen from the following: *Taking from what came to his hand* means taking from what had happened by plan and so from what had happened as a result of divine providence. What results from divine providence is divine, so taking from what came into his hand symbolizes divine qualities. A *gift* symbolizes introduction, as discussed below. And *Esau* represents goodness in the Lord's earthly divinity, as discussed in §§3302, 3322, 3504, 3599. In this case he represents heavenly goodness, because the Lord's earthly level had not yet become divine.

[2] The reason a gift symbolizes introduction is that it is intended to curry goodwill and favor. In earlier days the gifts and offerings people made had various meanings. Those they made on approaching monarchs and priests had one meaning; those they offered on the altar had another. The former symbolized introduction, but the latter symbolized worship (§349).

The word *gift* [or offering] was used for all kinds of sacrifices in general, but in particular for the minha, which consisted of bread and wine, or cakes accompanied by a libation. In the original language, minha means a gift.

[3] The practice of giving presents when approaching monarchs and priests appears many places in the Word, such as passages in which Saul consulted Samuel (1 Samuel 9:7, 8), some people who despised Saul failed to offer him a gift (1 Samuel 10:27), and the queen of Sheba came to Solomon (1 Kings 10:2). Others also came to Solomon, and the text says of them:

> All the earth was seeking the face of Solomon to hear his wisdom, and they were each offering their gift: vessels of silver and vessels of gold and clothes and weaponry and perfumes, horses and mules. (1 Kings 10:24, 25)

Since this was a sacred custom symbolizing introduction, the sages from the east who came to Jesus not long after he was born brought gifts: gold, frankincense, and myrrh (Matthew 2:11). Gold symbolized heavenly love; frankincense, spiritual love; and myrrh, both kinds of love on an earthly level.

[4] The custom had been commanded, as seen in Moses: "Jehovah's face shall not be seen by the empty-handed" (Exodus 23:15; Deuteronomy 16:16, 17). Other passages in the Word show that the gifts given to priests and monarchs were essentially for Jehovah.

Gifts that were sent symbolized introduction, as is evident from the gifts the twelve chieftains of Israel sent to dedicate the altar, or introduce it into use, after it was anointed (Numbers 7:1–end; the chieftains' gifts are referred to as a dedication in verse 88).

Two hundred she-goats and twenty he-goats; two hundred ewes and twenty rams symbolize divine goodness and the resulting divine truth. **4263** This is established by the symbolism of *she-goats* and *ewes* as goodness (discussed in §§3995, 4006, 4169) and from that of *he-goats* and *rams* as truth (discussed in §§4005, 4170). In this case they symbolize goodness and truth that are divine.

The reason for mentioning goodness and truth so often, and the reason so many objects symbolize them, is that everything belonging to heaven and to the church relates to them. Matters of love and charity relate to goodness, and matters of faith relate to truth. Still, there are different types and subtypes of goodness and truth, without number and even without limit. Consider that everyone with goodness is in the Lord's kingdom, and yet no community there has the same goodness as another. In fact, no individual in a community has the same goodness as another. No two people, let alone many, can have identical goodness. If they did, they would be one and the same person, not two people, let alone many. A unity always consists of differing parts brought together in heavenly agreement and harmony.

4264   *Thirty nursing camels and their offspring; forty heifers and ten young bulls; twenty jennies and ten foals* symbolize general and particular subservient attributes. This can be seen from the symbolism of *camels and their offspring,* of *heifers* and *young bulls,* and of *jennies* and their *foals* as properties of the earthly self. This symbolism has been discussed several times before: *camels,* §§3048, 3071, 3143, 3145; *young cattle,* §§1824, 1825, 2180, 2781, 2830; and *jennies,* §2781. For attributes of the earthly self being relatively menial, see §§1486, 3019, 3020, 3167. That is why these animals symbolize general and particular subservient attributes.

There are secrets regarding the number of animals—two hundred she-goats, twenty he-goats, two hundred ewes, twenty rams, thirty camels and their offspring, forty heifers, ten young bulls, twenty jennies, and ten of their foals—that cannot be laid open without lengthy explanation and extensive proofs. All numbers in the Word have a symbolic meaning (§§482, 487, 575, 647, 648, 755, 813, 1988, 2075, 2252, 3252), and the symbolism of each has been shown in earlier places where it occurs.

[2] To my astonishment, I have occasionally observed that when the speech of angels filters down into the world of spirits, it falls into rhythms of various different counts. I have also noticed that where people read a number in the Word, angels understand some attribute. Numbers can never reach heaven, because they measure dimension and space, and also time, and these belong to the world and nature. The heavenly counterparts of space and time are states and changes in state.

The earliest people, who were heavenly and communicated with angels, knew the symbolism of every number, even the multiples. So this symbolism was passed down to their descendants and to the offspring of the ancient church.

People in the church today hardly credit any of this, since they do not believe anything holier to be hidden away in the Word than what they see in the literal meaning.

4265   Genesis 32:16, 17, 18, 19, 20, 21, 22, 23. *And he gave into the hand of his servants a drove, a drove, by itself. And he said to his servants, "Cross before* *me, and you are to put space between drove and drove." And he commanded the first, saying, "Esau my brother might meet you and ask you, saying, 'Whose are you, and where are you going, and whose are these [animals] before you?' And you will say, 'Your servant Jacob's; this is a gift sent to my lord Esau. And look: he is behind us, too.'" And he commanded also the second, also the third, also all those going behind the droves, saying, "According to this word you will speak to Esau when you find him. And you will also say, 'Look: your servant Jacob is behind us'"; because he said, "I will appease his [angry] face with the gift going before me, and afterward I will see his face; maybe he will lift my face." And the gift crossed before him, and he spent the night that night in the camp. And he got up that night and took his two women and his two slave women and his eleven sons and crossed the crossing of the Jabbok. And he took them and sent them across the river and sent across what he owned.*

He gave into the hand of his servants a drove, a drove, by itself. And he said to his servants, "Cross before me, and you are to put space between drove and drove," symbolizes the way they would be arranged for introduction. *And he commanded the first, saying, "Esau my brother might meet you and ask you, saying, 'Whose are you, and where are you going?' and you will say, 'Your servant Jacob's; this is a gift sent to my lord Esau, and look: he is behind us, too,'"* symbolizes submissiveness. *And he commanded also the second, also the third, also all those going behind the droves, saying, "According to this word you will speak to Esau when you find him,"* symbolizes more of the same. *"And you will also say, 'Look: your servant Jacob is behind us'"; because he said, "I will appease his [angry] face with the gift going before me, and afterward I will see his face; maybe he will lift my face,"* symbolizes preparation for what was to come. *And the gift crossed before him* symbolizes the accomplishment of it. *And he spent the night that night in the camp* symbolizes what follows. *And he got up that night and took his two women and his two slave women and his eleven sons and crossed the crossing of the Jabbok* symbolizes the first infusion of a desire for truth, along with the truth that [the Lord] had acquired; *the crossing of the Jabbok* means a first infusion. *And he took them and sent them across the river and sent across what he owned* symbolizes a further infusion.

He gave into the hand of his servants a drove, a drove, by itself. And he said to his servants, "Cross before me, and you are to put space between drove and drove," symbolizes the way they would be arranged for introduction, as the following shows: *Giving something into someone's hand* means supplying something with power, a *hand* symbolizing power (see §§878, 3091, 3387, 3563). *Servants* symbolize traits of the earthly self, as discussed in

§§3019, 3020. Everything in the earthly or outer self is subordinate to the spiritual or inner self, so everything there is relatively menial and is called a servant or slave. A *drove* symbolizes secular concepts, religious concepts, and therefore doctrines, as discussed in §§3767, 3768. As long as these exist in the earthly, outer self, or its memory, before being implanted in the spiritual, inner self, they are symbolized by droves given into the hand of servants. *By itself* means each according to its category, or its type and subtype. *Crossing before me* and *putting space between drove and drove* means making way for the goodness that would be received—the theme here being the reception of the goodness that grows out of truth, and the union of goodness and truth in the earthly self.

The individual meanings make it clear that the whole taken together symbolizes the way things would be arranged for introduction.

[2] The introduction of truth into goodness in the earthly self is completely beyond being explained intelligibly, because religious people today do not even know what the inner or spiritual self is, although they have a lot to say about it. They also do not know that truth needs to be introduced into goodness in our outer, earthly self if we are to become truly religious people. Still less do they realize that anything in that self is rearranged by the Lord so that it can unite with the inner self. Even these broad concepts lie so deeply hidden that people are not aware of them. To explain in detail what the inner meaning says about this arrangement and introduction, then, would be to speak in pure riddles, or to say what is utterly unbelievable and therefore pointless. It would be like sowing a crop on water or sand. That is the reason for leaving out the particulars and explaining only the general outlines here and in the rest of this set of verses.

4267 *And he commanded the first, saying, "Esau my brother might meet you and ask you, saying, 'Whose are you, and where are you going, and whose are these [animals] before you?' and you will say, 'Your servant Jacob's; this is a gift sent to my lord Esau, and look: he is behind us, too,'"* symbolizes submissiveness. This too can be seen from the inner meaning of the individual words, which adds up to this overall meaning. Obviously the words involve submission, and submissive attitudes are being symbolized. After all, Jacob told his servants to call his brother a lord and himself a servant and to send the gift as if from a servant to his master.

Goodness is like a master, and truth is like a servant, and yet they are called brothers, as shown many times. Goodness and truth are called brothers because once they join together, an image of goodness appears within truth, so to speak, and they then work in tandem to produce an effect. Until they join together, though, goodness is called a master, and truth, a servant, especially when there is a dispute over their relative importance.

And he commanded also the second, also the third, also all those going behind the droves, saying, "According to this word you will speak to Esau when you find him," symbolizes more of the same—more of the rearrangement and submissiveness. This is clear without further explanation from the discussion just above at §§4266, 4267.

4268

"And you will also say, 'Look: your servant Jacob is behind us'"; because he said, "I will appease his [angry] face with the gift going before me, and afterward I will see his face; maybe he will lift my face," symbolizes preparation for what was to come. *And the gift crossed before him* symbolizes the accomplishment of it. And *he spent the night that night in the camp* symbolizes what follows. This can be seen from the inner meaning of all the words, which plainly refers to preparation in order to be well received.

4269

The situation in all this cannot be intelligibly explained in greater detail because as long as the broad outlines of a topic are unknown, no light can fall on its particulars; we are in the deepest shadow concerning them. General concepts have to come first. Until they are acquired, the details have no home to enter. In a home filled with pure shadow, they are invisible; in a home filled with falsity, they are rejected, smothered, or corrupted; and in a home filled with evil, they are ridiculed. It is enough to accept these general ideas:

> We have to be reborn before we can enter the Lord's kingdom (John 3:3).
> Until we are reborn, truth apparently takes first place, and goodness, second.
> Once we are reborn, the order reverses and goodness takes first place, while truth takes second.
> When the order reverses, the Lord provides and arranges for our earthly, outer self to receive truth from goodness and for truth to surrender to goodness.
> As a result we no longer act under the inspiration of truth but of goodness, or neighborly love.
> We act out of neighborly love when we live by religious truth and when we love doctrine for its effect on our life.

The sequence of subjects contained in the inner meaning here—the arrangement and introduction of truth and its submissiveness toward goodness—appears to angels in clear light. These are the subjects of angelic wisdom, even if people on earth see no hint of them. Nonetheless, people who live in simple goodness on the basis of simple faith possess the ability to learn it all. If they fail to grasp it during bodily life because of worldly cares and the dulled thinking that results, they succeed in the other life, where worldly and bodily concerns are taken away. In the other world such people become enlightened and enter into angelic understanding and wisdom.

4270   *And he got up that night and took his two women and his two slave women and his eleven sons and crossed the crossing of the Jabbok* symbolizes the first infusion of a desire for truth, along with the truth that [the Lord] had acquired, as the following shows: The *two women,* Rachel and Leah, symbolize a desire for truth, as discussed in §§3758, 3782, 3793, 3819. The *two slave women,* Bilhah and Zilpah, symbolize a relatively shallow desire for truth that serves as a middle ground, as discussed in §§3849, 3931. *Sons* symbolize truth, as discussed in §§489, 491, 533, 1147, 2623, 3373. And *the crossing of the Jabbok* symbolizes a first infusion.

The *Jabbok* means a first infusion because it was a border to the land of Canaan. All the borders of that land symbolized heavenly and spiritual qualities of the Lord's kingdom, depending on their relative distance and position (see §§1585, 1866, 4116, 4240). This includes the ford, or crossing, of the Jabbok, which was across the Jordan from Canaan and was a border of the inheritance belonging to Reuben's and Gad's descendants, as can be seen from Numbers 21:24; Deuteronomy 2:36, 37; 3:16, 17; Joshua 12:2; Judges 11:13, 22. It fell to these tribes as an inheritance because of Reuben's and Gad's representation. Reuben represented faith that belongs to the intellect, or doctrinal faith, which is the beginning of regeneration; or to put it more comprehensively, theological truth that leads to a good life (see §§[3860,] 3861, 3866). Gad represented good deeds stemming from faith (§3934). The truth espoused by faith (or doctrines) and the first deeds of faith to be performed are what introduce a regenerating person into goodness. That is why the crossing of the Jabbok symbolizes a first infusion, or introduction.

4271   *And he took them and sent them across the river and sent across what he owned* symbolizes a further infusion, as can be seen from the remarks just above. Jacob sent across not only his women, female slaves, and sons but also his herd and flock. So he sent everything he owned into the land of Canaan, where he met Esau. Since the theme of the inner meaning is the union of truth and goodness on the earthly level, going across the river actually symbolizes a first infusion. Here, where the text repeats the words and adds that Jacob sent across everything he owned, a further infusion is symbolized.

*   *   *   *

Genesis 32:24, 25. *And Jacob remained alone, and a man wrestled with*   4272
him till the rising of dawn. And [the man] saw that he did not prevail over
[Jacob] and touched the hollow of his thigh, and the hollow of Jacob's thigh
was dislocated in his wrestling with him.

Jacob remained alone symbolizes the truth-based goodness that had been acquired and was now at its end. *And a man wrestled with him* symbolizes a time when truth is tested. *Till the rising of dawn* means before the earthly goodness symbolized by Jacob united with the heavenly-spiritual dimension, or with divine goodness-from-truth. *And he saw that he did not prevail over him* means that [earthly goodness] won in its trials. *And touched the hollow of his thigh* means where heavenly-spiritual goodness connects with the earthly goodness symbolized by Jacob. *And the hollow of Jacob's thigh was dislocated in his wrestling with him* means that goodness-from-truth did not yet have the strength to establish full connection.

These same words also have to do with the man Jacob and his descendants, and in this case the words symbolize those people's character. Taken in this way, *he touched the hollow of his thigh* means where marriage love connects with earthly goodness. And *the hollow of Jacob's thigh was dislocated in his wrestling with him* means that the connection was profoundly damaged and disjointed in Jacob's descendants.

Jacob remained alone symbolizes the truth-based goodness that had   4273
been acquired and was now at its end. This can be seen from Jacob's current representation as goodness that comes of truth.

Previous discussions show what Jacob represented. He represented different elements on the earthly plane because the state of truth and goodness varies at its start, during its development, and at its end (§§3775, 4234). Here he symbolizes goodness based on truth.

There are several reasons for this representation. One is that the text now turns to Jacob's wrestling, which on an inner level symbolizes times of trial. Another is that Jacob receives the name Israel, and Israel represents a heavenly-spiritual person. Another is that the following story concerns Jacob's reunion with Esau, which symbolizes the introduction of truth to goodness. These are the reasons Jacob now represents truth-based goodness at an end on the earthly level.

4274   *And a man wrestled with him* symbolizes a time when truth is tested. This can be seen from the symbolism of *wrestling* as a trial. Spiritual trial is nothing less than a struggle or fight, because it is an attack on truth by evil spirits and a defense by the angels with us. Our awareness of that struggle is the trial (§§741, 751, 761, 1661, 3927, 4249, 4256).

We cannot undergo times of trial unless we have a goodness based on truth—that is, unless we have a love or desire for truth. If we do not love or desire truth as we know it, we do not care about it; but if we do love it, we are anxious that it not be harmed. The life of our intellect consists solely in what we believe to be true, and the life of our will, in what we have convinced ourselves is good. An attack on what we consider true is an attack on the life of our intellect, and an attack on what we are sure is good is an attack on the life of our will. When we are being tested, then, it is our life that is at stake.

[2] The battle first focuses on truth, or is waged over truth, because truth is the main thing we love. Whatever we love is what evil spirits assault. Once the pattern reverses and we come to love goodness more than truth, the goodness in us is put to the test.

Not many know what spiritual trial is, because not many today ever experience it. The only people who can be tested are those with goodness from faith, or with charity for their neighbor. If people who do not love their neighbor were tested, they would fail immediately, and those who fail learn to justify what is evil and to persuade themselves of what is false. Evil spirits then win in them and consequently form ties with them. That is why few today are ever allowed to undergo spiritual trial. They are exposed only to certain earthly anxieties, the goal of which is to extract them from love for themselves and materialism. Otherwise they would plunge into this love with abandon.

4275   *Till the rising of dawn* means before the earthly goodness symbolized by Jacob united with the heavenly-spiritual dimension, or with divine goodness-from-truth. This can be seen from the symbolism of *dawn* in the highest sense as the Lord, in a representative sense as his kingdom, and in the broadest sense as the heavenly quality of love (discussed in §2405). Here it symbolizes something heavenly and spiritual. When dawn did rise, Jacob was named Israel, and Israel symbolizes a heavenly-spiritual person. So before dawn rises means before the earthly goodness currently symbolized by Jacob unites with the heavenly-spiritual dimension.

The heavenly-spiritual dimension will be defined below at verse 28 [§4286], which talks about Israel.

And he saw that he did not prevail over him means that [earthly goodness] won in its trials, as is self-evident.

4276

And touched the hollow of his thigh means where heavenly-spiritual goodness connects with the earthly goodness symbolized by Jacob, as the following shows: A *thigh* symbolizes marriage love and therefore all heavenly and spiritual love, because these two kinds of love descend from marriage love as offspring from their parent (discussed in §3021). And the *hollow* or acetabulum—the socket of the hip joint—symbolizes a point of connection. In the current verse it refers to the connection between heavenly-spiritual goodness and the earthly goodness symbolized by Jacob. Nothing can be said about this connection until the reader knows the nature of the heavenly-spiritual goodness meant by Israel and of the earthly goodness meant by Jacob. Their nature will be described below at verse 28 (concerning Jacob, who by then is renamed Israel) and also where Jacob's descendants are discussed later on.

4277

And the hollow of Jacob's thigh was dislocated in his wrestling with him means that goodness-from-truth did not yet have the strength to establish full connection. This can be seen from the symbolism of being *dislocated,* which is that truth was not yet organized in such a way that together with goodness all of it could pass into heavenly-spiritual goodness. (This symbolism is discussed in the explanation of verse 31 below [§4302].) So goodness based on truth did not have the strength to establish full connection. The *hollow of the thigh* is the place where the two kinds of goodness connect, as noted just above in §4277.

4278

The explanation just given matches the highest and inner meanings but differs from the lower meaning, which deals with the character of Jacob and his future descendants.

4279

Because the Word is from the Lord and comes down to us from him through heaven, it is divine down to its smallest details. It also has the same character when climbing back up or rising to him through the heavens as it had when coming down from him.

People realize that there are three heavens, the inmost being called the third heaven; the middle one being called the second heaven; and the lowest, the first heaven. Whether the Word is ascending or descending, it is divine in the Lord, heavenly in the third heaven (since that heaven is heavenly), and spiritual in the second heaven (since that heaven is spiritual). In the first heaven it is heavenly and spiritual in an earthly way, and this heaven is also called heavenly-earthly and spiritual-earthly. In the church, among people on earth, the Word's literal meaning is earthly—in other words, worldly and physical.

[2] These remarks disclose the nature of the Word and show what happens when it is read by a person who is reverent, or who is devoted to goodness and truth. The Word appears to such a person as a worldly tale that nevertheless contains something holy. In the first heaven it appears to be heavenly and spiritual in an earthly way and yet to contain something divine. In the second heaven it is spiritual. In the third heaven it is heavenly. In the Lord it is divine.

Levels of meaning in the Word reflect the heavens. The Word's highest meaning, which concerns the Lord, exists for the third or inmost heaven. Its inner meaning, which concerns the Lord's kingdom, exists for the second or middle heaven. Its next lower meaning, which narrows the inner meaning to the nation mentioned there, exists for the first or lowest heaven. The lowest or literal meaning exists for people still living in the world. However, this meaning is such that the next deeper layer can communicate with it, as can the layer beyond that and the highest layer too. We ourselves communicate with the three heavens, because we were created in the image of them. In fact, when we live lives of love for the Lord and charity for our neighbor, we are a heaven in miniature. That is why people who live such lives have the Lord's kingdom inside them, as he himself teaches in Luke 17:21: "*Look! God's kingdom is within you.*"

[3] These comments have been made to show that the Word contains not only a highest and an inner sense but also a lower one, and that the lower one narrows the inner sense to the nation mentioned there. Places where the meaning is narrowed this way stand out clearly from context. Obviously, the man's wrestling with Jacob here and the dislocation and displacement of Jacob's thigh also have to do with Jacob himself and his descendants. Let me explain the passage according to that meaning.

In what follows, this meaning will be called the *inner narrative meaning*. I use this term because that meaning is sometimes presented in a living, visible way in the first heaven, as I have been privileged to witness on several occasions.

See the prefatory explanation in §4272, final paragraph.

4280   In this sense, *he touched the hollow of Jacob's thigh* means where marriage love connects with earthly goodness. This can be seen from the symbolism of the *hollow of the thigh* as a place where the bond of marriage love exists; see above at §4277. A connection there with earthly goodness is symbolized because the hollow is where the hip connects with the [legs and] feet. On an inner level, feet symbolize earthly goodness. (For this symbolism of feet, see §§2162, 3147, 3761, 3986.)

[2] The meaning of the thigh as marriage love and of the feet as earthly goodness is a piece of ancient lore that has been lost. It was perfectly well known to the ancient church, which used representation and symbolism. Such knowledge constituted their understanding and wisdom. This was true not only for people in the church but also for those outside it, as demonstrated by the ancient books of the Gentiles and by the stories we now call myths. Symbolism and representation were transmitted from the ancient church to these people, for whom the thighs and genital area likewise symbolized the realm of marriage, and the feet, the earthly dimension.

The thighs and feet acquire this symbolism from the correspondence all our limbs, organs, and viscera have with the universal human. Such correspondences are currently being discussed at the ends of the chapters. The correspondence of the thighs and feet in their turn will be stated below [§§4938–4952, 5050–5061], where the symbolism given for them here will be confirmed from life experiences.

[3] These ideas cannot help but seem baffling today, since (as noted) such knowledge is so old it has been completely lost, but it nonetheless surpasses other kinds of knowledge. The degree to which it surpasses them can be seen from several pieces of evidence. For one thing, the Word's inner meaning can never be known without it. For another, the angels present with us perceive the Word according to that meaning. For another, such knowledge gives us contact with heaven. Believe it or not, our inner self actually thinks the same way [as angels]. While our outer self is taking the Word at face value, our inner self is taking it according to its inner meaning, even though we are unaware of the fact as long as we live in our bodies. The best proof is that when we go to the other world and become angels, we come into this knowledge spontaneously, it seems, without being taught.

[4] For a definition of the marriage love symbolized by the thighs and also by the genital region, see §§995, 1123, 2727–2759. Marriage love is the basis for all love (§§686, 3021), so people who have real marriage love also have heavenly love (love for the Lord) and spiritual love (charity for their neighbor). The term *marriage love,* then, means not only this love itself but all heavenly and spiritual love as well. These types of love are said to connect with earthly goodness when the inner self unites with the outer self, or the spiritual self with the earthly. That connection is what the hollow of the thigh symbolizes.

In general, Jacob and his descendants lacked the connection, as the following will show (since that is the subject of the inner narrative meaning here).

4281   *The hollow of Jacob's thigh was dislocated in his wrestling with him* means that the connection was profoundly damaged and disjointed in Jacob's descendants. This can be seen from the symbolism of being *dislocated,* in this sense, as being disjointed and therefore damaged. The *hollow of the thigh* means a connection, as the discussion in §4280 above makes clear. And *Jacob* in the Word does not mean Jacob only but all his descendants too, as a large number of passages shows. Examples are Numbers 23:7, 10, 21, 23; 24:5, 17, 19; Deuteronomy 33:10; Isaiah 40:27; 43:1, 22; 44:1, 2, 21; 48:12; 59:20; Jeremiah 10:16, 25; 30:7, 10, 18; 31:7, 11; 46:27, 28; Hosea 10:11; Amos 7:2; Micah 2:12; 3:8; Psalms 14:7; 24:6; 59:13; 78:5; 99:4; and elsewhere.

[2] Jacob and his posterity were such that no connection of heavenly and spiritual love with earthly goodness was possible in them. In other words, their inner or spiritual self could not unite with their outer or earthly self. Every story about that nation in the Word makes this evident. They did not know and did not want to know what the inner, spiritual self was, so it was not revealed to them. They did not believe there was anything to a person besides the superficial, earthly level. In all their worship they focused exclusively on the earthly level—so exclusively that the worship of God among them was actually idolatrous. When inner worship is separated from outer, it is nothing but idolatry.

The religion established among them was not a religion but a mere representation of a religion, so it is called a representative religion. Among people like this, a representation of a religion is possible (see §§1361, 3670, 4208). [3] Representation implies nothing about a person, only about the attribute being represented. As a result, it was not only people that represented divine, heavenly, and spiritual traits but also nonliving things such as Aaron's garments, the ark, the altar, the sacrificed cattle and sheep, the lampstand and its lamps, the bread arranged on the golden table, the anointing oil, the frankincense, and so on. That is why evil monarchs represented the Lord's kingliness as much as the good ones did, and why evil high priests represented the functions of the Lord's divine priesthood as much as the good ones did, when they went through the motions of their job, carrying out the statutes and commandments.

Consequently, to preserve something representing a religion among them, statutes and laws that were purely representative were explicitly revealed to them. As long as they had those rules and observed them strictly, they could represent something; but when they turned aside from their statutes and laws—to those of other nations, for instance, and especially to the worship of another God—they forfeited the ability to represent anything. So they were forced to obey the truly representative laws and statutes through external coercion: captivities, disasters, threats, and miracles. They were not led by deeper means, as those are whose outward devotion contains inward reverence.

This is what "the hollow of Jacob's thigh was dislocated" symbolizes on the inner narrative level, which deals with Jacob and his descendants.

Genesis 32:26, 27, 28. *And [the man] said, "Let me go, because dawn is rising." And he said, "I won't let you go unless you bless me." And he said to him, "What is your name?" And he said, "Jacob." And he said, "No longer will your name be called Jacob, but Israel, because you have competed nobly with God and with humans and prevailed."* **4282**

He said, "Let me go, because dawn is rising," means that the trial ended when union arrived. *And he said, "I won't let you go unless you bless me,"* means that there had to be union. *And he said to him, "What is your name?" and he said, "Jacob,"* symbolizes the nature of the goodness that grows out of truth. *And he said, "No longer will your name be called Jacob, but Israel,"* means that it was now heavenly-spiritual on a divine level. *Israel* means a heavenly-spiritual person operating on the earthly level and therefore one who is earthly. (A genuinely heavenly-spiritual person, operating on the rational level, is meant by Joseph.) *Because you have competed nobly with God and with humans and prevailed* symbolizes continual victory in struggles regarding truth and goodness.

[2] In the *inner narrative meaning,* which deals with Jacob and his descendants, this is the symbolism: *Let me go, because dawn is rising* means that Jacob's descendants lost their representative role before they took up the representations belonging to the land of Canaan. *And he said, "I won't let you go unless you bless me,"* means they insisted on having a representative role. *And he said to him, "What is your name?" and he said, "Jacob,"* symbolizes their status as Jacob's descendants, along with their character. *And he said, "No longer will your name be called Jacob, but Israel,"* means that they could not represent [the church] as "Jacob," only on the basis of a new quality given to them. *Because you have competed nobly with God and with humans and prevailed* means on account of their obstinate cravings and delusions.

He said, "Let me go, because dawn is rising," means that the trial ended when union arrived, as the following shows: *Let me go* (that is, stop wrestling with me) means that the trial ended. *Wrestling* means trial (see above **4283** at §4274), and the fact that it ended is plain from what follows. *Dawn* symbolizes a union of the earthly goodness symbolized by Jacob with what is heavenly-spiritual, or divine truth-from-goodness (also discussed above, at §4275).

[2] The wrestling started before dawn rose and ended after it rose, and the text then goes on to say what happened after the sun came up—all because times of day, like seasons, symbolize states (§§487, 488, 493, 893, 2788, 3785). In this case they symbolize states of union achieved through times of trial. When our inner self unites with our outer self, day breaks on us, because we then enter a state that is spiritual, or heavenly. We can even see a dawnlike glow, if our state allows us to perceive it. If not, our intellect is at least enlightened, and we seem to ourselves like one who wakes from sleep in the morning, when dawn first brightens and begins the day.

4284 *And he said, "I won't let you go unless you bless me,"* means that there had to be union. This can be seen from the symbolism of *not letting you go* as not stopping (discussed just above in §4283) and from that of *blessing* as uniting (discussed in §§3504, 3514, 3530, 3584). As these considerations show, then, *I won't let you go unless you bless me* means that it would not stop until union took place. In other words, there had to be union.

4285 *And he said to him, "What is your name?" and he said, "Jacob,"* symbolizes the nature of the goodness that grows out of truth. This can be seen from the symbolism of a *name* as something's quality (discussed in §§144, 145, 1754, 1896, 2009, 2724, 3006) and from the representation of *Jacob* as goodness that grows out of truth (discussed above at §4273).

4286 *And he said, "No longer will your name be called Jacob, but Israel,"* means that it was now heavenly-spiritual on a divine level. *Israel* means a heavenly-spiritual person operating on the earthly level and therefore one who is earthly. A real heavenly[-spiritual] person, operating on the rational level, is meant by Joseph. All this can be seen from the remarks on Jacob, Israel, and Joseph below. First, though, I need to define the term *heavenly-spiritual.*

The church today knows that there is a spiritual self and an earthly self, or an inner and an outer self, but it does not yet know much about the spiritual or inner person, much less about a heavenly person and the way this differs from a spiritual person. Not knowing this, the church cannot know what the heavenly-spiritual person meant here by Israel is, so I need to explain briefly.

[2] People recognize that there are three heavens: the inmost, middle, and outermost, or to put the same thing another way, the third, second, and first. The inmost or third heaven is truly heavenlike, and the angels

there are called heavenly because they love the Lord and have the strongest bond with him. As a result they have more wisdom than any others. They are innocent and are therefore called innocences and wisdoms. Heavenly angels are divided into inner and outer kinds, the inner ones being more heavenly than the outer.

The middle or second heaven is spiritual, and the angels there are called spiritual because they have charity for their neighbor. That is, they possess mutual love, which consists in loving another more than one loves oneself. Because of this trait, they have understanding and are called understandings. These angels too are divided into inner and outer kinds, and the inner ones are more spiritual than the outer.

The outermost or first heaven is also heavenly and spiritual, but not to the same degree as the others. Earthliness still clings to its inhabitants, so they are called heavenly-earthly and spiritual-earthly. They too live in mutual love, but they love others as much as themselves, not more. They have a desire for goodness and a knowledge of truth and are likewise divided into inner and outer kinds.

[3] The term *heavenly-spiritual* also needs to be defined briefly. The angels called heavenly-spiritual are those just described as spiritual, who inhabit the middle or second heaven. They are called heavenly because of their mutual love, and spiritual because of the understanding they gain from mutual love. Joseph represents the inner ones, and the Word refers to them as Joseph, while Israel represents the outer ones, and the Word refers to them as Israel. The inner ones, referred to as Joseph, tend toward rationality, but the outer ones, referred to as Israel, tend toward earthliness. Such angels bridge the rational and earthly planes. This is the reason for saying that Israel means a heavenly-spiritual person operating on the earthly level, who is therefore earthly, and that Joseph means a real heavenly-spiritual person operating on the rational level. Speaking comprehensively, everything good associated with love and charity is called heavenly, and everything true that results and that is associated with faith and understanding is called spiritual.

[4] The point of these comments is to show what Israel stands for. But in the highest sense Israel symbolizes heavenly spirituality on a divine level in the Lord. In an inner sense, he symbolizes the Lord's spiritual kingdom in heaven and on earth. (The Lord's spiritual kingdom on earth is the church, which is called a spiritual religion.) Since Israel stands for the Lord's spiritual kingdom, he also stands for a spiritual person, because the Lord's kingdom exists in all such people. A person is a heaven in its smallest form and is also a church (§4279).

Jacob, on the other hand, represents both the heavenly and the spiritual aspects of the Lord's earthly plane, in the highest sense. In an inward sense he represents the Lord's kingdom as it exists in the outermost or first heaven. Consequently he also represents the [heavenly-earthly and spiritual-earthly aspects] of the church. Goodness on the earthly level is what is being called heavenly at this point, and truth there is what is being called spiritual.

This discussion shows what Israel and Jacob symbolize in the Word and explains why Jacob was renamed Israel.

[5] All the same, the discussion cannot help seeming opaque, mainly because few know what a spiritual person is, and hardly any, what a heavenly person is, so not many know there is any difference between the two. The reason for this ignorance is that people do not distinguish between the goodness associated with love and charity and the truth associated with faith. The reason for the failure to distinguish between them is that genuine charity no longer exists. Where a thing does not exist it cannot be perceived. Then there is the fact that people care little about the issues of life after death or about the heavenly realm, but a great deal about the issues of bodily life and about the worldly realm. If people took an interest in life after death and therefore in heaven, they could easily understand everything written above, because we have an easy time grasping and absorbing subjects we love but a hard time with subjects we do not love.

[6] The Word makes it quite plain that Jacob has one symbolism and Israel another, because its narrative and its prophetic books speak now of Jacob, now of Israel, and sometimes of both in a single verse. This fact suggests that the Word has an inner meaning, without which it is completely unknowable.

The following passages demonstrate that Jacob is called Jacob in some places and Israel in others:

> *Jacob* settled in the land of his father's immigrant journeys. These are the births of *Jacob:* Joseph was a son of seventeen years, and *Israel* loved Joseph above all his children. (Genesis 37:1, 2, 3)

Jacob here is first called Jacob and then called Israel. He is called Israel when the passage takes up the subject of Joseph. In another place:

> *Jacob* saw that there was grain in Egypt. *Jacob* said to his sons, . . . And *Israel's* sons came to buy, in the midst of those who came. (Genesis 42:1, 5)

Later:

> They went up from Egypt and came to the land of Canaan, to *Jacob* their father. When they told him all Joseph's words that he had spoken to them, the spirit of *Jacob* their father revived. And *Israel* said, "A great thing! Joseph my son is alive." (Genesis 45:25, 27, 28)

Further:

> And *Israel* set out, as did everything he owned. God said to *Israel* in visions at night, and he said, "*Jacob! Jacob!*" who said, "Here I am." *Jacob* rose from Beer-sheba, and the sons of *Israel* carried *Jacob* their father down. (Genesis 46:1, 2, 5)

In the same chapter:

> These are the names of *Israel's* sons as they came into Egypt, of *Jacob* and his sons. (Genesis 46:8)

In addition:

> Joseph brought *Jacob* his father in and stood him in front of Pharaoh. Pharaoh said to *Jacob*, . . . And *Jacob* said to Pharaoh, . . . (Genesis 47:7, 8, 9, 10)

In the same chapter:

> And *Israel* settled in the land of Goshen. And *Jacob* lived in the land of Egypt seventeen years. And *Israel's* days for dying came near; he called his son Joseph. (Genesis 47:27, 28, 29)

Once more:

> And it was announced to *Jacob*, and someone said, "Look: your son Joseph has come to you"; and *Israel* braced himself and sat up on the bed, and *Jacob* said to Joseph, "God Shaddai appeared to me in Luz." (Genesis 48:2, 3)

Israel is also mentioned in Genesis 48:8, 10, 11, 13, 14, 20, 21. And finally:

> *Jacob* called his children and said, "Assemble and listen, sons of *Jacob*, and listen to *Israel* your father." And when *Jacob* had finished commanding his sons, . . . (Genesis 49:1, 2, 33)

These examples plainly demonstrate several things: Jacob is called Jacob in one place, Israel in another. So Jacob means one thing, and Israel, another;

in other words, he symbolizes one thing when called Jacob and another when called Israel. And this secret is completely unknowable except from the inner meaning.

[7] The symbolism of Jacob and of Israel was mentioned above. In the Word, Jacob generally symbolizes the outer level of religion, and Israel, the inner core. After all, every religion has an outer level and an inner core; every religion is internal and is external. Since Jacob and Israel symbolize facets of religion, and every aspect of religion comes from the Lord, both Jacob and Israel in their highest sense mean the Lord. Jacob means the Lord's earthly divinity; Israel, the Lord's spiritual divinity. The outer level of the Lord's kingdom and his church, then, is Jacob, and the inner core is Israel. Further evidence may be found in the following passages, which also mention both, each with his own meaning. In the prophecy of Jacob, who by then was Israel:

> . . . by the hands of mighty *Jacob,* from whom comes the Shepherd, the Stone of *Israel.* (Genesis 49:24)

In Isaiah:

> Listen, *Jacob,* my servant, and *Israel,* whom I have chosen: I will pour my spirit out on your seed and my blessing on your offspring. This one will say, "I am Jehovah's," and this one will call himself by *Jacob's* name, and that one will write "Jehovah's" on his hand and surname himself by *Israel's* name. (Isaiah 44:1, 2, 3, 5)

Clearly Jacob and Israel stand for the Lord in this passage, and Jacob and Israel's seed and offspring stand for people who believe in him. In Balaam's prophecy in Moses:

> Who will count the dust of *Jacob,* or the number of a quarter of *Israel?* (Numbers 23:10)

Again:

> There is no divination against *Jacob* nor sorcery against *Israel;* at this time it will be said to *Jacob* and *Israel,* "What has God done?" (Numbers 23:23)

In addition:

> How good are your tents, *Jacob;* your dwellings, *Israel!* (Numbers 24:5)

Again:

> A star will rise out of *Jacob* and a scepter out of *Israel.* (Numbers 24:17)

In Isaiah:

> My glory I will not give to another. Pay attention to me, *Jacob,* and *Israel,* whom I called: I, the same—I am first; I am also last. (Isaiah 48:11, 12)

In the same author:

> *Jacob* will make those who are to come take root; *Israel* will bloom and flourish, and the face of the world will be filled with produce. (Isaiah 27:6)

In Jeremiah:

> Don't be afraid, *Jacob* my servant, and don't be terrified, *Israel,* because—look!—I have rescued you from afar. (Jeremiah 30:9, 10)

In Micah:

> I will unfailingly gather all of you, *Jacob;* I will unfailingly assemble the survivors of *Israel.* I will set them together like Bozrah's sheep. (Micah 2:12)

[8] The reason Jacob was renamed Israel was stated explicitly when he received the name: "No longer will your name be called Jacob, but Israel, *because you have competed nobly with God and with humans and prevailed.*" In the original language, Israel means "one who competes nobly with God"; and this phrase in an inner sense means that the Lord won in the struggles of his spiritual trials. Times of trial and victories in them were the means by which the Lord made his humanity divine (§§1737, 1813, and elsewhere). Trials and victory in trials are also what make a person spiritual, which is why Jacob was called Israel for the first time after he wrestled. (Wrestling means being tested; see §4274.) It is known that the church and the people of the Christian church call themselves Israel, but the only people in the church who are Israel are those who have become spiritual through times of trial. The name itself implies it.

It was later confirmed that Jacob would be called Israel, as can be seen further on, where these words appear:

> God appeared to *Jacob* again as he came from Paddan-aram, and blessed him, and God said to him, "Your name *Jacob*—your name will no longer be called *Jacob,* but *Israel* will be your name," and called his name *Israel.* (Genesis 35:9, 10)

The reason for this confirmation will be told below.

4287   *Because you have competed nobly with God and with humans and pre-vailed* symbolizes continual victory in struggles regarding truth and goodness, as the following shows: *Competing nobly* means winning in one's struggles, and in this case winning in the struggles brought on by times of trial, since they are the subject. And *with God and with humans* means regarding truth and goodness, as discussed below.

[2] Since the highest sense concerns the Lord, he is meant in that sense by the one competing nobly with God and humans. He endured all his trials by his own power, and through them he conquered the hells. One by one he took on all the hells, and even the angels, as will be discussed later. In this way he reduced everything in the heavens and the hells to order and finally glorified himself. That is, he made the humanity in himself divine.

[3] From this it is clear that on the highest level of meaning, Jacob and Israel mean the Lord, as shown just above in §4286. It is not just that he competed nobly; it is not just that he endured all his struggles and trials and won. He also endures them in each of us. But see what has already been stated many times about these struggles: The Lord bore the severest trials of all (1663, 1668, 1787, 2776, 2786, 2795, 2816); unlike any human, the Lord fought from divine love (1690, 1691 at the end, 1789, 1812, 1813, 1820); the Lord fought against the evil he inherited from his mother, until finally he was not her son; but he had no actual evil (1444, 1573, 2025, 2574, 2649, 3318 at the end); through his struggles and trials, and continual victory in them, the Lord rearranged everything in himself into a heavenly pattern (1928); by continual victory in the struggles of his crises he made his divine nature one with his human nature (1616, 1737, 1813, 1921, 2025, 2026, 2500, 2523, 2632, 2776); the Lord in us undergoes all our trials; he overcomes evil and subdues hell (987, 1661, 1692 at the end).

[4] The fact that competing with God and with humans means being tested in respect to truth and goodness is a secret invisible in the literal meaning. Anyone can see that God is not the one Jacob grappled with (as the explanation below will also clarify). No human being can be said to compete with God and prevail. We need the inner meaning to teach us what God and humans symbolize in this verse—that God symbolizes truth and humans symbolize goodness. The reason for the symbolism is that God symbolizes truth in the inner meaning, so when the text is speaking of truth, it mentions God (§§2586, 2769, 2807, 2822). When humans are mentioned, they mean goodness.

A human symbolizes goodness because the Lord is the only human. From him we acquire the name of human (§§49, 288, 565, 1894), and from him heaven is a person and is called the universal human (§§684, 1276, 3624–3649, 3741–3750). That is why the earliest church, which had heavenly goodness, was called "the human" (§478). [5] That is also why a human in the Word symbolizes goodness when the subject is goodness. In Isaiah, for example:

> I will render *mankind* more rare than gold, and *humanity* [more rare] than Ophir's gold. (Isaiah 13:12)

In the same author:

> The residents of the land will be destroyed by fire, and *mankind* remaining will be few. (Isaiah 24:6)

Mankind stands for spiritual goodness, or goodness that comes from truth. Humanity stands for goodness. In the same author:

> The paths have been devastated; the traveler on the way has ceased. They have nullified the compact; they have disdained the cities; they think nothing of *mankind*. (Isaiah 33:8)

In Jeremiah:

> I looked at the earth, and there—void and emptiness; and to the heavens, and these had no light. I looked, and there—*not a human!* And every bird of the sky had flown away. (Jeremiah 4:23, 25)

In the same author:

> "Look! The days are coming," says Jehovah, "on which I will sow the house of Israel and the house of Judah with the *seed of human* and the seed of animal." (Jeremiah 31:27)

In Ezekiel:

> Your dealers sold your trade goods *for the soul of a human* and vessels of bronze. (Ezekiel 27:13)

In the same author:

> You, my flock, flock of my pasture, *you are humanity;* I am your God. (Ezekiel 34:31)

In the same author:

> The devastated cities will be filled with a *flock of humanity*. (Ezekiel 36:38)

In these passages, humanity, [or a human,] stands for people with goodness and consequently for goodness itself, because goodness is what makes a person human. Truth that comes from goodness, though, is called mankind in the Word, and also a child of humankind.

4288   The same verses explained here also apply to the nation of Judah and Israel, which is called Jacob in the Word, as stated and shown above in §4279. In that sense, called the inner narrative meaning, the sentence *Let me go, because dawn is rising* means that Jacob's descendants lost their representative tradition before they entered the land of Canaan with all its representative features.

The character of that nation was demonstrated above: it had no inner worship, only superficial worship, so that the heavenly marriage was put out of its reach and it accordingly had no religion. All that could be established in it was a representation of a religion. See §4281.

[2] It is important, though, to know what a representative religion is and what a representation of a religion is. A representative religion exists when outward worship contains inward worship. A representation of a religion exists when there is no inward worship but there still is outward worship. Both have almost the same outward customs—the same statutes, laws, and commandments. In a representative religion, though, the outward customs correspond to inner content, forming a unified whole. In a representation of a religion no correspondence exists, because the outward customs either lack any inner content or disagree with it. In a representative religion, heavenly and spiritual love is the main thrust, but in a representation of a religion, bodily and worldly love is. Heavenly and spiritual love is the real inner dimension, but where it does not exist and only bodily and worldly love does, there is an outside with no inside.

The ancient church, which came after the Flood, was a representative religion. What was established among Jacob's descendants was merely a representation of a religion.

[3] To sharpen the distinction, let me illustrate it with some examples. Worship of God in the representative church took place on mountains because mountains symbolized heavenly love, and in the highest sense they symbolized the Lord (§§795, 1430, 2722, 4210). When the people

of that church held worship on mountains, they were in a holy frame of mind because they were feeling heavenly love.

Worship of God in the representative church took place in groves as well because groves symbolized spiritual love, and in the highest sense they symbolized the Lord's spiritual love (§2722). When the people of that church held worship in groves, they were in a holy frame of mind because they were feeling spiritual love.

When the people of the representative church worshiped God, they turned their faces toward the sunrise, because the rising sun also symbolized heavenly love (§§101, 1529, 1530, 2441, 2495, 3636, 3643). When they looked at the moon, a similar awestruck reverence pervaded them, because the moon symbolized spiritual love (§§1529, 1530, 1531, 2495, 4060). Likewise when they looked at the starry heavens, because this symbolized the angelic heaven, or the Lord's kingdom.

The people of the representative church had tents, or tabernacles, in which they held their worship of God, and their worship was sacred because tents, or tabernacles, symbolized the holy quality of love and worship (§§414, 1102, 2145, 2152, 3312). And so on in countless other cases.

[4] In the beginning, to be sure, the religion that represented a church also worshiped God on mountains and in groves; people faced the sunrise and gazed at the moon and stars; and worship took place in tents, or tabernacles. However, they took part in outward worship but lacked inward worship; that is, they indulged in bodily and worldly love, not in heavenly and spiritual love. So they would worship the mountains and groves themselves, the sun, moon, and stars, and their tents or tabernacles. As a result they took the rituals that had been sacred in the ancient church and made them idolatrous. The consequence of all this was that they were restricted to a single, shared religious practice. That is, they were restricted to the mountain where Jerusalem was and then Zion; to facing the sunrise from there and from the Temple; and to a shared tent, called the meeting tent, and later to the ark in the Temple. These practices were granted to the people in order to bring about a representation of religion when they were engaged in outward devotions; otherwise they would have profaned what is holy.

[5] From this you can see the difference between a representative church and a representation of a church. Broadly put, people in the representative church communicated with the three heavens in regard to their inner levels, and their outward acts served as a foundation for the inner levels.

People in the representation of a church, on the other hand, did not communicate with the heavens on their inner levels, but the outward acts they were held to could serve as a foundation. The Lord in his providence used these acts in a miraculous way to preserve some measure of communication between heaven and humankind through a likeness of the church. Without any communication between heaven and humankind through some shred of religion, the human race would perish.

What is that communication like, though, when it relies on outward acts devoid of inward content? This cannot be answered briefly, so it will have to be discussed later, by the Lord's divine mercy.

4289   As noted, *Let me go, because dawn is rising* means that Jacob's descendants lost their representative role before they took up the representations belonging to the land of Canaan. This can be seen from the series of ideas on the inner narrative level, which deals with Jacob's posterity. The state of their religion is depicted in the Word by evening, night, and morning, or *dawn*. Dawn portrays their state when they came into Canaan and therefore into their role representing the church there.

Let me explain. The representation of a church could not be established among them until they had been thoroughly purged, or until they no longer possessed any knowledge of deeper realities. If they had been aware of those realities, they could have been affected by them and therefore would have profaned them. Holy things—profound truth and goodness—can be profaned by people who know about and acknowledge them and especially by people who are moved by them; but they cannot be profaned by people who do not acknowledge them. See what has already been mentioned and explained concerning profanation: People who know about and acknowledge holy things can profane them, but people who do not know about or acknowledge them cannot: 593, 1008, 1010, 1059, 3398, 3898. People in the church can profane what is holy, but people outside the church cannot: 2051. So people who cannot permanently acknowledge and believe in goodness and truth are kept from doing so as far as possible: 3398, 3402. They are kept in ignorance so that they will not profane anything: 301, 302, 303. The danger of profaning what is holy: 571, 582. Worship is made shallow to keep its inner depths from being profaned: 1327, 1328. That is why deep truth was not disclosed to Jews: 3398.

[2] The Lord therefore provided for Jacob's descendants to cease representing the church in any genuine or inward way before they took up the representations belonging to Canaan—so much so that they knew

nothing at all about the Lord. They did believe the Messiah would come into the world, but with the aim of raising them to glory and supremacy over all the nations of the whole land, not of saving their souls forever. They knew nothing about the heavenly kingdom or life after death or even about neighborly love and faith.

In order to reduce them to this level of ignorance, they were held in Egypt for several hundred years. When they were called out of Egypt, they did not even know Jehovah's name (Exodus 3:12, 13, 14), and they had forgotten all the worship of the representative church. In fact, after the Ten Commandments had been issued from Mount Sinai in their presence, a month of days later they reverted to the Egyptian cult of a golden calf (Exodus 32).

[3] Because this was the nature of the nation brought out of Egypt, all the people in it died in the wilderness. All they had to do was obey the statutes and commandments in their outward form, since to do that much was to create the representation of a church; but the ones who had grown up in Egypt could not be forced to comply. Their children *could* be forced, although not very easily. The first inducements were miracles, while later ones were fear and captivity, as Joshua and Judges make plain.

Clearly, then, they lost any genuine or inward role representing a church before they entered Canaan, where an external representation of a church started up among them in its fullest form. The land of Canaan was the very land where representations of a religion could be produced, since all the sites and borders there had represented something since ancient times (see §3686).

In the inner narrative meaning, *he said, "I won't let you go unless you bless me,"* means that they insisted on having a representative role. *I won't let you go* symbolizes their insisting, and *being blessed* symbolizes a role representing the church.

4290

Far from being chosen over all other nations, Jacob's descendants *insisted* on representing the church, but this certainly cannot be seen very clearly from the literal meaning of the scriptural narratives. It cannot be seen clearly because the Word's stories in their literal meaning embrace secrets of heaven and therefore follow them in a series. Another reason is that the names have symbolic meaning. Many of them symbolize the Lord himself in their highest sense, and this includes Abraham, Isaac, and Jacob. (Many places in the preceding discussion show that these three symbolize the Lord on their highest level. See, for example, §§1965, 1989, [2010,] 2011, 3245, 3305 at the end, 3439.)

[2] The fact that Jacob's offspring were not chosen but insisted that the church exist among them can be seen from the inner narrative meaning in many Scripture passages, and openly in the following passages. In Moses:

> Jehovah spoke to Moses, "Go up from here—you and the people *whom you brought up from the land of Egypt*—to the land that I swore to Abraham, Isaac, and Jacob, saying, 'To your seed I will give it.' I will not go up in your midst—since you are a hard-necked people—for fear I will consume you on the way." When the people heard this evil word, they mourned and each put their finery off them. And Moses took the tent and spread it for himself outside the camp, moving it far away from the camp. Moses said to Jehovah, "Notice: *you are saying to me, 'Bring this people up,'* although you have not made known to me whom you are to send with me. Now therefore, please, if I have found favor in your eyes, please make your ways known to me, so that I may know about you, that I have found favor in your eyes. Notice also that this nation is your people." Therefore [Jehovah] said, "My face will go [with you] until I give you rest." (Exodus 33:[1, 3, 4, 7, 12, 13, 14])

This passage says that Moses brought the people up from the land of Egypt; that they took off their finery and mourned; that Moses spread his tent outside the camp; and that Jehovah yielded. Plainly, then, they insisted. [3] In the same author:

> Jehovah said to Moses, "How long will this people anger me, and how long will they not believe in me for all the signs that I have done in their midst? I will strike them with contagion and snuff them out and make you into a nation larger and stronger than they." But Moses pleaded; and Jehovah, prevailed on by his prayer, said, "I will be appeased, according to your word. Still, as I live, the whole earth will be filled with the glory of Jehovah. Because as for all the men who have seen my glory and my signs that I did in Egypt and in the wilderness, yet have tested me these ten times and have not obeyed my voice: if they see the land that I swore to their ancestors, . . . ! None of those angering me will see it; in this wilderness your bodies will fall. Your little children, however, I will bring in." (Numbers 14:[11, 12, 13, 20, 21, 22, 23, 29, 31])

This passage also shows that Jehovah wanted to obliterate them rather than establish the church among them but that they insisted, which is why it was done.

There are many other instances [in Scripture] as well when Jehovah would have liked to obliterate this nation that had rebelled so often, but every time, he permitted himself to be prevailed on by their entreaties.

[4] The fact that Balaam was not allowed to curse this people (Numbers 22; 23; 24) involves the same meaning. So do other passages saying that Jehovah regretted bringing this people into the land, that he was prevailed on by their prayers, and that he struck a new pact with them each time.

That is what is symbolized on the inner narrative level by the sentence "I won't let you go unless you bless me." The same is true of Jacob's tricking Esau out of his birthright and his blessing (Genesis 25; 27).

In the inner narrative meaning, *he said to him, "What is your name?" and he said, "Jacob,"* symbolizes their status as Jacob's descendants, along with their character. This can be seen from the symbolism of a *name* as a quality (discussed in §§144, 145, 1754, 1896, 2009, 2724, 3006) and from that of *Jacob* as his descendants (discussed above in §4281). **4291**

In the inner narrative meaning, *he said, "No longer will your name be called Jacob, but Israel,"* means that they could not represent [the church] as "Jacob," only on the basis of a new quality given to them. This can be seen from *Jacob's* symbolism in the Word as his descendants (discussed above in §4281) and from that of a *name* as a quality (noted just above in §4291). *Israel,* in an inner sense, means that new quality. Israel means a heavenly-spiritual person and therefore the inner person (§4286), and since Israel means these it also means the inner dimension of a spiritual religion. It is all the same whether you speak of a spiritual person or a spiritual religion, because a spiritual person is a church on a small scale, and a group of such people is a church on a larger scale. If an individual person were not a church, there would be no collective church. It is the congregation collectively that people usually refer to as a church, but every member of the congregation has to exemplify the church in order for there to be one. Every whole involves parts that are similar to it. **4292**

[2] Returning to the subject at hand—that Jacob's descendants could not represent [the church] as "Jacob," only on the basis of a new quality given to them, which is "Israel"—here is the situation: It was Jacob's descendants in particular who could represent the church. It was not Isaac's offspring in particular, because Isaac's offspring came from Esau as well as Jacob. Still less was it Abraham's offspring in particular, because Abraham's offspring came from Ishmael and Esau as well as Jacob, and also from his sons by Keturah, his second wife (Zimran, Jokshan, Medan, Midian, Ishbak, and Shuah), and from *their* sons (see Genesis 25:1, 2, 3, 4).

Now, seeing that Jacob's descendants insisted on playing a representative role (as shown directly above in §4290), they could not represent [the church] as "Jacob" or "Isaac" or "Abraham." They could not do so as "Jacob" because Jacob represented the outer level of the church, not the inner core. They could not do so as "Isaac" or "Abraham" for the reason cited just above. [3] If they were to represent the church, then, Jacob had to be given a new name, and through it he had to be given a new character symbolizing the inner spiritual self—in other words, the inner spiritual church. This new quality is "Israel." Every church of the Lord's has an inner and an outer dimension, as shown several times before [§§409, 1083, 1098, 1238, 1242]. The inner church is what is represented, and the outer church is what represents it. What is more, the inner church is either spiritual or heavenly. The inner spiritual church was represented by Israel, but the inner heavenly church was later represented by Judah. That is why a division arose, the Israelites making one kingdom by themselves, and the Judeans another by themselves. I will say more on this later, though, with the Lord's divine mercy.

These remarks clarify that Jacob—that is, Jacob's descendants—could not represent the church as Jacob, since to do so would be to represent religion's outer level alone. They could represent the church only as Jacob *and* Israel, since Israel means the inner part.

[4] That the inner depths are what are represented while the outer surface is what represents them has been shown in various earlier sections, and the same thing can be seen from humankind itself. Our words represent our thinking, and our deeds represent our will. Speech and action are outside us; thought and will are inside. In fact, our face represents both thought and will by putting on various expressions. Everyone recognizes that the face uses expressions to represent something, because in honest people those expressions reveal their inner moods. In short, everything our body does represents what is in our heart and mind.

[5] It is the same with the externals of the church, which resemble a body, while the inner levels resemble a soul. Take altars, for instance, and the sacrifices on them. People know that these were external, as were the loaves of showbread, the lampstand with its lamps, and the eternal flame; and anyone can recognize that they represented something internal. Likewise for all other rituals. These things could not represent the outer but the inner dimension, as the argument given shows. So Jacob could not [represent the church] as Jacob, because Jacob means the outer part of the church, but he *could* do it as Israel, because Israel means the inner part.

That is what is meant by the new quality given to Jacob's descendants so that they could represent [the church].

In the inner narrative meaning, *because you have competed nobly with God and with humans and prevailed* means on account of their obstinate delusions and obsessions. This can be seen from the symbolism of *God* and that of *humans* as truth and goodness (dealt with above at §4287). In this case the two words have the opposite meaning, because on this level they are ascribed to Jacob's posterity, who had no truth or goodness inside, as shown above. Instead, they had falsity and evil. Falsities are delusions because they come from delusions, and evils are obsessions because they come from obsessions.

[2] See above at §4290 for the idea that the people of this nation insisted on playing a representative role, which is to say they insisted that they were the church more truly than any other nation on the whole planet. This was permitted to them on account of their obstinate delusions and obsessions, which is the meaning in the current clause.

What their delusions and obsessions are like is impossible to know unless one has had some interaction with them in the other world. This was granted to me so that I could learn, and I have talked with them several times there. They love themselves and the riches of the world above all else, and in fact they worry above all else about losing that prestige and their assets. Today as in the past they despise everyone else in comparison with themselves, work energetically to acquire wealth, and are fearful. Having possessed such a character since ancient times, the people of this nation could be kept in greater outward reverence than others without having any inward reverence, so in superficial appearance they could represent the church and all it involves. These fantasies and cravings are what made them so intransigent.

[3] The same trait also appears in much of the information on them in the Word's narratives. After being punished, they could display a kind of outward humility no other nation could match. They could spend entire days throwing themselves prostrate on the ground and rolling in the dirt, refusing to rise till the third day. Day after day they could mourn aloud and go about in sackcloth and torn clothing, with ashes and dust sprinkled on their head. They could fast continuously for days on end, all the while bursting into bitter tears. But this sprang solely from a bodily and earthly passion and from fear that they would lose their supremacy and worldly wealth. Nothing profound could touch them, because they had no idea what lay inside and did not even want to know. They had no interest in life after death, for example, or in eternal salvation.

[4] This discussion shows that, in light of their character, it was absolutely necessary for them to be stripped of all inward devotion. Inward devotion is completely out of harmony with this kind of superficial holiness, because the two are exact opposites. The discussion also shows that they were better than others at simulating a church—that is, at representing holy things in outward form without any inward reverence. So a degree of communication with the heavens was possible through that nation; see §4288.

4294   Genesis 32:29, 30, 31, 32. *And Jacob asked and said, "Tell me your name, please." And he said, "Why are you asking this, as to my name?" And he blessed him there. And Jacob called the name of the place Peniel "because I saw God face to face and my soul was delivered." And the sun came up on him as he crossed Penuel, and he was limping on his thigh. Therefore the children of Israel do not eat the displaced joint's tendon—which is in the hollow of the thigh—to this day, because he touched the displaced joint's tendon in the hollow of Jacob's thigh.*

Jacob asked and said, "Tell me your name, please," symbolizes the heaven of angels and its nature. *And he said, "Why are you asking this, as to my name?"* means that heaven did not want to reveal itself. *And he blessed him there* symbolizes union with heavenly spirituality on a divine level. *And Jacob called the name of the place Peniel* symbolizes a state involving spiritual crises. *Because I saw God face to face and my soul was delivered* means that [the Lord] endured the most acute trials as if they came from his divine side. *And the sun came up on him* means internalizing what is good. *As he crossed Penuel* symbolizes a state in which truth lay within goodness. *And he was limping on his thigh* means that truth was not yet organized in such a way that together with goodness all of it could pass into heavenly-spiritual goodness. *Therefore the children of Israel do not eat the displaced joint's tendon, which is in the hollow of the thigh* means that nothing that contained falsity was adopted. *To this day* means that falsity would never attach, forever. *Because he touched the displaced joint's tendon in the hollow of Jacob's thigh* means because it was false.

[2] In the inner narrative meaning, which deals with Jacob's descendants, *Jacob asked and said, "Tell me your name, please,"* symbolizes evil spirits. *He said, "Why are you asking this, as to my name?"* means they did not recognize [that it came] from evil spirits. *He blessed him there* means so it happened. *Jacob called the name of the place Peniel* symbolizes the state in which they took on their representative role. *Because I saw God face to face and my soul was delivered* means that [the Lord] was present through representation. *The sun came up on him* means when they came into their

representative role. *As he crossed Penuel* means when they came into the land of Canaan. *He was limping on his thigh* means that goodness and truth were completely lost to those descendants. *Therefore the children of Israel do not eat the displaced joint's tendon, which is in the hollow of the thigh* means that the descendants ought to have known this. *To this day* means that they would be like this forever. *Because he touched the displaced joint's tendon in the hollow of Jacob's thigh* means because they had a heredity that could not be eliminated through rebirth, since they would not allow it.

And Jacob asked and said, *"Tell me your name, please,"* symbolizes the heaven of angels and its nature, as the following shows: *Jacob* represents the Lord's earthly divinity, as noted before. And the god (whose name he was asking for) and humans he competed nobly with and prevailed over symbolize truth and goodness. Accordingly they symbolize people who possess truth and goodness, as discussed in §4287. Since the angelic heaven is heaven on account of truth and goodness, that is the specific symbolism of the god and humans over whom the Lord prevailed.

In the Word, angels are called gods from time to time, and they are so called on account of their truth and goodness. In David, for instance:

> God stood in the *assembly of God;* in the midst of *the gods* he passed judgment. I have said, *"You are gods,* and you are all children of the Highest One." (Psalms 82:1, 6)

The assembly of God and the gods obviously mean heaven with its angels. In the same author:

> Who in heaven will compare with Jehovah, will be like Jehovah among the *children of gods?* (Psalms 89:6)

In the same author:

> Acclaim the *God of the gods,* acclaim the Lord of the lords! (Psalms 136:2, 3)

If you consider these quotations, and the fact that no one can compete nobly with God and prevail, and the fact that the being referred to as God did not want to reveal his name, you can see that what the Lord battled with was the heaven of angels.

The actual words "Why are you asking this, as to my name?" make it quite clear that a secret lies hidden in this verse, because if it had been Jehovah God, he would not have concealed his name. He would not have asked Jacob's name, either, since the only person (or people) who would ask for a name is someone other than God.

[2] It is a secret never before disclosed that the Lord in his trials eventually fought the angels themselves and in fact the entire angelic heaven. Here is the situation: Angels do enjoy the highest wisdom and understanding, but all of their wisdom and understanding comes from the Lord in his divinity. Left to themselves and their own devices, they have none, so the more truth and goodness they receive from the Lord's divinity, the wiser and more discerning they are.

Angels themselves openly admit that on their own they have no wisdom or understanding. They even become upset if others attribute any to them. They know and sense that to take credit for it would be to deny the Divine his divinity and lay claim to what is not theirs, which would be to commit the crime of spiritual theft. Angels also say that everything of their own is evil and false, whether they inherited it or acquired it by their life and deeds in the world when they lived as people there. They are not dissociated from or wiped clean of the evil and falsity and absolved in the process. No, it all remains with them, but the Lord withholds them from it and anchors them in goodness and truth (§1581). This every angel confesses. No one is allowed into heaven without knowing and believing it. People who do not do so cannot enjoy the light of wisdom and understanding that radiates from the Lord, which means that they cannot enjoy goodness and truth. These considerations also show how to understand the idea that heaven is not pure in God's eyes, as said in Job 15:15.

[3] This being so, the Lord sought to reduce all of heaven to heavenly order by allowing himself to be tested even by angels, who lacked goodness and truth to the extent they trusted in themselves alone. Such trials are the very deepest of all, because they focus exclusively on one's ultimate goals and act with a subtlety that is beyond detection. To the extent that angels *refrain* from trusting in themselves they enjoy goodness and truth and are incapable of testing anyone.

What is more, the Lord is constantly perfecting angels, although they can never, ever be perfected to the point where their wisdom and understanding can be compared to the Lord's divine wisdom and understanding. After all, they are finite and the Lord is infinite. There is no comparison between what is finite and what is infinite.

This discussion now shows what the god with whom Jacob competed nobly means and why he did not want to reveal his name.

4296   *Why are you asking this, as to my name?* means that heaven did not want to reveal itself. This can be seen from the remarks and proofs just above at §4295.

And he blessed him there symbolizes union with heavenly spirituality on a divine level. This can be seen from the symbolism of *blessing* as union, discussed in §§3504, 3514, 3565, 3584. The fact that the union was with heavenly spirituality on a divine level is established by the discussion above at §4286 concerning Jacob and his new name of Israel, which represents the Lord's heavenly spirituality on a divine level. Heavenly spirituality is also defined there.

4297

And Jacob called the name of the place Peniel symbolizes a state involving spiritual crises, as context shows. It used to be that when something extraordinary happened in a place, it would be given a name symbolic of the event that had occurred there and of the conditions involved (§§340, 2643, 3422). This spot was given a name that symbolized trying conditions because in this passage Jacob's wrestling and grappling depicts a state of trial.

4298

In the original language, Peniel means "the face of God." The next section will explain that seeing the face of God means sustaining the most acute trials.

Because I saw God face to face and my soul was delivered means that [the Lord] endured the most acute trials as if they came from his divine side, as the following shows: *Seeing God* means growing closer to him through inner qualities, or goodness and truth, so it symbolizes presence, as mentioned in §4198. The *face* symbolizes inner attributes, as discussed in §§1999, 2434, 3527, 3573, 4066, so it symbolizes thoughts and feelings. Both of these exist inside, because they exist in the heart and mind, and they display themselves in the face. And *my soul was delivered* means enduring—that is, enduring the divine presence.

4299

Only the direct and the remote causes of spiritual crisis can demonstrate this symbolism of the sentence—that [the Lord] endured the most acute trials as if they came from his divine side. The evils and falsities in us that bring on our times of trial—and therefore the evil spirits and demons who supply them—are the direct causes (§4249). However, the only people who can be tested, or undergo any spiritual trial, are those with a conscience. Spiritual trial is actually the torments of conscience, so we cannot be tested unless we have heavenly and spiritual goodness. People with goodness have a conscience; the rest do not, and do not even know what a conscience is.

[2] A conscience is a new will and a new intellect received from the Lord. It is the Lord's presence in us, which is more immediate the more we desire goodness or truth. If the Lord's presence is stronger than

our desire for goodness or truth, we come into trial. The reason for the trial is that the evil and falsity in us, which are moderated by the goodness and truth in us, cannot stand a more immediate presence—as circumstances in the other world can demonstrate. Evil spirits there can never approach any community of heaven without going into distress and agony. They also cannot stand to be observed by angels, at whose glance they instantly writhe, then fall down in a faint. Another piece of evidence is the distance hell maintains from heaven because it cannot bear heaven—in other words, the Lord's presence in heaven. That is why the Word says of hell's inhabitants, "Then they will start to say to the mountains, 'Fall on us!' and to the hills, 'Hide us!'" (Luke 23:30). In another passage, "They will say to the mountains and rocks, 'Collapse on us and conceal us from the face of the one sitting on the throne!'" (Revelation 6:16). There is also a dark, foggy aura wafting from the evils and falsities of hell's inhabitants that looks like a mountain or crag, and they hide under it (see §§1265, 1267, 1270).

[3] These comments now show that "I saw God face to face and my soul was delivered," symbolizes the most acute trials, which seem to come from the Divine.

Crises and torments seem to come from the Divine because they come about through the Lord's divine presence, as noted. Yet they come not from the Divine, or the Lord, but from evil and falsity in the person being tried or tormented. Nothing but sacred goodness, truth, and mercy emanates from the Lord. This holy goodness, truth, and mercy is what is unbearable to people involved in evil and falsity because it opposes or confronts them. Evil, falsity, and ruthlessness constantly intend harm to those sacred qualities, and the more they attack those qualities, the more torture they themselves suffer. When they attack and therefore suffer, they imagine it is the Divine that torments them. That is what is meant by "as if they came from his divine side."

[4] The ancients knew that no one can see Jehovah face to face and live, and this knowledge was passed down to Jacob's descendants. That is why their joy was so great when they saw an angel and lived through it. In Judges, for instance:

> Gideon saw that there was an angel of Jehovah, so Gideon said, "Lord Jehovih! *For I have seen an angel of Jehovah face to face!*" And Jehovah said to him, "Peace to you. Don't be afraid, *because you will not die.*" (Judges 6:22, 23)

In the same book:

> Manoah said to his wife, "*We will surely die, because we have seen God!*" (Judges 13:22)

And in Moses:

> Jehovah said to Moses, "*You cannot see my face, because no human shall see me and live.*" (Exodus 33:20)

[5] Moses is said to have spoken with Jehovah "face to face" (Exodus 33:11) and to have been known by Jehovah "face to face" (Deuteronomy 34:10), but that is because Jehovah appeared to him in a human form he could accept. That form was external, that of a bearded old man sitting with him, as angels have taught me. Consequently Jews always pictured Jehovah as a very elderly person with a long, white beard who was better than other gods at doing miracles. They did not think of him as particularly holy, since they did not know what holiness was. Still less could they ever have pictured any holy influence coming from him. This was because their passions were bodily, earthly, and devoid of any inner holiness (§§4289, 4293).

And the sun came up on him means internalizing what is good. This [4300] can be seen from the symbolism of the *sun's coming up* as the internalizing of goodness, or union with it. "Dawn rose" means when union arrives or begins (see §4283), so it follows that the sun's coming up means union itself. On an inner level, the *sun* symbolizes heavenly love (§§1529, 1530, 2441, 2495, 3636, 3643, 4060), so it symbolizes what is good, since goodness is a mark of heavenly love.

When heavenly love reveals itself in us—when we perceive it—the sun is said to come up on us, because we then internalize the goodness characterizing that love.

As he crossed Penuel symbolizes a state in which truth lay within good- [4301] ness. This can be seen from the symbolism of *Penuel* as a state in which truth lies within goodness. The Jabbok was what Jacob first crossed when he entered the land of Canaan, and it symbolizes the first infusion of a desire for truth (see §§4270, 4271). Penuel is what he now crossed, so it symbolizes a state in which goodness has been infused with truth. The theme here is the internalizing of goodness, and goodness is not good unless it contains what is true. Goodness takes its quality and form from truth— so much so that it cannot be called good in any person unless it contains truth. (On the other hand, truth takes its essence and therefore its life from goodness.) Because of this, and because the subject here is the internalizing of goodness, the text is also talking about a state in which truth is present within goodness.

[2] A state in which truth is present within goodness can be described, but it cannot be understood except by people with heavenly perception. People without such perception cannot even imagine a union between truth and goodness, because the truth is dark to them. In their vocabulary, truth is what they have learned from doctrine, and goodness is any event conforming with this truth. When people have perception, though, heaven's light shines on their intellect, or their mind's eye. They are drawn to truth that is united with goodness, just as physical vision, or the body's eye, is drawn to flowers that appear in gardens and meadows in the spring. People with still deeper perception are moved by it, as if it were a fragrance given off by spring flowers. Such is the state of an angel. As a result, these angels perceive all the different ways and means by which truth permeates goodness and is internalized by it. Compared to us, then, they see unlimited detail, because we do not even know that truth is ever instilled or united, or that this process renders us spiritual. [3] In order to supply some idea of the matter, then, let me say a few words.

The inner self has two components: the intellect and the will. Truth belongs to the intellect, and goodness belongs to the will. We use the term *truth* for what we know and understand to be so, and the term *goodness* for what we do willingly—in other words, for what we want to do. These two abilities [of intellect and will] form a single unit.

The situation can be illustrated by comparison with eyesight and the appealing, pleasant things we perceive by this sense. When our eye sees objects, it senses something delightful and pleasurable in them, depending on their form and color and therefore on the beauty in the whole and in each part. In other words, their appeal depends on their design or the arrangement of them into series. The appeal and pleasure belong not to the eye but to the heart and its desires. The more those sights appeal to us, the more we look at them and retain them in our memory. On the other hand, when our eye sees something for which it has no feeling, we overlook it and do not record it in our memory, so we form no bond with it. [4] Clearly, then, the sweetness and pleasure of our responses to the objects of outward sight determine whether we record them. They lodge within that sweet pleasure, because when it returns, they come back to mind, and likewise when we see the objects again, the pleasure comes back. It returns in different forms, depending on our frame of mind.

The case is exactly the same with the intellect, which is the inner eye. Its objects are spiritual and are called truths. The field holding those objects is the memory, and their appeal and pleasure to the inner eye is the goodness involved. Goodness is therefore the ground in which truth is sown and planted.

From this you can see to some extent how truth permeates goodness and is internalized by it, and what kind of goodness is under discussion here—a subject on which angels perceive countless things, where we perceive almost nothing.

And he was limping on his thigh means that truth was not yet organized in such a way that together with goodness all of it could pass into heavenly-spiritual goodness. This can be seen from the symbolism of *limping* as having goodness that does not as yet contain real truth, only general truth that can be filled in with real truth and does not clash with it. This symbolism is dealt with below. However, on the highest level, which has to do with the Lord, *limping on the thigh* means that truth was not yet organized in such a way that together with goodness all of it could pass into heavenly-spiritual goodness. The *thigh* means heavenly-spiritual goodness; see above at §§4277, 4278. **4302**

[2] The pattern that must be imposed on truth when it enters into goodness (heavenly-spiritual goodness, in this case) also cannot be explained in an intelligible way. First the reader needs to know what an orderly pattern is, what kind of pattern truth displays, what heavenly-spiritual goodness is, and how truth enters into it through goodness. Even if these points were elaborated, they would become clear only to people who possess heavenly perception. People with earthly perception alone would not understand them at all. Those with heavenly perception enjoy heaven's light, which comes from the Lord and contains understanding and wisdom. Those who see by earthly light have no understanding or wisdom, except to the extent that heaven's light flows into their earthly light and adapts it, enabling heavenly matters to be reflected in the objects of earthly light as if in a mirror, or in a kind of representative image. Earthly light never renders spiritual truth visible unless heavenly light flows into it.

[3] Here is the only thing that can be said about the pattern that must be imposed on truth if it is to gain entrance to goodness: In heaven, all truth (and goodness) in general and particular and even down to the smallest details is arranged in a pattern in which it all interrelates. It interrelates the way the limbs, organs, and viscera of the human body (or their functions) do in general and particular, down to the smallest details, forming

themselves into a unified whole. It is owing to this pattern imposed on truth and goodness that heaven itself is called the universal human. Its very life comes from the Lord, who by his nature organizes everything in this pattern. That is why heaven is his likeness and image. Therefore when truth is arranged in the same pattern that characterizes heaven, it is in the heavenly pattern and gains entrance to goodness. Truth and goodness display this pattern in every angel and are being arranged in this pattern in every human who is being reborn.

To sum up, the heavenly pattern is the pattern in which the truth that builds faith is arrayed within good done out of charity for one's neighbor, and in which this charitable goodness is arrayed within good done out of love for the Lord.

[4] As noted, *limping* means having goodness that as yet does not contain real truth but does contain general truth that can be filled in with real truth—provided it does not clash with real truth. The lame, then, are people who have goodness but not real goodness, because they do not know truth—the kind of goodness possessed by non-Christians who live lives of mutual neighborly love. These meanings can be seen from scriptural passages that mention the lame and limping in a positive sense. In Isaiah, for example:

> The eyes of the blind will be opened, and the ears of the deaf will be opened; then the *lame* will spring up like a deer, and the mute will sing with their tongue. (Isaiah 35:5, 6)

In Jeremiah:

> Watch: I am bringing them from the land of the north, and I will assemble them from the flanks of the land; among them are the blind and the *lame;* the pregnant one and the one in labor together. (Jeremiah 31:8)

In Micah:

> "On that day," says Jehovah, "I will gather the *limping,* and the stricken I will assemble, and I will turn the *limping* into a remnant, and the stricken into a populous nation, and Jehovah will reign over them on Mount Zion from now on forever." (Micah 4:6, 7)

In Zephaniah:

> At that time I will save the *limping* and assemble the stricken and make them an object of praise and a name. (Zephaniah 3:19)

Anyone can see that in these passages the lame and limping do not mean lame and limping people, since the texts say that they will spring up, be gathered, be turned into a remnant, and be saved. Instead, they symbolize people with goodness but not much truth, which describes upright non-Christians and people like them in the church as well.

[5] The same kind of people are meant by the lame of whom the Lord speaks in Luke:

> Jesus said, "When you make a banquet, call the poor, the maimed, the *lame,* and the blind. Then you will be fortunate." (Luke 14:13, 14)

Again in the same author:

> The householder said to his slave, "Go quickly into the streets and alleys of the city and bring the poor and the maimed and the *lame* and the blind in here." (Luke 14:21)

The ancient church created different categories of neighbor (or of their neighbors) for whom they were to perform acts of charity. They called some of these people maimed, some lame, some blind, and some deaf—meaning people who were spiritually so.

They also divided them into the hungry, thirsty, immigrant, naked, sick, and imprisoned (Matthew 25:35, 36), and into the widowed, orphaned, needy, poor, and wretched. By these categories they meant precisely those who were disadvantaged in regard to truth and goodness and who needed to be suitably taught and led to the proper path—in other words, to have their souls attended to. These days, though, faith rather than neighborly love constitutes the church, so people have no idea what is meant by such types in the Word. Nevertheless, anyone can see that it does not mean that the maimed, lame, and blind are to be called to banquets, and that the householder was not directing that people such as these be brought in, but people who are spiritually so. Everything the Lord said contains something divine and therefore a heavenly and spiritual meaning.

[6] The Lord's words in Mark have a similar meaning:

> If your foot makes you stumble, cut it off; it is better for you to enter life *lame* than, having two feet, to be thrown into fiery Gehenna, into fire unquenchable. (Mark 9:45; Matthew 18:8)

The foot that was to be cut off if it caused stumbling means the earthly plane, which always opposes the spiritual plane. It was to be destroyed if it tried to break truth up. Considering how out of step and antagonistic the earthly self is, then, simple goodness is preferable, even if it entails a denial of truth. That is what entering life lame symbolizes. For the meaning of a foot as something earthly, see §§2162, 3147, 3761, 3986, 4280.

[7] The lame in the Word also symbolize people without goodness and therefore without truth, as in Isaiah:

Then the plunder will be divided; those multiplying the number of *limpers* will plunder the plunder. (Isaiah 33:23)

In David:

When I limp, they rejoice and assemble; the *lame,* whom I do not know, assemble against me. (Psalms 35:15)

Because a lame person symbolizes people without goodness or truth, there was a prohibition against sacrificing anything *lame* (Deuteronomy 15:21, 22; Malachi 1:8, 13), and no one of Aaron's seed who was *lame* was to carry out the duties of the priesthood (Leviticus 21:18).

The case is the same with blindness as with lameness, because in a positive sense a blind person symbolizes people who do not know truth, and in a negative sense, those who subscribe to falsity (§2383).

[8] The original language has one word for "lame" and another for "limping." The lame, properly speaking, symbolize people who have an earthly kind of goodness in which physical appearances and sensory illusions block the inflow of spiritual truth. In a negative sense the lame symbolize people who have no earthly goodness, only evil, which is wholly impervious to spiritual truth. The limping, properly speaking, symbolize people with an earthly goodness that lets in general truths but not particular truths or their component details, because these are unknown. In a negative sense the limping symbolize people who wallow in evil and therefore do not allow even general truth in.

4303   *Therefore the children of Israel do not eat the displaced joint's tendon, which is in the hollow of the thigh* means that nothing that contained falsity was adopted. This can be seen from the symbolism of *eating* as being united and adopted (discussed in §§2187, 2343, 3168, 3513, 3596, 3832) and from that of a *tendon* as truth. The truth that is present within goodness resembles tendons within flesh—and in a spiritual sense, true concepts are tendons and goodness is flesh (§3813).

Tendons and flesh have the same symbolism in Ezekiel:

This is what the Lord Jehovih has said to these bones: "*I will put tendons on you* and bring flesh up over you and put breath in you." And

I looked, when there!—*tendons on them;* and flesh came up. (Ezekiel 37:[5,] 6, 8)

This is about our creation anew—that is, our rebirth—but when truth is twisted it ceases to be truth. As it is wrenched into its opposite, it approaches falsity, and that is why the displaced joint's tendon symbolizes falsity.

The hollow of the thigh is the point where marriage love connects with earthly goodness, so it is the point where spiritual truth acts on earthly goodness; see §§4277, 4280. These considerations show that *therefore the children of Israel do not eat the displaced joint's tendon, which is in the hollow of the thigh* means that nothing that contained falsity was adopted.

The reason this sentence speaks of the children of Israel is that Israel symbolizes heavenly spirituality on a divine plane (§4286), and children, [or sons,] symbolize truth (§§489, 491, 2623). So the truth belonging to heavenly spirituality on a divine plane did not adopt any falsity.

To this day means that falsity would never attach, forever. This is established by the symbolism of *to this day,* where the phrase appears in the Word, as that which is never-ending and eternal (discussed in §2838).   **4304**

Because he touched the displaced joint's tendon in the hollow of Jacob's thigh means because it was false. This can be seen from the fact that *touching in the hollow of Jacob's thigh* this time means because it was false. This meaning of touching in the hollow of Jacob's thigh can be seen from the remarks above at §§4277, 4278, 4303.   **4305**

The same sentences explained here also have to do with Jacob's descendants, and this sense is called the lower meaning, or the inner narrative meaning; see §§4279, 4288. How everything is to be understood in this meaning will now be explained.   **4306**

In the inner narrative meaning, *Jacob asked and said, "Tell me your name, please,"* symbolizes evil spirits, as can be seen from many indications on this level of meaning, which applies to Jacob's descendants here and in what follows. An inner meaning relates to the subject under discussion, you see.   **4307**

The being who wrestled Jacob symbolizes evil spirits rather than good ones, as stands to reason. Wrestling symbolizes times of trial (§§3927, 3928, 4274), and no trial is ever brought about by good spirits, only by evil ones, because a spiritual trial is an arousal of the evil and falsity inside us (§§741, 751, 761, 1820, 4249, 4299). Good spirits and angels never stir up evil and falsity but defend us against them and turn them to good. After all, good spirits are led by the Lord, and nothing but holy goodness and holy truth ever comes from him. The Lord never tests anyone, as is known from the received teachings of the church (and see §§1875, 2768). These points—and the fact that Jacob's descendants failed every trial, both in the wilderness and afterward—make it plain that the being who wrestled Jacob symbolizes evil spirits rather than good ones.

What is more, the nation symbolized here by Jacob did not exhibit any spiritual or heavenly love but only bodily and worldly love (§§4281, 4288, 4289, 4290, 4293). The presence of spirits with us depends on what we love. Good spirits and angels are present with those who love what is spiritual and heavenly, and evil spirits, with those who love only what is bodily and worldly. This fact is so consistent that if you want to know what kind of spirits are with you, just look at what kinds of things you love, or to put the same thing another way, what kind of aims you hold (since what we love is what we have as our goal).

[2] The reason this individual referred to himself as God is that Jacob believed him to be God. So did Jacob's posterity, who always believed that Jehovah was present in their outward devotion, although he would have been present only in a representative way, as will become clear from what follows [§4311]. They also believed that Jehovah led them into their crises, that everything bad came from him, and that when they were being punished, he was furiously angry. The Word is phrased this way because of their beliefs, despite the fact that Jehovah never leads anyone into trial, that nothing bad ever comes from him, and that he is never angry, let alone furious; see §§223, 245, 592, 696, 1093, 1683, 1874, 1875, 2395, 3605, 3607, 3614.

That is also why the one who wrestled with Jacob did not want to reveal his name.

The reason why heaven with its angels is meant in an inner, spiritual sense by the being who wrestled Jacob (§4295) is that the Lord—whom Jacob represents in the highest sense of this story—allowed even the angels to test him, and that the angels were then left to their own devices (as shown in that section).

4308 In the inner narrative meaning, *he said, "Why are you asking this, as to my name?"* means they did not recognize [that it came] from evil spirits. This can be seen from the discussion directly above in §4307.

4309 In the inner narrative meaning, *he blessed him there* means so it happened. This can be seen from the symbolism of *blessing* in this case as their creating the representation of a church—a symbolism discussed at §4290. *He blessed him there* accordingly means so it happened.

4310 In the inner narrative meaning, *Jacob called the name of the place Peniel* symbolizes the state in which they took on their representative role, as the following shows: *Calling something's name* symbolizes its quality, as noted many times before. A *place* symbolizes a state, as discussed in §§2625, 2837, 3356, 3387. And on this level of meaning, *Peniel* symbolizes taking on a representative role, since that is the theme in the verses that come before and after.

The symbolism of *Peniel* is explained by the words "because I saw God face to face and my soul was delivered," meaning that the Lord was present through representation, as discussed just below. Peniel, then, means that they took on a representative role.

Place-names, people's names, and the places and people themselves do not have the same symbolism on one level of meaning as they do on another. Take Jacob as an example. In a literal sense he means Jacob himself. In the inner narrative sense he symbolizes Jacob's descendants (§4281). In an inner, spiritual sense he symbolizes the earthly self of a person who has been reborn. In the highest sense he symbolizes the Lord's earthly divinity. This has been shown many times. The same is true of all other names, so it is true of Peniel.

In the inner narrative meaning, *because I saw God face to face and my soul was delivered* means that [the Lord] was present through representation. This can be seen from the symbolism of *seeing God face to face*, when applied to the state in which Jacob's descendants were, as the fact that the Lord was present in a representative way. To see God face to face in an outward form, with the body's eye, is not to see him present (§4299). He was not present [with Jacob's descendants] in the same way he is present with people who have been reborn and who therefore possess spiritual love and faith. This is plain from the description of that nation in §§4281, 4288, 4290, 4293 as a group of people who engaged in outward worship but not at the same time in inward worship. In other words, they indulged in bodily and worldly love, not in spiritual and heavenly love. In such people the Lord could be present only in a representative way.

[2] Representative presence needs to be defined briefly. People who love what is bodily and worldly and not what is spiritual or heavenly as well have no other spirits with them except evil ones, even when they are engaged in outward devotion. Good spirits cannot possibly join such a person, because they immediately sense what kinds of things the person loves. From the inner depths of such a person wafts an aura that spirits perceive as clearly as we perceive foul, disgusting particles flitting about us in the air by their smell. Such was the case with the nation under discussion here, in regard to goodness and truth, or love and faith. To enable them to create a representation of a church nonetheless, the Lord made a miraculous provision. When they were performing their superficial devotions while

4311

surrounded with evil spirits, their reverence, such as it was, would be lifted up into heaven. The good spirits and angels who lifted it up were not inside them but outside, because there was nothing inside them but emptiness, or else filthiness. As a result there was no contact with the actual person, only with the reverence itself that the person assumed while carrying out the statutes and commandments, all of which represented spiritual and heavenly attributes of the Lord's kingdom. This is what it means to say that the Lord was present with that nation through representation.

The Lord is present in a different way among people in the church who have spiritual love and therefore faith. In the case of people like this, good spirits and angels attend not only their outward worship but also their inward worship. So heaven communicates with the people themselves. The Lord flows by way of heaven through their inner levels into their outer levels. Reverent worship benefits the latter people but not the former in the other life.

[3] The case is the same with priests and ministers who preach what is holy but live badly and believe badly. They too have evil rather than good spirits with them, even when they are apparently conducting worship that is outwardly holy. What motivates them is love for themselves and the world, or love for winning high office, amassing wealth, and acquiring a reputation in the process. They project an interest in piety—sometimes so convincingly that no pretense can be detected in it. In fact, at that moment they themselves do not believe they are pretending. Yet they are in the midst of evil spirits, who are then in the same state and who influence and inspire them. Manifold experience (to be described in the treatises at the ends of chapters, by the Lord's divine mercy) has taught me that evil spirits can be and are in this kind of state when they are occupied with surface realities and when their self-love and materialism are being held in check. These [clergy members] likewise have no contact with heaven themselves, but the people listening to them and catching the words from their lips do have contact, if they are pious and reverent on the inside. It does not matter who utters a good word or a true one, as long as the speaker's life is not openly villainous (since this creates a scandal).

[4] Many scriptural passages reveal that the nation descended from Jacob was like this—that its people were surrounded by evil spirits, although the Lord could still be present with them through representation. They worshiped the Lord in anything but a heartfelt way, because as soon as the miracles stopped, they immediately turned to other gods and became idolaters. This was an obvious sign that they worshiped other gods in their hearts and merely claimed to believe in Jehovah. Indeed they did this much only to

gain supreme importance and superiority over all the nations around them. The golden calf Aaron made for this people offers plain testimony that they worshiped an Egyptian idol at heart and merely gave lip service to a belief in Jehovah, because of the miracles, and that Aaron joined them in doing so. The incident occurred just a month of days after they saw great miracles on Mount Sinai, in addition to those they had seen in Egypt. The story is told in Exodus 32, of which verses 2, 3, 4, 5, and especially 35 say clearly that Aaron had this character. Many other passages in Moses, Judges, Samuel, and Kings also provide evidence.

[5] The fact that their worship was all outward, never inward, can also be seen from their being forbidden to approach Mount Sinai when the law was being issued. If they touched the mountain, they would "surely die" (Exodus 19:11, 12, 13; 20:19), because they were unclean on the inside. Moses also says that Jehovah was to reside with them in the midst of their uncleanness (Leviticus 16:16). The Song of Moses too shows what that nation was like (Deuteronomy 32:15–43), as do many passages in the Prophets.

From this discussion the reader can see that no church existed with that nation, only the representation of a church, and that the Lord would have been present with them only in a representative way.

[6] See previous points made about these people as well: Among Jacob's descendants there was a representation of a religion but not a religion: 4281, 4288. The representation of a religion was not established among them until they had been thoroughly purged of inward reverence; otherwise they would have profaned what is holy: 3398, 4289. When they adhered to the statutes, they could play a representative role, but when they turned from them, they could not: 3881 at the end. Consequently they were held strictly to the rituals and were forced by superficial coercion to perform them: 3147, 4281. To enable them to create a representation of a religion, their worship was turned into an outward display without any inner content: 4281. On the same account, the inner depths of religion were not disclosed to them: 301, 302, 303, 2520, 3398, 3479, 3769. By nature they were better able than others to maintain outward reverence without any inward reverence: 4293. That is why they have been preserved to this day: 3479. Their outward sanctity has no effect on their souls: 349.

In the inner narrative meaning, *the sun came up on him* means when they came into their representative role. This can be seen from the fact that in this sense, which deals with Jacob's descendants, the *sun's coming up* means when they came into their representative role. The dawn's rising symbolized their state before taking up their representation (§4289).

4312

The sun is also said to come up in anyone who becomes a church and therefore also in one who comes to represent a church.

4313   In the inner narrative meaning, *as he crossed Penuel* means when they came into the land of Canaan. This can be seen from the fact that *Penuel* was Jacob's first stopping place after crossing the river Jabbok and that all borders had a symbolism depending on their relative distance and position (§§1585, 1866, 4116, 4240). Since Penuel was the first border, it means when he came into the land of Canaan.

4314   In the inner narrative meaning, *he was limping on his thigh* means that goodness and truth were completely lost to those descendants, as the following shows. Jacob—to whom *he* refers here—represents his descendants, as noted in §4281. And *limping on a thigh* symbolizes people who have no goodness and consequently no truth, as discussed in §4302. So *he was limping on his thigh* means that goodness and truth were completely lost to those descendants.

[2] The character that nation had is obvious from many things the Lord himself said in his parables, which on the inner narrative level applied to that nation. Take for instance the following parables:

The royal personage who settled the account of a slave who had no mercy himself for a fellow slave. (Matthew 18:23–end)

The householder who rented a vineyard out to some growers and went abroad. The growers seized the servants he sent, and beat, killed, and stoned them. Finally he sent his son, whom they threw out of the vineyard and killed. Hearing the parable, the scribes and Pharisees knew it was about them. (Matthew 21:33 and following verses, 45; Mark 12:1–9; Luke 20:9 and following verses)

The man who gave some talents to his slaves. The slave who received one talent, going off, hid it in the earth. (Matthew 25:14–30; Luke 19:13–26)

The people who came across a man wounded by robbers. (Luke 10:30–37)

The people who were called to a grand supper and all excused themselves. The Lord said of them, "I say to you that none of those men who were called will taste my supper." (Luke 14:16–24)

The rich man and Lazarus. (Luke 16:19–end)

The people who consider themselves superior to others. (Luke 18:10–14)

The two sons, one of whom said, "I will go into the vineyard"; but he did not. And Jesus said, "Truly, I say to you that the tax collectors and prostitutes will precede you into the kingdom of the heavens." (Matthew 21:28, 29, 30, 31, 32)

[3] The Lord explicitly says what that nation was like in Matthew 23:13 and following verses, ending with these words:

You testify against yourselves that you are the children of those who killed the prophets, and you fill the measure of your ancestors. (Matthew 23:13 and following verses, 31, 32, 33)

In Mark:

Jesus said to them, "Rightly Isaiah prophesied of you, 'This people honors me with their lips, but their heart is completely absent from me. In vain they worship me, teaching as teachings the commandments of humans, abandoning the command of God.'" (Mark 7:6–13)

In John:

The Jews answered Jesus that they were Abraham's seed. But Jesus said to them, "You are from your father, the Devil, and your father's desires you wish to do; he was a murderer from the start and did not stand on truth, because there is no truth in him. When he tells a lie, he is talking on his own, because he is a liar and the father of [a lie]." (John 8:33, 44)

Because this was their nature, they are also called a wicked and adulterous generation (Matthew 12:39) and a brood of vipers (Matthew 3:7; 23:33; Luke 3:7). And in Matthew:

Brood of vipers! How can you speak good things when you are evil? (Matthew 12:34)

[4] That nation did not even have any earthly goodness left, as symbolized by the fig tree spoken of in Matthew:

Jesus, seeing a fig tree along the way, came to it but found nothing on it except leaves alone. So he said to it, "May fruit not come from you from now to eternity!" Accordingly the fig tree instantly withered. (Matthew 21:19)

A fig tree means earthly goodness; see §217.

This evidence shows that goodness and truth were completely lost to that nation.

[5] Goodness and truth are said to be lost when they are lacking inside us. Outwardly visible goodness and truth draw their existence and life from

what lies inside. So the quality of the inner depths determines the quality of the outer surface, no matter what the surface looks like to the human eye. There are some I knew during their bodily life who seemed at the time to be zealous for the Lord, the church, their country and the common good, and justice and fairness. Yet in the other life they live among the hellish and, to my surprise, among the very worst there. The reason for their fate is that their inner reaches had been sordid and profane. They had put on a pretense of zeal for the sake of reputation, in order to obtain high office and amass riches—for selfish purposes, then, rather than for the reasons they had claimed. When they slough off this outer surface upon dying, the inner reality is exposed. They appear as they were on the inside, which they had hidden from the world while alive.

This is what it means to say that goodness and truth were completely lost.

4315   In the inner narrative meaning, *therefore the children of Israel do not eat the displaced joint's tendon, which is in the hollow of the thigh* means that the descendants ought to have known this. Consider that not eating it was a reminder to them of their own character. On that account, they ought to have known.

4316   In the inner narrative meaning, *to this day* means that they would be like this forever. This is established by the symbolism of *to this day*, where the phrase appears in the Word, as something permanent (discussed in §2838).

Jacob's descendants were like this from their earliest days, as his actual sons illustrate. *Reuben* lay with Bilhah, his father's concubine (Genesis 35:22). *Simeon* and *Levi* killed Hamor, Shechem, and all the men in Hamor and Shechem's city, and the *other sons* came upon those stabbed, and plundered the city (Genesis 34:1 and following verses, 27, 28, 29). The following is therefore what Jacob—who by then was Israel—said about them before he died. Of Reuben:

> You will not be eminent, for you climbed onto your father's beds, then you disgraced yourself; my pallet he climbed onto. (Genesis 49:4)

And of Simeon and Levi:

> Into their conspiracy my soul is not to come; with their band my glory is not to unite, because in their anger they killed a man, and in their premeditation they hamstrung an ox. A curse on their anger because it is fierce and on their fury because it is heavy! I will divide them among Jacob and scatter them among Israel. (Genesis 49:5, 6, 7)

[2] *Judah's* character can be seen from his marriage to a Canaanite woman (Genesis 38:1, 2). Such a marriage violated a commandment, as is evident from Abraham's speech to the servant sent to win Rebekah's promise to marry his son Isaac (Genesis 24:3, 6) and from many other passages in the Word. A third of Judah's clan came from the stock of his son Shelah, whose mother was the Canaanite (Genesis 38:11; 46:12; see also Numbers 26:20; 1 Chronicles 4:21, 22).

Reflect also on the unspeakable crime these and the other sons of Jacob committed against Joseph (Genesis 37:18–end).

The nature of their descendants in Egypt becomes clear from the account of them during their time in the wilderness, where they often rebelled, and afterward in the land of Canaan, where they often turned to idolatry. Their nature in the Lord's time was shown just above in §4314. Their modern nature is known to be such that they oppose the Lord, religious matters, neighborly kindness, and one another. Clearly, then, that nation has always been like this.

No one, then, should hold on to the view that any religion existed among them (only the representation of a religion did), let alone that they were chosen above anyone else.

In the inner narrative meaning, *because he touched the displaced joint's* **4317** *tendon in the hollow of Jacob's thigh* means because they had a heredity that could not be eliminated through rebirth, since they would not allow it. This can be seen from the symbolism of a *thigh* as marriage love and therefore as all heavenly and spiritual love (discussed in §4280). The *hollow* of the thigh means the point where marriage love (and all heavenly and spiritual love) connects with earthly goodness (§§4277, 4280). So *touching* it—in other words, hurting it badly enough to cause a limp— means destroying the goodness connected with those kinds of love. Since the dislocation was Jacob's, the clause means that his descendants received the trait from him, so it symbolizes their heredity. The *displaced joint's tendon* means falsity (see §4303) and in this case the falsity produced by inherited evil. From these considerations and the thread of the story, it follows that the heredity could not be eliminated from them through rebirth because they would not allow it.

[2] The fact that they had this heredity and that they could not be reborn is obvious from everything said about them in the Word and especially from the following verses in Moses:

Moses called all Israel and said to them, "You have seen everything that Jehovah has done in your eyes in the land of Egypt, to Pharaoh and all his servants and all his land. And *Jehovah has not given you a heart for knowing or eyes for seeing or ears for hearing, to this day."* (Deuteronomy 29:2, 4)

In the same author:

I know the people's designs that they are forming today, before I bring them into the land that I swore [to them]. (Deuteronomy 31:21)

Again:

I will hide my face from them, I will see what the latter days are, because they are a *generation of perversities*—offspring in whom there is no truth. I would exile them, I would make their memory cease from humankind if I did not fear the enemy's rage. For they are a nation whose counsel is dying out, and there is no understanding in them, since *from the grapevine of Sodom comes their grapevine, and from the fields of Gomorrah come their grapes; grapes of hemlock,* bitter clusters are theirs. The *poison of serpents* is their wine, and the cruel *head of asps.* Is it not stored up with me, sealed in my treasuries? (Deuteronomy 32:20, 26, 27, 28, 29, 30, 31, 32, 33, 34)

There are many other passages, too, particularly in Jeremiah.

[3] This symbolism of the touching of the hollow of Jacob's thigh and of his resulting limp is plain in Hosea:

Jehovah has a dispute with Judah, to exact punishment on Jacob according to his ways; and according to his deeds will [Jehovah] repay him. In the womb he supplanted his brother. In his trouble he competed with God and competed against an angel and prevailed; he wept and begged him. (Hosea 12:2, 3, 4)

On the inner narrative level of this verse, competing with God means demanding that they be allowed to represent the church (§§4290, 4293).

From the above discussion, then, it is clear that this is the character Jacob's descendants inherited from Jacob himself. There is still more evidence, but for the time being I pass it by.

[4] To deal specifically with heredity: People in the church currently believe that we inherit all our evil from our first ancestor and that therefore we have all been condemned for it; but this is not the case. The evil we each inherit takes its origin from our parents, their parents (our grandparents), and our great-grandparents in succession. As for the evil that people amass through the way they actually live—so much so that

frequent practice or habit makes it look like second nature—all of it is passed down to their children. In the children it becomes inherited evil and joins the evil implanted in the parents by the grandparents and great-grandparents. The evil we inherit from our father lies deep within, while that which we inherit from our mother lies on the surface. The former cannot be uprooted very easily, but the latter can. When we regenerate, the inherited evil rooted in us by our most immediate ancestors is eradicated, but if we do not or cannot regenerate, it remains in us.

This, then, is what inherited evil is. See also §§313, 494, 2122, 2910, 3518, 3701.

People who reflect on it can see this on their own. The same thing is evident from the fact that every clan has some unique weakness or strength that distinguishes it from other clans. This unique trait comes from the parents and grandparents, as is recognized.

Likewise with the Jewish nation as it survives today. We can distinguish Jews and tell them apart from all other nations, of course, not only by their particular bent of mind but also by their customs, speech, and appearance.

[5] Nevertheless, few know what inherited evil is. The general opinion is that it means doing what is evil, but it really means intending and therefore planning what is evil. It resides in our very will and therefore in our thoughts. It is the actual impetus that lurks inside, and even when we do what is good it latches on. We can recognize it by the pleasure we feel when something bad happens to another. Its root lies deeply hidden. The inner vessel that receives goodness and truth from heaven—or rather through heaven from the Lord—is itself corrupt and "warped," as they say, so that when something good or true flows in from the Lord, it is shoved aside, corrupted, or smothered. That is why in modern times we are not given a perception of what is good and true but a conscience instead, once we have been reborn; and conscience defines goodness and truth as that which we learn from our parents and teachers.

The results of inherited evil are to love ourselves more than others, to wish evil on others if they do not show us respect, to feel pleasure in revenge, and to love the world more than heaven—along with all the cravings, or evil desires, that ensue.

We are unaware that such things lurk inside us, let alone that they are opposed to heavenly desires. In the other world, though, we are shown clearly how much evil we have appropriated from our inheritance by the way we actually live, and how far we have distanced ourselves from heaven by the resulting negative desires.

[6] The fact that the evil heredity of Jacob's descendants could not be eliminated from them through rebirth because they would not allow it can also be seen from scriptural narratives. They failed in every trial in the wilderness (see [the books of] Moses), and afterward in the land of Canaan, whenever they stopped seeing miracles. Yet these trials were external, not internal, or spiritual. Jacob's descendants could not be tested on a spiritual level because they did not know inner truth, and they did not have inner goodness, as already shown, and we can be tested only in regard to what we know and possess. Times of trial are the true, real means of being reborn.

That is what it means to say they would not allow rebirth.

Concerning their condition and lot in the other world, see §§939, 940, 941, 3481.

The Universal Human
and Correspondence (Continued):
Correspondence with the Senses in General

4318   ONE of the most important kinds of intelligence angels have is to know and perceive that all life comes from the Lord, that heaven as a whole corresponds to his divine humanity, and consequently that all angels, spirits, and people correspond to heaven. It is also to know and perceive *how* they correspond.

These are the fundamentals of the intelligence in which angels excel, compared to us. It enables them to have immeasurable knowledge and perception about the heavens and therefore about the world, since the phenomena of the world and nature are means and results flowing from heavenly phenomena as their origins. The whole material world is a theater representing the Lord's kingdom.

4319   A great deal of experience has shown me that people, spirits, and angels do not think, say, or do anything on their own but only from others. These others do not do so on their own, either, but only from yet others, and so on. Each and every one of us functions under the power of the source of all life, the Lord, despite the wholly convincing appearance that we do so on our own.

This fact has often been demonstrated to spirits who believed and proved to themselves during bodily life that everything existed within themselves. In other words, they believed that they thought, spoke, and acted on their own, from their soul, which seems to be infused with life.

Through vivid experience (of a kind existing in the other life but impossible in the world), it has also been demonstrated that evil people think, will, and act under the inspiration of hell, and good people, under the inspiration of heaven, or rather of the Lord working through heaven. Yet the evil and the goodness both seem to come from the people themselves.

Christians know from doctrine based on the Word that evil comes from the Devil and goodness from the Lord, but few of them believe it. Since they do not believe it, they adopt as their own the evil they think, will, and do. The goodness does not become theirs, because people who consider themselves the source of goodness lay claim to it and attribute it to themselves. They see themselves as earning credit for it. Christians also know from the church's doctrine that we cannot do anything good on our own, that in fact whatever we do on our own, by our own devices, is evil, no matter how good it looks. But few believe this either, even though it is true.

[2] Some bad characters who had hardened themselves in the opinion that life was their own and accordingly that whatever they thought, willed, or did came from themselves were shown that reality is in complete accord with the doctrine [just mentioned above]. They said they now believed it but were told that knowing is not believing. Belief runs deep and cannot exist except in the presence of a desire for what is good and true. So it can exist only in people dedicated to doing good out of charity toward their neighbor. These same spirits, because they were evil, kept insisting that they now believed it, because they had seen it, but the question was investigated through a technique that is common in the other life: angels looked inside them. When they were inspected, the crown of their head seemed to be removed, and their brain looked shaggy and dark. This experiment made plain the inner nature of people whose faith is not true faith but mere knowledge, and reinforced that knowing is not believing. With people who both know and believe, the head looks human and the brain looks well ordered, snow-white, and translucent, because they receive heaven's light. However, some people merely know something and imagine they believe it when they do not, because they lead evil lives. As a result they do not receive heaven's light or the understanding and wisdom contained in that light. When they go near communities of angels—that

is, near heavenly light—the light turns into darkness for them. That is why their brain looked dark.

4320   Life, which comes from the Lord alone, appears as if it were inherent in us all because of the Lord's love or mercy toward the whole human race. He wants to give us each as our own what he possesses as his own and to grant us each eternal happiness. Love gives everything it has to the beloved, as people know, because love manifests itself in the beloved and makes itself present there. What, then, would divine love not do?

The fact that the evil also receive life from the Lord is like the situation with objects in the world, which all receive light from the sun and therefore color, according to their forms. Objects that absorb the light and sully it look black or ugly, but they still take their blackness and ugliness from the sunlight. It is the same with the light that is life from the Lord in the evil. This life is not life but spiritual death, so to speak.

4321   Although these claims seem bewildering and unbelievable to people on earth, they should not be denied, because actual experience provides authority for them. If we were to deny everything whose causes were unknown, we would deny countless facts of nature, since we barely recognize the causes of one thing out of ten thousand. Nature holds so many secrets of such major importance that what we know is almost nothing compared to what we do not know. What, then, of the secrets that exist in a realm transcending nature—in the spiritual world? They include the following:

> There is only one life force, and we all live off it, each of us in a different way from the next. The evil also live off the same life, as do the hells.
>
> The operation of the inflowing life depends on the way it is received.
>
> The Lord organizes heaven in such a way that it resembles a human being, which is why it is called the universal human. As a result, everything in us corresponds to that human. Without the inflow of the universal human into everything in us, we could not survive a moment.
>
> All individuals in the universal human maintain their own constant position in accord with the nature and condition of the truth and goodness they possess. Location there is not location but state, so that those who appear on the left always appears on the left; those on the right, always on the right; those in front, in front; those at the back, at the back; those on a level with the head, the chest, the back, the hips, or the legs, above the head or below the feet, in a straight line or at an angle, at a smaller or greater distance—they

appear there no matter how much or in what direction a spirit [who is seeing them] turns.

The Lord as the sun always appears on the right at a moderate height a little above the level of the right eye. Everything there leads back to the Lord as the sun and center and therefore to the one only source of everything's existence and survival. Since in the Lord's eyes all [spirits] appear in their own constant position according to the state of their goodness and truth, they appear the same way to every individual there, because the Lord's life (and therefore the Lord himself) is in everyone in heaven.

Not to mention countless other secrets.

Who today does not believe that we spring from seed and egg through a physical process? That from the beginning of creation the seed has contained the power to reproduce such forms, first within the egg, then in the uterus, and afterward on its own? Who believes that divinity produces anything anymore? **4322**

The reason people view the matter this way is that no one knows that there is any inflow from heaven, or rather from the Lord through heaven. People do not know it because they do not want to know there is such a thing as heaven. Scholars in their rooms openly debate among themselves the existence of hell and so of heaven, and because they question the existence of heaven, they cannot take as an axiom the idea that the Lord flows in through heaven. This inflow, though, is what produces everything in earth's three kingdoms—especially in the animal kingdom, and particularly in the human race—and maintains it in a form compatible with its purpose.

As a result, people also cannot learn that there is any correspondence between heaven and the human being. Still less can they see that this correspondence is responsible for bringing everything in them into being, down to the smallest detail. Since it is responsible for the emergence of these things, it is responsible for their continued existence. Continued existence is constant emergence; to preserve the connectedness and form of anything is to create it continually.

At the end of the preceding chapters I undertook to show from personal experience in the world of spirits and heaven that everything in us corresponds with heaven. The purpose was to let people see what brings them into existence and keeps them in existence and also to teach that there is a constant inflow into them from that source. **4323**

Later, and again from experience, I will show that we reject the inflow from heaven (that is, from the Lord through heaven) and welcome an inflow from hell. It will also be shown, however, that the Lord always keeps us in correspondence with heaven, so that if we choose to, we can be led from hell to heaven and through heaven to the Lord.

4324 The correspondence of the heart and lungs and of the brain with the universal human has already been dealt with at the ends of earlier chapters. Now the pattern needs to be continued in a treatment of the correspondence with that human's external sense organs: the organs of sight (the eye), of hearing (the ear), and of smell, taste, and touch. I start, though, with sensation in general.

4325 Sensation in general, or general sensation, is distinguished into voluntary and involuntary types. Voluntary sensation is the domain of the cerebrum; involuntary, of the cerebellum. The two types of general sensation are united in the human being, but they are still distinct. The nerve fibers that run from the cerebrum create general voluntary sensation, and those from the cerebellum create general involuntary sensation. Fibers from both sources come together in the two appendages [to the brain] called the medulla oblongata and the spinal cord. Through these appendages they extend into the body, shaping its limbs, viscera, and organs. Most of the fibers going to the parts that envelop the body (muscles and skin) and to the sense organs come from the cerebrum. From them arise our senses and therefore our voluntary activity. In contrast, the fibers going to the parts within that envelope or wrapping, which are called the internal organs, come from the cerebellum. As a result we have no sensation in those organs and no voluntary control over them.

This discussion to some extent defines general voluntary sensation (or voluntary sensation in general) and general involuntary sensation.

There are several other important pieces of information, too: Something general has to exist in order for anything particular to do so. The particular cannot possibly emerge or survive without the general. In fact, the particular survives *within* the general. And the nature of the particular depends on the quality and condition of the general. This holds true for sensation in a human being, and it holds true for motion.

4326 I heard a low thundering that descended from high above the back of my head and kept echoing throughout that whole area. Wondering who the spirits were, I was told that they correlated with general involuntary sensation. I also learned that they were good at picking up on a person's thoughts but did not want to reveal or express them. This is like the cerebellum, which perceives everything the cerebrum does but does not make it public.

Once they stopped acting in a perceptible way on the back of my head and all around it, I was shown how far their action reached. At first it was directed toward my entire face. Then it narrowed down to the left side of my face and eventually to the left ear. This movement symbolized what the functioning of general involuntary sensation was like in primeval times among people on this earth and how it developed.

[2] The influence of the cerebellum mainly suffuses the face, as is evident from the fact that our disposition is etched on our face. Emotions also appear on our face—usually without our choice. These include fear, awe, shame, and different kinds of happiness and sadness, not to mention other emotions that our face broadcasts to the observer. So others know from our face what we are feeling, and how our mood and mind are changing. These signals come from the cerebellum through its nerve fibers when pretense is absent.

I have been shown, then, that in the remotest past, among the earliest people, general sensitivity filled the whole face; that afterward it gradually came to fill only the left side of the face; and that after this it finally moved outside the face, until today hardly any general involuntary sensation remains in the face.

The right side of the face, including the right eye, corresponds to a desire for goodness. The left side corresponds to a desire for truth. The area around the ear corresponds to obedience alone, without desire.

[3] The earliest people, whose era was called the Golden Age, lived in a state of wholeness, of love for the Lord, and of mutual love, like angels. In them, every involuntary impulse of the cerebellum accordingly lay open in the face. In those days people had no idea how to express anything in their face except whatever was flowing from heaven into their involuntary urges and therefore into their will.

The ancients, whose era was called the Silver Age, were in a state of truth and therefore showed charity to their neighbor, so in them the involuntary impulses of the cerebellum were not visible in the right side of the face, only in the left. Their descendants, however, whose era was called the Iron Age, spent their lives not in a desire for truth but in obedience to truth. As a result, involuntary impulses no longer showed anywhere in their face but withdrew to the area around the left ear.

I learned that the fibers of the cerebellum consequently altered their path into the face and that fibers from the cerebrum moved in to take their place. Now the cerebrum's fibers control those of the cerebellum. This is because of the effort to make one's facial expression conform with the will's deliberate choices—the will having its seat in the cerebrum.

People do not see that this is the way matters stand, but it is quite plain to angels from the way heaven flows in and from correspondence.

4327   That is what general involuntary sensation is like today among people with the goodness and truth belonging to faith. Among people immersed in evil and the resulting falsity, no general involuntary sensation reveals itself any longer—not in the face or in speech or in gestures. What reveals itself is voluntary sensation, which mimics involuntary sensation, or "second nature," so called, and which they have developed by practice or habit, starting in childhood.

The nature of this sensation among such people was demonstrated to me by the silent inflow of a chill across my whole face, both the right and left sides, which then condensed around my eyes and reached from my left eye out into my face. This activity symbolized the fact that the fibers from the cerebrum had invaded and would take control of the cerebellar fibers. The result is that artifice, pretense, lies, and deception reign inwardly, while on the outside all looks sincere and virtuous. The concentration toward the left eye and from there back into the face meant that they have an evil purpose and use their intellect to achieve it. The left eye symbolizes the intellect.

[2] The spirits who constitute general involuntary sensation today are mostly of this type. In ancient times they were the most heavenly of all, but now they are the most criminal and come mainly from the Christian world. There are large numbers of them, and they appear under the occiput and along the back, where I have seen and perceived them many times.

After all, the spirits who currently relate to this kind of sensation are those who think deceitful thoughts and plot evil against their neighbor. They don a mask of friendship—close friendship—and put on a pantomime as well. They speak sweetly, as if endowed with an especially rich store of neighborly love, when all the while they are the most hostile foes, not only of the person they are dealing with but also of the human race.

Their thoughts were communicated to me, and I found them wicked and horrendous, full of cruelty and savagery.

4328   I was also shown how matters stand in general with the will and the intellect. The earliest people, who constituted the Lord's heavenly church (discussed in §§1114–1123), had a will containing goodness and an intellect containing truth produced by goodness. These two were unified in them. The ancients, who formed the Lord's spiritual church, had a will that was entirely beyond recall, but their intellect was sound. In it the Lord shaped a new will through regeneration, and through this in turn he formed a new intellect. (See §§863, 875, 895, 927, 928, 1023, 1043, 1044, 1555, 2256.)

[2] The nature of the goodness that existed in the heavenly church was illustrated to me by a pillar coming down from the sky. It was blue, and on the left side was a luminous glow resembling the fiery halo of the sun. These features represented those people's first stage. The blue color represented goodness in their will, and the fiery halo represented their intellect.

Later the blue of the pillar turned into a dark fiery color, which represented their second stage. It showed that their two life forces, that of the will and that of the intellect, still acted in unison, but with less clarity in regard to goodness from the will. Blue symbolizes goodness, and a fiery glow, the truth produced by goodness.

[3] Afterward the pillar turned completely black and was circled by a halo that glowed white in places and projected colors. This symbolized the state of the spiritual church. The black pillar symbolized a will that was utterly depraved and wholly made up of evil. The halo with white parts symbolized an intellect containing a new will from the Lord. In heaven, the intellect is represented by something glowing.

Some spirits came to me at a certain height. It sounded as though there were a lot of them, and from the concepts they were thinking and talking about (which were transmitted to me) I discovered that they did not seem to have any clear, distinct ideas, only the general thinking of a large group. I decided that no distinct perception could be gained from them, only a vague, general idea and therefore an obscure one. That is what I then considered to be the nature of any general idea. Their thinking *was* general, or comprehensive, as I could clearly tell from the ideas flowing from them into my own thoughts.

[2] However, they were given an intermediary through whom they could talk with me, because this kind of generalization could not be put into words except through other spirits. When I talked with them through the intermediary, I voiced my opinion: that generalities cannot produce a clear idea on any subject, only one that is so vague as to be almost nonexistent. Over the next quarter hour, though, they showed me that they had a well-defined idea of general concepts and of many components within the general concepts. This they demonstrated mainly by carefully and

4329

accurately observing all the variations and changes in my thoughts and feelings in such detail that no spirits could ever manage better.

I was able to conclude that there are two very different kinds of general thought. One kind is obscure, and it is held by people who know little and are therefore in the dark about everything. The other kind is clear, and it is held by people who have learned about truth and goodness and fitted all they have learned into its place in the pattern and arrangement of the general whole. Truth and goodness are organized in such a way in them that from the whole they can see everything distinctly.

[3] These are the inhabitants of the other world who constitute general voluntary sensation. By learning about goodness and truth, they have acquired the ability to view subjects from a general standpoint and fully ponder a range of ideas at once, instantly discerning their truth or falsity. It does seem as though they see matters dimly, because they view the particulars involved from a general standpoint, but since such matters are arranged within the general whole in a well-defined way, the spirits still see them clearly. This general voluntary sensation is available only to the wise.

This characteristic of theirs is also something I found out about for myself. They looked at one of my deductions from every angle and on this basis were able to draw conclusions about the inner depths of my thoughts and feelings. So skillful were they at drawing their conclusions that I started to shrink from engaging in further thought; they were uncovering things in me that I did not know were there but could not help acknowledging in light of their conclusions. As a result I sensed inside myself a reluctance to talk with them. As soon as they noticed the reluctance, there appeared a sort of hairy object accompanied by something that spoke indistinctly. I was told that this symbolized a general bodily capacity for sensation that corresponded to these spirits.

The next day I talked with them again and discovered anew that they had a generalized perception that was not vague but clear. I also learned that as a general whole and its circumstances varied, so did the particulars and their circumstances, since the particulars recapitulated the whole in their pattern and series.

[4] I was told that forms of general voluntary sensation still more perfect exist in a deeper realm of heaven and that when angels grasp a general or universal thought, they also grasp the details, which the Lord arranges within the universal idea in a clear and distinct way. A general whole and a universal whole are nothing unless they contain particulars and details,

of which they consist and which allow them to be called comprehensive. The more individual parts they contain, the more general or universal they are. Plainly, then, the Lord's overall providence is absolutely nothing without the minute concerns it contains and comprises. It is stupid to assert the existence of a universal capacity in the Divine and then deprive it of its specific instances.

The three heavens together constitute the universal human, and all the limbs, viscera, and organs of the body correspond to it according to their functions and purposes, as noted above [§4321]. As a consequence, it is not only the outward, visible aspects that correspond to the universal human but also the inward, invisible aspects; it is the elements of the outer self and of the inner self.

4330

The communities of spirits and angels that elements of the outer self correspond to are drawn mostly from this planet. Those to which elements of the inner self correspond come mainly from elsewhere. All these heavenly communities form a unit, just as the outer and inner self do in a person who has been reborn.

However, not many people coming into the other world from this planet today have an outer self that forms a unit with their inner self. Most people here focus on their senses. In fact, few believe there is anything more to us than our outer self. They think that when our outer self withdraws, as it does when we die, hardly anything living remains. Still less do they believe that an inner dimension lives within the outer one, and that when the outer dimension withdraws, the inner one is particularly alive.

[2] Personal experience showed me how these people oppose the inner self. There was a multitude of spirits from our planet who had been like this when they lived in the world. Into their field of vision came some spirits relating to a person's inner sensory self. Immediately the first set of spirits started to harass them, almost like irrational people assaulting the rational. They talked and argued endlessly, relying on sensory illusions, the resulting misconceptions, and pure guesswork, crediting nothing but what they could prove by their physical senses, and jeering at the inner self. [3] The spirits relating to the inner sensory self, completely unmoved by these antics, marveled at the others' insanity and even stupidity.

Surprisingly, when the outer sensory spirits went near the inner sensory spirits, almost entering the environment of the inner spirits' thinking, their breathing became labored. (Spirits and angels breathe, just as people do, but their breathing is relatively internal; §§3884, 3885 and following sections, 3893.) Nearly suffocating, they left. Because they could breathe more easily the farther they went from the inner sensory spirits, calm and quiet increased among them as well. The closer they approached, the less calm and quiet they had. [4] The reason was that when outer sensory spirits are wrapped up in their illusions, delusions, and theories and therefore in falsity, they are at peace. When this thinking is ripped from them—as it is when the inner self brings the light of truth to bear on them—they lose their tranquillity. Auras consisting of thought and feeling exist in the other world, where they are communicated back and forth, depending on a spirit's presence or approach (§§1048, 1053, 1504–1512, 1695, 2401, 2489).

The conflict lasted several hours and showed how people on this planet today oppose the inner self. Empirical evidence is almost all they care about.

4331   More on the universal human and correspondence appears at the end of the next chapter, where correspondence with specific senses is discussed [§§4403–4421].

Genesis 33

[Matthew 24:36–41]

A T the head of the previous chapter I explained the Lord's predictions in Matthew 24:32, 33, 34, 35 concerning his Coming, which means the last days of the previous church and the first stage of a new one, as shown there [§§4229–4231] and in various earlier sections [§§728, 2405, 2441, 3353, 4060]. The final days (or end) of the previous church and the first stage (or beginning) of a new one have already been discussed; see the head of Genesis 31, §§4056–4060, and Genesis 32, §§4229–4231. Now I need to explain the words that follow in verses 36–41 of the same chapter in that Gospel:

4332

> But of that day and hour no one knows (not even the angels of the heavens) except my Father alone. As the days of Noah were, though, so will be the Coming of the Son of Humankind. For as they were in the days before the Flood—eating and drinking, marrying and giving in marriage, up to the day on which Noah entered into the ark, and did not know till the Flood came and carried them all away—so also will be the Coming of the Son of Humankind. Two will then be in the field; one will be taken and one left. Two grinding in the mill; one will be taken and one left. (Matthew 24:36, 37, 38, 39, 40, 41)

What these words symbolize on an inner level will become clear from the explanation that follows, showing that they depict future conditions, when the old church is rejected and a new one is established. The rejection of the old church and the establishment of a new one is meant by the close of the age and the Son of Humankind's Coming, and by the Last Judgment generally, and this has been demonstrated many times before. So has the idea that this kind of last judgment has happened several times on our globe. The *first* was when the Lord's heavenly church— the earliest church—perished among the people who lived just before the Flood. This church died in a deluge of evil and falsity, which is what a flood means in an inner sense. [2] The *second* was when the spiritual church that came after the Flood ended of its own accord. This church

4333

was called the ancient church and pervaded much of the Near East. The *third* was when the representation of a church among Jacob's descendants was destroyed. This occurred when the Ten Tribes were taken into permanent captivity and scattered among the nations, and finally when Jerusalem was destroyed and the people of Judah were also dispersed.

Since an era was brought to a close after the Lord came on earth, much of what he said in the Gospels about the close of that age can also be applied to the Jewish nation. Many people today so apply it. However, the main, specific message there has to do with the culmination now at hand, which is the end of the Christian church (described also by John in the Book of Revelation). This will be the *fourth* of the last judgments taking place on our earth.

The implications of the words contained in verses 36–41, quoted above, will be evident from the inner meaning of those words, which is as follows:

4334   *But of that day and hour no one knows* means that no one on earth or in heaven will be able to see what the state of goodness and truth in the church will then be. The day and hour do not mean a day and hour, or time, but a state of goodness and truth. For periods of time in the Word symbolizing states, see §§2625, 2788, 2837, 3254, 3356. A day symbolizes a state (§§23, 487, 488, 493, 893, 2788, 3462, 3785), so an hour does too, but it symbolizes a particular one. A state of goodness and truth is meant because the topic of discussion is the church, and goodness and truth constitute the church.

[2] *(Not even the angels of the heavens) except my Father alone* means that heaven does not know the specific state of goodness and truth in the church; only the Lord does. He alone also knows when that state in the church will come. The Father means the Lord himself (see §§15, 1729, 2004, 2005, 3690). Divine goodness in the Lord is called the Father, and divine truth growing out of divine goodness is called the Son (§§2803, 3703, 3704, 3736). People who believe that the Father is one person and the Son another and distinguish them do not understand the Scriptures.

[3] *But as they were in the days before the Flood* symbolizes a state in which people in the church are being spiritually devastated, which resembles the state of devastation in the first or earliest church. The close of the age or last judgment for the earliest church is portrayed in the Word as a flood—a flood symbolizing a deluge of evil and falsity and therefore the close of that era; see §§310, 660, 662, 705, 739, 790, 805, 1120. For the idea that days mean states, see above.

[4] *Eating and drinking, marrying and giving in marriage* symbolizes their state when they adopt evil and falsity and then internalize them. Eating means adopting goodness, and drinking means adopting truth—see §§3168, 3513 at the end, 3596—so in a negative sense they mean adopting evil and falsity. Marrying means uniting with evil, and giving in marriage means the same in regard to falsity. This can be seen from the discussion and explanation of marriage and marriage love in §§686, 2173, 2618, 2728, 2729, 2737, 2738, 2739, 2803, 3132, 3155, showing that in an inner sense it is a union of goodness and truth. In the negative sense used here it is a union of evil and falsity.

Everything the Lord said was divine, so its inner meaning is not the same as its literal meaning. When he speaks of eating and drinking in the Holy Supper, for instance, in its spiritual sense it does not mean eating and drinking but adopting the goodness that comes from his divine love (§§2165, 2177, 2187, 2343, 3464, 3478, 3735, 4211, 4217). For another instance, when he associates marriage with the church and his kingdom, it means a union between love's goodness and faith's truth. Because of this union, the Lord's kingdom is called a heavenly marriage in the Word.

[5] *Up to the day on which Noah entered into the ark* symbolizes the end of the previous church and the beginning of a new one. Noah symbolizes the ancient church in general, which replaced the earliest church after the Flood (§773 and other places). The ark symbolizes the church itself (§639). A day, which is mentioned several times in these verses, symbolizes a state, as shown just above.

[6] *And did not know till the Flood came and carried them all away* means that people in the church will not then know that they have been deluged with evil and falsity. Because of the evil and falsity they succumb to, they will not be able to identify the goodness that belongs to love for the Lord and to charity for one's neighbor. They will not know what the truth that belongs to faith is, or that it develops out of love and charity, or that it exists only in people who live lives of love and charity. They will also be unaware that what saves or damns us is what we have inside, not what we are like outside separated from what we have inside.

[7] *So will be the Coming of the Son of Humankind* means that divine truth will not be welcome. The Son of Humankind's Coming is divine truth that will then be revealed, as noted before at verses 27 and 30 [§§3900, 4060], in §§2803, 2813, 3704, and in §§3004, 3005, 3006, 3008, 3009.

[8] *Two will then be in the field; one will be taken and one left* symbolizes people in the church devoted to goodness and people in the church devoted to evil. Those devoted to goodness will be saved, and those devoted to evil will be damned. A field means the church in regard to goodness; see §§2971, 3196, 3310, 3317, 3766.

[9] *Two grinding in the mill; one will be taken and one left* means that people in the church who focus on truth (or desire truth) for good reasons will be saved, while people in the church who focus on truth (or desire truth) for evil reasons will be damned. This symbolism of grinding and a mill in the Word will become clear from the discussion that follows directly.

This evidence now shows that the words above depict future conditions for goodness and truth in the church when the church is rejected and a new church is adopted.

4335   In the Word, *millers* mean people in the church who focus on truth because they want what is good. In a negative sense they mean people in the church who focus on truth because they want what is evil. These meanings can be seen from the following passages. In Isaiah:

> Go down and sit in the dirt, virgin daughter of Babylon. Sit on the earth. There is no throne, daughter of the Chaldeans. *Take a mill and grind meal;* uncover your hair; bare your foot; uncover your thigh; cross rivers. (Isaiah 47:1, 2)

The daughter of Babylon stands for people who on the outside seem devout and good but inside are profane and evil (§§1182, 1326). The daughter of the Chaldeans stands for people who on the outside seem devout and filled with truth but inside are profane and filled with falsity (§§1368, 1816). Taking a mill and grinding meal stands for hatching doctrine out of truth by twisting it. Meal consists of wheat or barley, so it symbolizes truth resulting from goodness, but in an opposite sense it symbolizes truth that people twist in order to lead others astray. In Jeremiah:

> I will destroy from them the voice of joy and the voice of gladness, the voice of the bridegroom and the voice of the bride, *the voice of millstones* and the light of a lamp. And this whole land will become a wasteland and a ruin. (Jeremiah 25:10, 11)

[2] And in John:

> No artisan of any art will be found in Babylon any longer; *no voice of a millstone will be heard in it any longer,* and the light of a lamp will not

shine in it any longer, and the voice of bridegroom and bride will not be heard in it any longer. (Revelation 18:21, 22, 23)

"The voice of a millstone will not be heard in Babylon any longer" means that truth will not be heard; "the light of a lamp will not shine" means that no understanding of truth will shine either. In Lamentations:

> They have raped women in Zion; young women in the cities of Judah. Chieftains have been hung by their hands; the presence of the old has not been honored. *Young people have been taken away to grind,* and youths fall down on the wood. (Lamentations 5:11, 12, 13, 14)

The grinding for which the young people were taken stands for the fabrication of falsity, with a touch of truth added to make it convincing. [3] In Moses:

> Every firstborn in the land of Egypt will die, from Pharaoh's firstborn sitting on his throne *to the slave woman's firstborn who is behind the millstones.* (Exodus 11:5)

The firstborn of Egypt stand for religious truth detached from neighborly kindness. This truth turns into falsity (§3325). The slave woman's firstborn who is behind the millstones stands for a desire for this kind of truth, which is the source of the falsity. That is what this piece of the story represented. [4] In the same author:

> No one shall take *millstones* and *grindstone* as collateral, because they are the soul of the one who pawns them. (Deuteronomy 24:6)

This law was laid down because millstones symbolized doctrines, and a grindstone symbolized doctrinal truth. These two things are being called the soul of the one who pawns them. Plainly the law would not have been given and the stones would not have been described as the borrower's soul if millstones and a grindstone were not spiritually symbolic.

[5] Grinding takes its symbolism from representations occurring in the world of spirits, as I have been shown. I saw some people there who seemed to be grinding and was told that they symbolize people who collect truth in large quantities without any useful purpose, just for their own pleasure. When people acquire truth in this way, it fails to touch them with its goodness. It looks true on the outside, but since it lacks any inner content, it is a mirage. If its inner content is evil, it is used to justify evil, and the connection with evil turns it into falsity.

Genesis 33

1. And Jacob raised his eyes and looked, and here, Esau came, and with him four hundred men. And he divided the children among Leah and Rachel and the two slave women.
2. And he put the slaves and their children first, and Leah and her children after them, and Rachel and Joseph after them.
3. And he himself crossed before them and bowed down to the earth seven times until he brought himself near, right to his brother.
4. And Esau ran to meet him and hugged him and fell on his neck and kissed him, and they cried.
5. And he raised his eyes and saw the women and the children and said, "Who are these that you have?" And he said, "The children with whom God has favored your servant."
6. And the slaves drew near, they and their children, and bowed down.
7. And Leah and her children also drew near and bowed down. And afterward Joseph and Rachel drew near and bowed down.
8. And he said, "What is this whole camp of yours that I have come across?" And he said, "To find favor in the eyes of my lord."
9. And Esau said, "I have plenty, my brother; let what is yours be yours."
10. And Jacob said, "Please, no; please, if I have found favor in your eyes, may you also accept my gift from my hand, because I have seen your face, like seeing the face of God, and you have welcomed me.
11. Please accept my blessing that I have brought you, because God has favored me, and because I have everything," and he urged him, and [Esau] accepted.
12. And [Esau] said, "Let's set off and go, and I will go at your side."
13. And [Jacob] said to him, "My lord knows that there are tender children and unweaned flocks and herds with me; and let anyone drive them for one day and all the flocks will die.
14. Please let my lord cross before his servant, and I will advance slowly at the pace of the work that is before me, and at the pace of the children, till I come to my lord, to Seir."
15. And Esau said, "Please let me station with you some of the people who are with me," and he said, "Why should this be? Let me find favor in the eyes of my lord!"

16. And Esau returned that day to his way to Seir.

17. And Jacob traveled to Succoth and built himself a house, and he made huts for what he had gained; therefore he called the name of the place Succoth.

18. And Jacob came to Salem (the city of Shechem, which is in the land of Canaan) as he came from Paddan-aram; and he camped before the face of the city.

19. And he bought the portion of the field where he had spread his tent, from the hand of the children of Hamor, Shechem's father, for a hundred kesitahs.

20. And he established an altar there and called it El-Elohe-Israel.

Summary

THE theme of the inner meaning is the union of divine goodness on the earthly plane (Esau) with goodness that comes of truth (Jacob). The chapter talks about the submissiveness of the latter, and the way it is instilled into divine goodness on the earthly plane. The process by which it happens is delineated. The final subject is the acquisition of inner truth. **4336**

Inner Meaning

WHERE the previous chapters spoke of Jacob, the inner meaning dealt with the acquisition of truth on the earthly plane. Truth is acquired in order that it can unite with goodness, because that is the purpose of all truth. Jacob in an inner sense means such truth, and Esau means the goodness with which truth must unite. **4337**

Before they unite, truth appears to take first place, but after their union, goodness really does take first place; see §§3539, 3548, 3556, 3563, 3570, 3576, 3603, 3701, 3995. That is also what is meant by Isaac's prophetic saying to Esau: "By your sword you will live, and your brother you will serve; and it will happen when you gain the dominance that you will tear his yoke off your neck" (Genesis 27:40). The topic of discussion is now that state, which is why Jacob calls Esau his lord, and himself, Esau's servant, in verses 5, 8, 13, 14 of the current chapter.

[2] It needs to be known that Jacob now represents goodness based on truth, but viewed in itself, truth-based goodness is only truth. As long as truth exists in our memory alone, it is called truth. When it exists in our will and in our actions, it is called truth-based goodness. Putting truth into practice is exactly this. Whatever comes from the will is called good, because the vital essence of the will is love and therefore desire, and everything that results from love and its desire is called good.

Truth cannot unite with the goodness that flows through our inner self and is divine in origin (represented here by Esau) until the truth is present in our will and our actions—that is, until it is truth-based goodness. The goodness that flows in through our inner self and is divine in origin flows into our will, where it meets up with truth-based goodness, which is instilled through our outer self.

4338   Genesis 33:1, 2, 3. *And Jacob raised his eyes and looked, and here, Esau came, and with him four hundred men. And he divided the children among Leah and Rachel and the two slave women. And he put the slaves and their children first, and Leah and her children after them, and Rachel and Joseph after them. And he himself crossed before them and bowed down to the earth seven times until he brought himself near, right to his brother.*

Jacob raised his eyes and looked symbolizes perception and focus, on the part of truth-based goodness, which is *Jacob. And here, Esau came* means that divine goodness in its earthly form came. *And with him four hundred men* symbolizes a state. *And he divided the children among Leah* means arranging outer truth within the scope of a desire for such truth. *And Rachel* means arranging inner truth within the scope of a desire for such truth. *And the two slave women* means within the scope of a desire for that which serves both. *And he put the slaves and their children first, and Leah and her children after them, and Rachel and Joseph after them* symbolizes the hierarchy, starting with the general attributes that contain the rest. *And he himself crossed before them* symbolizes what is universal, and therefore everything. *And bowed down to the earth seven times* means that it all submitted. *Until he brought himself near, right to his brother* symbolizes union on the part of truth-based goodness (Jacob).

4339   *Jacob raised his eyes and looked* symbolizes perception and focus, on the part of truth-based goodness, which is *Jacob.* This can be seen from the symbolism of *raising the eyes and looking* as perceiving and focusing. Lifting the eyes is an outward gesture that corresponds to the inward act of raising the mind. So it corresponds to perception, and looking corresponds to a focus.

To see that *Jacob* now represents goodness based on truth, look just above at §4337.

Esau came means that divine goodness in its earthly form came. This is established by the representation of *Esau* as divine goodness on the earthly plane, discussed in §3576.

And with him four hundred men symbolizes a state—a state of union between divine goodness and truth on the earthly plane, since that union is the current subject. In the Word, *four hundred* symbolizes a state of trial and however long it lasts (§§1847, 2959, 2966), and since times of trial are always the means for uniting goodness with truth, a state of union is what is meant. On the point that trials bring goodness and truth together, see §§2272, 3318. Trials occur when goodness starts to take the leading role (§§4248, 4249). The Lord's divine nature became one with his human nature through his trials (§1737).

[2] The actual goodness to be united with truth is not tested, but truth *is* tested. Truth is tested not by goodness but by falsity and evil. It is also tested by illusions and errors (which cling to truth on the earthly plane) and by our attachment to them. When goodness flows into us— taking an inner route, through our inner, rational self—the notions our earthly self has formed from sensory illusions and the deceptions they lead to cannot stand its approach. They are out of harmony with it, which creates anxiety in our earthly self, and a crisis. That is what the inner meaning of this chapter depicts by the fear and distress and consequently the submissive, humble state that Jacob came into when Esau arrived with four hundred men. Goodness and truth never form a bond by any other means.

These considerations show that *four hundred men* symbolize a state of trial. *Four hundred* symbolizes the actual state, but the *men* symbolize truth on the rational level that is united with goodness when goodness flows into the earthly level. For the idea that men symbolize traits of the intellect and reason, see §§265, 749, 1007, 3134.

[3] However, these concepts are ones that land in the dark in the human mind, because while we are living in our body we cannot see the difference between the rational and earthly dimensions. If we have not been reborn we cannot tell the difference at all, but even if we have, we see very little of it, because we do not reflect on it or even care about it. Long ago, the only thing people in the church had to know about if they wanted intelligence was a human being's inner depths, but such knowledge has been almost entirely obliterated.

Nonetheless, the concepts can be seen to some extent from previous explanations of the rational mind and its inflow into the earthly plane: The earthly plane is regenerated by means of the rational plane (§§3286, 3288), and the rational plane accepts truth before the earthly plane does (§§3368, 3671). This truth, which flows from the rational to the earthly plane in company with goodness, is what the four hundred men accompanying Esau symbolize on an inner level.

4342 *And he divided the children among Leah* means arranging outer truth within the scope of a desire for such truth. This can be seen from the symbolism of *dividing among* as arranging, from that of *children* or sons as truth (discussed in §§489, 491, 533, 1147, 2623, 3373), and from the representation of *Leah* as a desire for outer truth (discussed in §§3793, 3819). These children or sons accordingly mean truth associated with a shallow desire and therefore outer truth.

The truth called sensory truth is said to be external. It is the truth that comes to us directly from the world through our physical senses. The inner truth symbolized by Rachel's children lies higher on the earthly level, more directly under the gaze of the rational level. Illusion and error do not cling to it as much as they do to sensory truth, because the further inward truth goes, the more it is purified of worldly and earthly taint.

4343 *And Rachel* means arranging inner truth within the scope of a desire for such truth. This is established by the representation of *Rachel* as a desire for inner truth (discussed in §§3758, 3782, 3793, 3819). Her children, or sons, mean inner truth in this case. See the remarks on inner truth just above at §4342.

4344 *And the two slave women* means within the scope of a desire for that which serves both, as the following shows: *Slave women* symbolize desires for secular and religious knowledge (as discussed in §§1895, 2567, 3835, 3849). They also symbolize a middle ground that serves to unite the outer and inner self (as discussed in §§3913, 3917). And Zilpah and Bilhah, the slaves here, represent shallow desires that serve as means (as discussed in §§3849, 3931).

4345 *And he put the slaves and their children first, and Leah and her children after them, and Rachel and Joseph after them* symbolizes the hierarchy, starting with the more general attributes that contain the rest. This can be seen from the discussion just above concerning the symbolism of the slaves, Leah, Rachel, and their children: The slaves mean desires for secular and religious knowledge, Leah means a desire for outer truth, and

Rachel means a desire for inner truth. A desire for secular and religious knowledge is the most superficial because such knowledge is what truth grows out of and consists in. A desire for outer truth comes next and is deeper, and a desire for inner truth is still deeper. The shallower things are, the more general they are; the deeper they are, the less general. Deeper levels are said to be particular and minutely detailed, by comparison.

[2] What is general is called general because it is made up of particulars and therefore contains particulars. Something general without anything particular is not general, and it is because of the particular that it can be called general. It is like a whole and its parts. The whole cannot be called a whole unless there are parts, because the whole is made up of the parts.

There is nothing in the universe that does not emerge and endure from something other than itself. What emerges and endures from something else is referred to as general, and what it consists of and is sustained by is referred to as particular. By nature, what is external consists of what is internal, so external qualities are general in relation to internal ones. The case with a human being's capacities is that the more external they are the more general they are, because outward abilities consist of inward ones, which consist of the inmost ones, in sequence.

[3] The body itself with all that belongs to it—what are called the physical senses, for instance, and actions—is very general, by comparison. The earthly mind with all that belongs to it is less general because it is more inward, and it is described as being relatively specific. The rational mind with all that belongs to it is still more inward and is minutely detailed, by comparison.

All of this lies open to plain and vivid sight when we put off our body and become a spirit. It is then obvious to us that our physical parts were simply the overall compound of what exists in our spirit, and that the physical parts had their origin and continued existence from the things of our spirit. So we perceive that what belonged to our spirit was relatively detailed. When we as that same spirit become an angel—in other words, when we are lifted into heaven—we see and feel in clear detail what we saw and felt in a vague, general way before. There are then countless individual elements that we previously saw and felt as a single whole.

[4] The same thing can also be seen when we are living as a person in the world. What we see and feel in early childhood is very general. What

we see and feel in youth and early adulthood are the particulars that make up those generalities. And what we see and feel as a full adult are the minute details that make up the particulars. As we grow up, we insert particulars into the general ideas we had as a child, and then we insert fine detail into the particulars, because we gradually advance inward, filling in the general with the particular, and the particular with the detailed.

From this discussion it can now be seen what is meant by the hierarchy starting with the general attributes that contain the rest, as symbolized by Jacob's putting the slaves and their children first, Leah and her children after them, and Rachel and her child after them.

[5] When we are being reborn, or to put it another way, when truth is uniting with goodness in us, the same process happens in us as is depicted here. Generalized desires and the truth that goes with them (the slaves and their children) are instilled into goodness first, then those that are less general, or relatively specific (Leah and her children), and finally the ones that are still less general, or are finely detailed by comparison (Rachel and Joseph). During rebirth, you see, we pass through something analogous to the stages of life—early childhood first, then youth and early adulthood, and finally full adulthood.

4346   *And he himself crossed before them* symbolizes what is universal, and therefore everything. This can be seen from the representation of Jacob *(he)* as goodness that comes of truth, or truth in our will and in our actions (discussed in §4337). Goodness that grows out of truth is the most universal of all. The general, particular, and minutely detailed (discussed just above) all belong to it because it contains them.

4347   *And bowed down to the earth seven times* means that it all submitted. This is established by the symbolism of *bowing down to the earth* as a feeling of humility (discussed in §2153) and therefore as submissiveness. *Seven times* symbolizes the highest degree of submissiveness. The fact that it was Jacob who bowed down means that it all submitted, because Jacob represents what is the most universal of all, as noted just above at §4346.

[2] As for humility and submissiveness, few know why we have to display them toward the Lord when we are worshiping, so not many know what they accomplish. People who do not know about deeper dimensions cannot help thinking that the Divine wishes for our humility and submission in the same way a person who craves prestige would. They believe the Divine seeks glory from our worship and is moved by the praise we offer. The reality is just the opposite, though. The Divine has no desire

for glory. What luster can we add, after all? It is not for his own sake but for ours that he wants us to be humble and submit. When we are committed to humility, we become averse to the evil and falsity in ourselves (§§2327, 2423, 3994), so we get rid of them. Once they are gone, the Divine can flow in with goodness and truth.

We can all see this in ourselves. If we are vain, we love ourselves; and not only do we place ourselves ahead of others, we care nothing for the Divine. Consequently we reject any inflow of goodness and any union of goodness with truth. This is the real reason for us to be humble before the Divine.

[3] Plainly, then, goodness cannot bond with truth, and we cannot be reborn, unless we humble ourselves and surrender.

Humility and submissiveness are attributes of truth, because truth enters by way of our outer self, while goodness enters by way of our inner self. What flows in through the outer self brings with it illusion and therefore falsity, along with a desire for falsity. What flows in through the inner self does not do so, because divine qualities are what enter by this route and seek truth out in order to unite with it.

This discussion now shows what is meant by the fact that it all submitted, as symbolized by Jacob's bowing down to the earth seven times until he brought himself near, right to his brother.

Until he brought himself near, right to his brother symbolizes union on the part of truth-based goodness (Jacob), as the following indicates: *Bringing himself near* means doing so in order to unite. Esau, the *brother,* represents divine goodness on the earthly level, as mentioned above at §4337. And Jacob represents goodness that comes of truth, as also mentioned above at §4337.

Section 4347 just above explains how these matters stand.

Genesis 33:4. *And Esau ran to meet him and hugged him and fell on his neck and kissed him, and they cried.*

Esau ran to meet him symbolizes an inflow of divine goodness on the earthly level. *And hugged him* symbolizes a first bond of love. *And fell on his neck* symbolizes a second bond uniting everything in that universal entity. *And kissed him* symbolizes a deeper bond produced by love. *And they cried* symbolizes the outcome.

Esau ran to meet him symbolizes an inflow of divine goodness on the earthly level. This can be seen from the symbolism of *running to meet* as an inflow, and from the representation of *Esau* as divine goodness on the earthly level (noted in §§4337, 4340). *Running to meet* means an inflow, because divine goodness flows in through the inner self and meets up with truth (which enters through the outer self) in order to unite with it. This is also evident from the remaining phrases, because the text proceeds to say that he hugged him, fell on his neck, and kissed him, which symbolizes union through love, as you will see.

4351 *And hugged him* symbolizes a first bond of love. This can be seen from the symbolism of *hugging* as affection (discussed in §3807). Since affection is an aspect of love, and love seeks union, the phrase symbolizes a bond of love. It is a first bond of love because the text goes on to say that he fell on his neck and kissed him—actions that symbolize deeper, closer types of union resulting from love.

It is clear without further explanation that hugging is the result of a loving closeness and consequently that it means such closeness in an inner sense. The contents of the inner meaning are presented through outward actions and objects in the Word.

4352 *And fell on his neck* symbolizes a second bond uniting everything in that universal entity. This can be seen from the symbolism of *falling on his neck* as a tighter bond, since it is a closer embrace. On an inner level, moreover, a *neck* symbolizes inflow and communication between inner and outer planes, and therefore connection (see §§3542, 3603). The bond is one that unites everything or unites *with* everything in that universal entity because Jacob (to whom *his* refers) means what is the most universal of all in regard to truth (§4346).

[2] The union of goodness with truth on the earthly level is being depicted here, and these are the facts of the matter: Goodness flows through the inner self into the outer self, where it unites with truth that is instilled through the outer self. The goodness that flows in through the inner self is a loving goodness, because there is no such thing as spiritual and heavenly goodness that is not loving. Love is the source of the goodness in us and is the reason it is called good. Love itself, which inhabits and accompanies goodness, is what creates a bond. If love did not inhabit and accompany it, there could never be any union, because love is nothing but spiritual togetherness, being the means of that togetherness.

The love comes exclusively from the Lord, because he is the spring and source of all heavenly and spiritual love and therefore of all the resulting goodness.

This love comes in two kinds: heavenly and spiritual. Heavenly love is love for the Lord, and spiritual love is love for one's neighbor, which is called charity. These two kinds of love are the origin of all heavenly and spiritual goodness, and they unite with the truth described as the truths of the faith. Religious truth viewed without love is merely a lifeless string of words, but it receives life through love and therefore through union with a loving goodness.

Clearly, then, faith can exist only in people with a loving goodness; and faith's quality depends on love.

[3] Since faith never exists except in people who possess a loving goodness, neither does confidence or trust. In anyone who lacks love and charity, the trust or confidence that people associate with faith is a sham. Either that or it is the kind that even devilish spirits can have in a state of fear or anguish or in a state of self-serving conviction prompted by self-love and materialism.

People today have considered faith without acts of neighborly kindness to be a saving faith, even though from their distant perspective they are still able to tell that the truths of the faith do not have the power to save, because they exist as well among those who are evil. As a consequence, they acknowledge the existence of confidence and trust and call *this* faith, not knowing what it is. They do not realize that that too can exist even in the evil. There is no spiritual confidence except that which flows in through the goodness belonging to love and charity. It flows in not when we are suffering fear and anguish, or when self-love and materialism inspire us to talk ourselves into believing, but when we are in a state of freedom. Such confidence exists only in people in whom goodness has united with truth and taken root as a result of their whole previous course of life, rather than in times of sickness, misfortune, mortal danger, or impending death. If the assurance or trust that shows up under pressure saved us, all mortals would be saved. To this kind of trust any of us could easily be reduced. The Lord, who wants to save us all, would not fail to supply it to anyone. However, the confidence and trust that is called faith—its identity and nature and who possesses it—needs to be discussed elsewhere [§§9239–9245], the Lord in his divine mercy willing.

And kissed him symbolizes a deeper bond produced by love. This can be seen from the symbolism of *kissing* as union resulting from love (discussed in §§3573, 3574, 4215). Here it symbolizes a deeper bond.

This verse deals generally with the union between divine goodness on the earthly plane (Esau) and the truth there (Jacob), but the following verses deal with it more specifically.

4353

As for the union itself, it is what constitutes human rebirth. We are regenerated by having the truth we know connected to goodness, or the components of faith joined with those of neighborly love. The whole of the process is depicted here and in what follows.

Of course the passage is about the Lord and the way he was making his earthly level divine, and therefore about the way he was uniting divine goodness to truth on the earthly plane. But since human rebirth is an image of the Lord's glorification (§§3138, 3212, 3296, 3490), regeneration is also a focus of the inner meaning. Rebirth is accessible to human thought but the Lord's glorification is not very accessible, so let me use the former to shed light on the latter.

[2] The information already laid open shows that the connecting of goodness with truth through which we are reborn moves constantly inward; truth unites with goodness on deeper and deeper levels. The purpose of regeneration is the union of the inner self with the outer, of the spiritual through the rational with the earthly. Unless the two levels join together, there is no rebirth; and the union cannot take place until goodness unites with truth on the earthly level. The earthly dimension needs to be a platform, and the contents of that dimension need to correspond. That is why the connection between goodness and truth grows progressively deeper as our earthly part is being reborn. The spiritual level unites first with the deepest aspects of the earthly level and then through these with the more superficial ones.

What is more, our inner part cannot unite with our outer part unless the truth known to our outer part becomes truth-based goodness, or truth in our will and in our actions (§4337). That is when our inner and our outer part are first capable of banding together. The Lord acts on us through our inner self and specifically through the goodness there. Goodness in our inner self can unite with goodness in our outer self, but goodness cannot unite directly with truth. [3] From this it is evident that the truth we know has to become truth in our will and in our actions, or truth-based goodness, before any bond between our rational and earthly planes, or between our inner and outer selves, can come into existence.

How does truth turn into truth-based goodness? Anyone who pays attention can see. All divine truth concerns two commandments: to love God above all, and to love our neighbor as ourselves [Matthew 22:36–40; Mark 12:29–31]. These commandments are the source, the aim, and the focus of truth, directly or indirectly. So when we put truth into action, it is gradually incorporated into its own first origin and ultimate goal, which is charity for one's neighbor and love for the Lord. As a result it becomes goodness, which is called truth-based goodness. When that happens, it can be united with or integrated into the inner self, and the union gradually grows deeper as more and more inward truth is implanted in that goodness.

The act comes first; our will to do it comes afterward. What we do at the urging of our intellect we eventually do with our will and finally take on as a habit. At that point it is infused into our inner, rational self. Once it has been infused we no longer do what is good from truth but from goodness, because we start to feel a certain bliss and to sense something of heaven in it. This feeling remains with us after death, and through it the Lord lifts us into heaven.

And they cried symbolizes the outcome. This can be seen from the symbolism of *crying* as the outcome of grief and the outcome of joy (discussed in §3801). Here it is an outcome of joy over the union of goodness and truth through love.

4354

Genesis 33:5, 6, 7. And he raised his eyes and saw the women and the children and said, "Who are these that you have?" And he said, "The children with whom God has favored your servant." And the slaves drew near, they and their children, and bowed down. And Leah and her children also drew near and bowed down. And afterward Joseph and Rachel drew near and bowed down.

4355

He raised his eyes symbolizes a perception. *And saw the women and the children* means of different desires for truth and of the truth that goes with those desires. *And said, "Who are these that you have?"* symbolizes recognition. *And he said, "The children with whom God has favored your servant,"* symbolizes truth supplied by divine providence. *And the slaves drew near, they and their children, and bowed down* symbolizes facts derived from sense impressions, the truth that comes of them, and their subordination. *And Leah and her children also drew near and bowed down* symbolizes a desire for the outer aspects of religious truth, the truth that goes with that desire, and its subordination when being introduced. *And afterward Joseph and Rachel drew near and bowed down* symbolizes [two] kinds of desire for the inner aspects of religious truth, and their subordination when being introduced.

He raised his eyes symbolizes a perception. This is established by the symbolism, dealt with in §§4083, 4339, of *raising one's eyes* as perception.

4356

4357   *And saw the women and the children* means of different desires for truth and of the truth that goes with those desires, as the following shows: The *women*—the slaves, Leah, and Rachel—symbolize different kinds of desire for truth, as discussed in §§3758, 3782, 3793, 3819, 4344. And the *children* or sons symbolize truth, as discussed in §§489, 491, 533, 1147, 2623, 3373. In this case they symbolize truth belonging to those desires.

4358   *And said, "Who are these that you have?"* symbolizes recognition. This is visible from the fact that questions on the literal level of meaning are not questions on the highest level. The Lord is the focus of the highest meaning, and he has no need to ask a person anything, because he knows absolutely everything. This question, *Who are these that you have?* symbolizes recognition because Esau represents the divine goodness of the Lord on the earthly plane. Divine goodness instantly recognizes the truth that is going to unite with it.

Goodness always recognizes truth because it cannot exist without that which it calls true, just as truth cannot exist without that which it calls good. They unite spontaneously. The quality of the goodness determines what kind of truth unites with it, because goodness is what recognizes truth and forms an intimate connection with it as a husband with his wife. The bond that goodness has with truth is what marriage means in a spiritual sense (§§2508, 2618).

For the idea that goodness recognizes the truth that goes with it, and truth recognizes the goodness that goes with it, and that they unite, see §§3101, 3102, 3161, 3179, 3180.

4359   *And he said, "The children with whom God has favored your servant,"* symbolizes truth supplied by divine providence, as the following shows: *Children,* or sons, symbolize truth, as noted just above in §4357. And *with whom God has favored your servant* means that it comes from divine providence. Any favor God lavishes on us is part of his providence.

4360   *And the slaves and their children drew near and bowed down* symbolizes facts derived from sense impressions, the truth that comes of them, and their subordination—as the following shows: *Slave* women symbolize a desire for secular and religious knowledge, which belongs to the outer self, as discussed above at §4344. So they symbolize facts derived from sense impressions, which are discussed below. *Children,* or sons, symbolize truth, as mentioned above at §4357. And *bowing down* means being subordinate.

Facts gleaned from sense impressions, symbolized by the *slave* women, are the knowledge of external, worldly subjects and are therefore the most general knowledge of all (§4345). This kind of knowledge enters directly through the physical senses and is picked up from the senses themselves. The knowledge possessed by little children is always this kind. It serves as a foundation for the knowledge of deeper earthly subjects, but later as a foundation for the knowledge of spiritual subjects too. Spiritual matters rest on a foundation of earthly matters and are represented in them.

True ideas unite with goodness in sequence, starting with the more general ones, as shown above in §4345, and that is why the passage mentions the bowing (or subordination) of the slaves and their children first.

And Leah and her children also drew near and bowed down symbolizes a desire for the outer aspects of religious truth, the truth that goes with that desire, and its subordination when being introduced—as the following establishes: *Leah* represents a desire for outer truth (as discussed in §§3793, 3819) and therefore a desire for the outer aspects of religious truth. *Children,* or sons, symbolize truth, as mentioned just above. And *bowing down* symbolizes subordination—that is, subordination when being introduced into divine goodness on the earthly plane, which is represented by Esau.

4361

And afterward Joseph and Rachel drew near and bowed down symbolizes [two] kinds of desire for the inner aspects of religious truth, and their subordination when being introduced, as the following establishes: *Joseph* represents the heavenly-spiritual dimension, as discussed in §4286. *Rachel* represents a desire for inner truth, as dealt with in §§3758, 3782, 3793, 3819. And *bowing down* symbolizes subordination when being introduced, as noted just above in §4361.

4362

The discussion above of verse 2 explained how this matter stands [§§4342–4345].

Genesis 33:8, 9, 10, 11. *And he said, "What is this whole camp of yours that I have come across?" And he said, "To find favor in the eyes of my lord." And Esau said, "I have plenty, my brother; let what is yours be yours." And Jacob said, "Please, no; please, if I have found favor in your eyes, may you also accept my gift from my hand, because I have seen your face, like seeing the face of God, and you have welcomed me. Please accept my blessing that I have brought you, because God has favored me, and because I have everything," and he urged him, and [Esau] accepted.*

4363

He said, "What is this whole camp of yours that I have come across?" symbolizes the resulting specifics. *And he said, "To find favor in the eyes of my lord,"* means being introduced in a pleasing way. *And Esau said, "I have plenty, my brother; let what is yours be yours,"* symbolizes tacit acceptance, in order to instill a desire for the goodness that comes of truth. *And*

Jacob said, "Please, no," symbolizes the origin of the desire. *Please, if I have found favor in your eyes, may you also accept my gift from my hand* symbolizes a reciprocal desire that it be instilled. *Because I have seen your face, like seeing the face of God, and you have welcomed me* symbolizes that desire [for goodness] present in one's conscious awareness, so far as it has been stimulated in response. *Please accept my blessing that I have brought you* symbolizes divine traits that need to be connected with divine goodness on the earthly level. *Because God has favored me* means as a result of providence. *And because I have everything* symbolizes the spiritual riches belonging to [truth-based goodness]. *And he urged him, and he accepted* means that [a desire for truth] would be instilled by truth-based goodness through a desire inspired by divine goodness.

4364   *He said, "What is this whole camp of yours that I have come across?"* symbolizes the resulting specifics. This can be seen from the fact that the *camp* symbolizes specifics, because they are the items mentioned in verses 14, 15 of the previous chapter: "two hundred she-goats and twenty he-goats; two hundred ewes and twenty rams; thirty nursing camels and their offspring; forty heifers and ten young bulls; twenty jennies and ten foals." These meant goodness and truth and everything subservient to them, which enabled [divine goodness] to be introduced; see §§4263, 4264. So they mean specifics. The specifics in this case are simply confirmation that truth is true and goodness is good. They second the thoughts and feelings a person has, or the things a person knows and loves, that prompt her or him to favor and affirm an idea. In ancient times in the church, the offerings people gave to monarchs and priests carried the same implications. Everyone knows that we bring another around to our way of thinking, to what we say is good and true, by both rational and emotional persuasion. The confirmatory details are what are meant by specifics and are symbolized here by the camp. That is why Jacob says the camp was intended "to find favor in the eyes of my lord," and "Please, if I have found favor in your eyes, may you accept my gift from my hand."

[2] The process is the same in spiritual affairs, or in matters of faith, when they are being tied to goodness that comes of neighborly love. People believe that goodness and truth flow directly into them from heaven, without any means on their part, but they are greatly mistaken. The Lord leads us each by our inclinations, bending us by his silent providence, because he guides us in freedom (§§1937, 1947). All freedom is a matter of desire, or love (see §§2870, 2873), so goodness unites with truth only in freedom, not under pressure (§§2875, 2876, 2877, 2878, 2881, 3145, 3146,

3158, 4031). When we are freely led to goodness, then, we welcome truth, and it is implanted in us. We start to feel moved by it and little by little are introduced into heavenly freedom.

If people who have been reborn—people who love their neighbor, and especially those who love the Lord—reflect on their life until now, they will find that they have been guided in much of their thinking and many of their emotions.

[3] Examples will make it easier to see exactly what is meant by the resulting specifics mentioned here. One true idea that needs to be introduced into goodness is that people live on after death. Nobody accepts this idea unless it is confirmed by specifics such as the following: We are capable of thinking not only about what we can see and touch but also about what we cannot see or touch. We are able to be moved by such things and through that emotion form a connection with them. So we can bond with heaven and even with the Lord himself, and no one who can be united with the Divine can ever die. These considerations and many others like them are specifics that occur to us before the true idea is introduced into any form of goodness—in other words, before it is fully believed. The truth does present itself first, but the specifics enable it to be accepted.

[4] To take another example: We are spirits, and our spirit is clothed with a body while we are living in the world. This is also a true idea needing to be introduced into goodness, because if it is not, we have no interest in heaven, since we think of ourselves the same way we think of unreasoning animals. However, the idea can be introduced only through specifics such as the following: The body we carry around serves various purposes here. It enables us to see with physical eyes what exists in the world and to do things with physical muscles whose strength is equal to the burdens here. Inside us, though, we have a part that thinks and wills, and the body is its physical tool or instrument. The spirit is the person, the real person, which does and senses things through that instrument. We can confirm this to ourselves through much experience if we only believe it is so. All these arguments are specifics that come first and cause the truth to be introduced into goodness; and they result from [that truth].

These considerations and others like them are what are symbolized by the camp.

And he said, "To find favor in the eyes of my lord," means being introduced in a pleasing way, as is self-evident. After all, to *find favor* is to be acceptable, and what is acceptable is introduced in a pleasing way.

4365

4366   *And Esau said, "I have plenty, my brother; let what is yours be yours,"* symbolizes tacit acceptance, in order to instill a desire for the goodness that comes of truth. This can be seen from the fact that the refusal here involves assent, since Esau accepted anyway. The point in refusing, when one would accept, is sometimes to inspire and heighten interest, transforming good thoughts into good intent. The Lord guides us in our spiritual life by almost the same means we use in secular life to lead others. In worldly life it is common to turn people down in hopes that they will act more eagerly, inspired not just by their thoughts but also by their will. If their offer were truly refused, the purpose they intend would die, so the purpose itself urges that they think more intently and in the process develop a heartfelt wish.

[2] The reason this phenomenon is not as visible in regard to spiritual life as secular life is that there are not many people in whom goodness unites with truth—that is, not many who are being reborn. And the few who are being reborn do not reflect on such things. They cannot, since they do not know what spiritual goodness is because they do not know what neighborly love and the neighbor are in the genuine sense. Not knowing this, they cannot have a very deep idea of the truth that composes faith. What is more, they set such a wide gulf between spiritual and secular life that they do not dare draw a lesson about one from the other. That the two correspond, and that spiritual life is represented in secular life, they have no notion at all. In fact, some of them reject the comparison. The reality, though, is that we cannot form any picture of spiritual life except from the experiences of secular life. Take these away and our idea of spiritual life falters, until finally we no longer believe in it. As clear evidence, consider that people no longer think spirits and angels have the kind of social interactions we do, or conversations either. They do not believe spirits and angels debate what is honest and seemly, just and fair, good and true as we do, and much more perfectly—let alone see, hear, or get to know each other, form communities, live together, and much more.

4367   *And Jacob said, "Please, no,"* symbolizes the origin of the desire. This can be seen from the remarks just above to the effect that refusal to accept a gift sparks desire. Desire shows in Jacob's words *please, no,* so the phrase plainly symbolizes the origin of the desire.

4368   *Please, if I have found favor in your eyes, may you also accept my gift from my hand* symbolizes a reciprocal desire that it be instilled. This can be seen from the context above and below. The theme is the union of goodness with truth on the earthly level, so the passage concerns the desire sparked in truth by goodness. That is why Esau rejected the gift Jacob sent—in order to instill desire in truth, as shown above in §4366. That is why the previous phrase, "Please, no," symbolizes the origin of the desire (§4367). That is why the current sentence, *Please, if I have found favor in your eyes, may you also accept my gift from my hand* symbolizes a reciprocal desire that it be instilled—since Jacob says this in all goodwill—in other words, with desire. That is why the text goes on to say "he urged him."

[2] When I mention a reciprocal desire that is instilled into truth (Jacob) by goodness (Esau), I mean a desire for truth. There are two heavenly types of desire: a desire for goodness and a desire for truth. These have already been discussed several times [§§1904, 1997, 2718]. A desire for truth traces its origin to goodness, and goodness alone. The desire itself comes from there because truth has no inherent life but takes its life from goodness. When truth appeals to us, then, what moves us is not truth but the goodness that flows into truth and creates the desire. That is what is meant by a reciprocal desire that it be instilled.

The public recognizes that there are many people in the church who are devoted to the Lord's Word and spend a lot of time reading it, but few of them do so in order to learn what is true. Most of them stick to their creed and simply work at confirming it from the Word. It seems as though they have a desire for truth, but they do not. The only people with a desire for truth are those who love to be taught truth, or to know what is true, and to examine the Scriptures for this purpose. No one has this desire except a person who possesses goodness, or charity for his or her neighbor and particularly love for the Lord. In such a person, goodness itself flows into truth and creates desire, because the Lord is present in that goodness.

[3] The following examples can illustrate:

Take people who do the work of genuine neighborly kindness and read these words addressed to Peter by the Lord:

> I say to you that you are Peter, and on this rock I will build my church, and the gates of hell will not prevail over it. And I will give you the keys to the kingdom of the heavens; and whatever you bind on earth will be bound in the heavens, and whatever you unbind on earth will be unbound in the heavens. (Matthew 16:15, 16, 17, 18, 19)

These people, whose desire for truth springs from good done out of true charity, love to be taught what the passage means. They learn that faith growing out of neighborly love is symbolized by the rock on which the church will be built and therefore by Peter, so that this faith is given the keys to open and close heaven. (See the preface to Genesis 22.) When they hear these things, they rejoice, and the truth of it moves them, because it means that this power belongs to the Lord alone, the source of faith. When people's desire for truth does not spring from good done out of true charity but from some other kind of goodness—even more so if it arises out of self-love and materialism—they are not drawn to this truth. Instead they feel dismayed and angry, because they want to claim for the priesthood the right to open and close heaven. They are angry because the teaching deprives them of control, and they are dismayed because it deprives them of [others'] deference.

[4] For another example, take people with a desire for truth stemming from genuine neighborly kindness who hear that religion consists in neighborly love, not in faith detached from it. They accept this truth with joy. People with a desire for truth that stems from self-love and materialism do not accept it.

Again, when people with a desire for truth springing from good done out of genuine neighborly love hear that charity begins not with themselves but with the Lord, they rejoice. People with a desire for truth springing from love for themselves and for worldly advantages do not accept this truth but fiercely defend the idea that love for their neighbor starts with themselves. So they do not know what it is to love their neighbor as themselves.

When people whose desire for truth comes from good done out of genuine neighborly love hear that heavenly bliss is to do good to others out of goodwill, not for any selfish purpose, they rejoice. But people whose desire for truth comes from love for themselves and for worldly advantages do not like it and do not even understand it.

[5] When people whose desire for truth comes from good done out of true charity are taught that the deeds of the outer self are worthless unless they arise from the inner self and therefore from good intent, they accept it with joy. People whose desire for truth stems from self-centered and worldly kinds of love praise the deeds of the outer self but disregard any good intent in the inner self. In fact, they do not even know that the good intentions of the inner self survive death, or that when the deeds of the outer self are isolated from those intentions they are dead and therefore cease to exist.

Likewise in all other cases.

This evidence shows that religious truth cannot possibly be internalized by any but those who do the work of true neighborly kindness, so it can unite only with goodness. It also shows that all genuine desire for truth comes from charitable goodness.

Anyone can see the same thing confirmed by everyday experience—that people dedicated to evil do not believe, but people dedicated to goodness do. Quite plainly, then, religious truth unites with goodness, never with evil.

Because I have seen your face, like seeing the face of God, and you have welcomed me symbolizes desire present in one's conscious awareness, so far as it has been stimulated in response, as the following shows: *Seeing a face like the face of God* symbolizes desire present in one's conscious awareness. A *face* symbolizes inner depths (§§358, 1999, 2434, 3527, 3573, 4066), and the *face of God* symbolizes everything good (§§222, 223), which imparts perceptible desire when it flows in. And *welcoming me* symbolizes desire that has been stimulated. The fact that the sentence is referring to desire that has been stimulated can be seen from the discussion of this subject just above [§§4366–4368] and accordingly from context.

4369

Please accept the blessing that I have brought you symbolizes divine traits that need to be connected with divine goodness on the earthly level. This can be seen from the meaning of the *blessing* as the items mentioned in verses 14, 15 of the previous chapter, Genesis 32, symbolizing divine goodness and truth and everything subservient to them, which enabled them to be introduced; see §§4263, 4264. These need to be connected with divine goodness on the earthly level, as explained above in §4364.

4370

Because God has favored me means as a result of providence. This can be seen from the fact that the clause symbolizes providence, as above in §4359.

4371

And because I have everything symbolizes the spiritual riches belonging to [truth-based goodness]. This can be seen from the symbolism of *everything he had* as spiritual riches, because what he had was flocks and herds, which symbolize goodness and truth, as shown before [§§4364, 4370]. Goodness and truth are called spiritual riches. Spiritual riches have to do with truth, and the use of them has to do with goodness.

4372

And he urged him, and he accepted means that [a desire for truth] would be instilled by truth-based goodness through a desire inspired by divine goodness. This can be seen from the explanations presented so far, starting with §4364. The actual desire inspired by divine goodness in truth-based goodness is testified to by the words *he urged him*. See above at §4366.

4373

To discuss the desire for truth further, since it is a theme of these verses: It is important to know that this desire seems to come from truth and therefore to inhere in truth, but it does not come from truth. It comes from goodness, because the only life present in truth is that which it receives from goodness. The appearance that it comes from truth can be compared to the life present in the body. Life is not the body's but the soul's, and it is not even the soul's but comes through the soul from the origin of life, which is the Lord; yet it appears to belong to the body. It also resembles a reflection in a mirror, which seems to be *in* the mirror, although the image actually comes from outside.

[2] To see that this is the inner meaning of the current and preceding words is not easy for people who focus their attention on the story line, admittedly, because they think about Esau and Jacob and the advance gift. They do not realize that Esau represents divine goodness on the earthly level, and Jacob, truth that was to unite with divine goodness on that level. They do not see that the amicable conversation between the two symbolizes a desire aroused in truth by goodness. However, when people on earth read the story, angels take these elements in no other sense. Angels think only in spiritual terms, and among them the narrative level of meaning is turned into a spiritual idea. That is how angelic thoughts correspond with human thoughts. There are unending correspondences of this kind, which make the Word holy and divine. As the literal meaning rises, it becomes spiritual, until it reaches the Lord, where it becomes divine.

That is what inspiration is.

4374   Genesis 33:12, 13, 14, 15, 16. *And [Esau] said, "Let's set off and go, and I will go at your side." And [Jacob] said to him, "My lord knows that there are tender children and unweaned flocks and herds with me; and let anyone drive them for one day and all the flocks will die. Please let my lord cross before his servant, and I will advance slowly at the pace of the work that is before me, and at the pace of the children, till I come to my lord, to Seir." And Esau said, "Please let me station with you some of the people who are with me," and he said, "Why should this be? Let me find favor in the eyes of my lord!" And Esau returned that day to his way to Seir.*

He said, "Let's set off and go," symbolizes what came next. *And I will go at your side* means that they were to unite. *And he said to him, "My lord knows that there are tender children,"* symbolizes truth that had not yet acquired divine life. *And unweaned flocks and herds with me* symbolizes inner goodness and earthly goodness that had not yet acquired divine life.

And let anyone drive them for one day and all the flocks will die symbolizes a pause for development, without which they would not live; in other words, they needed to be prepared for union. *Please let my lord cross before his servant* symbolizes a broader presence. *And I will advance slowly* symbolizes a further stage of preparation. *At the pace of the work that is before me* means allowing for broad generalities. *And at the pace of the children* means allowing for the truth they contain. *Till I come to my lord, to Seir,* means until they could bond; *Seir* means a union of spiritual and heavenly attributes on the earthly plane. *And Esau said, "Please let me station with you some of the people who are with me,"* means that some truth marked by goodness would be united. *And he said, "Why should this be? Let me find favor in the eyes of my lord!"* symbolizes enlightenment as a result of a presence within. *And Esau returned that day to his way to Seir* symbolizes the state of divine goodness on the earthly level at that point, to which truth-based goodness had been attached; a *way* means a relatively truth-based goodness.

He said, "Let's set off and go," symbolizes what came next—what came next in the union of goodness with truth. This can be seen from the symbolism of *setting off* and *going,* which clearly involve progression to further stages. Progression and development come up in the inner meaning of the next few verses. **4375**

And I will go at your side means that they were to unite. This can be seen from the symbolism of *going beside you* as being attached, in this case meaning that they were to unite, said of goodness and truth. **4376**

And he said to him, "My lord knows that there are tender children," symbolizes truth that had not yet acquired divine life, as the following shows: *Children,* or sons, symbolize truth, as discussed in §§489, 491, 533, 1147, 2623, 3373. And *tender* means fresh and new and therefore having received some life but not yet genuine life—or in this case divine life, since the topic of discussion is the glorification of the Lord's earthly divinity. **4377**

These ideas can be illustrated by the experiences of people who are being reborn, since human regeneration is an image of the Lord's glorification. People who are regenerating run through the same stages of life they do when they are born: childhood, youth, early adulthood, and full adulthood. After all, those who are regenerating are being born anew. When they are in their [spiritual] infancy, the truth they know does have life but not spiritual life as yet. At that point there is only general truth—truth devoid of particulars and fine detail—for goodness to unite with. So the bond is merely a shallow not a deep one. It deepens gradually as they advance through the rest of the stages.

This childlike stage is symbolized by the tender children and also by the next few words: "and unweaned flocks and herds with me; and let anyone drive them for one day and all the flocks will die."

4378   *And unweaned flocks and herds with me* symbolizes inner goodness and earthly goodness that had not yet acquired divine life, as can be seen from the following: *Flocks* symbolize inner goodness, as discussed in §§2566, 3783. *Herds* symbolize outer, earthly goodness (§2566; and §§2180, 2781). And *unweaned* also means fresh and new. In this case the unweaned symbolize spiritual qualities being born on the earthly level. In the childlike stage of human rebirth, spiritual qualities are present in potential, since spiritual life gradually advances with each stage, as if from an egg. Childhood serves as a kind of egg for adolescence, which serves as a kind of egg for young adulthood, which serves as a kind of egg for full adulthood. It is as if we are constantly being born. These remarks show what is meant by inner goodness and earthly goodness that have not yet acquired divine life, symbolized by the unweaned flocks and herds. See also the comments just above at §4377 on the state of [spiritual] infancy.

4379   *And let anyone drive them for one day and all the flocks will die* symbolizes a pause for development, without which they would not live; in other words, they needed to be prepared for union, as can be seen from context. Earlier verses, you see, dealt with the union of goodness and truth in general terms; the current passage deals with the same union in specific terms. The actual process by which truth is introduced into goodness is being described in the inner meaning here. The general outlines of the process are visible to some extent from the explanation given, but not its secrets, which are countless. These are revealed only to people who see by heaven's light; and a certain crude likeness of the secrets appears to people who see by the world's light when heaven's light is allowed in.

[The need for gradual development] is fairly evident from the fact that when people are being reborn they run through the same stages of life they do upon birth, and that an earlier stage always serves as a kind of egg in relation to a later stage. We are constantly being conceived and born. This happens not only while we are living in the world but also when we go to the other world, to eternity. Even so, we cannot improve past the point of being like an egg for the limitless stages yet to come.

This discussion shows how much is involved in human regeneration, though we know hardly anything about it. You can see, then, how much the inner meaning holds here, where the subject is the evolving states and methods by which goodness is introduced into truth.

Please let my lord cross before his servant symbolizes a broader presence. **4380** This can be seen from the symbolism of *crossing before someone.* In this instance, which has to do with the bond between goodness and truth, it symbolizes a broader presence.

In regeneration, which is accomplished by the coming together of goodness and truth, goodness is what acts and truth is what allows itself to be acted upon. When goodness has been applying itself to truth and uniting with it to some small extent, truth appears to react. It is not truth that reacts, however, but the goodness united or connected with it, which reacts *through* truth. This connection is what is meant by a broader presence.

I talk about a bond between goodness and truth, but what I mean is a person in whom goodness and truth exist. Goodness and truth cannot be spoken of apart from a medium in which they exist, and that medium is the human being. Heaven's inhabitants think and talk in these kinds of abstracts because they do not attribute goodness or truth to themselves but to the Lord, and because goodness and truth from the Lord fill all of heaven. The ancients regularly spoke in that fashion.

And I will advance slowly symbolizes a further stage of preparation. **4381** This can be seen from the symbolism of *advancing slowly.* Here, where the topic is the introduction of goodness into truth and truth's acceptance of what is good, the phrase symbolizes a further stage of preparation.

At the pace of the work that is before me means allowing for broad gen- **4382** eralities, as the preceding discussion shows. The *pace of the work* refers to the last few clauses: "that there are tender children and unweaned flocks and herds with me; and let anyone drive them for one day and all the flocks will die." The discussion of these clauses above shows they mean that [the rate of progress] allows for broad generalities.

The text talks about the *pace,* [or "foot,"] *of the work* and then the *pace,* [or "foot,"] *of the children* because a *foot* symbolizes the earthly dimension (see §§2162, 3147, 3761, 3986, 4280) and the current focus is on that dimension.

And at the pace of the children means allowing for the truth they con- **4383** tain. This can be seen from the symbolism of *children,* or sons, as truth (mentioned several times above).

"The truth they contain" means the truth that broad generalities contain. Broad generalities are what were compared above in §4378 to an egg, because they contain specifics, which contain minute details (§§4325 at the end, 4329, 4345). The first, childlike stage contains a potential for specifics, which contain a potential for details. Later the specifics and details emerge and manifest themselves in action, so there is develop-ment. When we are being reborn—when the Lord is leading us—we are provided with general concepts containing future ideas, which gradually emerge in a pattern and sequence that defies comprehension. Each and every one of them is foreseen by the Lord, who knows what they will be like into the infinite future. Accordingly, general truth is never united to goodness in us unless it is capable of accommodating specific truth that is capable of accommodating finely detailed truth.

[2] These specifics, though, and even the details of the specifics, are nothing more than generalizations by comparison with all that remains. In the smallest details there is still endlessly more.

Although the wisdom of angels outstrips ours so greatly that what they know and perceive is inexpressible, they themselves confess that all their knowledge is extremely general by comparison [with the Lord's]. The num-ber of things they do not know is limitless—they do not dare say "infinite," because no ratio exists between what is finite and what is infinite.

From these considerations the reader can draw conclusions about the nature of the Word: Because it is divine, the Word contains infinite truth from its original source, then the ineffable truth of angelic wisdom, and only in the end the kind of truth suited to the human mind.

4384   *Till I come to my lord, into Seir,* means until they—the truth that is Jacob and the goodness that is Esau—could bond. This can be seen from the symbolism of *Seir* as a union on the earthly plane of spiritual and heavenly attributes, that is, of the truth that composes faith and the goodness that composes neighborly love. In the following Scripture pas-sages, Seir properly symbolizes goodness united with truth on the earthly level, and in the highest sense, goodness in the Lord's earthly divinity united with truth there. In Moses' prophetic utterance concerning the children of Israel:

> Jehovah came from Sinai and *dawned from Seir on them;* he shone out from Mount Paran and came with the holy myriads. (Deuteronomy 33:2, 3)

In Balaam's prophecy:

> I see him, but not yet; I view him, but he is not near. A star will rise out of Jacob, and a scepter will spring up from Israel. And Edom will be an

inheritance, and *an inheritance will Seir be* for its enemies, and Israel will do a powerful deed. (Numbers 24:17, 18)

In the song of Deborah and Barak:

Jehovah, when you came out from Seir, when you marched from the field of Edom, the earth trembled, mountains streamed down. This is Sinai, in the presence of Jehovah, the God of Israel. (Judges 5:4, 5)

In Isaiah:

One is shouting to me from Seir, "Guard, what is [left] of the night? Guard, what is [left] of the night?" The guard said, "Morning comes, and also night." (Isaiah 21:11, 12)

See the information and the quotations concerning Seir in §4240.

And Esau said, "Please let me station with you some of the people who are with me," means that some truth marked by goodness would be united. This can be seen from the symbolism of *stationing with you* as uniting, and from that of the *people who are with me* as some truth marked by goodness. *People* mean truth (see §§1259, 1260, 2928, 3295, 3581), so the *people who are with me* mean truth marked by goodness.

Truth marked by goodness, or based on goodness, has been defined several times before. It is truth that rises out of goodness, truth that goodness brings with it when it flows through the inner self into the outer self. This truth is symbolized by the four hundred men Esau had with him (see above at §4341). So the current verse is talking about *some* of that truth, since it says *some of the people who are with me.*

And he said, "Why should this be? Let me find favor in the eyes of my lord!" symbolizes enlightenment as a result of a presence within. This can be seen from the implications of this deferential way of speaking. It rejects a direct presence but agrees to a less direct one, which is the same as a presence within, resulting in enlightenment.

And Esau returned that day to his way to Seir symbolizes the state of divine goodness on the earthly level at that point, to which truth-based goodness had been attached, as the following shows. A *day* symbolizes a state (as discussed in §§23, 487, 488, 493, 893, 2788, 3462), so a *return that day* means the state he then took on. *Esau* represents divine goodness on the earthly level, as noted above in §4340. A *way* symbolizes truth in the will and in actions (§§4337, 4353). And *Seir* symbolizes a union of truth with goodness, as discussed above in §4384. Gather all of this into one meaning and it is plain that the sentence symbolizes the state of divine goodness on the earthly level at that point, to which truth-based goodness had been attached.

[2] It is by no means apparent from the narrative level of meaning in these words that they have such a symbolism, yet that is what they involve in a spiritual, inner sense. The angels present with us—the heaven within us [Luke 17:21]—have no interest whatever in worldly narratives. They do not know what Esau is or Seir. They do not think about the day on which Esau returned or the way to Seir. Instead, they form ideas from the spiritual qualities corresponding to such things and extract the spiritual meaning instantly. Correspondences produce this effect. It is almost the same as when another person speaks in a foreign tongue and we immediately understand the meaning, as if we heard it in our own tongue. The strange sound and pronunciation of the words do not hinder us. So it is with the Word's inner meaning, which coincides exactly with the universal language angels use, or their spiritual thought-speech. Angels' speech is spiritual because their thoughts come from heaven's light, which comes from the Lord.

4388 Genesis 33:17, 18, 19, 20. *And Jacob traveled to Succoth and built himself a house, and he made huts for what he had gained; therefore he called the name of the place Succoth. And Jacob came to Salem (the city of Shechem, which is in the land of Canaan) as he came from Paddan-aram; and he camped before the face of the city. And he bought the portion of the field where he had spread his tent, from the hand of the children of Hamor, Shechem's father, for a hundred kesitahs. And he established an altar there and called it El-Elohe-Israel.*

Jacob traveled to Succoth symbolizes the state of life then experienced by the goodness that grows out of truth. *And built himself a house* symbolizes an increase during that state in the goodness that grows out of truth. *And he made huts for what he had gained* means likewise [an increase] in goodness and truth in general, benefiting the goodness that now grows out of truth. *Therefore he called the name of the place Succoth* symbolizes the nature of the state. *And Jacob came to Salem, the city of Shechem,* symbolizes inner religious truth marked by calm. *Which is in the land of Canaan* means in the Lord's kingdom. *As he came from Paddan-aram* means after the previous state. *And he camped before the face of the city* means applying oneself. *And he bought the portion of the field* means making the goodness that comes of that truth one's own. *Where he had spread his tent* symbolizes something holy. *From the hand of the children of Hamor, Shechem's father,* symbolizes the descent of that truth from divine stock that is unrelated. *For a hundred kesitahs* symbolizes completeness. *And he established an altar there* symbolizes inward worship. *And called it El-Elohe-Israel* means that it came from spiritual divinity.

Jacob traveled to Succoth symbolizes the state of life then experienced by the goodness that grows out of truth, as the following shows: *Jacob* represents truth-based goodness, as discussed above [§4337]. At present he represents the goodness now growing out of truth because of what was connected to it by the goodness that is Esau, as already described. *Traveling* symbolizes the pattern and customs of a life, as noted in §1293, so it symbolizes a state of life. And *Succoth* symbolizes the nature of the state, as will be discussed later, in §§4391, 4392.

4389

And built himself a house symbolizes an increase during that state in the goodness that grows out of truth. This can be seen from the symbolism of *building a house* as supplying the outer self with understanding and wisdom, as discussed in §1488. Since understanding relates to truth, and wisdom to goodness, the building of the house symbolizes an increase in the goodness that grows out of truth. For the meaning of a *house* as goodness, see §§2233, 3128, 3142, 3652, 3720. The goodness that grows out of truth is defined above at §§4337, 4353 as truth in our will and in our actions. This truth is what is called goodness, and a conscience formed of that goodness is called a conscience for truth.

4390

This goodness based on truth grows in proportion to the charity we express in action as a result of goodwill, so its increase depends on how much and how well we love our neighbor.

[2] The reason for mentioning goodness and truth so often in the explanations is that everything in heaven and therefore everything in the Lord's church relates to truth and goodness. These two attributes embrace everything in general having to do with theology and with the way one lives. Truth has to do with theology, and goodness with the way one lives. Without exception, all the things that the human mind focuses on relate to truth and goodness. Its intellect focuses on matters of truth and its will on matters of goodness. The words *truth* and *goodness*, then, clearly have a very broad meaning and branch off into an inexpressibly large number of derivative forms.

That is why truth and goodness are mentioned so often.

And he made huts for what he had gained means likewise in general, benefiting the goodness that now grows out of truth, as the following shows. *What he had gained* symbolizes goodness and truth in general. And the

4391

symbolism of *making huts* or tents is similar to that of building a house: receiving an increase in the goodness that grows out of truth. The difference is that building a house is relatively specific and therefore more inward, while making huts or tents is relatively general and therefore more outward. The house was for Jacob, his women, and the children; the huts were for the slaves, flocks, and herds.

In the Word, *huts* or tents strictly speaking symbolize the holy effect of truth. They are distinguished from shelters, which are also called tents, the distinction being that shelters symbolize the holy effect of goodness (§§414, 1102, 2145, 2152, 4128). In the original language, the huts are called *succoth;* the shelters, *ohalim.*

The holy effect of truth is the goodness that comes of truth.

[2] The following passages in the Word also show that this is the symbolism of huts, or tents, which are called *succoth.* In David:

Jehovah God rode upon a guardian being and flew and was borne on the wings of the wind; he turned the dark into his hideout, and *his environs into his tent*—watery darkness, *the clouds of the heavens.* (Psalms 18:10, 11)

In another place:

He tilted the heavens when he came down, and thick darkness was under his feet. And he rode upon a guardian being, and flew and was borne on the wings of the wind, and turned the dark around him into *tents*— watery bundles, *the clouds of the heavens.* (2 Samuel 22:10, 11, 12)

This is about divine revelation, or the Word. Tilting the heavens when he came down stands for hiding the Word's inner depths. The thick darkness under his feet means that what we are capable of seeing is relatively dark—as the literal meaning of the Word is. Riding upon a guardian being means that providence arranged it so. Turning the dark around him into tents, or his environs into his tent, stands for hiding the holy power of truth away, deep inside the literal meaning. Watery bundles and the clouds of the heavens mean the Word in its literal text. For the idea that the clouds of the heavens mean the Word in its literal text, see the preface to Genesis 18, §4060.

[3] This passage in Isaiah symbolizes something similar:

Jehovah will create over the whole dwelling place of Mount Zion and over its convocations a *cloud by day,* and smoke and the radiance of a fiery flame by night, for over all the *glory* there will be a canopy. And a *tent* will serve as shade by day, and as a refuge and hideout against the deluge and rain. (Isaiah 4:5, 6)

Here too the cloud means the Word's literal meaning, and the glory, its inner meaning, as they do in Matthew 24:30; Mark 13:26; Luke 21:27. Once more the tent stands for the holy effect of truth.

The reason for saying that deep truth is hidden is that if it had been disclosed, people would have profaned it; see §§3398, 3399, 4289. This is also explained by the following words in David:

You conceal them in the hiding place of your presence because of the conspiracies of man; *you place them out of sight in a tent* because of the quarrel of tongues. (Psalms 31:20)

[4] The meaning of a tent as the holy effect of truth is also clear in Amos:

On that day I will *raise up David's fallen tent* and wall up the breaches, and the wreckage I will raise up, and I will rebuild it as in the days of old. (Amos 9:11)

Raising up David's fallen tent stands for restoring truth's holy effect after it has been destroyed. David stands for the Lord and his divine truth (§1888), because a monarch means divine truth (§§2015, 2069, 3009).

Since a tent symbolized the holy effect of truth, and living in tents symbolized the resulting worship, a feast of tents, which is called the Feast of Tabernacles, was established in the religion of Judah and Israel (Leviticus 23:34, 42, 43; Deuteronomy 16:13, 16; where it is also called the Festival of Sukkot, or tents).

Therefore he called the name of the place Succoth symbolizes the nature of the state. This is established by the symbolism of *calling something's name* as its quality (discussed in §§144, 145, 1754, 1896, 2009, 2724, 3006, 3421) and from that of a *place* as a state (discussed in §§2625, 2837, 3356, 3387, 4321). The nature of the current state—the state of the holy effect now belonging to the truth that comes of goodness—is what "Succoth" involves, because Succoth means tents, and tents symbolize the holy effect of truth, as shown just above in §4391.

Succoth has the same symbolism in David:

I will split Shechem, and the valley of *Succoth* I will measure out. I own Gilead, and I own Manasseh, and Ephraim is the strength of my head; Judah is my lawgiver. (Psalms 60:6, 7; 108:7, 8)

4393   *And Jacob came to Salem, the city of Shechem,* symbolizes inner religious truth marked by calm. This can be seen from the symbolism of *Salem* as peaceful calm (discussed below) and from that of the *city of Shechem* as inner religious truth (discussed in the next chapter where Shechem and his city are dealt with; for the meaning of a *city* as religious truth, see §§402, 2268, 2449, 2451, 2712, 2943, 3216).

The symbolism of Salem as peaceful calm can be seen in David:

> God is known in Judah; in Israel his name is great, *and in Salem is his tent,* and his dwelling place is in Zion. There he broke the bow's blazing missiles, the shield, and the sword—and war. (Psalms 76:1, 2, 3)

In this passage Salem plainly means peace and calm, because the text says that there God broke the bow's blazing missiles, the shield, the sword, and war. The symbolism can also be seen from the word's meaning in the original language, since Salem means calm and wholeness. For a definition of peace and calm, see §§1726, 3696. Peace and calm are the abode of inner truth—in other words, of people whose beliefs and life are filled with inner truth. As long as people stay in outer truth, and more particularly when they pass from outer to inner truth, their state lacks calmness, because they then face the struggles of spiritual crisis.

Jacob provides an illustration of this in the current passage. Having experienced fear and anxiety over Esau he has now reached a state of calm.

4394   *Which is in the land of Canaan* means in the Lord's kingdom. This is established by the symbolism of the *land of Canaan* as the Lord's kingdom (discussed in §§1413, 1437, 1607, 3038, 3481, 3705).

When our beliefs and life are filled with inner truth, we are in the Lord's kingdom and in a calm state, at which point we view outer issues the way a person on a towering hill observes the sea heaving below.

4395   *As he came from Paddan-aram* means after the previous state. This can be seen from the symbolism of *as he came,* which means after, and from that of *Paddan-aram* as a knowledge of goodness and truth (discussed in §§3664, 4107, 4112), but an outer knowledge that serves to introduce real goodness and truth. Laban lived there, and he represents a desire for superficial, introductory goodness; see §§3612, 3665, 3778, 3974, 3982, 3986 at the end, 4063, 4189, 4206. The text says *as he came from Paddan-aram,* then, because progress had been made from outward to inward truth and goodness and accordingly from an earlier stage to the current one.

And he camped before the face of the city means applying oneself to the **4396**
goodness accompanying [inner religious] truth, as the following shows:
Camping properly means being arranged in an orderly pattern, as discussed
in §4236. Here, though, it means applying oneself, because in this case
camping means establishing a home base with the herds and flocks, which
were called a camp above in §4364. And *before the face of the city* means
to the goodness accompanying that truth. A *face* symbolizes inner depths
(§§358, 1999, 2434, 3527, 3573, 4066) and therefore desires for goodness
and truth, which shine out from one's face. A *city* means truth; see §§402,
2268, 2449, 2451, 2712, 2943, 3216.

And he bought the portion of the field means making the goodness that **4397**
comes of that truth one's own. This can be seen from the symbolism of
buying something as making it one's own and from that of a *portion of a
field* as the goodness growing out of that truth. A *field* means the church
in respect to goodness, and therefore goodness itself; see §§2971, 3196,
3317, 3500, 3508, 3766.

Where he had spread his tent symbolizes something holy. This can be **4398**
seen from the symbolism of a *tent* as something holy (discussed in §§414,
1102, 2145, 2152, 3210).

From the hand of the children of Hamor, Shechem's father, symbolizes **4399**
the descent of that truth from divine stock that is unrelated. This will
become clear from information to be given in the next chapter, where
Hamor and Shechem are discussed.

For a hundred kesitahs symbolizes completeness. This is indicated by **4400**
the symbolism of a *hundred* as a complete state (discussed in §2636) and
therefore as completeness. Actually, a hundred properly symbolizes a large
amount here, because the topic is adoption of the goodness that grows
out of inner truth, such truth being symbolized by the sons of Shechem's
father Hamor (§4399). On an inner level, *kesitahs,* which were coins, also
symbolize this truth. What is more, the word comes from one that means
truth (Psalms 60:4).

The union of goodness with this kind of truth will be discussed below
at §4402.

And he established an altar there symbolizes inward worship. This can be **4401**
seen from the symbolism of *establishing an altar* as worship. The altar was
the main object representing the Lord (§§921, 2777, 2811), so it was also the
main object used in worship. In this case worship means inward worship
from spiritual divinity—the next subject of discussion.

4402   *And called it El-Elohe-Israel* means from spiritual divinity—inward worship from spiritual divinity. This can be seen from the symbolism of *El-Elohe-Israel* (discussed just below), and from that of *Israel* as what is spiritual (discussed in §§4286, 4292).

Now to put in perspective the explanations given from verse 17 of the current chapter onward.

The chapter deals in its highest sense with the way the Lord made his earthly level divine. Since the things the highest meaning has to say about the Lord transcend the thoughts of the human mind, being divine, let me shed light on them through a subject more readily grasped. That subject is the way the Lord regenerates our earthly dimension. The inner meaning here also describes the rebirth of a person's earthly level, you see, since human rebirth is an image of the Lord's glorification (§§3138, 3212, 3296, 3490). The Lord followed a divine plan in glorifying himself, or making himself divine, and he follows the same plan in regenerating us, or making us heavenly and spiritual. Here [the text depicts] the way he makes us spiritual, because *Israel* symbolizes a spiritual person.

[2] Our spiritual self is not our inner rational self but our inner earthly self. Our inner rational self is the one called the heavenly person. The difference between a spiritual and a heavenly person has been described many times before. What makes people spiritual is the uniting of truth and goodness in them, or the uniting of faith's attributes with charity's. The union takes place on the earthly level, where first outer truth and then inner truth comes together with goodness. Verses 1–16 of the chapter were about the union of outer truth [to goodness] on the earthly level, and verses 17 to the end are about the union of inner truth to goodness.

The only way inner truth can be united with goodness is by a stream of light that flows through the inner self into the outer. By this light one can see divine truth, but only as to its broad outlines, in approximately the same way the eye sees a multitude of objects as a single dim whole, without any distinction among the parts. This illumination, which renders truth visible in a general way only, is symbolized by Esau's statement to Jacob, "Please let me station with you some of the people with me," and by Jacob's reply, "Why should this be? Let me find favor in your eyes!" (For a discussion of these words, see §§4385, 4386.) [3] Conditions are relatively dim for our spiritual self (see §§2708, 2715, 2716, 2718, 2831,

2849, 2935, 2937, 3241, 3246, 3833), which is the self that Israel represents (§4286).

This spiritual self is so called for the following reason: Heaven's light, which holds understanding and wisdom, shines on the objects of worldly light in us. This enables what is seen by heavenly light to be represented in objects seen by worldly light and to correspond with them. Regarded in itself, spirituality is the divine light itself shed by the Lord, so it is an understanding of truth, and therefore it is wisdom. In spiritual people this light falls on the ideas that compose their faith and that they believe to be true, but in a heavenly person it falls on the goodness that love urges.

These points may be clear to people who see by heaven's light, but they are dark and dim to those who see by the world's light. To most people today, then, they are obscure, and perhaps so obscure as to be mostly unintelligible. Since they are the focus of the inner meaning, though, and are as described, they must not be passed over but revealed. The time is coming when light will shine.

[4] The altar was called *El-Elohe-Israel* and symbolized inward worship from spiritual divinity because in its highest sense *El Elohe* is the same as spiritual divinity and as Israel. Israel means the Lord's spiritual divinity, and in a representative sense it means the Lord's spiritual church or, to put it another way, a spiritual person; see §§4286, 4292. *El Elohe* in the original language means God the God, or more literally translated, God of the gods.

In many Scripture passages Jehovah, or the Lord, is called *El* in the singular, or *Eloah,* and he is also called *Elohim* in the plural—sometimes both forms occurring in the same verse or same string of verses. People who do not know the Bible's inner meaning cannot tell why this happens. *El* involves one idea, *Eloah* another, and *Elohim* another, as anyone can conclude from the fact that Scripture is divine, or traces its origins to the Divine. So every word in it, and in fact the smallest tip of a letter of every word, is inspired.

[5] What the name *El* implies where it is used, and what the name *Elohim* implies, can be seen from remarks in various earlier sections showing that the text speaks of *El* and *Elohim,* or God, when the subject is truth. See §§709, 2586, 2769, 2807, 2822, 3921 at the end, 4287. That is why *El* and *Elohim* on the highest level of meaning symbolize divine spirituality. Divine spirituality is the same as divine truth, with

the difference that *El* symbolizes truth in our will and in our actions, which is identical with truth-based goodness (§§4337, 4353, 4390).

Elohim is plural because by divine truth is meant everything true that comes from the Lord. Sometimes the Word also calls angels *elohim,* or gods (§4295), as will be evident in the Scripture quotations below.

Now, since on the highest level *El* and *Elohim* symbolize the Lord's truth, they also symbolize his power. Truth is what power is attributed to, because goodness works through truth when wielding power (§§3091, 4015). Where the Word is dealing with the power that comes from truth, then, the Lord is called *El* and *Elohim,* or God. For the same reason, *El* in the original language also means a strong person.

[6] The following passages can show still more clearly that Scripture refers to *El* and *Elohim,* or God, when dealing with divine spirituality—in other words, with divine truth, and therefore with divine power. In Moses:

> God said to Israel in visions at night, "I am *God of the gods (El Elohe)* of your father; you are not to be afraid of going down into Egypt, because I will turn you into a great nation there." (Genesis 46:2, 3)

This is addressed to Israel, whom God promises to turn into a great nation, so it has to do with truth and its power. Accordingly the passage speaks of *El Elohe,* which in its most direct sense means God of the gods. In the same author it can also be seen that the immediate reference of *Elohim* is to gods, because they are mentioned in connection with truth and the power it yields:

> There Jacob built an altar, and he called the place *El-bethel,* because there *the Elohim* were revealed to him as he fled before his brother. (Genesis 35:7)

And in another place in the same author:

> Jehovah our God is *God of the gods* and Lord of the lords, *God (El)* the great, the mighty, and the fearsome. (Deuteronomy 10:17)

God of the gods in this verse is expressed as *Elohe Elohim,* and then God as *El,* to whom greatness and might are ascribed. [7] In David:

> A great *God (El)* is Jehovah, and a great monarch over all *gods (Elohim),* in whose hand are the explorations of the earth; and the strength of the mountains is his. (Psalms 95:3, 4)

Here God or *El* is mentioned, because the passage is talking about divine truth and the power it supplies, and then gods, because it is talking about

the true ideas that result. A monarch, on an inner level, symbolizes truth
(§§1672, 2015, 2069, 3009, 3670), so you can see what "a great monarch
over all gods" implies. Explorations of the earth are also true ideas in the
church, which are called the strength of the mountains because of the
power they have from goodness. In the same author:

> Who in the sky will compare themselves to Jehovah, will be like Jehovah,
> among the *children of gods (Elim)? God (El)* is strong in the private [coun-
> cil] of the holy. Jehovah, *God* Sabaoth, who is like you, a mighty Jah?
> (Psalms 89:6, 7, 8)

The children of gods, or of the *Elim,* stand for divine truth, which is
plainly credited with power, since the passage says, "God *(El)* is strong;
Jehovah, God of Armies, who is mighty like you?" [8] Again elsewhere in
the same author:

> Give Jehovah—you *children of gods*—give Jehovah glory and *strength!*
> (Psalms 29:1)

In Moses:

> They fell on their faces and said, "*God of the gods (El Elohe)* of the spirits
> of all flesh!" (Numbers 16:22)

In David:

> I have said, "You are *gods (Elohim),* and you are all children of the
> Highest One." (Psalms 82:6; John 10:34)

Truths are the reason the people here are called gods. Children, [or
sons,] mean truths (§§489, 491, 533, 1147, 2628, 3373, 3704). In the same
author:

> Acclaim the *God of the gods (Elohe Elohim),* acclaim the Lord of the
> lords! (Psalms 136:2, 3)

In Daniel:

> The king will act according to his pleasure and lift himself and exalt
> himself over every *god (El);* and against the *God of gods (El Elohim)* he
> will speak strange things. (Daniel 11:36)

This evidence shows that the most direct meaning of *El Elohe* is
God of the gods, and that in the inner meaning, gods refer to truths
from the Lord.

[9] *El,* or God, is used in the singular where the text is talking about the power that comes of divine truth—in other words, of the Lord's divine spirituality—as the following passages show. In Moses:

> I wish my hand were as *God (El)* to do you evil! (Genesis 31:29)

In another place:

> Nor is [your] hand as *God (El).* (Deuteronomy 28:32)

And in Micah:

> Their hand is as *God (El).* (Micah 2:1)

A hand as God means an attempt at power. For a hand meaning power, see §§878, 3387; and that a hand is spoken of in connection with truth, §3091. In David:

> On the sea I will put his *hand,* and on the rivers, his *right hand.* The name he will give me is "You are my Father, my *God (El),* the Rock of my salvation." (Psalms 89:25, 26)

This is about the power that comes of truth. In the same author:

> Scoundrels say in their heart, "*God (El)* has forgotten, has hidden his face; he will never see." Rise, Jehovah *God (El)!* Raise your *hand!* Why does a scoundrel despise *God (Elohim)?* (Psalms 10:11, 12, 13)

Likewise. [10] In the same author:

> Jehovah is my rock and my fortress and my rescuer, my *God (El),* my towering rock. (Psalms 18:2)

This is about power. In Isaiah:

> The remainder will return, the remainder of Jacob, to the *mighty God (El).* (Isaiah 10:21)

In the same author:

> A child has been born for us, a son has been given to us, on whose shoulder will be sovereignty; they will call his name Miraculous, Counselor, *God (El), Mighty One,* Eternal Father, Prince of Peace. (Isaiah 9:6)

In the same author:

> Look: the *God (El)* of my salvation! I will trust and not be afraid, because he is my *strength.* (Isaiah 12:2)

In the same author:

> I am *God (El)* even from [this] day; I am he, and there is no one snatching from my hand. I do something, and who will reverse it? (Isaiah 43:12, 13)

This is about power. In Jeremiah:

> *God (El) the great, the mighty,* whose name is Jehovah of Armies. (Jeremiah 32:18)

In 2 Samuel:

> With my *God (El)* I will leap the wall. *God (El)*—his way is upright; Jehovah's speech is pure. Who is *God (El)* besides Jehovah? Who is a rock besides our *God (Elohim)?* The *God (El)* of my refuge is *strength.* (2 Samuel 22:30, 31, 32, 33)

[11] In Moses:

> *God (El)* is not a man and would tell lies, nor is he the offspring of humankind and would have regrets. Has he said a thing and not done it, or spoken and not secured it? He brought them out of Egypt; he has strength like that of a unicorn. At that time it will be said to Jacob and Israel, "What has God done?" (Numbers 23:19, 21, 22, 23)

In an inner sense this is about power and truth. In the same author:

> *God (El),* who brought them out of Egypt—he has strength like that of a unicorn. He will devour the nations, his foes, and their bones he will break and the arrows of [a foe] he will crush. (Numbers 24:8)

Horns, and the strength of a unicorn, symbolize the power truth acquires from goodness; see §2832. Not to mention many other passages.

As most words in Scripture also have a negative meaning, so do *god* and *gods,* which are referred to as such when the theme is falsity and the power it yields. In Ezekiel, for instance:

> The *gods (Elim) of the mighty* will speak to him in the middle of hell. (Ezekiel 32:21)

In Isaiah:

> You grew hot for your *gods (Elim)* under every green tree. (Isaiah 57:5)

They are called gods because of falsity. There are other similar passages.

The Universal Human
and Correspondence (Continued):
Correspondence with the Eye and Light

4403 I was able to observe and learn what spirits were like, and which area of the body they belonged to, by their position and location in me, their horizontal level, and their remoteness on that level.

The ones who appeared near me were usually the agents of entire communities. Communities delegate spirits to visit others, whose thoughts and feelings they perceive through those spirits. That is how they communicate with others. By the Lord's divine mercy, though, the so-called proxies, or emissary spirits, will be discussed separately.

I have observed the following about them: The ones who appear above the head and close to it are those who teach and readily allow themselves to be taught. The ones low at the back of the head are those who act quietly and discreetly. The ones near the back are similar. The ones at the thorax, or chest, are those who possess neighborly love. The ones in the groin are those with marriage love. The ones by the lower legs are earthly spirits, and the ones by the feet are the coarser ones of this kind.

The spirits near the face are of different types, according to their correspondence with the facial sense organs. The ones by the nostrils, for instance, are those who have the skill of perception. The ones by the ears are the obedient. The ones by the eyes are those with understanding and wisdom. And so on.

4404 The five outer senses—touch, taste, smell, hearing, and sight—each correspond with inner senses, but hardly anyone today knows about correspondences. After all, people do not realize that there is such a thing as correspondence, let alone that it exists between what is spiritual and what is earthly—in other words, between attributes of the inner and outer selves.

To describe the correspondence of the senses: The sense of touch in general corresponds with a desire for goodness; the sense of taste, with a desire to know; the sense of smell, with a desire to perceive; the sense of hearing, with a desire to learn, and with obedience; while the sense of sight corresponds with a desire to have understanding and wisdom.

4405 The reason the sense of sight corresponds with a desire to have understanding and wisdom is that the sight of the body corresponds perfectly to the sight of its spirit and therefore to the intellect.

There are two kinds of light: one that the world receives from the sun, and one that heaven receives from the Lord. Worldly light does not contain intelligence, but heavenly light does. The more the objects of the world's light are illuminated in us by the objects of heaven's light—the more they correspond, then—the more understanding and wisdom we have.

Since eyesight corresponds to intellect, the intellect is also said to have sight, which is called intellectual sight. Ideas that we discern are called objects of that sight. Even in everyday language we say we see those ideas when we understand them, and the intellect is said to have light, enlightenment, and therefore clarity, or conversely shadow, darkness, and therefore obscurity.

4406

These and other expressions like them have come into use in our speech because they correspond. Our spirit lives in heaven's light, our body in the world's light, and our spirit is what lives in our body and does its thinking. Consequently many inner attributes have slipped down into our language in this way.

The eye is the most wonderful organ in the face and communicates more directly with the intellect than any other sense organ in a human. A more rarified atmosphere acts on the eye than on the ear, so the sights we see penetrate to the inner seat of sensation in our brain by a shorter, deeper route than that taken by the speech we perceive with our ear.

4407

That is why some animals lacking an intellect have two surrogate "brains" in their eye sockets: their intellect depends on their vision. People do not work this way. We are endowed with a large brain, so our intellect does not depend on our sight but the other way around.

It is quite clear that our sight depends on our intellect. Consider that our earthly emotions are reflected in our face but our deeper emotions, which involve our thoughts, appear in our eyes. They show themselves as a kind of vital spark with its radiating light, which gleams out in the presence of thought-filled emotion.

This is a phenomenon we recognize and observe, even though we are not given any formal education in it. We recognize it because our spirit associates with spirits and angels in the other world, who know about it from unmistakable perception. (On the point that everyone's spirit associates with spirits and angels, see §§1277, 2379, 3644, 3645.)

To people who reflect, it is obvious that eyesight corresponds with the sight of the intellect. Worldly objects all draw on sunlight, enter through the eye, and store themselves in the memory, evidently in a form closely related to the visual; when we retrieve them, we see them inwardly. That is the source of human imagination, whose images are

4408

referred to by philosophers as material ideas. When the objects present themselves on a still deeper plane, they facilitate [higher-level] thought. In this case as well they appear in some kind of visual image, but a more refined one. The images involved in [higher-level] thought are called immaterial ideas, or intuitional ones.

Plainly, inner light is the light that contains life and therefore understanding and wisdom. It illuminates the inner eye and reaches out to objects that have entered through outer vision. The way inner light operates is determined by the way impressions from worldly light are arranged inside a person.

Information entering through the ear also turns into semi-visual images from the world's light once it arrives inside a person.

4409 Since eyesight corresponds to intellectual sight, it also corresponds to truth, because everything about the intellect relates to truth. It also relates to goodness, so that the intellect not only knows what is good but is also affected by it.

Everything involved in physical sight also relates to truth and goodness, because it relates to the symmetry of objects and so to their beauty and appeal.

Any keen-sighted person can see that absolutely everything in the physical world relates to truth and goodness. Such a person can also recognize, as a result, that the whole material world is a theater representing the Lord's kingdom.

4410 The sight of the left eye corresponds to truth in the intellect; the right eye corresponds to a desire for truth, which also belongs to the intellect. Consequently the left eye corresponds to faith in what is true, and the right eye, to faith in what is good. A great deal of experience has shown all of this to me.

The reason for the correspondence is that light from the Lord contains not only light but also warmth. The actual light is truth emanating from the Lord, and the warmth is goodness. From this fact, and from the inflow into the two hemispheres of the brain, comes the correspondence. People who possess goodness are on the Lord's right, while those who possess truth are on his left.

4411 Each and every aspect of the eye corresponds to something in the heavens. This includes the three humors—aqueous, vitreous, and crystalline—and not only the humors but also the membranes and in fact every part of the eye.

The deeper parts of the eye have more beautiful, appealing correspondences, although they differ from heaven to heaven. When light radiating from the Lord flows into the third and inmost heaven, it is received as goodness, which is called charity. When it flows directly and indirectly into the second, middle heaven, it is received as the truth that comes of charity. When this truth flows directly and indirectly into the first and outermost heaven, it is received as a substance, in the form of a paradisal garden, or a city with palaces in it. That is the order in which the correspondences follow one another till they end with the angels' outer eyesight.

It is similar in humankind. In the outermost element of human sight—the eye—[truth] is presented in the form of matter, by means of that sight whose objects are the things of the visible world.

An individual with love and charity and consequently faith has similar inner levels, because such a person corresponds to the three heavens and is a miniature heaven.

A man I had known in bodily life—though I had not known his disposition or deeper feelings—talked with me several times in the other life, but only briefly and from a distance. He revealed himself in a general way through entrancing representations. He was able to create pleasures for the eye (such as colors of every kind and lovely colored shapes), to insert images of little children wearing beautiful adornments, as angels do, and to add many other attractive, agreeable sights. He worked by exerting a soft, gentle influence on a membrane in the left eye. By these methods he gained access to the feelings of other people, in order to please them and enhance their lives. **4412**

Angels told me that people like this are associated with the membranes of the left eye, and that they provide a link with paradisal kinds of heavens, where truth and goodness are represented in the form of substance, as noted above in §4411.

Heaven's light contains understanding and wisdom; and what appears to angels' eyes as light is the insight to see what is true, and the wisdom to see what is good, radiating from the Lord. This I was allowed to learn through personal experience. I was lifted into a light that sparkled as if it were shimmering with diamonds, and while I was kept in that light I seemed to myself to be drawn away from body-centered thinking. I felt as though I was being drawn into spiritual thinking and therefore to the ideas that make it possible to understand truth and goodness. Thoughts that had their origin in the world's light appeared distant from me and essentially irrelevant, even though they were dimly present. **4413**

From this experience I was able to see that as we come into heaven's light we come into intelligence. So it is that the more insight angels have, the fuller and brighter the light they enjoy.

4414   There are as many different kinds of light in heaven as there are angelic communities composing heaven and in fact as there are angels in each community. The reason is that heaven is organized according to differences in goodness and truth, and therefore according to states of understanding and wisdom, and so according to the acceptance of light from the Lord. As a result, the light is never exactly the same in any two places in all of heaven. Rather, it differs in its blend of fiery red and bright white and in its strength. Understanding and wisdom is actually an exquisite modification of the heavenly light from the Lord.

4415   Recently-arrived souls—that is, newcomer spirits, or people who arrive in the other life several days after physical death—are astounded to find light there. They bring with them the misconception that light comes only from the [physical] sun and its fiery matter. Still less do they realize there is such a thing as light to illuminate the intellect, since they were not aware of it during bodily life. Still less again do they realize that this light enables us to think and generates any activity in our intellect by flowing into images acquired from worldly light.

If these newcomers have been good [on earth], they are taken up into heavenly communities and ushered from one to another in order to be taught. The goal is for them to see by personal experience that light exists in the other world and that it is stronger than any possible light in the world. The intent is also for them to perceive that the more light they live in there, the more insight they have.

Some who had risen into the realms of heavenly light spoke with me from there, confessing that they had never believed anything like it, and that worldly light was murky by comparison. From where they were they also gazed through my eyes into the light of the world, which they perceived simply as a dark cloud. "That's the kind of light people on earth have!" they said sympathetically.

These comments make it clear why the Word refers to heavenly angels as angels of light. They also make it clear that the Lord is our light and therefore our life (John 1:1–9; 8:12).

4416   The kind of light shining on spirits in the other world indicates their character, because the light they see by corresponds to the light they perceive by, as was said.

Those who knew the truth [in the world] and confirmed it to themselves but lived an evil life appear in a light that is snow-white but cold, like winter light. When they approach spirits surrounded by heaven's light, their own light is blotted out and turns dark. When they remove themselves from the heavenly light, it is replaced by a yellow glow like that of sulfur, in which they resemble ghosts. The truth they possess resembles a mirage now, because their belief in it had been dogmatic. Owing to the very nature of dogmatism, they believed what they believed because it brought them status, wealth, and prestige. They did not care what was true, only what was orthodox.

[2] Spirits engaged in evil and therefore in falsity appear in the kind of glow a coal fire emits. The glimmer turns pitch dark in the presence of heaven's light. However, the actual types of meager light by which they see vary with the falsity and evil they engage in.

This evidence also showed me why people who live an evil life can never have sincere, heartfelt faith in divine truth. They live in that smoky luminescence, which, when heavenly light falls on it, turns dark for them. They end up unable to see with either their eyes or their mind, in addition to which they writhe in pain, and some almost faint. That is why truth can never be accepted by the evil, only by the good.

[3] People on earth who live an evil life cannot believe they are in this light, because they cannot see the light that is shining on their spirit. All they can see is the light on which their eyesight and therefore their earthly mind depends. If the glimmer in which their spirit lives had the genuine light of truth and goodness flowing into it from heaven, it would change. And if they saw that glimmer and experienced the changes, they would clearly recognize how far they are from accepting matters of genuine light—that is, of faith—let alone from absorbing attributes of charity. So they would see how distant they are from heaven.

I once had a conversation with some spirits about life—that we have no life on our own, only from the Lord, although we seem to be alive on our own. (Compare §4320.) The first question we discussed was what life is. We said that life consists in understanding and willing; and since all intellect relates to truth, and all will to goodness (§4409), that to live is to understand what is true and will what is good. **4417**

Some argumentative spirits questioned this, though. There are spirits who have to be called argumentative, because no matter what the proposition, they argue over its validity. They are usually in the dark on all questions of truth. These arguers, as I was saying, maintained that people who do not understand anything true or will anything good are still alive. "In fact, such people consider themselves more alive than others," they said.

"It is true that the vitality evil people have seems like life to them," I was allowed to answer, "but it is a kind of life that is called spiritual death. You can see this by considering that understanding what is true and willing what is good constitutes life from the Divine. So understanding what is false and willing what is evil cannot constitute life, because evil and falsity are opposed to true life."

[2] For proof, they were shown what their life was like. Presented visually, it looked like the glow from a coal fire, obscured by smoky haze. When they are bathed in this glow, they cannot help thinking that the life force of their thought and will is the only kind of life there is. Even more convincingly, the light that goes with an understanding of truth (which is the light of real life) is completely incapable of being seen by them. As soon as they come into that light, it turns into their own darkened glimmer. As a result, they absolutely cannot see or therefore perceive anything.

They were also shown what the state of their vital energy then was. This was done by cutting off all their pleasure in falsity, which in the other world is accomplished by isolating them from the spirits they live among. On completion of the process their faces appeared to be drained of color, like corpses, so that you could say they were portraits of death.

Life in animals will be dealt with separately, by the Lord's divine mercy.

4418   People in hell are said to be in the dark, but they are said to be in the dark because they dwell in falsity. Just as light corresponds to truth, darkness corresponds to falsity.

A yellow glimmer like that of burning sulfur and coal surrounds them, as noted above, and this glimmer is what is meant by the darkness. The dull glow, and the visibility it provides, determines the reach of their intellect, because [light, sight, and intellect] correspond.

Another reason for calling their weak light darkness is that it becomes dark in the presence of heavenly light.

4419   There was a spirit with me who had known a great deal when he lived in the world and had therefore believed he was wiser than anyone else. As a result he developed the bad habit of wanting to control everything wherever he went. A certain community sent him to me to serve as their proxy, or their contact (§4403), and also to get him out of their way. His efforts to dominate them with his intelligence were aggravating.

While he was with me, I was given the opportunity to talk with him about intellectual conceit. This conceit is so ingrained in the Christian world, I said, that people consider all intelligence to be self-derived. They do not believe any of it comes from God—although when they speak from faith and doctrine, they say that everything true and good comes from heaven and accordingly from the Divine. They acknowledge that all ability to understand does too, since truth and goodness are what need to be understood.

The spirit did not want to listen, so I said it would help if he left, since his air of [superior] intelligence was irksome; but since he was sure he was smarter than anyone else, he did not wish to go.

[2] Then some angels showed him what self-derived and divinely derived intelligence are like. They used different kinds of light to demonstrate, since in the other world such phenomena are presented in a marvelous visual way as varieties of light.

The angels illustrated self-derived intelligence as a glimmer resembling swamp light ringed by darkness, reaching only a short distance from its source. They also showed how it was snuffed out instantly when a community of angels looked at it, just as swamp light does in the presence of daytime sunlight.

Then they showed what intelligence from the Divine was like, again using light. This light was brighter and more radiant than the sun at noon and reached unlimited distances, ending in outer space as sunlight does. Understanding and wisdom, they said, enter from all directions into the halo of that light, making it possible to perceive truth and goodness with almost unlimited insight—depending on what kind of truth one acquires from goodness.

From this evidence it can be seen that in the human being, features of worldly light correspond to features of heavenly light. So the vision of our outer self, or eyesight, corresponds to the vision of our inner self, or intellectual sight.   **4420**

It can also be seen that different kinds of light in the other world make the nature of one's intelligence visible.

There is more on correspondence with the eye and light at the end of the next chapter [§§4523–4534].   **4421**

Genesis 34

[Matthew 24:42–51]

4422 THIS chapter will be introduced with an explanation of the Lord's words in Matthew 24, from verse 42 to the end—the chapter's final words on the close of the age, or the Lord's Coming. The literal words are these:

> Be watchful, then, because you do not know at what hour your Lord is coming. Know this, though: that if the householder knew in which watch the thief is coming, he would certainly be watchful and not let his house be broken into. Therefore you be ready too, because at an hour that you do not imagine the Son of Humankind will come. Who, then, is the faithful servant, and wise, whom his lord set over his domestics, to give them their food on time? Fortunate is that servant whom his lord, coming, finds doing so. Truly, I say to you that [his lord] will set him over all his goods. But if that evil servant says in his heart, "My lord puts off coming," and starts to beat his fellow servants and to eat and drink with the drunkards, the lord of this servant will come on a day that he does not expect and in an hour that he does not realize. And [his lord] will cut him in two and put his portion with the hypocrites. In that place there is lamentation and the gnashing of teeth. (Matthew 24:42, 43, 44, 45, 46, 47, 48, 49, 50, 51)

Context clarifies what these words involve. After all, the whole Gospel chapter has been about the church's final days—this being what the close of the age and the Lord's Coming mean in an inner sense. The explanations of the chapter's entire contents show this to be true. See the explanations at the head of the last few chapters: chapter 26, §§3353–3356; chapter 27, §§3486–3489; chapter 28, §§3650–3655; chapter 29, §§3751–3757; chapter 30, §§3897–3901; chapter 31, §§4056–4060; chapter 32, §§4229–4231; chapter 33, §§4332–4335.

[2] Those discussions also laid out the sequential thread of the contents, which predicted what would happen when the Christian church

that was established after the Lord's Coming started to destroy itself, falling away from goodness:

1. People would start to forget what was good and true and would quarrel over it.
2. They would despise it.
3. Next they would refuse to acknowledge it at heart.
4. Then they would profane it.
5. Since religious truth and neighborly kindness would survive among certain people referred to as the chosen, the text depicts the state of faith at that point
6. and afterward the state of neighborly love.
7. Finally it treats of the start of a new church and
8. the condition of goodness and truth in the so-called church when that church is rejected and a new church is adopted.

This series suggests what is involved in the passage quoted above—the closing part of that chapter. It encourages people in the church to do the good that faith requires, and warns that if they do not, they will be destroyed.

Hardly anyone knows what happens when an old church is rejected and a new one is adopted. Some people know nothing about the inner dimension of a human being or the state of that dimension, so they do not know about a person's state after death. Such people necessarily figure that individuals in the old church who are stripped of goodness and truth—that is, who no longer pay heartfelt tribute to goodness and truth—will perish, in a flood like the antediluvians or by exile from their land like the Jews or in some other way.

In reality, though, when a church has been devastated—in other words, when it no longer does the good required by faith—it perishes mainly in terms of its inner state. So it perishes mainly in regard to its state in the other world. Heaven then detaches from the people of that church (as does the Lord) and shifts to another group of people, whom it adopts in their place. This is because heaven has no means of contact with humankind if the church does not exist somewhere on earth. The church is like the heart and lungs of the universal human on earth (§§468, 637, 931, 2054, 2853).

[2] People who are then in the old church and have consequently been banished from heaven are in a flood in regard to their inner reaches, and the water even goes over their head. They themselves are unaware of the deluge while living in their body, but they enter it after death. In the

other world the flood is obvious. In fact, it looks like a thick fog enveloping them and separating them from heaven.

The situation of people wrapped in that misty fog is that they absolutely cannot see to identify religious truth, let alone religious goodness. Heaven's light, which contains understanding and wisdom, cannot penetrate their cloud.

Such is the state of a devastated church.

4424   The inner meaning of the Lord's words quoted above is self-evident. The Lord is not speaking so much in a representative and symbolic way as in metaphors. All that needs to be explained is the symbolism of the words in the last verse: *He will cut him in two and put his portion with the hypocrites. In that place there is lamenting and the gnashing of teeth.*

He will cut him in two means being separated and isolated from goodness and truth. People who know what is good and true, as those in the church do, and yet who live evil lives, are said to be cut in two when that knowledge is taken from them. In the other world they are deprived of the knowledge of goodness and truth and are held in the grip of evil and therefore of falsity. The purpose is to prevent them from making contact with heaven through their knowledge of goodness and truth and with hell through evil and the resulting falsity. If they did that, they would hang suspended between the two. Another purpose is to prevent them from profaning what is good and true, which happens when goodness and truth are mixed with falsity and evil.

The same idea is symbolized by the Lord's words to the man who hid his talent in the earth:

> Take the talent from him and give it to the one who has ten talents. Because those who have something will be granted everything, so as to overflow with it. But from those who do not have anything, even what they have will be taken. (Matthew 25:28, 29)

This is also true of statements the Lord makes elsewhere in Matthew (13:12), and in Mark (4:25) and Luke (8:18).

[2] *And put his portion with the hypocrites* symbolizes such people's fate (their portion) among those who seem outwardly to adopt a true theology and live a good life but inwardly believe nothing that is true and intend no good (that is, hypocrites). Such people are accordingly "cut in two." When their outer veneer is taken from them, which happens to everyone in the other life, they appear as they are on the inside, devoid of faith and neighborly love. These are qualities they had displayed in order to dupe others into bestowing honors, wealth, and reputation on them.

Almost all who are in the devastated church are like this. They have the outward appearance [of goodness] but nothing inside. So their inner depths are immersed in a flood, as discussed just above in §4423.

[3] *In that place there will be lamentation and the gnashing of teeth* symbolizes their state in the other life. Lamentation is the state of their evil, and the gnashing of teeth is the state of their falsity.

Teeth in the Word symbolize what lies on the lowest earthly level—in a positive sense, truth on that level, and in a negative sense, falsity. That is also what teeth correspond to. The gnashing of teeth, then, is falsity's clash with truth. Some people concentrate on the earthly realm alone, and concentrate on it as a result of sensory illusions, believing only what their senses allow them to see. These people are said to gnash their teeth. In the next life they even seem to themselves to be gnashing their teeth when they are drawing conclusions about religious truth on the basis of their illusions.

In a religion stripped of goodness and truth, people like this are numerous.

The gnashing of teeth has the same symbolism elsewhere, as in Matthew:

> The children of the kingdom will be cast out into outer darkness; in that place there will be lamentation and the *gnashing of teeth*. (Matthew 8:12)

The children of the kingdom are people in a devastated religion. The darkness means falsity (§4418) because they are in the dark when they are in the thick fog described above. The gnashing of teeth is the clash between falsity and truth there. Likewise in other passages, such as Matthew 13:42, 50; 22:13; 25:30; Luke 13:28.

Genesis 34

1. And Dinah—daughter of Leah, whom she bore to Jacob—went out to see the daughters of the land.

2. And Shechem—son of Hamor the Hivite, a chieftain of the land—saw her and took her and lay with her and humbled her.

3. And his soul clung to Dinah, Jacob's daughter, and he loved the girl and spoke to the girl's heart.

4. And Shechem said to Hamor his father, saying, "Take me this girl for my woman."

5. And Jacob heard that [Shechem] had defiled Dinah, his daughter. And his sons were with his property in the field. And Jacob kept quiet until their coming.

6. And Hamor, Shechem's father, went out to Jacob to speak with him.

7. And Jacob's sons came from the field when they heard it, and the men grieved, and [anger] blazed in them strongly because [Shechem] had done folly in Israel, to lie with Jacob's daughter, and this must not happen.

8. And Hamor spoke with them, saying, "Shechem my son—his soul has a desire for your daughter; would you please give her to him for his woman?

9. And may you unite in kinship with us; may you give your daughters to us and take our daughters for yourselves.

10. And with us may you settle, and the land will be before you; settle it, travel it on business, and have a possession in it."

11. And Shechem said to [Dinah's] father and to her brothers, "Let me find favor in your eyes, and what you say to me I will give.

12. Multiply dowry and gift greatly on me, and I will give as you say to me; and may you give me the girl for my woman."

13. And Jacob's sons answered Shechem and Hamor his father in deceit and spoke, because he had defiled Dinah, their sister.

14. And they said to them, "We cannot do this thing, to give our sister to a man who has a foreskin, because this is a disgrace to us.

15. Nonetheless, in this we will concede to you if you become like us by circumcising every male among you.

16. And we will give our daughters to you, and your daughters we will take for ourselves, and we will settle with you, and we will become one people.

17. And if you don't listen to us, to be circumcised, we will take our daughter and go."

18. And their words were good in the eyes of Hamor and in the eyes of Shechem, Hamor's son.

19. And the youth was not slow to do the thing, because he took pleasure in Jacob's daughter. And he was more honored than anyone in his father's household.

20. And Hamor and Shechem his son came to the gate of their city and spoke to the men of their city, saying,

21. "Those men are peaceful toward us, and they will settle in the land, and travel it on business. And the land—look, it is wide in extent before them. Their daughters we could take for ourselves as our women, and our daughters we could give to them.

22. Nonetheless, in this the men will concede to us, to settle with us, to become one people: if every male among us is circumcised, as they are circumcised.

23. Their property and their purchases, and every animal of theirs—is it not ours? Only let's concede to them, and they will settle with us."

24. And they listened to Hamor and to Shechem his son—everyone going out the gate of [Shechem's] city—and circumcised every male, everyone going out the gate of [Shechem's] city.

25. And it happened on the third day, while they were in pain, that two sons of Jacob—Simeon and Levi, Dinah's brothers—each took his sword and came upon the city boldly and killed every male.

26. And Hamor and Shechem his son they killed by the mouth of the sword and took Dinah from Shechem's house and went out.

27. Jacob's sons came upon those stabbed, and plundered the city, because [the residents] had defiled their sister.

28. Their flocks and their herds and their donkeys and whatever was in the city and whatever was in the field they took.

29. And all their riches and every little child of theirs and their women they captured and plundered, and everything that was in the house.

30. And Jacob said to Simeon and to Levi, "You have caused me trouble, to make me stink with the inhabitant of the land—the Canaanite and the Perizzite—and my numbers are few. And they will gather against me and strike me, and I will be destroyed, I and my household."

31. And they said, "Shall he treat our sister as a whore?"

Summary

THE inner meaning of this chapter deals with Jacob's descendants and their obliteration of all the doctrinal truth known to the ancient church. Hamor, Shechem, and the people of their city represent that truth. The representation of a religion existing among Jacob's descendants lay only in outward appearances, devoid of inner content; the representative religion existing among the ancients lay in outward appearances combined with inner content.

4425

Inner Meaning

4426 GENESIS 34:1, 2, 3, 4. *And Dinah—daughter of Leah, whom she bore to Jacob—went out to see the daughters of the land. And Shechem—son of Hamor the Hivite, a chieftain of the land—saw her and took her and lay with her and humbled her. And his soul clung to Dinah, Jacob's daughter, and he loved the girl and spoke to the girl's heart. And Shechem said to Hamor his father, saying, "Take me this girl for my woman."*

Dinah went out symbolizes a desire for everything faith espouses, and the religion that results. *Daughter of Leah, whom she bore to Jacob,* means on an external level. *To see the daughters of the land* means to learn about different kinds of desire for truth and about the religions growing out of them. *And Shechem saw her* symbolizes truth. *Son of Hamor the Hivite* means from the ancients. *A chieftain of the land* symbolizes the most important [truth] among those religions. *And took her and lay with her and humbled her* means that in no other way could it unite with the desire for the truth symbolized by Jacob's sons, her brothers. *And his soul clung to Dinah, Jacob's daughter,* symbolizes a favorable leaning toward union. *And he loved the girl and spoke to her heart* symbolizes love. *And Shechem said to Hamor his father* symbolizes thinking based on truth known to the ancients. *Saying, "Take me this girl for my woman,"* symbolizes a wish to unite with the desire for that truth.

4427 *Dinah went out* symbolizes a desire for everything faith espouses, and the religion that results. This can be seen from the representation of *Dinah* as a desire for all truth and as the religion resulting from this desire (discussed in §§3963, 3964). Jacob's twelve sons represented all aspects of faith and therefore everything that goes to make up a religion (§§2129, 2130, 3858, 3926, 3939). Dinah, then, who was born after the ten sons Jacob had with Leah and the slaves, symbolizes a desire for those things. So she symbolizes the church, because the church comes from a desire for truth. In fact, it is all the same whether you say a desire for truth or the church. A desire for truth is what causes a person to *be* a church.

4428 *Daughter of Leah, whom she bore to Jacob,* means on an external level, as the following shows: *Leah* represents a desire for outer truth, as discussed in §§3793, 3819. And in the highest sense *Jacob* represents the Lord—specifically, divine truth on the Lord's earthly plane—as discussed in §§3305, 3509, 3525, 3546, 3576, 4234, 4273, 4337. In a secondary sense he represents an external religion, or the outer level of a religion, as discussed in §§3305, 4286. This clarifies that *daughter of Leah, whom she bore to Jacob,* symbolizes a desire for truth on an external level.

To see the daughters of the land means to learn about different kinds of desire for truth and about the religions growing out of them, as the following shows: *Seeing* symbolizes knowing, as mentioned several times before. *Daughters* symbolize different kinds of desire and the resulting religions, as discussed in §§2362, 3024, 3963. And the *land*—the land of Canaan, in this case—symbolizes an area where the church exists, and therefore the religion itself, as discussed in §§662, 1066, 1068, 1262, 1733, 1850, 2117, 2118, 2928, 3355, 3686, 3705.

4429

[2] What follows will make it possible to see the symbolism involved in the current verse, which has to do with the representation of a religion that was to be established among Jacob's descendants. The representation could not be established among them until inner truth had been totally destroyed in them—in other words, until they no longer had any knowledge of it; see §4289. Inner truth consists in everything represented and symbolized by the rituals commanded of Jacob's descendants. All their rituals represented and symbolized something in the Lord's kingdom in the heavens and therefore something in his kingdom on earth, which is to say, in the church. The things symbolized and represented here are the inner truths.

Absolutely everything commanded of Jacob's descendants when the representation of a church was being established among them, as described in the books of Moses (especially Exodus and Leviticus), represented and symbolized heavenly and spiritual attributes of the Lord's kingdom. This has been demonstrated throughout the exegesis. Jacob's descendants knew nothing about it, because they would have profaned it had they been aware of it (§§301, 302, 303, 2520, 3398, 3479, 3769, 4281, 4293). So they did not take up these representative duties until they had been completely stripped of inner truth.

The theme of the current chapter, then, is inner truth and their extinguishing of its light.

[3] The representative acts commanded of Jacob's posterity were not new but had mostly been in earlier use among the ancients. The ancients did not worship outward appearances, though, as was done by Jacob's offspring, who were the inhabitants of Judah and Israel. Instead they worshiped inner realities, in which they recognized the Lord himself. A remnant of the church from ancient times was still in existence in the

land of Canaan, particularly among the people called Hittites and Hivites. So those nations represent truth that had been known to the church.

These considerations can now clarify to some extent what is symbolized by "Dinah—Jacob's daughter by Leah—went out to see the daughters
of the land." Dinah represents the external type of religion that was being
established among Jacob's descendants, and the daughters of the land symbolize different religions among the ancients. For the symbolism of daughters throughout the Word's inner meaning as religions, see §§2362, 3024,
where the meaning is illustrated. For the symbolism of the land as an area
and nation in which the church exists and therefore as the church, see
§§662, 1066, 1068, 1733, 1850, 2117, 2118, 2928, 3355, 3686, 3705.

4430   *And Shechem saw her* symbolizes truth. This can be seen from the representation of *Shechem* as truth—in this case, truth that the church possessed
from ancient times. Shechem represents such truth because the church
still survived in the nation Shechem belonged to. His nation was one of
the upright ones, as proved by Hamor and Shechem's sincerity when they
spoke to Jacob and his sons (verses 8, 9, 10, 11, 12) and by the compliance
the people showed in order that Shechem could marry Dinah (verses 18,
19, 20, 21, 22, 23, 24). This being so, they represented the church's truth.

In addition, the city of Shechem was Abram's first stopping place
when he arrived in Canaan from Syria (Genesis 12:6). Now, on Jacob's
arrival from Syria, it was also *his* first stopping place, where he spread
his tent, made huts, and established an altar (Genesis 33:17, 18, 19, 20).
Abraham's and Jacob's journeys or travels represented progress in religious
truth and a loving goodness—progress by the Lord, in the highest sense,
and by a person the Lord is regenerating, in a secondary sense. This has
been explained a few times already. So Shechem symbolized the beginning of light (§§1440, 1441) and consequently inner truth, since inner
truth is the beginning of light.

[2] The current chapter, however, deals in its inner meaning with
Jacob's descendants and the way they extinguished this first light or inner
truth in themselves. On this level of meaning—an inner narrative level—
Jacob's sons stand for all his progeny. The Word's inner meaning, you see,
concerns itself only with matters of the Lord's kingdom and therefore
of his church. Jacob's actual children did not constitute a religion. Their
descendants did, but not till after they left Egypt and in fact not till they
entered the land of Canaan.

[3] As for this city named after Shechem, in ancient times it had been
called Salem. The previous chapter makes this clear: "Jacob came to *Salem,*

the city of Shechem, which is in the land of Canaan" (Genesis 33:18). Salem symbolizes calm, the city of Shechem symbolizes inner religious truth, and we come into a state of calm when we arrive at that truth; see §4393. Later the same city was called Shechem, as can be seen in Joshua:

> Joseph's bones, which the children of Israel brought up from Egypt, they buried in *Shechem,* in the part of the field that Jacob had bought from the children of Hamor, Shechem's father, for a hundred kesitahs. (Joshua 24:32)

And in Judges:

> Gaal, son of Ebed, said to the citizens of *Shechem,* "Who is Abimelech— and who is Shechem—that we should serve him? Isn't he Jerubbaal's son, and isn't Zebul his deputy? Serve the men of Hamor, Shechem's father! And why must we serve this one?" (Judges 9:28)

[4] The same city was eventually called Sychar, as is plain in John:

> Jesus came into a city of Samaria called *Sychar,* near the field that Jacob gave Joseph his son. Jacob's spring was there. (John 4:5, 6)

These passages and others mentioning the city show that it symbolizes inner truth. So does this one in Hosea:

> Gilead is a city of evildoers, polluted by blood; and as a man awaits troops, [they await] a company of priests. They kill on the way *to Shechem* because they have done an enormity. In the house of Israel I saw a vile thing. (Hosea 6:8, 9, 10)

"They kill on the way to Shechem" means that they obliterate truth all the way to its inner forms, so that everything remaining is superficial. The obliteration of inner truth is also symbolized by Abimelech's action in destroying that city and sowing it with salt (Judges 9:45).

Son of Hamor the Hivite means from the ancients, as the following **4431** shows: The *son,* Shechem, symbolizes inner truth, as discussed just above. (For the meaning of a son as truth, see §§489, 491, 533, 1147, 2623, 3373, 4257.) And *Hamor* represents the father of that truth, so he represents its origin among the ancients.

The truth within the [Israelites'] rituals and representative objects came from the church of ancient times, and because it did, Hamor is also called a *Hivite.* The Hivite nation symbolized inner truth among the ancients, because it had possessed such truth since ancient times. That is why Hamor is called a Hivite here. All the nations in the land of Canaan symbolized some good or true characteristic of the church in early times, because the earliest church, which was heavenly, was located there (§3686). Later they turned aside to idolatry, as did all the other nations in which the church existed. As a consequence the same nations also symbolize different forms of idolatry. However, the Hivites had symbolized inner truth from early on, and they were among the more upright nations, whose wickedness had not been as complete as the others'; that is, religious truth had not been blotted out so entirely in them. So the Lord in his providence preserved the Gibeonite Hivites through a pact that Joshua and his chieftains struck with them (Joshua 9:15; to see that the Gibeonites were Hivites, consult Joshua 9:7; 11:19).

These remarks now show that Shechem, son of Hamor the Hivite, symbolizes inner truth from the ancients.

4432 *A chieftain of the land* symbolizes the most important [truth] among those religions. This can be seen from the symbolism of a *chieftain* as that which is most important (discussed in §§1482, 2089) and from the symbolism of the *land* as a religion (discussed in §§662, 1066, 1068, 1262, 1733, 1850, 2117, 2118, 2928, 3355, 3686, 3705).

4433 *And took her and lay with her and humbled her* means that in no other way could it unite with the desire for the truth symbolized by Jacob's sons, her brothers. This can be seen from the symbolism of *taking her, lying with her, and humbling her* as uniting but not in the lawful way, which is by betrothal.

It is impossible, without knowing the facts of the matter, to see how these words mean that this uniting could not happen any other way. The inner truth from the ancients symbolized by Shechem, son of Hamor the Hivite, is truth that had been core to the church among the ancients. It was core to their statutes, judgments, and laws—in other words, to their rituals and so on. That truth constituted the doctrine they lived by. More specifically, it constituted the doctrine of neighborly love, because people belonging to the genuine church of those ancient days had no other doctrine. As it relates to theology, it can be called inner religious truth, but as it relates to life it can be called goodness.

If any church was going to be established in the nation descended from Jacob, its people had to be introduced into this kind of truth and goodness. There is no church unless there is an inner dimension within the outer dimension. That is, there is no church unless people think about deeper implications while going through the outward motions and are moved by those deeper levels—or at least are moved by the outward acts because of their inner content. The inner depths make the church, because the Lord is in them. It is there that spiritual and heavenly qualities from him are found.

[2] However, the nation descended from Jacob, the nation of Israel and Judah, could not be introduced to inner truth in the lawful way, by betrothal, because the outward worship of that nation's people did not correspond to it. From Abraham, Isaac, and Jacob, their ancestors, they received a form of worship started by Eber, which on the face of it was at variance with the worship of the ancient church (see §§1238, 1241, 1343, 2180). Since their worship was at variance, the inner truth known to the ancients could not unite with it in the lawful way, by betrothal, but in the manner depicted here. From this you can understand what it means to say that in no other way could inner truth unite with the desire for the truth symbolized by Jacob's sons, Dinah's brothers.

[3] Even though a law recorded in Exodus 22:16 and Deuteronomy 22:28, 29 and also known to the ancients did allow couples to come together this way, that nation flatly refused to accept a connection between the inner truth passed on by the ancients and the outward acts of worship among [its members], the descendants of Jacob (§§4281, 4290, 4293, 4307, 4314, 4316, 4317). As a result, no religion could be set up in that nation but rather a mere representation of a religion (see §§4281, 4288, 4307). The fact that the people of that nation not only were unable to accept inner truth but even annihilated it in themselves is represented by several events here: Jacob's sons answered Shechem and Hamor in deceit (verse 13); then Simeon and Levi struck the city with the mouth of the sword and killed Hamor and Shechem (verses 25, 26); and the other sons came upon those stabbed, plundered the city, and took the flocks and herds and whatever was in the city, field, and house (verses 27, 28, 29).

These comments show what the prophetic words of Jacob, who by then was Israel, symbolize:

> Simeon and Levi are brothers; tools of violence are their blades. Into their conspiracy my soul is not to come; with their band my glory is not to unite, because in their anger they killed a man, and in their pleasure they hamstrung an ox. A curse on their anger because it is fierce and on their fury because it is heavy! I will divide them among Jacob and scatter them among Israel. (Genesis 49:5, 6, 7)

And his soul clung to Dinah symbolizes a favorable leaning toward union. This can be seen from the symbolism of a *soul's clinging* as a leaning. Clearly the leaning is toward union, because in an inner sense, anything

4434

connected with marriage love involves spiritual union—the union of truth with goodness and of goodness with truth. The reason anything connected with marriage love in its inner meaning involves spiritual union is that marriage love has its origin in the marriage of truth with goodness and of goodness with truth; see §§2618, 2727, 2728, 2729, 2737, 2803, 3132. Adultery mentioned in the Word, then, means the adulteration of what is good, and whoredom means the falsification of what is true (§§2466, 2729, 2750, 3399). From these considerations it stands to reason that nothing the current chapter has to say about Shechem and Dinah means anything else in its inner sense than the union of the truth that Shechem represents with the desire for truth that Dinah represents. So it stands to reason that the words *his soul clung to Dinah* symbolize a favorable leaning toward union.

[2] This whole chapter is about Shechem's love for Dinah, looking to marriage, and his efforts to make her his woman. In view of this, and because anything connected with marriage love symbolizes spiritual union, let me prove from the Word that what it says about marriage and related topics involves such a meaning. In John:

> Let us rejoice and exult and give the glory to him—because the time came for the *Lamb's wedding*, and *his wife* prepared herself—as people who have been called to the supper of the *Lamb's wedding*. (Revelation 19:7, 9)

In the same author:

> I saw the holy city New Jerusalem coming down from God out of heaven, prepared as a *bride adorned for her husband*. One of the seven angels spoke with me, saying, "Come, I will show you the *bride, the Lamb's wife*." He took me away in spirit onto a mountain big and high and showed me the great city, Jerusalem the Holy, coming down out of heaven from God. (Revelation 21:2, 9, 10)

In fact, the material about the bride and the marriage here symbolizes a bond between the Lord and the church—a bond formed by truth and goodness. This is plain to see, because the holy city, the New Jerusalem, is actually the church. A city means the church's truth (see §§402, 2268, 2449, 2451, 2712, 2943, 3216), and Jerusalem means a spiritual religion (§§402, 2117, 3654). [3] In Malachi:

> Judah committed treachery, and an abominable thing was done in Israel and in Jerusalem, because Judah profaned Jehovah's holiness; for *he loved and betrothed to himself the daughter of a foreign god*. Jehovah has stood as witness between you and *the wife of your youth*, against whom you committed treachery. (Malachi 2:11, 14, 15)

Loving and betrothing [to oneself] the daughter of a foreign god means uniting with or internalizing falsity rather than truth, which is the wife of one's youth. [4] In Ezekiel:

> You took *your sons and your daughters* whom you *bore* to me and sacrificed them to be devoured. Was there too little of your *whoring?* You are the daughter of your mother, who showed disgust for *her husband* and *her children;* and you are the sister of your sisters, who showed disgust for *their husbands* and *their children.* (Ezekiel 16:20, 45)

This is about Jerusalem's abominations, which resulted from evil and falsity and are therefore depicted in that chapter by behavior that violates marriage: adultery and whoredom. The husbands who were treated with disgust are goodness, the sons are truth, and the daughters are desire for truth. [5] In Isaiah:

> Sing, *infertile woman!* (She had not *given birth.*) Break into song and shout for joy (she has not *gone into labor*), because the *children of the desolate one* are more numerous than the *children of the married one.* The reproach of your *widowhood* you will remember no longer, because the name of *your husbands,* your makers, is Jehovah Sabaoth; and your redeemer, the Holy One of Israel, is called God of the whole earth. For Jehovah has called you as a *woman abandoned* and afflicted in spirit and as the *consort of his youth* when she is divorced, your God has said. All *your children* will be taught by Jehovah, and great will be the peace of *your children.* (Isaiah 54:1, 4, 5, 6, 13)

Seeing that marriage symbolizes the union of truth with goodness and of goodness with truth, you can tell what is symbolized by husband and wife, sons and daughters, widows, and the divorced, and by giving birth, being in labor, being desolate, and being infertile, because they all have to do with marriage. The spiritual symbolism of each of these images has been demonstrated many times in various explanations. [6] In the same author:

> For Zion's sake I will not keep quiet, and for Jerusalem's sake I will not rest. No longer will you be named *Abandoned,* but your land will be called *Married,* for Jehovah will take pleasure in you, and your land will be *married.* Because *a young man will marry a young woman, your sons will marry you,* and there will be the joy of a *bridegroom* over a *bride;* your God will rejoice over you. (Isaiah 62:1, 4, 5)

Anyone who does not know the Word's inner meaning might suppose that these images in the Word are mere metaphors, like those used frequently in everyday language. Such a person might imagine that the church is being compared to a daughter, young woman, or wife, and accordingly that matters of faith and charity are being compared to various aspects of marriage. In the Word, though, everything represents spiritual and heavenly qualities and genuinely corresponds to them. The Word came down from heaven, and because it did, it is divinely heavenlike and spiritual from its outset. The elements of the literal meaning correspond to this plane. As a consequence, traits of the heavenly marriage (which is the union of goodness and truth) come down into images that correspond to them and therefore into aspects of marriage on earth.

[7] That is why the Lord compared the kingdom of the heavens (or his kingdom in heaven) and his kingdom on earth (or the church) to a royal personage who *gave a wedding* for his son and invited many guests to it (Matthew 22:2 and following verses). He also compared his kingdom to ten *unmarried young women* who, taking lamps, went out to meet the *bridegroom* (Matthew 25:1 and following verses). In addition the Lord called people in the church the sons of the wedding:

> Jesus said, "Can the *sons of the wedding* mourn while the *Bridegroom* is with them? But the days will come when the *Bridegroom* will be taken from them, and then they will fast." (Matthew 9:15)

[8] For the same reason, a desire for goodness and a desire for truth are called the joy and gladness of bridegroom and bride, because heavenly joy springs from those desires and lies in them. In Isaiah, for instance:

> Your sons will *marry* you, and there will be the joy of a *bridegroom* over a *bride;* Jehovah your God will rejoice over you. (Isaiah 62:5)

In Jeremiah:

> The voice of joy and the voice of gladness, and the voice of the *bridegroom* and the voice of the *bride,* the voice of those who say, "Acclaim Jehovah, because Jehovah is good!" (Jeremiah 33:11)

In the same author:

> I will bring an end in the cities of Judah and in the streets of Jerusalem to the voice of joy and the voice of gladness, the voice of the *bridegroom* and the voice of the *bride,* because the earth will turn into a wasteland. (Jeremiah 7:34; 16:9; 25:10)

And in John:

> The light of a lamp will not shine in Babylon any longer, and the voice of *bridegroom* and *bride* will not be heard in it any longer. (Revelation 18:23)

[9] Since through true marriage love, marriages on earth correspond to the heavenly marriage—the marriage of goodness and truth—the laws concerning betrothal and marriage laid down in the Word are in complete correspondence with spiritual laws concerning the heavenly marriage. An example is the requirement that a man marry only one wife (Mark 10:2–8; Luke 16:18). It is the same in the heavenly marriage: goodness can unite only with its truth, and truth with its goodness. If goodness formed a bond with any truth other than its own, it could not possibly survive but would be torn in two and destroyed. In a spiritual religion, a wife represents what is good, and a man represents what is true; but in a heavenly religion, a husband represents what is good, and a wife, what is true. Moreover—and this is a secret—they not only represent those things but actually correspond to them.

[10] Laws concerning marriage laid down in the Old Testament likewise correspond with the laws of heavenly marriage. Examples appear in Exodus 21:7, 8, 9, 10, 11; 22:16, 17; 34:16; Numbers 36:6; Deuteronomy 7:3, 4; 22:28, 29. There are also the laws about the degrees of forbidden relations in Leviticus 18:6–20. The particulars will be discussed elsewhere, with the Lord's divine mercy.

In Ezekiel it is plain that degrees of relationship in marriage and the laws governing them trace their source to laws concerning truth and goodness (which are the laws of the heavenly marriage) and reflect those laws:

The priest-Levites shall *not take themselves a widow* or *divorced woman as wives,* but *virgins* from the seed of Israel's house. And the *widow* who was a *widow* of a priest they shall take. (Ezekiel 44:22)

This verse is about the holy city—the new Jerusalem—and the heavenly Canaan. Obviously these stand for the Lord's kingdom and his church, so the Levites do not mean Levites, nor the widow or divorced woman, a widow or divorced woman, but the concepts to which they correspond.

And he loved the girl and spoke to her heart symbolizes love, as is self-evident.

4435

And Shechem said to Hamor his father symbolizes thinking based on truth known to the ancients. This is established by the symbolism of *saying,* in scriptural narrative, as perceiving and therefore thinking (mentioned in §3395) and from the representation of *Shechem, Hamor's son,* as truth known to the ancients (discussed in §§4430, 4431). These meanings show that *Shechem said to Hamor his father* means thinking based on truth known to the ancients.

4436

4437   *Saying, "Take me this girl for my woman,"* symbolizes a wish to unite with the desire for that truth. This can be seen from the symbolism of the *girl,* Dinah, as a desire for the truth symbolized by Jacob's sons, her brothers (discussed in §§4427, 4433), and from that of *taking as his woman* as uniting (discussed above in §4434).

4438   Genesis 34:5, 6, 7. *And Jacob heard that [Shechem] had defiled Dinah, his daughter. And his sons were with his property in the field. And Jacob kept quiet until their coming. And Hamor, Shechem's father, went out to Jacob to speak with him. And Jacob's sons came from the field when they heard it, and the men grieved, and [anger] blazed in them strongly because [Shechem] had done folly in Israel, to lie with Jacob's daughter, and this must not happen.*

Jacob heard that he had defiled Dinah, his daughter, means uniting in an unlawful way; *Jacob* in this case means the outer ancient church. *And his sons were with his property in the field* means that his descendants were absorbed in their religiosity. *And Jacob kept quiet until their coming* means consulting the religious truth he and his descendants possessed. *And Hamor, Shechem's father, went out to Jacob to speak with him* symbolizes counsel taken by the truth known to that religion. *And Jacob's sons came from the field* means that they consulted their own religiosity. *And the men grieved, and [anger] blazed in them strongly* means that they were immersed in evil directed against truth as it was known to the church among the ancients. *Because he had done folly in Israel, to lie with Jacob's daughter, and this must not happen* symbolizes a union they saw as unlawful that violated the truth they possessed.

4439   *Jacob heard that he had defiled Dinah, his daughter,* means uniting in an unlawful way—uniting with the desire for the truth known to the outer church represented at this point by Jacob—as the following shows: *Defiling* means uniting unlawfully. Marriage symbolizes lawful union (§4434), so the defilement of marriage symbolizes a union that is not lawful (concerning which, see §4433). *Dinah* represents a desire for everything faith espouses, and the religion that results, as discussed in §4427. And *Jacob* in this case represents the outer ancient church.

Jacob symbolizes the outer ancient church here because that church was to have been established among his descendants. It would have been established, too, if his descendants had accepted the inner truth possessed by the ancients. Jacob's representation as that church here can also be seen from the context of the current chapter. He was not in league with his sons when they struck the city and killed Hamor and Shechem. That is why he said to Simeon and Levi in verse 30, "You have caused me trouble, to make me stink with the inhabitant of the land." And in the prophecy he uttered before dying, "Into their conspiracy my soul is not to come; with their band my glory is not to unite, because in their anger they killed a man, and in their pleasure they hamstrung an ox" (Genesis 49:6). Jacob represents the outer ancient church in many other Scripture passages as well (§§422, 4286), because in the highest sense he represents the Lord's earthly divinity, to which the outer church corresponds.

Jacob's sons stand for his descendants, though, who wiped out the truth they possessed from the ancients. In the process they destroyed any trace of religion. All that remained to them was the representation of a religion, as discussed in §§4281, 4288, 4289, 4311.

And his sons were with his property in the field means that his descendants were absorbed in their religiosity. This can be seen from the symbolism of *his sons* as his posterity; from that of *property* as outer truth (discussed in §§1435, 4391); and from that of a *field* as the church (discussed in §§2971, 3766). So *his sons were with his property in the field* means that they were absorbed in their religiosity. The kind of religion that existed among them has to be called a religiosity, because it consisted in outward worship devoid of inward content. **4440**

And Jacob kept quiet until their coming means consulting the religious truth he and his descendants possessed, as the following shows: *Keeping quiet* means thinking about and silently consulting. And *until their* (his sons') *coming* means the religious truth he and his descendants possessed. Sons mean truth; see §§489, 491, 533, 1147, 2623, 3373, 4257. The consultation was to be with Jacob's sons and consequently with the truth they symbolized, so the truth known to Jacob and his descendants is what was consulted. **4441**

And Hamor, Shechem's father, went out to Jacob to speak with him symbolizes counsel taken by the truth known to that religion, as the following indicates: *Hamor, Shechem's father,* represents the truth of the ancient people, as discussed in §§4430, 4431. *Jacob* represents the outer ancient church, as discussed just above in §4439. And *speaking with him* symbolizes consulting. So the clause symbolizes counsel taken by the truth known to that religion. **4442**

Anyone who does not know that names in the Word symbolize something will be surprised at this meaning of the words *Hamor, Shechem's father, went out to Jacob to speak with him*—that the truth known to the church as it existed among the ancients consulted the version of truth belonging to the ancient church that was to be established among Jacob's descendants. On the other hand, it will not be a surprise to anyone who knows that the Word has this kind of inner meaning, especially not to those who have learned from the books of the ancients about their manner of writing. It was quite common for them to introduce abstract qualities such as Wisdom, Understanding, Knowledge, and so on as if they were conversing with each other. They would also give them names symbolizing the qualities. That is exactly what the gods and demigods of the early people were, as were the human figures they created in order to weave the subject matter into a story.

[2] The sages of old took this custom from the ancient church, which was scattered throughout much of the Near East (§§1238, 2385), since the people of the ancient church used representations and symbols in their sacred texts.

The ancient church received this practice from the mouth of the earliest people, who came before the Flood (§§920, 1409, 1977, 2896, 2987), and they received it from heaven, because they had contact with heaven (§§784, 1114–1125). The first heaven—the lowest of the three heavens—engages in this kind of representation and symbolism, which is why the Word was composed in the same mode. The Word has a unique characteristic, setting it above the writings of the early people, though. All the topics in unbroken sequence represent heavenly and spiritual aspects of the Lord's kingdom and, in the highest sense, the Lord himself. Even the narrative parts are like this. What is more, they are genuine correspondences coming from the Lord without interruption through the three heavens.

4443   *And Jacob's sons came from the field* means that they consulted their own religiosity, as the following shows: *Jacob's sons* symbolize the nation descended from them, among whose people a representation of a religion was established. And a *field* symbolizes a religiosity, as noted above in §4440. *Coming from* it means consulting it, as follows from context. It also follows from the consideration that their religious culture is what they are said to come from.

4444   *When they heard it, and the men grieved, and [anger] blazed in them strongly* means that they were immersed in evil directed against truth as it was known to the church among the ancients. This can be seen from the current symbolism of *grieving* and *blazing strongly* as being immersed in evil. That the evil was directed against truth as it was known to the church among the ancients follows from the fact that it was directed against Shechem, Hamor's son, who symbolizes truth among the ancients, as noted above at §§4430, 4431.

Subsequent verses make it clear that these people were immersed in evil. They spoke in deceit (verse 13), and after Shechem and Hamor had complied with their request, they killed them both (verses 26–29). As a result, their grieving and blazing strongly means that they were steeped in evil. It looks as though they were feeling zeal over Shechem's lying with their sister, as in the next few clauses: "Because he had done folly in Israel, to lie with Jacob's daughter, and this must not happen." And at the end of the chapter: "They said, 'Shall he treat our sister as a whore?'" (verse 31). It was not zeal, though. Zeal can never exist in anyone controlled by evil, only in a person committed to goodness, because zeal contains goodness (§4164).

[2] The religiosity of their descendants did harbor something good, because each and every component of it represented heavenly and spiritual attributes, which belong to the Lord's kingdom. However, as far as the people in it went, it contained nothing good. They concentrated on outward appearances alone aside from any inward reality, as shown above [§§4433, 4440].

It resembles the religiosity in which the people of that nation are still immersed today. They acknowledge Moses and the Prophets and therefore the Word, and in itself this is holy, but in regard to the people themselves, the religion is not holy. At every point in the Word they focus on themselves, so they make it worldly and even earthbound. If there is anything heavenly in the Word, they do not know or care about it. People in this kind of state cannot dwell in goodness when they are practicing their religiosity, only in evil. Nothing heavenly influences them, because they smother it in themselves.

[3] A law that was also known to the ancient church allowed a man who had humbled an unmarried woman to give a dowry and take her as his wife, in keeping with these words in Moses:

> If a man persuades a virgin who is not betrothed, and he lies with her, he shall endow her with a dowry as his wife. If her father firmly refuses to give her to him, he shall pay silver equaling the dowry of virgins. (Exodus 22:16, 17)

And in another place:

> If a man finds a girl, a virgin, who is not betrothed, and seizes her and lies with her, and they are caught, the man who lay with her shall give the girl's father fifty pieces of silver, and she shall become his wife, in exchange for his humbling her; and he cannot divorce her all his days. (Deuteronomy 22:28, 29)

What Shechem said to the girl's father and brothers shows plainly that the same law was known to the ancients:

> Shechem said to her father and to her brothers, "Let me find favor in your eyes, and what you say to me I will give. Multiply dowry and gift

greatly on me, and I will give as you say to me; and may you give me
the girl for my woman." (verses 11, 12)

Shechem was willing to fulfill the law, and Dinah's brothers conceded, providing Shechem became like them by circumcising every male, in accord
with these subsequent words:

> Nonetheless, in this we will concede to you if you become like us by
> circumcising every male among you; and we will give our daughters to
> you, and your daughters we will take for ourselves, and we will settle
> with you, and we will become one people. (verses 15, 16)

This being so, the brothers' actions were obviously not inspired by the
law and therefore not by anything good. They were acting against the law
and consequently from evil motive.

[4] The law did forbid them to enter into marriage with the surrounding nations, as recorded in Moses:

> You are not to take any of their daughters for your sons, or to let their
> daughters whore after their gods and make your sons whore after their
> gods. (Exodus 34:16)

And in another place:

> You shall not contract kinship with the nations; your daughter you shall
> not give to their son, and their daughter you shall not take for your son,
> because they will lead your son or daughter astray from [walking] after
> me to serve other gods. (Deuteronomy 7:3, 4)

This law concerned idolatrous nations, though, and was laid down to
keep the people from being drawn away from true representational worship to idolatrous worship through marriage. When the Israelites became
idolaters, they could not represent heavenly and spiritual attributes of
the Lord's kingdom any longer, only the opposite qualities, such as exist
in hell. As idolaters they were calling up from hell a particular devil,
whom they were worshiping and to whom they were attaching divine
representations. That is why the quotation says they were not to whore
after the nations' gods. Another reason they were not to intermarry is that
the nations symbolized evil and falsity, and the goodness and truth the
Israelites represented was not to be mixed with it; what belonged to the
Devil and to hell was not to be mixed with what belonged to heaven and
the spirit (§3024 at the end).

[5] There never was a ban on marrying into nations that accepted the
worship of [Jacob's descendants] and that acknowledged Jehovah after

they were circumcised. [Jacob's descendants] referred to such people as immigrants residing with them. Moses has this to say about them:

> If *an immigrant should reside with you* and wish to perform the Passover to Jehovah, *every male of his shall be circumcised,* and then he shall approach to perform it, and he will be as an inhabitant of the land. *One law there shall be for the inhabitant and for the immigrant who resides in your midst.* (Exodus 12:48, 49)

And in another place:

> When *an immigrant resides with you,* he shall perform the Passover to Jehovah according to the statute of the Passover; and according to its statutes, so he shall perform it. *One statute there shall be for you, both for the immigrant and for the native of the land.* (Numbers 9:14)

The reason they were called immigrants residing in the midst of and with [Jacob's descendants] was that immigrating symbolized being taught, and an immigrant symbolized people who let themselves be taught the statutes and doctrines. For this symbolism of immigrating and an immigrant, see §§1463, 2025, 3672. In the same author:

> For *if there resides with you an immigrant* who makes a fire offering for a restful smell to Jehovah—as you do it, so he shall do it. As for the congregation, *one statute there shall be for you and for the resident immigrant,* an eternal statute throughout your generations. *As you are, so shall the immigrant be before Jehovah. One law and one judgment shall there be for you and for the immigrant residing with you.* (Numbers 15:14, 15, 16)

And in other places:

> *The immigrant residing with you shall be to you as the native-born of you.* (Leviticus 19:34)

> *One judgment there shall be for you; as for the immigrant, so for the native shall it be.* (Leviticus 24:22)

[6] This statute was known not only to Jacob and his children but also to Shechem and Hamor, as their words demonstrate. The statutes, judgments, and laws given to the nation of Israel and Judah were not new ones but ones that had previously existed in the ancient church. The same regulations also existed in the second ancient church, which was named the Hebrew church, after Eber, as shown in several places. As a consequence, the law currently under discussion was known. This is clear

from the words of Jacob's sons: "Jacob's sons said to Hamor and Shechem, 'We cannot do this thing, to give our sister to a man who has a foreskin, because this is a disgrace to us. Nonetheless, in this we will concede to you if you become like us by circumcising every male among you; and we will give our daughters to you, and your daughters we will take for ourselves, and we will settle with you, and we will become one people'" (verses 14, 15, 16). It is also clear from the words of Hamor and Shechem. Not only did they concede, they also had themselves and every male of their city circumcised (verses 18, 19, 20, 21, 22, 23, 24). [7] Plainly, then, Shechem acquired the same status as an immigrant, a situation addressed in the law, and accordingly could take Jacob's daughter as his woman. So the sons' murder of [Shechem's people] was an unspeakable deed, as Jacob testified before his death (Genesis 49:5, 6, 7).

Scriptural narrative reveals that Judah, Moses, the kings of the Judeans and Israelites, and many others of the people also married non-Jewish wives. There should be no doubt that these women accepted the statutes, judgments, and laws of [Jacob's descendants] and were acknowledged as immigrants.

4445   *Because he had done folly in Israel, to lie with Jacob's daughter, and this must not happen* symbolizes a union they saw as unlawful that violated the truth they possessed. This can be seen from the symbolism of *doing folly, to lie with Jacob's daughter,* as an unlawful union. *Lying with* her and defiling her in the process means uniting unlawfully; see above at §4439. The text says *in Israel* because *Israel* symbolizes an inner plane of religion. It then says *Jacob's daughter* because Jacob symbolizes an outer plane of religion. On the point that Israel means the inner part of the church, and Jacob the outer, see §§4286, 4292, 4439.

The fact that they saw it as unlawful, though it was lawful, can be seen from the discussion and proof just above in §4444 and elsewhere.

4446   Genesis 34:8, 9, 10, 11, 12. *And Hamor spoke with them, saying, "Shechem my son—his soul has a desire for your daughter; would you please give her to him for his woman? And may you unite in kinship with us; may you give your daughters to us and take our daughters for yourselves. And with us may you settle, and the land will be before you; settle it, travel it on business, and have a possession in it." And Shechem said to [Dinah's] father and to her brothers, "Let me find favor in your eyes, and what you say to me I will give. Multiply dowry and gift greatly on me, and I will give as you say to me; and may you give me the girl for my woman."*

Hamor spoke with them, saying, symbolizes goodness belonging to the church among the ancients. *Shechem my son* symbolizes the truth that grows out of it. *His soul has a desire for your daughter; would you please give her to him for his woman?* symbolizes a longing to unite with this new [religion], which on the face of it appears to resemble the ancient one. *And may you unite in kinship with us; may you give your daughters to us and take our daughters for yourselves* symbolizes the oneness of goodness and truth. *And with us may you settle* symbolizes life. *And the land will be before you; settle it* symbolizes a church that would be united. *Travel it on business, and have a possession in it* symbolizes creeds they share that will harmonize. *And Shechem said to her father and to her brothers* symbolizes truth of an ancient, divine stock consulting the goodness and truth characterizing this religiosity. *Let me find favor in your eyes, and what you say to me I will give* means that if they were likeminded on their part, he was too, on his part. *Multiply dowry and gift greatly on me; I will give as you say to me* means that he would welcome what they had to offer and make it his own. *And may you give me the girl for my woman* means as long as there was union.

Hamor spoke with them, saying, symbolizes goodness belonging to the church among the ancients. This can be seen from the representation of *Hamor* as something from the ancients, as discussed in §4431. To be specific, he represents the religious goodness they passed on. The goodness of a religion is a father, and the truth that grows out of it (Shechem, in this case) is a son, which is why a father in the Word symbolizes goodness, and a son, truth.

The phrase being used is "the goodness belonging to the church among the ancients," rather than "the goodness of the ancient church." The reason is that "the church among the ancients" means a religion that developed out of the earliest church, which came before the Flood. "The ancient church" means a religion that came after the Flood. These two churches have been discussed in several earlier places. In those places I showed that the earliest church, which came before the Flood, was a heavenly one, but that the ancient church, which came after the Flood, was spiritual. The difference between what is heavenly and what is spiritual has also been dealt with many times [§§1824, 2048, 2088, 2227, 2654, 3240, 3691, 3887].

[2] A remnant of the earliest, heavenly church still survived in the land of Canaan, particularly among the people there called Hittites and Hivites. It survived there, not elsewhere, because the earliest church, which was called Humankind, or Adam (§§478, 479), was located in Canaan. So that is where the Garden of Eden was. In the story, the Garden of Eden symbolized the understanding and wisdom of the people in that church (100, 1588), and the trees in the garden symbolized their ability to perceive

(103, 2163, 2722, 2972). Since the garden, or paradise, symbolized understanding and wisdom, it also means the church itself. Since it means the church, it means heaven, and since it means heaven, in the highest sense it means the Lord. That is why the land of Canaan in its highest sense symbolizes the Lord; in a secondary sense, heaven and the church; and in an individual sense, a person in the church (1413, 1437, 1607, 3038, 3481, 3705). It is also why the symbolism is the same when the Word refers simply to "the land" (566, 662, 1066, 1068, 1413, 1607, 3355). A new heaven and new earth, [or land,] are the inner and outer dimensions of a new religion (1733, 1850, 2117, 2118 at the end, 3355 at the end).

Because the earliest church was situated in the land of Canaan (see §567), locations there necessarily developed a representative meaning. That is why Abram was commanded to move there and his descendants through Jacob were given the land—to preserve the representative meaning of the places, since this meaning would be used in the writing of the Word (§3686). So all the sites there, the mountains and rivers, and all the surrounding borders took on representative meanings (§§1585, 1866, 4240).

[3] From these considerations you can see what I mean by the church among the ancients: the surviving remnant of the earliest church. Because this remnant survived among the Hittites and Hivites, a burial place was secured for Abraham, Isaac, Jacob, and their wives among the Hittites in Hittite territory (Genesis 23:1–end; 49:29, 30, 31, 32; 50:13), and for Joseph among the Hivites (Joshua 24:32). Hamor, Shechem's father, represented the remnant of the earliest church, so he symbolizes the goodness belonging to the church among the ancients and consequently the origin of inner truth from a divine stock (§4399).

For the difference between the earliest church, which predated the Flood, and the ancient church, which came after it, see §§597, 607, 608, 640, 641, 765, 784, 895, 920, 1114–1128, 1238, 1327, 2896, 2897.

4448   *Shechem my son* symbolizes the truth that grows out of it. This can be seen from the representation of *Shechem* as inner truth (discussed in §4430) and therefore as truth growing out of it—out of the goodness that is Hamor (§4447). All the truth a religion possesses comes from its goodness. Truth never comes from any other source.

The truth represented by Shechem is called inner truth and is in its essence simply the doing of good out of neighborly love. The earliest church, being heavenly, devoted itself to the doing of good out of love for the Lord and was accordingly able to perceive all truth. The people of that church were almost like angels, and had contact with angels, which is where their perception came from. For that reason, they never argued about religious truth but said yes to it, because they perceived from heaven that it was so. In fact, they did not even want to use the word "faith" but preferred to substitute "charity"; see §§202, 337, 2715, 2718, 3246. That is why inner truth here means charitable goodness. On the point that a remnant of the earliest church survived with Hamor the Hivite and his son Shechem, see the previous section, §4447.

[2] The situation was different with the ancient church, which was spiritual. The people of that church were dedicated not to love for the Lord, as the earliest church was, but to charity for their neighbor. They could arrive at charity only through religious truth, of which they did not have a perception, as the earliest people did. That is when people started inquiring into the validity of truth.

On the difference between heavenly people, who have perception, and spiritual people, who do not, see §§2088, 2669, 2708, 2715, 3235, 3240, 3246, 3887.

His soul has a desire for your daughter; would you please give her to him **4449** *for his woman?* symbolizes a longing to unite with this new one, which on the face of it appears to resemble the ancient one, as the following shows: *A soul's desiring* symbolizes a longing. Dinah, the *daughter,* represents a desire for truth and therefore a religion, since a desire for truth is what makes a religion religious. A religion is what "this new one" refers to. And *giving her for his woman* symbolizes union, as discussed in §4434.

[2] In regard to the superficial resemblance between this new religion established among Jacob's descendants and the ancient one, here is some necessary information: The statutes, judgments, and laws commanded of the Israelite and Judean nation by Moses were not very different from the statutes, judgments, and laws in force in the ancient church. This includes regulations concerning betrothal and marriage, slaves, which animals were to be eaten and which were not, cleansings, feasts, booths, eternal flames, and many other subjects. It also includes the official regulations of the second ancient church, founded by Eber, concerning altars, burnt offerings, sacrifices, and libations.

The Word's narratives make it quite plain that these were familiar before they were commanded of that nation. [3] To take up just the altars, burnt offerings, and sacrifices: Balaam is reported to have ordered that seven altars be built and that burnt offerings and sacrifices of young bulls and rams be offered on them (Numbers 23:1, 2, 14, 15, 29). Concerning the surrounding nations, many passages say their altars were destroyed [Exodus 34:13; Deuteronomy 7:5; 12:3; Judges 2:2]. And the prophets of Baal executed by Elijah are said to have offered sacrifices. Such evidence shows that the sacrifices commanded of the people of Jacob were not new. Neither were their other statutes, judgments, and laws.

These rules became idolatrous among the nations, though, particularly because they would employ them in the worship of some profane god, turning that which had a divine representation to hellish purposes. They also added new ones. Because of this, and in order to restore the representative worship of the ancient church, the regulations were revoked.

From this it can be seen that the new religion established among Jacob's descendants appeared on the face of it to resemble the ancient one.

4450 *And may you unite in kinship with us; may you give your daughters to us and take our daughters for yourselves* symbolizes the oneness of goodness and truth. This can be seen from the symbolism of *uniting in kinship* as becoming one (discussed in §4434) and from that of *daughters* as desires and therefore as forms of goodness (discussed in §§489, 490, 491, 2362, 3963). The fact that truth is what they become one with is symbolized by *may you give to us* and *may you take for yourselves.* Shechem and the sons of Jacob symbolize truth, as shown above.

Clearly, then, this sentence symbolizes the oneness of goodness and truth. In other words, this new religion would come to resemble the ancient church, not only in its outer face but also in its face within, through oneness.

4451 *And with us may you settle* symbolizes life. This can be seen from the symbolism of *settling* as living, as discussed in §§1293, 3384, 3613. *Settling with us,* then, means living together and making a single religion.

4452 *And the land will be before you; settle it* symbolizes a church that would be united. This is established by the symbolism of the *land* as a church (discussed in §§566, 662, 1066, 1068, 1413, 1607, 3355, 4447) and from that of "settling with us" as living together (discussed just above at §4451). So the meaning is that there would be a single church.

4453 *Travel it on business, and have a possession in it* means that creeds they share will harmonize, as the following shows: *Doing business* symbolizes acquiring and sharing religious knowledge, as discussed at §2967. So *traveling the land on business* means entering into a knowledge of goodness and truth—the knowledge symbolized by Shechem, Hamor's son, and his city. And *having a possession in it* symbolizes being unified and therefore harmonizing. People who possess a land in common are unified and in harmony.

Doing business means acquiring and sharing religious knowledge because no trade of any kind occurs in heaven, where Scripture is taken in its inner sense. They have no gold there, no silver, none of the goods we deal in on earth. So when the term *business* comes up in the Word, it is understood in a spiritual sense, and the kind of thing that corresponds to it is perceived. The general meaning is the acquisition and sharing of religious knowledge. The particular meaning is the commodity mentioned. If gold is mentioned, goodness that comes of love and wisdom is meant (§§113, 1551, 1552). If it is silver, the truth associated with understanding and faith is meant (§§1551, 2048, 2954). If it is ewes, rams, kids, or lambs—the ancient medium of exchange—then the qualities that ewes, rams, kids, and lambs symbolize are meant. And so on.

[2] In Ezekiel, for instance:

Say to Tyre, "You are one who lives at the entries to the sea, the *peoples' dealer* to many islands. Tarshish was *your merchant* for the abundance of all your riches; for silver, for iron, for tin and lead they sold *your market goods.* Javan, Tubal, and Meshech were *your dealers;* for human souls and vessels of bronze *they sold your cargo.* The children of Dedan were your *dealers.* Many islands were *your merchandise at hand.* Syria was *your merchant* for the abundance of your works. Judah and the land of Israel were *your dealers* in wheat, minnith, and pannag; and for honey and oil and balsam *they sold your cargo.* Damascus was *your merchant* for the abundance of your works from the abundance of all your riches—for the wine of Helbon and wool of Zahar. Dan and Javan gave you thread for *your market goods.* Dedan was *your dealer* in free-moving clothes for the chariot. The Arab and all the chiefs of Kedar were *your merchants at hand* for lambs and rams and he-goats; for these they were *your merchants.* The *dealers* of Sheba and Raamah were *your dealers* in the finest of every perfume; and for every precious stone and gold they sold *your trade goods.* Haran and Canneh and Eden were the *dealers* of Sheba; Assyria, Chilmad, *your dealer.* These were *your dealers* in perfect things, in bolts of blue-violet fabric, and embroidery, and in treasure chests of costly garments, in tied ropes and cedar timbers among *your merchandise.* So you were filled and received great honor in the heart of the seas." (Ezekiel 27:1–end)

[3] This passage and many others in the Word make it apparent that the trade goods, cargo, merchandise, and wares actually mean supplies of knowledge about goodness and truth. What does scriptural prophecy have to do with Tyre's tradings, unless they symbolize something spiritual and heavenly? This being so, it is quite plain that not only do the

wares symbolize other things but the nations mentioned there symbolize people in whom those things exist. It is clearly from the inner sense alone that the meaning can be known. Tarshish, Javan, Tubal, Meshech, the children of Dedan, Syria, Judah, Israel, Dan, Javan, Dedan, the Arab, Sheba, Raamah, Haran, Canneh, Eden, Assyria, and Chilmad have their symbolism. Then there is the symbolism of their goods, such as silver, iron, tin, lead, vessels of bronze, wheat, minnith, pannag, honey, oil, balsam, wine of Helbon, wool of Zahar, thread, free-moving clothes for the chariot, lambs, rams, he-goats, perfume, precious stone, gold, bolts of blue-violet fabric, embroidery, tied ropes, and cedar timbers. These and similar items symbolize the goodness and truth of the church and of the Lord's kingdom, and a knowledge of them. That is why Tyre is the subject, because Tyre symbolizes religious knowledge (§1201).

The presence of such commodities—in other words, goodness and truth in the church and the Lord's kingdom—was the reason for the name for the land of Canaan, which symbolizes the church and the Lord's kingdom. From ancient times this land was named for its wares or merchandise, since that is what Canaan means in the original language.

These remarks now show what traveling the land on business symbolizes.

4454   *And Shechem said to her father and her brothers* symbolizes truth of an ancient, divine stock consulting the goodness and truth characterizing this religiosity, as the following indicates: At this point *saying* symbolizes consulting. *Shechem* represents truth of an ancient, divine stock, as discussed above at §4447. The *father,* Jacob, symbolizes truth-based goodness, as discussed in §§4273, 4337. And the *brothers,* Jacob's sons, symbolize truth, as noted above [§4450].

The evidence offered above in §4447 shows that Shechem means truth of an ancient, divine stock. Hamor the Hivite, along with his nation and family, you see, was living among the survivors of the earliest church—a heavenly church—in the land of Canaan. This church more than any other in the whole world had a divine origin, because its people exhibited a goodness from love for the Lord. Their will and intellect formed a unit and therefore composed an undivided mind, so they were able to perceive truth on the basis of goodness. By an internal path the Lord flowed into the goodness in their will and through this into the goodness in their intellect, or truth. That is why this church above all others was referred to as Humankind (§§477, 478, 479) and as God's likeness (§§51, 473, 1013).

This explains why Hamor and Shechem are said to be of an ancient, divine stock, as also earlier at §4399.

The earliest church, called Humankind or (in Hebrew) Adam, was located in the land of Canaan, as noted above in §4447. This is quite plain from the church's descendants, called Nephilim in Genesis 6:4, who are said in Numbers 13:33 to have lived in Canaan; see §581. But Canaan was at that time the name of all the land from the river of Egypt to the river Euphrates (Genesis 15:18).

Let me find favor in your eyes, and what you say to me I will give means that if they were likeminded on their part, he was too, on his part. This can be seen from the symbolism of *finding favor in someone's eyes* as a stock phrase implying an inclination (discussed in §3980). Here it means an inclination to *give whatever they would say to him*. The statement means that he was of a mind on his part, if they were likeminded on their part, and this is clear from the context of the inner meaning. In an inner sense, *giving what they say* means joining forces with them in regard to truth and goodness.

4455

Multiply dowry and gift greatly on me, and I will give as you say to me means that he would welcome what they had to offer and make it his own. In other words, their religious outwardness would unite with his greater depth, and together they would make a single church. This can be seen from the symbolism of *giving as you say,* which means joining forces with them in regard to truth and goodness, as discussed just above in §4455. The actual *dowry and gift* that he said they should *multiply on him* symbolizes an agreement to form a single whole. The dowry given to a betrothed woman was a token of an agreement on both sides.

4456

He says they should multiply dowry and gift greatly on him (meaning above the established amount, fifty pieces of silver) because he had lain with her before adopting their religiosity. In addition, it was Jacob's role to consent or refuse, according to a law with which the ancients were also familiar, recorded in Exodus 22:16, 17. The main reason [for multiplying the dowry], though, was the desirability of the union between inner truth (Shechem) and the longing for outer truth (Dinah).

A dowry was a token of agreement and therefore confirmation of entry [into marriage] because paying or giving silver was a sign of ownership by the payer—a sign that the woman was his—while accepting the silver would be a reciprocal gesture. So these were signs that the bride was the bridegroom's, and the bridegroom was the bride's.

4457   *And may you give me the girl for my woman* means as long as there was union. This can be seen from the symbolism of *giving her for his woman* as union (discussed at §4434). In this case it means as long as there was union, since the pact had not yet been sealed.

4458   Genesis 34:13, 14, 15, 16, 17. *And Jacob's sons answered Shechem and Hamor his father in deceit and spoke, because he had defiled Dinah, their sister. And they said to them, "We cannot do this thing, to give our sister to a man who has a foreskin, because this is a disgrace to us. Nonetheless, in this we will concede to you if you become like us by circumcising every male among you. And we will give our daughters to you, and your daughters we will take for ourselves, and we will settle with you, and we will become one people. And if you don't listen to us, to be circumcised, we will take our daughter and go."*

Jacob's sons answered Shechem and Hamor his father in deceit symbolizes evil thinking and evil intentions concerning the truth and goodness belonging to the church among the ancients. *And spoke, because he had defiled Dinah, their sister,* means that since there was no other way to enter into union, it would be done by conforming. *And they said to them, "We cannot do this thing,"* means that they disapproved. *To give our sister to a man who has a foreskin* means unless [Shechem's people] viewed religious truth and goodness as consisting in the representation of it and turned away from the qualities symbolized by the representations. *Because this is a disgrace to us* means that it undermined them. *Nonetheless, in this we will concede to you if you become like us* symbolizes compliance with their religiosity. *By circumcising every male among you* symbolizes the outward representation alone, which would make [Shechem's people] pure in the eyes of [Jacob's offspring]. *And we will give our daughters to you, and your daughters we will take for ourselves* symbolizes the resulting union. *And we will settle with you* means in regard to life. *And we will become one people* means in regard to theology. *And if you don't listen to us, to be circumcised* means unless they turned away from the truth they possessed and conformed with outward representation. *We will take our daughter and go* means there would be no union.

4459   *Jacob's sons answered Shechem and Hamor his father in deceit* symbolizes evil thinking and evil intentions concerning the truth and goodness belonging to the church among the ancients, as the following shows: *Shechem* represents truth known to the ancients, or truth of an ancient, divine stock, as discussed in §§4399, 4454. *Hamor* represents the goodness from which that truth came, as discussed in §§4399, 4431, 4447, 4454. And *deceit* symbolizes evil thinking and evil intentions. Deceit in general involves evil directed against another person and against what that person says and does. The thinking and intentions of people engaged in deceit are quite different from that of their victims, as the outcome of this chapter's events illustrates. From these considerations it can be seen that *Jacob's sons answered Shechem and Hamor his father in deceit* symbolizes evil thinking and evil intentions concerning the truth and goodness belonging to the church among the ancients.

[2] Jacob's children, or descendants, were not able to harbor any thought or intent but an evil one toward truth and goodness in the inner self because they concentrated on outward appearances devoid of inward reality (§§4281, 4293, 4307, 4429, 4433). They were also dismissive of the inner dimension and consequently held it in utter contempt.

That nation is that way today too. So is anyone who cares only about the surface dimension. People wholly engrossed in what is external do not even know what it is to be alive to inner realities because they do not know what the inner plane is. If anyone mentions the inner plane in their presence, they might agree that it exists, because they know from doctrine that it does, but their agreement is a lie. Alternatively, they deny it with their lips as they do in their heart. They do not venture beyond the sense impressions of their outer self. As a result they do not believe there is any life after death. Neither do they believe there can be any resurrection, unless they are to rise in their body. They are allowed to have this picture of resurrection because otherwise they would have none. After all, they assign all life to the body, not knowing that the life of their body springs from the life of their spirit, which lives after death.

These are the only beliefs possible for people who focus on outer levels alone. In them, concrete realities stifle all thinking about and therefore all belief in inner realities.

[3] Since this kind of ignorance reigns supreme today, I need to explain what a concentration on outward appearances apart from inner realities is. Everyone lacking in conscience concentrates on the surface alone because the inner self reveals itself through conscience. And people always lack conscience when they think and do what is true and good not for the sake of truth and goodness but for the sake of themselves and their own status and wealth. The same is true of people who do so only out of fear of the law or fear for their life. Such people would plunge without scruple into every unspeakable crime if it did not endanger their reputation, position, resources, or life.

This fact is obvious from people in the other world who were this way during bodily life. Because one's inner depths lie open in the other world, such people are constantly trying to destroy others. As a consequence, they live in hell, where they are held in check by spiritual restraints.

[4] I wish to explain further what it is to be focused on the surface and what it is to be focused on what is within. I want to show that people who stay on the surface cannot grasp what the inner depths are and accordingly cannot form a desire for them—since we never form a desire for things we do not grasp.

Take, for example, the idea that to be least is to be greatest in heaven, that to be humble is to be exalted, that to be poor and needy is to be rich and prosperous. People who focus on the surface alone cannot comprehend this. They do not see how being least can ever mean being greatest, how being humble can mean being exalted, how poverty can be wealth, how need can be abundance. Yet this is exactly how matters stand in heaven. Since they cannot comprehend the situation, they cannot desire it; and when they reflect on it from the viewpoint of the bodily and worldly concerns that occupy them, they find it repellent. They do not see at all that this is the case in heaven, and as long as they restrict themselves to superficialities, they do not want to see it. In fact, they *cannot*.

Those in heaven who know, acknowledge, and believe at heart—which means with warm acceptance—that they have no strength on their own, but that all their strength comes from the Lord, are called the least. Nonetheless they are the greatest, because they have power from the Lord. Those who are humble are likewise exalted. The humble are those who warmly acknowledge and believe that they have no strength on their own, no understanding or wisdom on their own, and no goodness or truth on their own. They are gifted by the Lord with more power, more understanding of truth, and more wisdom about goodness than any others. The poor and needy are likewise rich and prosperous. The ones called poor and needy are those who believe at heart, with warm acceptance, that they possess nothing on their own, have no knowledge or wisdom on their own, and cannot do anything on their own. In heaven they are rich and prosperous because the Lord gives all wealth to them. They are wiser than others, more affluent than others, live in the grandest palaces (§§1116, 1626, 1627), and have access to the treasuries holding all of heaven's riches.

[5] For another example, people who stay on the surface cannot possibly grasp that heavenly joy is to love one's neighbor more than oneself and to love the Lord above all—the amount and quality of this love

determining one's happiness. People who focus on mere superficialities love themselves more than their neighbor. If they love others, it is only because those others curry their favor; so they love others for their own sake. They love themselves in others, and others in themselves. People like this cannot see what it is to love others more than oneself. They do not even want to see, and cannot. When you tell them heaven consists in this love (§548), they balk. In consequence, people who were such in physical life can never go near a heavenly community. If they do, their negativity causes them to throw themselves headlong into hell.

[6] Few people today know what it is to be focused on the surface and what it is to be focused on what is within, and most believe the two are mutually exclusive, so let me supply one more example by way of illustration.

There is nourishment for the body and nourishment for the soul. People who care only for superficial pleasure fuss over their skin, indulge their belly, love to live sumptuously, and feel that the height of pleasure lies in rich edibles and exquisite potables. People focused on inner matters also take sensual pleasure in these things, but their dominant desire in nourishing their body with delicious food is to keep it healthy, the aim being a healthy mind in a healthy body. So their main goal is mental health, to which bodily health serves as a means. Spiritual people do not stop there but regard the health of the mind, or soul, as a means of absorbing understanding and wisdom—not for the sake of reputation, position, or wealth but for the sake of life after death. Those who are spiritual to an even higher degree consider understanding and wisdom to be an intermediate goal that enables them to serve as useful members in the Lord's kingdom. Those who are heavenly seek to serve the Lord. To such a person, physical food is a means to the enjoyment of spiritual food, and spiritual food is a means to the enjoyment of heavenly food. Since the different types of food are designed to serve one another in this way, they also correspond with each other—which is why they are referred to here as food.

This discussion shows what it is to be focused only on the surface and what it is to be focused on what is within.

[7] Aside from the members of it who died as little children, the nation of Judah and Israel (the focus of the inner narrative meaning in the current chapter) for the most part has this character. Its people are more focused on what is external than any others because of their greed. People who love gain and profit only for the gold and silver and for no other purpose, and

who place all life's joy in possessing these, live at the outermost, lowliest level. What they love is like the absolute dust of the earth. By contrast, people who love gold and silver for some higher purpose raise themselves out of the dust in proportion to that purpose. The very purpose we love circumscribes our life and distinguishes us from others. An evil purpose makes us hellish. A good purpose makes us heavenly. Not that the purpose itself does so but our love for that purpose. In what we love lies our life.

4460   *And spoke, because he had defiled Dinah, their sister,* means that since there was no other way to enter into union, it would be done by conforming. This can be seen from the explanation of the words "he took her and lay with her and humbled her," which meant that in no other way could he unite with the desire for the truth symbolized by Jacob's sons, her brothers; see §4433. *He had defiled her* involves a similar meaning.

4461   *And they said to them, "We cannot do this thing,"* means that they disapproved, as is self-evident.

4462   *To give our sister to a man who has a foreskin* means unless [Shechem's people] viewed religious truth and goodness as consisting in the representation of it and turned away from the qualities symbolized by the representations. This can be seen from the symbolism of a *foreskin* as an outward representation—a sign that they were [not] part of the church. Because of this meaning it was common to use the terms *circumcision* and *foreskin* to distinguish between people in the church and people not in the church. Circumcision symbolizes leaving behind any tainted love (any self-love or materialism) and approaching heavenly love (love for the Lord or for one's neighbor). So it symbolizes moving toward the church, which is why the clause symbolizes compliance with the religiosity of [Jacob's offspring]. The result of this compliance would be that [Shechem's people], like [Jacob's offspring], would view religious truth and goodness as consisting in the representation of it and turn away from the inner qualities symbolized. Otherwise they would not resemble [Jacob's offspring] as required in the next sentence: "In this we will concede to you if you become like us."

On the point that circumcision is a sign of purification from unclean types of love, see §§2039, 2632. On the point that people with unclean kinds of love are described as having a foreskin, see §§2049, 3412, 3413.

[2] Hardly anyone today knows the specific meaning of circumcision, so it needs to be spelled out. The genitals in both sexes symbolize—and not only symbolize but actually correspond to—different aspects of the

union between goodness and truth. The end material in several chapters has shown that all human organs and limbs correspond with spiritual qualities in heaven [§§3624–3649, 3741–3750, 3883–3896, 4039–4055, 4218–4228, 4318–4331, 4403–4421]. This includes the organs and parts dedicated to reproduction, which correspond with the marriage of goodness and truth. From this marriage descends marriage love; see §§2618, 2727, 2728, 2729, 2803, 3132, 4434.

Since the foreskin covers a genital organ, it corresponded to the masking of goodness and truth in the earliest church and to the contamination of them in the ancient church. In the people of the earliest church, goodness and truth could be masked but not contaminated, because they were people of depth. The people of the ancient church were relatively shallow, so goodness and truth could be contaminated in them. Shallowness and specifically shallow kinds of love are what introduce contamination. That is why people of the earliest church knew nothing about circumcision; only those of the ancient church did.

[3] From the ancient church, circumcision spread to many other nations. It was imposed on Abraham and his descendants not as something new but as a practice that had been dropped and was to be restored. It was to become a sign to his posterity that they belonged to the church. However, the nation of Abraham's descendants did not know what circumcision symbolized and did not want to know, because they considered religiosity to be identical with representative acts, which are external. So they condemned the uncircumcised generally. In reality, though, circumcision was merely a sign representing purification from self-love and materialism. People who have been purified of these are spiritually circumcised; their hearts are said to be circumcised. In Moses, for instance:

> *Jehovah God will circumcise your heart and the heart* of your seed, [to cause you] *to love* Jehovah your God with all your heart and with all your soul. (Deuteronomy 30:6)

In the same author:

> *You shall circumcise the foreskin of your heart,* and you shall no longer harden your neck. (Deuteronomy 10:16, 18)

In Jeremiah:

> Till untilled ground for yourselves and *remove the foreskin of your heart!* (Jeremiah 4:3, 4)

[4] People wallowing in love for themselves and for worldly advantages are called foreskinned, even if they were circumcised, as in Jeremiah:

> Watch! The days are coming when I will inflict punishment on everyone *circumcised in the foreskin*—on Egypt and on Judah and on Edom and on the children of Ammon and on Moab and on all who have trimmed the corners [of their hair and beard] and live in the wilderness, because *all the nations are foreskinned* and the whole house of Israel are *foreskinned at heart.* (Jeremiah 9:25, 26)

This passage also shows that many other nations were circumcised, since it says, "I will inflict punishment on everyone circumcised in the foreskin." So to repeat, circumcision was not an innovation or an exclusive mark of Jacob's descendants differentiating them. The Philistines were the ones who were uncircumcised, so "the foreskinned" usually refers to them (1 Samuel 14:6; 17:26, 36; 31:4; 2 Samuel 1:20; and elsewhere).

4463 *Because this is a disgrace to us* means that it undermined them. This can be seen from the symbolism of a *disgrace* as something undermining their religiosity and therefore themselves.

4464 *Nonetheless, in this we will concede to you if you become like us* symbolizes compliance with their religiosity, as the following shows: *Conceding* symbolizes complying. And *becoming like them* symbolizes dwelling on superficialities alone rather than inner qualities, since in doing so [Shechem's people] would have resembled [Jacob's descendants]; see just above at §4459.

Section 4459 showed what it is to be focused solely on the surface and what it is to be focused on what is within. Here I should say why we ought to focus on what is within. Anyone who reflects can see that we have contact with heaven through our inner depths, because all of heaven lies within. If we are not in heaven in regard to our thoughts and feelings, or in regard to the contents of our intellect and will, we cannot go there after death, because we have no contact. We develop communication with heaven during our bodily life through truth in our intellect and goodness in our will, and if we do not develop it then, it does not develop later. The doors to the inner reaches of our mind cannot open after death if they were not open during our physical life.

[2] Without our awareness, we are surrounded by a kind of spiritual aura that reflects our desires. Angels can detect this aura more capably than the keenest nose on earth detects a scent. Some people have concentrated only on the outer level of life; that is, they have indulged in the satisfaction

of hating their neighbor, the revenge and cruelty this leads to, adultery, a sense of superiority and contempt for others, fraud, greed, deceit, decadence, and so on. The spiritual aura that envelops people like this is as offensive as the earthly stench given off by corpses, dung, ripe garbage, and so on; and people who had lived this way take the aura with them when they die. Since they are saturated through and through with it, they cannot live anywhere but hell, where such auras exist. Concerning auras in the other life and their source, see §§1048, 1053, 1316, 1504–1519, 1695, 2401, 2489.

[3] Others have concentrated on an inner level, though. They are the ones who have enjoyed practicing goodwill and charity toward their neighbor, and especially those who have found bliss in loving the Lord. They are surrounded by a pleasant, agreeable aura that is the atmosphere of heaven itself, and accordingly they are in heaven.

Auras perceived in the other life always rise out of the different types of love and resulting desires we had nurtured. So auras rise out of our life—love and its attendant desire being the substance of life itself. Since they rise out of varieties of love and desire, they rise out of the aims and goals inspiring us to will and act as we do. We always aim at what we love, so our goals constitute our life and determine its quality. This is the main source of our aura. It is perceived in exquisite detail in heaven because the whole of heaven abides in an atmosphere of purpose.

These remarks show the nature of a person focused on what is within and the nature of a person focused on the surface. They also demonstrate the reason why we ought to engage not only with what is on the surface but also with what is within.

[4] When the outer dimension monopolizes people's attention, they do not care about this information, no matter how sharp a genius they possess in the affairs of public life and no matter how strong a reputation for scholarship they have gained from knowing facts. They do not care because they do not believe in anything they cannot see with their eyes or touch with their hands. So they do not believe in heaven or hell. If you told them that right after death they were going to the other world, where they would see, hear, speak, and sense by touch more perfectly than in their body, they would reject it as nonsense or a fantasy. Nonetheless it is the actual truth. The same thing would happen if you told them that the real person is the soul or spirit that lives on after death rather than the body it carries around in the world.

[5] The consequence is that people who are wholly absorbed in superficialities do not care what you say about the inner plane, even though

inner qualities are what will render them fortunate and happy in the kingdom where they are going and will live forever. Most Christians share this disbelief.

The failure of Christians to believe is something I was permitted to learn about by talking to people arriving in the other life from the Christian world. In the next life they are not able to hide what they have thought, because one's thoughts lie open to view there. Neither are they able to hide what they have held as their goals—which is to say, what they have loved—because it reveals itself in their aura.

4465   *By circumcising every male among you* symbolizes the outward representation alone, which would make [Shechem's people] pure in the eyes of [Jacob's offspring]. This can be seen from the symbolism of *circumcising every male* as an outward representation—a sign that [the circumcised] were part of the church. In this case it was a sign that they were part of the religious culture of [Jacob's offspring], as noted above in §4462. It follows that this would make [Shechem's people] pure in their eyes, because Jacob's descendants identified purity and holiness not with internals but with externals.

4466   *And we will give our daughters to you, and your daughters we will take for ourselves* symbolizes the resulting union. This can be seen from statements on marriage at §4434 above saying that in a spiritual sense marriage is the union of goodness and truth. To *give our daughters to you and take your daughters for ourselves* is to create ties of marriage with each other.

4467   *And we will settle with you* means in regard to life—that is, union in regard to life. This is established by the symbolism of *settling with you* as living together, discussed in §§1293, 3384, 3613, 4451.

4468   *And we will become one people* means in regard to theology—that is, union in regard to theology. This is established by the symbolism of a *people* as truth known to the church and therefore as theology (discussed in §§1259, 1260, 3295, 3581). *Becoming one people*, then, means union through theology.

There are two things that bring the people of the church together: life and theology. When the way they live their lives brings them together, theology does not divide them. If theology alone brings them together (as it does in the church today), they part ways and form as many sects as theologies. Yet doctrine exists for the sake of life, and life is based on doctrine. Evidence that people separate if theology alone unites them is the fact that adherents of one doctrine condemn others, sometimes even damning them to hell. Evidence that theology does not divide if life unites is the fact that people who live good lives do not condemn anyone with a different

opinion but leave it up to that person's beliefs and conscience. They extend
the same tolerance even to people outside the church. They say in their
hearts that ignorance cannot condemn anyone who lives a life of innocence
and mutual love, as children do—and children are also ignorant when they
die young.

And if you don't listen to us, to be circumcised means unless they turned
away from the truth they possessed and conformed with outward representation. This can be seen from the explanation above at §4462.

4469

The meaning of the words spoken by Jacob's sons in these verses is
at odds with the meaning taken by Hamor and Shechem, so it is also at
odds with the inner meaning, as the explanations make plain. The reason
is that Jacob's sons spoke in deceit, as verse 13 says, and when people speak
deceitfully, they are feeling something quite different than is felt by the
person they are addressing (§4459).

We will take our daughter and go means there would be no union. This
can be seen from the symbolism of marriage as the union of goodness and
truth (discussed above at §4466). *Taking our daughter and going* means
not giving her in marriage, so it means that there would be no union.

4470

Jacob's sons speak as if they were Jacob their father here, since they
say "we will take our daughter" rather than "our sister." The reason is visible from the inner meaning. It was the father's role to refuse or accept,
in keeping with the law laid down in Exodus 22:16, 17. Since the current
focus is on Jacob's descendants and their religiosity, though, the sons (representing that religiosity) answer for their father. Jacob could not respond
himself because he currently represents the ancient church (§4439).

Genesis 34:18, 19, 20, 21, 22, 23, 24. *And their words were good in the
eyes of Hamor and in the eyes of Shechem, Hamor's son. And the youth was
not slow to do the thing, because he took pleasure in Jacob's daughter. And
he was more honored than anyone in his father's household. And Hamor
and Shechem his son came to the gate of their city and spoke to the men of
their city, saying, "Those men are peaceful toward us, and they will settle
in the land, and travel it on business. And the land—look, it is wide in
extent before them. Their daughters we could take for ourselves as our women,
and our daughters we could give to them. Nonetheless, in this the men will
concede to us, to settle with us, to become one people: if every male among
us is circumcised, as they are circumcised. Their property and their purchases, and every animal of theirs—is it not ours? Only let's concede to
them, and they will settle with us." And they listened to Hamor and to
Shechem his son—everyone going out the gate of [Shechem's] city—and circumcised every male, everyone going out the gate of [Shechem's] city.*

4471

Their words were good in the eyes of Hamor symbolizes complying as
to their way of life. *And in the eyes of Shechem, Hamor's son, means* as to
their theology. *And the youth was not slow to do the thing* symbolizes a
longing to embrace it. *Because he took pleasure in Jacob's daughter* means
directed toward the religiosity of that church. *And he was more honored
than anyone in his father's household* symbolizes the most important point
in all the truth known to the church among the ancients. *And Hamor
and Shechem his son came to the gate of their city* symbolizes what was
good and true in the theology of the church among the ancients. *And
spoke to the men of their city, saying,* symbolizes persuasion. *Those men are
peaceful toward us* symbolizes harmony. *And they will settle in the land*
means as to their way of life. *And travel it on business* means as to their
theology. *And the land—look, it is wide in extent before them* symbolizes
its reach. *Their daughters we could take for ourselves as our women, and our
daughters we could give to them* symbolizes union. *Nonetheless, in this the
men will concede to us, to settle with us* means that they would harmonize
in their lives. *To become one people* means in their theology. *If every male
is circumcised, as they are circumcised* means if [Shechem's people] were
initiated by those means into the purely superficial representative and
symbolic practices of [Jacob's offspring]. *Their property and their purchases* means their truth. *And every animal of theirs* means their goodness.
Is it not ours? means that these were the same in reality and appearance.
Only let's concede to them, and they will settle with us means "if we comply." *And they listened to Hamor and to Shechem his son* symbolizes consent. *Everyone going out the gate of his city* means that they turned away
from the theology of the church among the ancients. *And circumcised
every male, everyone going out the gate of his city* symbolizes compliance
with superficiality.

4472   *Their words were good in the eyes of Hamor* symbolizes complying as to
their way of life. This can be seen from the symbolism of the *words being
good* as compliance, and from the representation of *Hamor* as goodness in
the church among the ancients (discussed in §4447). Hamor represents
a way of life here, because life has to do with goodness, just as theology
has to do with truth—theology being meant by Shechem, as mentioned
next. The reason Hamor now represents a way of life rather than goodness is that he had stooped to the shallow ways of Jacob's sons.

4473   *And in the eyes of Shechem, Hamor's son,* means as to their theology. This
can be seen from the representation of *Shechem* as truth in the church among
the ancients, which grew out of the goodness that is Hamor (discussed in

§4454). At this point Shechem means theology, for the reason given just above in §4472.

And the youth was not slow to do the thing symbolizes a longing to embrace it. This can be seen from the symbolism of *not being slow to do* what he was told as a longing to comply with it and therefore to embrace it.

4474

Because he took pleasure in Jacob's daughter means directed toward the religiosity of that church. This is established by the representation of Dinah— *Jacob's daughter*, here—as a desire for the truth of the ancient church, the church *Jacob* is representing (§4439). There was a longing for union with the desire for this church's truth, or to put it another way, with this church. However, at present Jacob's sons, speaking for their father (§4470), represent this church, which turned completely shallow among Jacob's descendants; and Hamor and Shechem agreed to embrace it. So Jacob's daughter now symbolizes its religiosity.

4475

And he was more honored than anyone in his father's household symbolizes the most important point in all the truth known to the church among the ancients. This can be seen from the symbolism of being *more honored than anyone* as being the most important. One who is honored above all is almost the same as a chieftain, which symbolizes the most important thing; see §§1482, 2089. But the text says *more honored than anyone in his father's household*, not "chieftain," because Hamor and Shechem were from the remnant of the earliest church (§§4447, 4454). The individuals who were called chieftain in the ancient church were referred to as honored in the earliest church.

4476

The most important point in all the truth known to the church among the ancients is symbolized because the clause applies to Shechem, who represents truth known to the church among the ancients; see §4454.

And Hamor and Shechem his son came to the gate of their city symbolizes what was good and true in the theology of the church among the ancients. This is established by the representation of *Hamor* as goodness in the church among the ancients (discussed in §4447); by that of *Shechem* as the truth growing out of it (discussed in §4454); and by the symbolism of the *gate of a city* as what is true in a theology (discussed in §2943).

4477

And spoke to the men of their city, saying, symbolizes persuasion. This can be seen from the symbolism of *speaking* as willing and as influencing (discussed in §§2951, 3037). Here it symbolizes persuading, because people who will something wish to persuade others about it, and those whose passion inspires them to exert an influence communicate their persuasion. The *men of the city* are people engrossed in the truth of a theology. In this

4478

case they are people subscribing to the same truth as Shechem. In ancient times, a city was simply one clan out of a whole nation. The shared living space of those belonging to the same clan was called a city. On an inner level it does not mean a clan but the nature of the clan's life and theology, so a city symbolizes what is true in a theology, and the residents symbolize what is good in it; see §§402, 2268, 2449, 2451, 2712, 2943, 3216. When a city's residents are called *the men of the city*, though, they symbolize the truth of a theology rather than the goodness in it. In the Word, men mean truth (§3134).

4479   *Those men are peaceful toward us* symbolizes harmony—here, harmony as to their teachings, as the following shows: *Men* symbolize truth, as dealt with in §3134, so they symbolize teachings. When the truths known to a religion are gathered together and acknowledged, they are called teachings. And *peaceful* means that they harmonize. People who are in harmony concerning a church's teachings and creeds are called peaceful, in a spiritual sense.

4480   *And they will settle in the land* means as to their way of life. This can be seen from the symbolism of *settling* as life, as noted above at §4467. The *land* symbolizes the church, here as elsewhere (§§662, 1066, 1068, 1262, 1733, 1850, 2117, 2118 at the end, 2928, 3355, 4447), so *settling in the land* symbolizes the compatibility of lives in keeping with a church's values.

Everything written in the Word is inherently and essentially spiritual. People know that the Word is spiritual, but its spirituality is not evident in its literal meaning. Its literal meaning contains worldly material, especially in the narratives, but when people on earth read what is there, the worldly element of it becomes spiritual in the spiritual world—in other words, among angels. Angels cannot think about any concept—including that of settling in the land—except in spiritual terms.

To think in spiritual terms is to think in terms of the Lord's kingdom and therefore in terms of the church.

4481   *And travel it on business* means as to their theology. This is established by the symbolism of *traveling the land on business* as entering into a knowledge of goodness and truth (discussed in §4453) and therefore as taking up a theology, since theology contains and teaches that knowledge.

4482   *And the land—look, it is wide in extent before them* symbolizes its reach—the reach of the truth in their theology. This can be seen from the symbolism of the *land* as the church (mentioned just above in §4480) and from that of *wide in extent* as the reach of truth and therefore of the truth in a theology.

When the Word describes the measurements of an object, in an inner sense they do not mean measurements but the qualities of a state. Measurement involves space, and there is no space in the other life, just as there is no time. Instead, states correspond to space and time; see §§2625, 2837, 3356, 3387, 3404, 4321. This being so, length and width and height, which are spatial measurements, symbolize different aspects of a state. Length symbolizes holiness; height, goodness; and width, truth; see §§650, 1613, 3433, 3434. That is why a *land wide in extent* symbolizes the reach of the truth in a church's theology.

[2] The claim that a land wide in extent symbolizes the reach of the truth in a church's theology will necessarily astonish people who do not realize there is anything spiritual in the Word other than what appears in the literal meaning. Nevertheless this is the symbolism, as the following Scripture passages using the word *breadth* can illustrate. In Isaiah, for instance:

> Assyria will go through Judah, he will flood in and pass over, he will reach all the way to their neck, and the spread of his wings will be the fullness of the *land's breadth*. (Isaiah 8:8)

In David:

> Jehovah, you did not shut me up in the hand of my enemy; you made my feet stand *in a broad place*. (Psalms 31:8)

In the same author:

> In tight-bound anguish have I called on Jah; he answers me *with a broad place*. (Psalms 118:5)

In Habakkuk:

> I am raising up the Chaldeans, a nation bitter and swift, walking through the *breadth of the land*. (Habakkuk 1:6)

The breadth actually symbolizes truth known to the church.

[3] The reason breadth has this symbolism is that the Lord is the center of everything in the spiritual world, or heaven, because he is the sun there. People in a good state live on progressively more inward levels,

depending on the amount and type of goodness they possess, so height is spoken of in connection with goodness. People at the same level of goodness are also at the same level of truth, so they are at the same distance [from the center], or in the same ring, so to speak. That is why width is spoken of in connection with truth. As a result, when people on earth read the Word, the angels with them take width to mean nothing else. For example, when the Word's narratives deal with the ark, the altar, the Temple, or the spaces outside cities, angels perceive the measurements of length, width, and height as states of goodness and truth. The same is true in the treatment of the new land, the new Jerusalem, and the new temple in Ezekiel 40, 41, 42, 43, 44, 45, 46, 47, which symbolize heaven and a new church, as the details there show. Likewise in John, where he says the New Jerusalem will be square, its length as great as its *width* (Revelation 21:16).

[4] What lies farther within in the spiritual world is depicted as being higher, and what is more outward is depicted as lower (§2148). This is our only way of grasping inner and outer levels when we are in the world, because we exist in space and time. Concepts of space and time have entered our thoughts and permeated most of them. In a spiritual sense, then, different kinds of measurement—which is a spatial limitation—such as height, length, and width, clearly mean properties that define states of desire for goodness and of desire for truth.

4483   *Their daughters we could take for ourselves as our women, and our daughters we could give to them* symbolizes union. This can be seen from the explanation above at §4466, where similar words occur.

4484   *Nonetheless, in this the men will concede to us, to settle with us* means that they would harmonize in their lives. This can be seen from the symbolism of *conceding* as harmonizing, and from that of *settling* as life (discussed above at §§4451, 4452).

4485   *To become one people* means in their theology. This can be seen from the symbolism of a *people* as a theology (also discussed above, at §4468).

4486   *If every male is circumcised, as they are circumcised* means if [Shechem's people] were initiated by those means into the purely superficial representative and symbolic practices of [Jacob's offspring]. This can be seen from the symbolism of *being circumcised* as an outward representation—a sign that [the circumcised] were part of the church. In this case it was a sign that they were part of the same religious culture as Jacob's descendants, a subject discussed in §4462. Because they embraced the

religiosity of Jacob's descendants, which consisted solely in external practices (§§4281, 4293, 4307), the text adds *as they are circumcised*. These
remarks show that *every male's being circumcised, as they are circumcised*
means if [Shechem's people] were initiated by this means into the purely
superficial representative and symbolic practices of [Jacob's offspring].
Other implications of the clause will come out in what follows.

Their property and their purchases means their truth. This is established   **4487**
by the symbolism of *property and purchases* as truth. The distinction is this:
When *property* also means the smaller livestock, it stands for truth-based
goodness, since this is the symbolism of such livestock. Truth-based goodness is truth in our will and in our actions (§§4337, 4353, 4390). A *purchase*, which is expressed in other passages as a "purchase of silver," stands
for truth. The former, or truth-based goodness, is called heavenly truth,
while the latter is called spiritual truth (§2048). The former, or heavenly
truth, is truth integrated into one's life, while the latter, or spiritual truth,
is truth belonging to one's theology.

Every animal of theirs means their goodness. This is established by the   **4488**
symbolism of an *animal* as goodness (discussed in §§45, 46, 142, 143, 246,
714, 715, 1823, 2179, 2180, 2781, 3218, 3519).

Is it not ours? means that these were the same in reality and appear-   **4489**
ance. This can be seen from context. The goodness and truth of the earliest church, some of which remained in existence among Hamor, Shechem,
and their clans, harmonized with the goodness and truth that Jacob's posterity received from the ancient church. The rituals established among
Jacob's descendants, after all, were simply the outward representations
and symbols of inward qualities the earliest church had possessed. *Is it not
ours?* then, means that they were the same in reality and appearance.

[2] Let an example be used to illustrate. The altar on which [Jacob's
descendants] sacrificed was the main object representing the Lord (§§921,
2777, 2811), so it was a foundation of worship in the ancient church that
was called the Hebrew church. Therefore every component in the con-
struction of an altar had a representation: the dimensions of height, width,
and length; the stones, bronze latticework, and horns; the flame kept constantly burning on it; and the sacrifices and burnt offerings. What they
represented was truths and varieties of goodness belonging to the Lord
and coming from him. These constituted the inner plane of worship, and
because they were represented in the outward object, they were the same
in reality and appearance as the truths and good qualities of the earliest

church. The dimensions of height, width, and length were general symbols of goodness, truth, and the resulting holiness (see §§650, 1613, 3433, 3434, 4482). Stones were a specific symbol of lowly kinds of truth (1298, 3720). The bronze of which the latticework around the altar was made symbolized earthly goodness (425, 1551). Horns symbolized the strength truth has from goodness (2832). Fire on the altar symbolized love (934). Sacrifices and burnt offerings symbolized heavenly and spiritual traits, according to their various types (922, 1823, 2180, 2805, 2807, 2830, 3519). From this it is possible to see that the outer features had something inside, and that the inner content was the same [as in the earliest church]. Likewise for all the other [outward representations].

[3] The people of the earliest church did not care about these outward objects, though. They were people of depth, and the Lord flowed into them from within, teaching them to recognize goodness. The categories of goodness and the distinctions among them were truths to those people, so they knew what each and every thing in the world represented in the Lord's kingdom. The whole world, or all creation, is a theater representing the Lord's kingdom (§§2758, 3483).

The people of the ancient church were not deep but shallow, so it was not from within, only from the outside, that the Lord could flow into them and teach them to recognize goodness. At first he did so through representation and symbolism, and this gave rise to a representative religion. Later he did so through doctrines teaching about the goodness and truth that were represented and symbolized, and this gave rise to Christianity. In its essence and inner form, Christianity is the same as the representative religion, but the representations and symbolism of that religion were abolished after the Lord came into the world. They were abolished because they all represented him and therefore represented various facets of his kingdom—since these are from him and *are* him, so to speak.

[4] The difference between the earliest church and the Christian is like the difference between daytime sunlight and the nighttime glimmer of the moon or stars. Seeing goodness by an inner or primary way is like seeing by sunlight in the day. Seeing by an outer or secondary way is like seeing by the glint of the moon or stars at night. The difference between the earliest church and the ancient was almost as great. It is just that Christians could have enjoyed fuller light if they had acknowledged an inner level—in other words, if they had believed in and acted on the truth and goodness the Lord taught. Goodness itself is the same for both [the earliest church and the others]. The only question is whether the goodness is seen clearly or

dimly. People who see clearly see endless secrets, almost as angels in heaven do, and are moved by what they see. People who see dimly, on the other hand, see hardly anything with certainty. What they do see merges with the shadows of night, or falsity, and is not capable of moving them deeply.

Now, since goodness is the same for both churches, so is truth. That is why *Is it not ours?* means that the goodness and the truth were the same in reality and appearance. After all, Hamor and Shechem were from the remnant of the earliest church, as noted, while Jacob's offspring were from the ancient church that was called the Hebrew church—although they engaged only in its outer practices.

However, Hamor and his son Shechem sinned grievously in accepting circumcision, as §4493 below will demonstrate.

Only let's concede to them, and they will settle with us means "if we comply and our lives are then connected." This can be seen from the symbolism of *conceding* as complying, and from that of *settling with us* as living together, or connecting one's life with another's (discussed in §4467). **4490**

And they listened to Hamor and to Shechem his son symbolizes consent, as can be seen without explanation. **4491**

Everyone going out the gate of his city means that they turned away from the theology of the church among the ancients. This can be seen from the symbolism of *going out* in the current case as turning away, and from that of the *gate of a city* as a theology (discussed in §§2943, 4477). Here it symbolizes the theology of the church among the ancients because it was the gate of *his* city—Shechem's—and Shechem represents truth known to the church among the ancients (§4454). By the church among the ancients I mean a religion that developed out of the earliest church, as was also mentioned before [§4447]. **4492**

The comments in the next section will reveal what is involved here.

And circumcised every male, everyone going out the gate of his city symbolizes compliance with superficiality, as the following shows: *Circumcising every male* symbolizes being initiated by this means into the purely superficial representative and symbolic practices of Jacob's descendants, as noted in §4486. And *going out the gate of the city* symbolizes turning away from the theology of the church among the ancients, as noted just above in §4492. Since rejection of that theology and acceptance of superficiality is being symbolized, the text twice says "going out the gate of his city" without adding "and coming in it," as occurs in other passages. "Coming in" would mean conforming with that theology and turning away from outward concerns, but here we have the opposite. **4493**

[2] The situation in all this needs explaining. The people of the earliest church, whose survivors included Hamor, Shechem, and their clans, possessed a completely distinct and different mentality and character than the men of the ancient church. The people of the earliest church had a will marked by wholeness, but the men of the ancient church did not. So the Lord could flow into the people of the earliest church through their will, or by an inner way, but not so into the men of the ancient church, because their will was depraved. Instead, he flowed into their intellect and therefore by an outer way rather than an inner one, as noted above in §4489. To flow through the will is to do so through the good impulses of love, since all goodness belongs to the volitional side. To flow through the intellect, though, is to do so through the true ideas of faith, since all truth belongs to the intellectual side. This side, the intellectual side, is where the Lord formed a new will in the men of the ancient church when he regenerated them.

Goodness and truth were planted in the volitional side of the people in the earliest church (see §§895, 927) but in the intellectual side of the men of the ancient church (§§863, 875, 895, 927, 2124, 2256, 4328). A new will is formed in the intellectual side (§§928, 1023, 1043, 1044, 4328). There is a parallelism between the Lord and the goodness in us but not between the Lord and the truth in us (§§1831, 1832, 2718, 3514). So the men of the ancient church lived in relatively dim conditions (§§2708, 2715, 2935, 2937, 3246, 3833). Clearly, then, the people of the earliest church had a completely distinct and different mentality and character than the men of the ancient church.

[3] That was why individuals in the earliest church were deep and had nothing superficial in their worship, while individuals in the ancient church were shallow and did have superficiality in their worship. Those in the earliest church could look through the inner plane at the outer plane and see it in broad daylight, so to speak, while those in the ancient church looked through the outer plane at the inner and saw it as if by the glow of the moon and stars at night. As a consequence the Lord appears in heaven as a sun to the former but as a moon to the latter (§§1521, 1529, 1530, 1531, 2441, 2495, 4060). The former are the ones called heavenly in these explanations, and the latter are the ones called spiritual.

[4] Let me use an example to illustrate the difference. If people in the earliest church had read the narrative or prophetic part of the Word without previous instruction or any explanation, they would have seen its inner meaning. In fact, the inner meaning's heavenly and spiritual content

would have occurred to them immediately, but hardly anything in the literal meaning would have entered their consciousness. So the inner meaning would have been clear to them, and the literal meaning, dim. They
would be like a person listening to someone talk and absorbing only the
meaning, without paying attention to the speaker's words. If people in
the ancient church had read the Word, on the other hand, they could
not have seen its inner meaning without previous instruction or explanation. The inner meaning would have been dim to them, and the literal
meaning, clear. They would be like a person listening to someone talk
and thinking only about the words, without also paying attention to the
meaning, which is therefore lost.

But when people in the Jewish religion read the Word, they pick up
nothing but the literal meaning. They do not realize there is any inner
meaning and even deny its existence. So do people in the Christian religion today.

[5] These examples can show what the difference was. Those whom
Hamor and Shechem represent were among the remnant of the earliest
church and therefore cared about what was on the inside rather than the
outside. Those whom Jacob's sons symbolize cared about what was on
the outside rather than the inside. It can also be seen that Hamor and
Shechem could not have conformed to and embraced the shallow ways
of Jacob's sons without shutting off their own inner depths and perish-
ing forever.

[6] This is the secret reason Hamor, Shechem, and their clans were
killed, which otherwise would not have been permitted. The fact does not
absolve Jacob's sons of guilt for committing an outrageous crime, though.
They knew nothing of the secret reason, and that reason was not *their*
aim. We are each judged by our aim or intent. Their intent was deceitful, as verse 13 explicitly says. When the Lord permits something like this
to happen, it is done by the evil, hellish beings who prompt it. However, whatever harm the evil intend and do to the good, the Lord turns it
into a benefit, as in this case Hamor and Shechem were granted salvation
together with their clans.

Genesis 34:25, 26, 27, 28, 29. *And it happened on the third day, while they*   **4494**
were in pain, that two sons of Jacob—Simeon and Levi, Dinah's brothers—
each took his sword and came upon the city boldly and killed every male.
And Hamor and Shechem his son they killed by the mouth of the sword and
took Dinah from Shechem's house and went out. Jacob's sons came upon
those stabbed, and plundered the city, because [the residents] had defiled their

sister. Their flocks and their herds and their donkeys and whatever was in the city and whatever was in the field they took. All their riches and every little child of theirs and their women they captured and plundered, and everything that was in the house.

It happened on the third day symbolizes what developed, right to the end. *While they were in pain* symbolizes cravings. *That two sons of Jacob, Simeon and Levi,* symbolizes faith and love. *Dinah's brothers* symbolizes the truth and goodness of that religion. *Each took his sword* symbolizes falsity and evil. *And came upon the city boldly and killed every male* means that they wiped out truth in the theology of the church among the ancients. *And Hamor and Shechem his son, by the mouth of the sword* means the church itself. *And took Dinah from Shechem's house and went out* means that they did away with the desire for truth. *Jacob's sons came upon those stabbed, and plundered the city* means that all of Jacob's descendants destroyed the theology. *Because he had defiled their sister* means that they sullied the truth of which faith is composed. *Their flocks and their herds* means that they destroyed goodness on the rational and earthly planes. *And their donkeys* means the truth growing out of it. *And whatever was in the city and whatever was in the field they took* means everything true and good in the church. *And all their riches* means all the knowledge acquired by people in the church. *And every little child of theirs* means all innocence. *And their women* symbolizes neighborly love. *They captured and plundered* means they deprived those people of it all and twisted it. *And everything that was in the house* means everything belonging to the church.

4495   *It happened on the third day* symbolizes what developed, right to the end. This can be seen from the symbolism of a *third day* as something complete, from beginning to end (discussed in §2788), and therefore as the whole continuity, too. This symbolism of a third day will be hard to believe for anyone who views Bible stories as mere worldly histories whose only holiness comes from their presence in a sacred volume. However, scriptural narratives hold spiritual and heavenly contents that are not evident in the literal meaning—and not only the narratives themselves but also all the words, including all the numbers. This has been demonstrated in preceding explanations. It will stand out even more clearly (the Lord in his divine mercy willing) in the prophetic parts, which do not draw the mind to the thread of the literal meaning as strongly as the narrative portions do.

No one who examines the deeper levels of the Word can help seeing that the number three, like the numbers seven and twelve, involves secrets. If these numbers hold secrets, it follows that all the other numbers in the Word do too, since the Word is holy throughout.

[2] In talking with angels I have sometimes seen numbers apparently written before my very eyes, just like a person reading them on a piece of paper in broad daylight, and I have perceived that the topics the angels were discussing were expressed in those numbers. This experience has also enabled me to see that every number in the Word contains some secret. The fact is plain to see from the following in John:

> He measured the wall of Jerusalem the Holy at *one hundred forty-four cubits*, which is the measure of a human, that is, of an angel. (Revelation 21:17)

And in another place:

> Let one who has understanding calculate the number of the beast, since it is the number of a human. To be specific, *its number is six hundred sixty-six*. (Revelation 13:18)

Of course the first of these two numbers, 144, is 12 times 12; and 666 is a multiple of 3 and of 6. The sanctity embedded in them can be seen from the holiness of the number 12 (see the comments at §§577, 2089, 2129 at the end, 2130 at the end, 3272, 3858, 3913; for the holiness of the number 3, §§720, 901, 1825, 2788, 4010).

[3] Because this last number, three, symbolized something complete, all the way to its end, it symbolized a single period large or small. So the representative church embraced the number and used it whenever this idea was meant. The number is used the same way in the Word, where absolutely everything has a symbolic meaning, and the following places illustrate this:

> [The children of Israel] were to go a *journey of three days* and hold a sacrifice. (Exodus 3:18; 5:3)

> They were to be ready for the *third day* because on the *third day* Jehovah was to come down onto Mount Sinai. (Exodus 19:11, 15, 16, 18)

> None of the meat of the sacrifice was to remain till the *third day*. (Leviticus 7:16, 17, 18; 19:6, 7)

> The water for removing [sin] was to be spattered on an unclean person on the *third day* and on the seventh day (Numbers 19:11–end), and

those who had touched anyone killed in battle would be cleansed on the *third day* and on the seventh day. (Numbers 31:19–25)

[4] Joshua commanded the people to cross the Jordan *within three days.* (Joshua 1:11; 3:2)

Jehovah called Samuel *three times,* and *three times* Samuel ran to Eli, and the *third time* Eli understood that Jehovah was calling Samuel. (1 Samuel 3:1–8)

Jonathan told David to hide himself in the field on the *third* evening, and he, Jonathan, would send to David *the third day from then* and reveal his father's state of mind. Jonathan then shot *three arrows* to the side of a stone. And after that David bowed *three times* to the earth before Jonathan. (1 Samuel 20:5, 12, 19, 20, 35, 36, 41)

Three options were set before David for him to choose among: famine would come for seven years, or for *three months* he would flee before his foes, or there would be contagion for *three days* in the land. (2 Samuel 24:11, 12, 13)

[5] Rehoboam told the assembled people of Israel, who sought to be relieved of his father's yoke, to go away for *three days* and come back. And they came to Rehoboam on the *third day,* as the king had said: "Come back to me on the *third day.*" (1 Kings 12:5, 12)

Elijah stretched himself out on the widow's son *three times.* (1 Kings 17:21)

Elijah said to pour water on the burnt offering and pieces of wood a *third time,* and a *third time* they did so. (1 Kings 18:34)

Jonah was in the sea monster's belly *three days and three nights.* (Jonah 1:17; Matthew 12:40)

The Lord spoke about a person who had planted a vineyard, saying the person sent slaves *three times* and then a son. (Mark 12:2, 4, 5, 6; Luke 20:12, 13)

He said Peter would *three times* deny [knowing] him. (Matthew 26:34; John 13:38)

He said to Peter *three times,* "Do you love me?" (John 21:15, 16, 17)

[6] These and many other places in the Word show that the number three held a secret and that it was therefore adopted in the ancient churches

as one of their symbols. Plainly it symbolizes a whole time span of the church and of events in the church and therefore either a long or a short period. So it symbolizes something complete and also the whole continuity, right to the end. This is especially clear in Hosea:

> Jehovah will bring us to life after two days, and on the *third day* he will raise us up, and we will live before him. (Hosea 6:2)

While they were in pain symbolizes cravings. This can be seen from the symbolism of the *pain* following circumcision as a craving. The reason for the symbolism is that circumcision symbolizes purification from love for oneself and for worldly advantages (§§2039, 2044, 2049, 2632, 3412, 3413, 4462). All the cravings of the flesh stem from those two kinds of love. That is why the pain has this symbolism. When we are being purified of such love, as is the case when we are being reborn, we suffer pain and anguish. The cravings that are being removed are what cause the sensation.

When a ritual represents some secret process, everything about the ritual up to its very end involves some facet of that process, as for instance the fact that the knives or daggers used for circumcision were made of stone (§§2039 at the end, 2046 at the end, 2799). [Something is also symbolized] by the blood involved, by the method used, and also by what the person goes through. This also applies to the rituals of cleansing, ordination, consecration, and the other ceremonies.

In this case the pain following circumcision symbolizes the craving of Hamor, Shechem, and the men of his city for the superficial ways of Jacob's descendants, as discussed above at §4493.

That two sons of Jacob, Simeon and Levi, symbolizes faith and love. This can be seen from the representation of *Simeon* as faith belonging to the will (discussed in §§3869, 3870, 3871, 3872) and from that of *Levi* as spiritual love, or charity (discussed in §§3875, 3877). That is what Simeon, Levi, and the tribes named for them symbolize in a positive sense, but in a negative sense they symbolize falsity and evil. Falsity is opposed to the truth that builds faith, and evil is opposed to the good done by charity. This is what Simeon and Levi represent in relation to the Jewish nation, which had eradicated from itself all the faith and all the charity within its worship. The fact will become clearer in what follows, where the text says that they killed Hamor, Shechem, and the men of the city, and that Jacob's sons came upon those stabbed, and plundered everything.

4496

4497

The purpose of Simeon and Levi's behavior was to represent the fact that religious truth and charitable goodness were turned into falsity and evil. When truth turns into falsity in a religion, and goodness turns into evil, that religion is finished.

4498 *Dinah's brothers* symbolizes the truth and goodness of that religion. This can be seen from the symbolism of *brothers* as truth and goodness, or faith and charity (discussed in §§367, 3303, 3803, 3815, 4121, 4191, 4267), and from the representation of *Dinah* as a desire for truth and therefore as the church (discussed in §§3963, 3964, 4427).

4499 *Each took his sword* symbolizes falsity and evil. This can be seen from the symbolism of a *sword* as truth engaged in battle and therefore as the defense of truth, and in a negative sense as falsity engaged in battle and therefore as the devastation of truth (discussed in §2799). The sword symbolizes evil as well because Levi was also involved. Levi represented charity and therefore goodness. When goodness turns evil, the falsity that comes of evil is its weapon, and anything it then does is evil.

4500 *And came upon the city boldly and killed every male* means that they wiped out truth in the theology of the church among the ancients, as the following indicates: A *city* symbolizes the theology of a religion, as discussed in §§402, 2449, 2943, 3216, 4478, and in this case the theology of the church among the ancients. That is the religion represented by Hamor and Shechem, whose city it was. *Boldly* means with confidence—here, confidence in falsity and evil. And a *male* symbolizes truth, as discussed in §§749, 2046, 4005. Clearly, then, *they came upon the city boldly and killed every male* means that with confidence in falsity and evil they wiped out truth in the theology of the church among the ancients.

The church among the ancients, which had developed out of the earliest church, was the one that was intended to be established among Jacob's posterity, because the ancient church had started to die. However, Jacob's descendants had obliterated all religious truth and charitable goodness in themselves and therefore the whole inner content of their worship, so no religion could be established among them. That is what the inner meaning describes here. The consequence, since they obstinately insisted, was that a mere representation of a religion was established among them; see §§4281, 4288, 4289, 4290, 4293, 4307, 4314, 4316, 4317, 4429, 4433, 4444.

4501 *And Hamor and Shechem, by the mouth of the sword* means the church itself, as the following shows: *Hamor* represents goodness in the church among the ancients, as dealt with in §4447. *Shechem* represents truth in the church among the ancients, as dealt with in §§4454, 4472, 4473. And the *mouth of the sword* symbolizes falsity and evil engaged in battle, as mentioned in §4499, and accordingly the means by which [Jacob's descendants] annihilated the church in themselves.

And took Dinah from Shechem's house and went out means that they did away with the desire for truth. This is clear from the representation of *Dinah* as a desire for truth (dealt with above in §4498). The most readily apparent inner meaning is that they did away with the desire for truth in people still remaining from the earliest church. After all, the text says *from Shechem's house,* and Shechem's house symbolizes the truth-based goodness of that church. The theme, though, is the eradication of truth and goodness in Jacob's descendants, symbolized here by his sons. For that reason, seeing that the meaning always relates to the theme at hand, Shechem's house now actually symbolizes truth-based goodness, as it had existed in the people of the earliest church. So the meaning is that this kind of goodness was eliminated in the nation descended from Jacob. The qualities symbolized on an inner level by a word or name in Scripture depends on the nature of the people in whom they exist.

At the same time these words symbolize a breakdown of goodness and truth in Hamor, Shechem, and his clan due to their compliance with superficiality, as shown in §4493.

[2] The validity of the explanations so far concerning Simeon and Levi can be seen from Jacob's prophetic utterance before dying, which includes this:

> *Simeon and Levi are brothers; tools of violence are their blades. Into their conspiracy my soul is not to come; with their band my glory is not to unite, because in their anger they killed a man, and in their pleasure they hamstrung an ox. A curse on their anger because it is fierce and on their fury because it is heavy! I will divide them among Jacob and scatter them among Israel.* (Genesis 49:5, 6, 7)

Simeon and Levi symbolize the religious truth that turned into falsity in Jacob's descendants and the charitable goodness that turned into evil (as above in §§4499, 4500). They are called brothers because goodness is truth's brother; that is, charity is faith's brother (4498). "Tools of violence are their blades," or swords, means that falsity and evil inflicted violence on truth and goodness (4499). "Into their conspiracy my soul is not to come" and "with their band my glory is not to unite" symbolize a rift over life and over theology. The Word mentions a soul in connection with the way people live (1000, 1040, 1742, 3299) and glory in connection with theology. "Because in their anger they killed a man, and in their

4502

pleasure they hamstrung an ox," means that with their premeditated evil they wiped out the church's truth and goodness. A man means the church's truth (3134), and an ox means its goodness (2180, 2566, 2781). "A curse on their anger because it is fierce, and on their fury because it is heavy!" symbolizes punishment for turning away from truth and goodness. Cursing means turning away, and being punished for it (245, 379, 1423, 3530, 3584). Anger means abandonment of truth, and fury means abandonment of goodness (357, 3614). "I will divide them among Jacob and scatter them among Israel" means that there will no longer be goodness or truth on the outward or inward planes of their religion. To divide and scatter means to detach and uproot it from them (4424). Jacob means the outer part of a religion, and Israel means its inner part (4286).

[3] These things are said of Simeon and Levi in Jacob's utterance because the two of them symbolize the church's overall truth and goodness. When these disappear, and particularly when falsity and evil take their place, the church becomes defunct. No other message is involved, as can be seen from the fact that the tribes of Simeon and Levi were no more cursed than any of the other tribes. Levi's tribe was taken for the priesthood, and Simeon's coexisted with the other tribes of Israel on an equal footing.

4503   *Jacob's sons came upon those stabbed, and plundered the city* means that all of Jacob's descendants destroyed the theology. This can be seen from the symbolism of *Jacob's sons* as his descendants (discussed above [§4430]); from that of *plundering* as destroying; and from that of a *city* as a church's theology (discussed above in §4500).

The fact that Simeon and Levi went out after killing every male in the city including Hamor and Shechem, and that Jacob's sons then came upon those stabbed, and plundered the city, contains a secret that only the inner meaning reveals. [2] The secret is this: After the church's truth and goodness (represented by Simeon and Levi) had been eradicated and replaced with falsity and evil, more falsity and evil (symbolized in a negative sense by Jacob's other sons) were added. Each of Jacob's sons represented a general aspect of faith and charity (as shown in §§2129, 3858, 3913, 3926, 3939, 4060; for Reuben's representation, see §§[3860,] 3861, 3866, 3870; for Judah's, 3881; for Dan's, 3921, 3922, 3923; for Naphtali's, 3927, 3928; for Gad's, 3934, 3935; for Asher's, 3938, 3939; for Issachar's, 3956, 3957; for Zebulun's, 3960, 3961). Once the church's truth and goodness have been destroyed, the general aspects of faith and charity represented by these other sons become generalized falsity and evil, which are then added on. These constantly increase in the church after it has been corrupted and destroyed. That is what is symbolized by Jacob's sons' coming upon those stabbed and plundering the city after Simeon and Levi had killed every male in the city (including Hamor and Shechem), taken Dinah, and gone out.

[3] In the Word, victims of stabbing symbolize annihilated truth and goodness, as the following passages illustrate. In Isaiah:

> You were thrown out of your grave like a despicable offshoot, [like] the garment of the slain, [who were] *stabbed with a sword,* who drop to the stones in the pit like a trampled corpse. (Isaiah 14:19)

This is about Babylon. The people stabbed with a sword stand for those who have profaned the church's truth. In the same author:

> Grant that *their victims of stabbing* be thrown out and the stench of their corpses rise. (Isaiah 34:3)

The subject here is falsity and evil plaguing the church, which is what the victims of stabbing stand for. [4] In Ezekiel:

> The violent among the nations will unsheathe a *sword* over the loveliness of your wisdom and profane your beauty. Down into the pit they will send you, and you will *die the deaths of the stabbed* in the middle of the seas. (Ezekiel 28:7, 8)

This is about the ruler of Tyre, who symbolizes the most important items of knowledge about truth and goodness. Dying the deaths of the stabbed in the middle of the seas stands for people who use facts to hatch falsity, contaminating the church's truth. [5] In the same author:

> Also these will go down with them into hell to those *stabbed by the sword,* when you have been made to go down with the trees of Eden into the underground realm, [when] in the midst of the uncircumcised you lie with those *stabbed by the sword.* (Ezekiel 31:17, 18)

In the same author:

> Go down and lie with the uncircumcised; in the midst of those *stabbed by the sword* they will fall. The principal ones of the powerful will speak to him in the middle of hell. (Ezekiel 32:19, 20, 21)

This is about Pharaoh and Egypt. Those stabbed by the sword stand for people who lose their sanity to secular knowledge, allowing it to squelch any belief they may have in religious truth. [6] In David:

> I have been reckoned with those going down into the pit; I have become like a man [who has] no strength, disregarded among the dead, like *victims*

of stabbing lying in the grave, whom you remembered no longer and who were cut off from your hand. (Psalms 88:4, 5)

Victims of stabbing in hell, in the pit, and in the grave stand for people who have destroyed truth and goodness in themselves through falsity and evil. It is not because they were stabbed by a sword that they are in hell, as anyone can see. [7] In Isaiah:

City of riots, jubilant city, [your victims of stabbing were] *not stabbed by the sword* and not killed in war; all who were found in chains together in you fled from far away. (Isaiah 22:2, 3)

This is about illusions produced by sense impressions, which make people blind to religious truth. Any who therefore doubt and deny this truth are described as stabbed, but not by a sword. [8] In Ezekiel:

I am bringing a *sword* on you and destroying your high places; and your altars will be wrecked and your pillars broken, and I will lay *your victims of stabbing* before your idols. When the *stabbed* fall down in your midst, you will recognize that I am Jehovah. Then you will know, when the *stabbed* lie amid their idols, around their altar. (Ezekiel 6:3, 4, 7, 13)

The stabbed stand for people who are devoted to theological falsity. [9] In the same author:

Defile the House and fill the courtyards with the *stabbed*. They went out and struck people in the city. (Ezekiel 9:7)

This was a prophetic vision. Defiling the House and filling the courtyards with the stabbed stands for profaning what is good and true. In the same author:

You multiplied *your victims of stabbing* in this city and filled its streets with the *stabbed,* for which reason the Lord Jehovih has said, "*Your victims of stabbing* that you put in its midst—they are the flesh, and [the city] is the pot"; and he will bring you out from its midst. (Ezekiel 11:6, 7)

[10] Since victims of stabbing symbolized people who wiped out religious truth in themselves through falsity and evil, it was the case in the representative religion that those who had touched such a victim were unclean. This is what Moses says about them:

Everyone who has [gone] on the open field [and] touched one *stabbed by a sword,* or a dead body, or a human bone, or a grave will be unclean seven days. (Numbers 19:16, 18)

That was the reason for the investigation and the atonement involving a heifer described in the same author:

> If a *victim of stabbing* is found lying in a field and it is not known who struck the victim, then the city's elders and judges shall go out and measure [the distance] to the cities that surround the *stabbing victim*. It shall happen, at the city nearest the *stabbing victim*, that the elders of that city shall take a heifer-ox by which no work has been done, which has not pulled anything in a yoke, and bring it down to a river or valley and break the neck of the heifer there and wash their hands over the heifer whose neck was broken and say, "Our hands did not shed blood, and our eyes did not see it. Expiate the guilt of your people Israel, Jehovah, and do not put innocent blood in the midst of your people!" And the blood will be expiated for them. (Deuteronomy 21:1–8)

[11] Each part of the inner meaning shows that these laws were laid down because a victim of stabbing symbolizes the twisting, destroying, and profaning of the church's truth through falsity and evil. The law speaks of a victim lying in a field because a field symbolizes the church; see §§2971, 3310, 3766. A heifer by which no work has been done symbolizes innocence in an uninformed outer self. If these details of the inner meaning were not divulged, anyone would have to wonder why such a procedure should have been required for atonement.

Because he had defiled their sister means that they sullied the truth of which faith is composed. This can be seen from the symbolism of *defiling* as sullying, and from that of a *sister* as truth (dealt with in §§1495, 2508, 2524, 2556, 3386). In this case a sister symbolizes the truth composing faith, since Dinah, the sister, symbolizes a desire for everything having to do with faith (§4427).

The reason why "Shechem had defiled their sister" means that they sullied the truth of which faith is composed is that Dinah represents a desire for all truth and therefore represents religion itself (§§3963, 3964). Dinah's brothers did not give her to Shechem as his woman but kept her with them in her defilement, so she subsequently represented something negative, as her brothers did. What she came to represent was a desire for all falsity and therefore a corrupted religion. That is why "he had defiled their sister" means that they sullied the truth of which faith is composed.

Their flocks and their herds means that they destroyed goodness on the rational and earthly planes. This is established by the symbolism of *flocks* as goodness on the rational plane and of *herds* as goodness on the earthly plane (discussed in §2566).

4504

4505

4506   *And their donkeys* means the truth growing out of it—out of earthly and rational goodness. This can be seen from the symbolism of *donkeys* and of jennies' foals and mules as truth on the earthly and rational planes (discussed in §2781).

4507   *And whatever was in the city and whatever was in the field they took* means everything true and good in the church, as the following indicates. A *city* symbolizes doctrine and therefore truth known to the church (discussed in §§402, 2268, 2449, 2712, 2943, 3216, 4492, 4493). And a *field* symbolizes the church in regard to goodness and therefore goodness in the church (discussed in §§2971, 3310, 3766, 4440, 4443). So *whatever was in the city and whatever was in the field* means everything true and good in the church.

4508   *And all their riches* means all the knowledge acquired by people in the church. This can be seen from the symbolism of *riches* as knowledge, a symbolism that is clear in many Scripture passages. Spiritual riches, and consequently riches understood in a spiritual sense, are nothing but [concepts of goodness and truth]. So far as these concepts are known, they are part of the church's knowledge. In the Lord's kingdom and therefore in the church they serve as wealth. With the Lord's divine mercy, this will be proved from the Word in another place.

4509   *And every little child of theirs* means all innocence. This can be seen from the symbolism of a *little child* as innocence (discussed at §§430, 2126, 3183).

4510   *And their women* symbolizes neighborly love. This can be seen from the symbolism of *women* and wives as desires for truth and desires for goodness. They symbolize desires for truth when a spouse is mentioned by name and is called a husband, and desires for goodness when a spouse is not named but is referred to as a man (§§915, 1468, 2517, 3236). Here they symbolize desires for goodness because they were the women of the city's men, who symbolized truth (§4478 at the end). What is more, the city is always referred to as Shechem's, and he represented truth known to the church among the ancients (§4454).

A desire for spiritual goodness is the same as neighborly love, so the women here symbolize that love.

4511   *They captured and plundered* means they deprived those people of it all and twisted it, as the context in its inner meaning shows.

4512   *And everything that was in the house* means everything belonging to the church. This is established by the symbolism of a *house* as goodness in the church (discussed at §§1795, 3720) and accordingly as everything belonging to the church. Because this is the symbolism of the phrase, it comes last.

Genesis 34:30, 31. *And Jacob said to Simeon and to Levi, "You have caused me trouble, to make me stink with the inhabitant of the land—the Canaanite and the Perizzite—and my numbers are few. And they will gather against me and strike me, and I will be destroyed, I and my household." And they said, "Shall he treat our sister as a whore?"*

4513

Jacob said symbolizes the outer part of the ancient church. *To Simeon and Levi* symbolizes a representation of spiritual and heavenly qualities. *You have caused me trouble, to make me stink with the inhabitant of the land* means that people in the ancient church would loathe [him]. *The Canaanite and the Perizzite* symbolizes people with goodness and truth. *And my numbers are few* means easily. *And they will gather against me and strike me, and I will be destroyed* means that in this way the ancient church perishes. *I and my household* means in regard to truth and goodness. *And they said* symbolizes the answer. *Shall he treat our sister as a whore?* means that they had no desire.

Jacob said symbolizes the outer part of the ancient church. This can be seen from the representation of *Jacob* as the ancient church (discussed in §4439). Like any church, the ancient church has an outer part and an inner part, so in the Word, Jacob represents the outer part, and Israel, the inner part.

4514

To Simeon and Levi symbolizes a representation of spiritual and heavenly qualities. This can be seen from the representation of *Simeon* as faith but in a negative sense as falsity, and from that of *Levi* as love but in a negative sense as evil. These are discussed above at §§4497, 4502, 4503. At this point, then, they symbolize a representation of spiritual and heavenly qualities, because anything having to do with faith is called spiritual, and anything having to do with love is called heavenly.

4515

I say that Simeon and Levi symbolize a representation of these qualities because representing them is not the same as having them. Representation relates not to the person but to the quality represented (§§665, 1097 at the end). So it made no difference what kind of person had the representation (§3670). A representation of the church was able to be established among Jacob's descendants regardless of their character, as long as they strictly observed the letter of the statutes (§§3147, 4208, 4281, 4292, 4307, 4444). That is why Simeon and Levi symbolize a representation of spiritual and heavenly qualities at present.

of the eye. [2] People with expertise in both anatomy and physics can investigate and see that it is not just sense organs that correspond to the phenomena of earthly creation in regard to their physical composition. It is also motor organs and all the other viscera. Thus the whole body is an organ put together from the most deeply hidden elements of all things in earthly creation according to their secret active forces and the astounding ways they have of exerting their influence.

That is why the ancients referred to the human being as a miniature world, or microcosm.

[3] If you know this you can also see that nothing whatever in the world of nature comes into existence on its own but from something prior to itself. Neither can this prior entity emerge on its own but only from something prior to *it,* and so on all the way back to the first origin, from which everything that follows emerges in order. Since this is what brings everything into existence, it is also what keeps everything in existence. Lasting existence is perpetual emergence. It follows, then, that absolutely everything down to the outermost aspects of the physical world not only springs from but also is sustained by the first origin. Unless everything constantly came into being from the ultimate origin and maintained an uninterrupted connection to and with that origin, it would instantly dissolve and disappear.

4524   Now since everything in the world of nature emerges and keeps emerging—or survives—from something prior to itself, it follows that it emerges and survives from a realm beyond the physical world. This realm is called the spiritual world. There has to be an unbroken link with it for things to last, or keep emerging, so it follows that the spiritual world is the source for the purer or deeper components of the physical world and therefore of a human. It also follows that the purer or deeper components are the kinds of forms that the spiritual world can act on.

There can be only one spring of life, just as nature has only one source of light and heat; so all life plainly comes from the Lord, who is the beginning of life. This being so, everything in the spiritual world in whole and in part corresponds to the Lord. Consequently everything in the human being does too, since a human is a miniature spiritual world on the smallest scale. As a result, the spiritual self is also an image of the Lord.

4525   This discussion shows that everything—especially in a human—has something corresponding to it in the spiritual world. Without this correspondence it could not last even a moment, because without correspondence nothing would be continuous with life's very Being, the Lord. So it would be disconnected, and what is disconnected dissolves as if it were nothing.

The correspondence with a human is more direct and therefore closer, because people were created to use the Lord's life as their own. This means they were created with the capacity for the Lord to lift their thoughts and feelings above the earthly realm, so they have the power to think about God, feel affection for the Divine, and unite with him. They are unlike the creatures of the earth in this regard. Those who can unite with the Divine in this way do not die when the bodily dimension belonging to the world detaches, because the inner dimension remains united.

To continue with the correspondence of eyesight (the subject begun at the end of the previous chapter [§§4403–4421]): It needs to be known that eyesight corresponds with the activity of the intellect. The intellect is the inner eye, and this inner eye sees by a higher kind of light than the world's. We can acquire understanding through objects we see in worldly light because the higher light, heaven's light, flows into impressions from worldly light and makes them appear as representations or correspondences. You see, the light that is higher than worldly light is what shines from the Lord, who illuminates all of heaven. Understanding and wisdom from the Lord are actually seen as light there. This light is what creates our intellect or inner eye. When it flows in through our intellect into the impressions we have from worldly light, it causes them to appear as representations and correspondences and so as something to be understood. **4526**

Since the eyesight of the earthly realm corresponds to the intellectual sight of the spiritual realm, it corresponds to religious truth. Religious truth is part of a genuine intellectual ability, because truth gives us all our ability to understand. Consider that all thinking revolves around the idea that a thing is so or not so, true or not true.

On the point that eyesight corresponds to religious truth and goodness, see §4410 above.

I talked with several people a few days after they had died, and since they were newcomers, they had a moderate amount of light. As far as they were concerned, it was not very different from the world's light, and since that is how the light appeared to them, they doubted it could be coming to them from anywhere else [than the world]. As a consequence they were taken up just barely into heaven, where the light was much brighter. Speaking with me from there they said that they had never seen such light. This happened long after the sun had set. **4527**

They then expressed surprise that a spirit has eyes for seeing. During bodily life they had believed a spirit's life consisted solely in thought, not to say abstract thought, without an agent to do the thinking. They had been unable to conceive of an agent of thought because they had never seen one. Under these circumstances, their perception had been simply that since a spirit's life consisted in thought alone, it would vanish together with the body in which it existed, just like a gust of air or a tongue of flame, if the Lord did not hold it together in some miraculous way and keep it in existence. The newcomers then saw how easily scholars fall into error about life after death, and how the well-educated above all others believe only what they see.

So they marveled that they possessed not only thought but sight as well, and all the rest of the senses. It was particularly surprising to appear to themselves as completely human, to see, hear, and converse with each other, and to feel their limbs, with keener sensitivity than during physical life. They were dumbfounded that people have no idea of this while living in the world. They pitied the human race for its ignorance on the subject—an ignorance due to lack of belief, especially among the most enlightened, which is to say among people in the church who have the Word.

[2] Some of them had simply believed that people would be like ghosts after death, and had been confirmed in the opinion by specters they had heard about. The stories led them to conclude that [the soul] is just some coarse animating element floating out from the life of the body at first but sinking back into the corpse, where it is extinguished.

Others had believed they would not rise again till the time of the Last Judgment at the end of the world, when they would rise with their body (which would then reassemble, even if it had decayed into dust) and therefore with their flesh and bones. And since [people] have waited in vain for this Last Judgment or doomsday for many centuries, they had fallen into the error that they would never rise again. They were overlooking what they had learned from Scripture. In fact, they were forgetting about their own occasional assertion on the basis of Scripture that when a person dies the soul is in God's hand, living among the happy or unhappy, depending on the life the person had known. They were also neglecting what the Lord said about the rich man and Lazarus.

However, they were taught that we each have a last judgment when we die. We then seem to ourselves to be equipped with a body, as in the world. We enjoy all the senses we enjoyed in the world, too, although they are purer and sharper, because the body does not get in the way and objects of worldly light no longer cast shadow on objects of heavenly light. So we have a purified body, so to speak. After death we could never cart around a body of flesh and bone as we did in the world, because to do so would be to find ourselves wrapped once again in a layer of earthly dust.

[3] There were some people I discussed this with on the very day their bodies were interred. Through my eyes they saw their cadaver, the bier, and the burial. They rejected the body, they would tell me. It had served them usefully in the world in which they had lived, and they were now living in a body that served them usefully in the world of their new life.

They wanted me to tell this to their near and dear, who were now mourning. "If I did, they would ridicule it," I was allowed to answer. "When they cannot see something with their own eyes, they don't believe it is real. So they would dismiss it as a delirious apparition. They cannot be led to believe that spirits see one another with their eyes just as people on earth see one another with theirs; that people see spirits only with the eyes of their own spirit; or that people see spirits when the Lord opens their inner eyes—as happened with the prophets, who saw spirits and angels, and many things in heaven. Would people alive today have believed it had they lived in the prophets' days? There is room to doubt it."

The eye, or rather its power of vision, has a particularly strong correspondence with the communities in the other world devoted to the beauties of paradise. These communities appear high up, out in front, and a little to the right, where living displays of gardens are presented to view. The gardens contain trees and flowers of so many genera and species that by comparison the number of different kinds on our whole physical planet is small. Every object in those gardens incorporates some element of understanding and wisdom, which shines out from it. You might even say that along with [the flowers], specimens of understanding and wisdom fill these parks. These are the things that move the community members from deep inside, gladdening not only their eyes but also their mind.

[2] Such paradises exist in the first heaven, on the very threshold of its inner depths. They are representations that filter down from a higher heaven when angels in the higher heaven discuss religious truth among themselves with real understanding. The language of the angels there is based on spiritual and heavenly images, which serve in place of words for them. Their talk consists in an unbroken series of representations, which are so beautiful and delightful that there is no way to express it. The beauty and charm of their words is what is represented as the glories of paradise in the lower heaven.

[3] This heaven is divided into several heavens, to which every feature in the chambers of the eye corresponds. There is the heaven with paradisal gardens, just described. There is a heaven with atmospheres of different colors, where all the air seems to sparkle with gold, silver, pearls, precious stones, miniature flowers, and countless other things. There is a rainbow heaven with gorgeous rainbows large and small in the most magnificent hues.

Light from the Lord, which holds understanding and wisdom within it, creates all of this. So every object in these heavens contains some understanding of truth and some wisdom about goodness, portrayed in a representative way.

[4] When people have had no image of heaven and no idea of its light, it is hard to convince them that phenomena like this exist there. If people carry such skepticism with them into the next life but have lived lives of religious truth and goodness, angels take them to those areas. The sight astounds them. To learn about botanical wonders, atmospheres, and rainbows, see the earlier lessons of experience in §§1619–1626, 2296, 3220. Representations are constantly appearing in the heavens: §§1807, 1808, 1971, 1980, 1981, 2299, 2763, 3213, 3216, 3217, 3218, 3222, 3350, 3475, 3485.

4529 There was a man who was famed and renowned in the scholarly realm for his skill in botany. After he died, he heard in the other world that there too flowers and trees were available to be seen. He was stunned. Since this had been the joy of his life, he burned with desire to see whether it was true and was therefore taken up into a paradisal area. There he saw exquisitely beautiful groves and enchanting flower beds laid out in a huge array. Feeling an intense, passionate pleasure, he was allowed to wander the grounds, not only looking at each and every plant but also plucking samples, holding them up to his eye, and examining whether they were real.

[2] Then he talked with me and said, "I never would have believed it. If we had heard anything like it in the world, we would have considered it bizarre.

"Here," he went on to say, "you can see an unlimited abundance of flowering plants never seen in the world, barely comprehensible by any stretch of the imagination. Each of them glows with an incredible luster because it is produced by the light of heaven." He was not yet able to tell that the glow had a spiritual origin. In other words, he could not tell that a measure of understanding and wisdom about truth and goodness was present in each plant, making it shine.

"People on earth simply will not believe this," he added. Not many of them believe that heaven and hell exist, and those who do believe it know only that there is joy in heaven. Few of these know that in the other world there are things such as eye had never seen, ear had never heard, and mind could never have considered. Yet they know from the Word that the prophets saw astonishing sights, like the many things John observed and wrote about in Revelation. These were nothing but the representations that constantly spring up in heaven and that appeared to him when his inner eyes were open.

[3] They are relatively trivial, though. People who have the genuine understanding and wisdom that bring such objects into being are in such a happy state that they consider the items mentioned fairly trivial.

Some of those experiencing the lush gardens said it made them happier than anything. So they were taken higher and farther to the right into a heaven that gleamed still more radiantly, and eventually to one where they also perceived the bliss of understanding and wisdom present in the vegetation. While there they spoke with me again to say that what they had seen before was relatively trifling. Finally they were taken to a heaven where they could hardly bear the depth of their ecstasy. The rapture had penetrated to their inmost marrow, virtually dissolving it, so that they started to sink into a holy faint.

In the other life one also observes colors, whose brightness and gleam so far outshine the radiance of colors in our world that there is hardly any comparison. They result from variegation of the light and shadow there. Since understanding and wisdom from the Lord is what appears as light to the eyes of angels and spirits, and since it also illuminates their intellect from within, the colors are essentially changes in or modifications of understanding and wisdom.

More times than I can easily count I have seen colors in that world not only beautifying the flowers, lighting up the air, and composing the rainbows but separated out into other manifestations as well. Their brightness comes from the truth associated with understanding. Their gleam comes from the goodness associated with wisdom. The hues themselves are produced by the brilliance and dimness of both faculties, so that, like differences of color in the world, they arise out of light and shadow.

[2] That is why the colors mentioned in the Word represented aspects of understanding and wisdom. This includes the colors of the precious stones on Aaron's breastplate and of his holy garments; in the curtains of the tent where the ark was kept; in the New Jerusalem's foundation stones, described by John in Revelation; and elsewhere. Their individual representations will be discussed in the explanations, by the Lord's divine mercy.

In general, the brighter a color in heaven is and the more white it has, the more it comes from the truth associated with understanding. The more it glows and the more red it has, the more it comes from the goodness associated with wisdom.

Colors based on heavenly ones also belong to the areas of the eyes.

4531 Since understanding and wisdom from the Lord is what appears as light in heaven, angels are called angels of light. Foolishness and insanity from arrogant self-reliance reigns supreme in hell, so the names used for its inhabitants have to do with the dark. Hell is not dark, admittedly, but it is lit with a dull glimmer like that from a coal fire, which enables the inhabitants to see each other. Otherwise they could not survive.

The illumination they do have rises out of heaven's light, which turns into this glimmer when it falls on their craziness—their distortions and cravings.

The Lord and his light are present everywhere, including the hells. Otherwise the spirits there would lack all ability to think or speak. However, the level of light meets the demand for it.

This dim light is what the Word calls the shadow of death, comparing it to darkness. It even turns into darkness for hellish spirits who go near heaven's light; and when they are in darkness, they are in folly and stupidity.

Darkness plainly corresponds to falsity, then, just as light corresponds to truth; and people who subscribe to falsity are said to be blind.

4532 Some people think they understand goodness and truth on their own, so they trust themselves alone and consider themselves wiser than everyone else. In reality they are ignorant of goodness and truth. Some even refuse to understand what is good and true and are therefore prey to falsity. Sometimes in the other life these people—especially the latter group—are sent off into the dark, where they talk nonsense, because they are given to stupidity. I have been told that a lot of people are like this, including some who felt they had been granted tremendous light—which is how it seemed to others, as well.

4533 The wonders of the other life include this: that evil spirits appear entirely different when the angels of heaven look at them than they appear to each other.

When evil spirits and demons are off by themselves in their own swamp light, which resembles the light of a coal fire, as I said, they see themselves in human form. This form is not ugly, from their deluded point of view. But when heaven's angels look at the same spirits and demons, the swamp light vanishes immediately, and they appear with a completely different face, each according to her or his bent of mind. Some are as dark and pitch-black as devils. Some have faces as livid as corpses. Some have almost no face but something hairy instead. Some look like a set of teeth; some like a skeleton. Even more strangely, some actually look like monsters, deceivers look like snakes, the worst liars look like vipers, and so on.

As soon as angels take their eyes off such beings, however, they appear in their old form, the form they have in their own dim light.

Angels look in on the evil whenever they notice them climbing up out of their hells into the world of spirits, attempting harm to others. The evil are then exposed and cast back into hell.

This potency in an angel's gaze is due to the correspondence between intellectual sight and eyesight. The correspondence lends insight to their scrutiny, which scatters the faint glimmer of hell and reveals the true form and character of its inhabitants.

There will be more about the universal human and correspondence at the end of the next chapter [§§4622–4634].

Genesis 35

[The Close of the Age]

4535 THE previous chapters from Genesis 26 up to here were introduced with explanations of the Lord's predictions about his Coming, or the *close of the age.* Several times in those explanations it was shown that his Coming, or the close of the age, symbolizes the church's final days, which in the Word are also called the Last Judgment. People who fail to see beyond the literal meaning necessarily understand the Last Judgment to be the end of the world. This notion comes chiefly from the Book of Revelation, where [John] says that he saw a *new heaven* and a *new earth, for the first heaven and the first earth passed away* and the sea no longer existed. Moreover he saw the holy city New Jerusalem coming down from God out of heaven (Revelation 21:1, 2). The idea also comes from Isaiah's visionary sayings, which contain a similar statement:

> Look—I am *creating new heavens* and a *new earth!* Therefore the earlier ones will not be remembered or rise into one's heart. Rejoice and be glad forever [in] what I am creating! Look—I will be creating Jerusalem as a joy, and its people as gladness. (Isaiah 65:17, 18; 66:22)

[2] People who fail to see beyond the literal meaning cannot help thinking that the whole heaven along with this earth is destined to collapse into nothingness. They inevitably believe the dead will first rise at that time but live in a new heaven, on a new earth. These parts of the Word are not to be understood in such a way, though, as can be seen in many other Scripture passages mentioning the heavens and the earth.

People who have some belief in an inner meaning can see clearly that the new heaven and the new earth mean a new religion that is to take over when the earlier one passes away (see §§1733, 1850, 3355). They can see that heaven means the inner dimension of the new religion, and the earth, its outer dimension.

[3] This final era of the previous religion and first era of the new religion is what is also called the close of the age—which the Lord talked about in Matthew 24—and his Coming. It is a time when the Lord leaves behind the previous religion and comes to the new one.

Other passages in the Word also show that this is what the close or culmination of the age is. In Isaiah, for instance:

> On that day the survivors will return, the survivors of Jacob, to the mighty God. For although your people Israel is like the sand of the sea, [only] survivors of it will return. It is a *definite culmination*, overflowing with justice. For the Lord Jehovih Sabaoth is making a *culmination* and a *determined end* on *all the earth*. (Isaiah 10:21, 22, 23)

In the same author:

> Now, do not mock, or your punishments might intensify, because I have heard from the Lord Jehovih Sabaoth of a *culmination* and *final decision on the whole earth*. (Isaiah 28:22)

In Jeremiah:

> This is what Jehovah has said: "*All the earth* will be devastated, yet I will not make a *culmination*." (Jeremiah 4:27)

In Zephaniah:

> I will reduce people to distress, and they will go about like the blind of [Jerusalem], because they have sinned against Jehovah, and their blood will be shed like dust, and their flesh, like dung; because Jehovah will make a *culmination* and indeed a speedy one *with all the inhabitants of the land*. (Zephaniah 1:17, 18)

Every one of these quotations makes it clear that the culmination referred to means the final period of the church and that the earth means the church.

[4] The earth [or land] means the church because the land of Canaan was the land where the church had existed since earliest times and where a representation of the church later existed among Jacob's descendants. When a culmination is said to have come on this land, the meaning is not that it came on the nation there but on the sacred worship of the nation in which the church existed. The Word is spiritual, and spirituality does not have to do with land itself or with the nation inhabiting a land but with qualities belonging to the church.

For the idea that the land of Canaan was the land where the church had existed since earliest times, see §§567, 3686, 4447, 4454, 4516, 4517. For the idea that the earth [or land] in the Word consequently symbolizes the church, §§566, 662, 1066, 1068, 1262, 3355, 4447. This clarifies what is meant in Isaiah by making a culmination on all the earth, and in Zephaniah, by a speedy culmination with all the inhabitants of the land.

The Jewish nation was the inhabitant of that land, and it was not brought to a culmination, but its type of sacred worship was, as is recognized.

[5] This meaning of a culmination is still more evident in Daniel:

> Seventy weeks have been decreed upon your people and upon your holy city, to *culminate* transgression, and to seal up sin, and to atone for wickedness, and to introduce everlasting justice, and to seal up vision and prophet, and to anoint the Holiest Place. In the middle of the week he will put an end to sacrifice and oblation. Then at last upon the ruinous bird will come ruination; and all the way to a *culmination* and *final decision*, [ruination] will shower down on the wasteland. (Daniel 9:24, 27)

[6] From this evidence you can now see that the final days of the church are precisely what is meant by the close of the age, concerning which the disciples asked the Lord, "What will be the sign of your coming and of the *close of the age?*" (Matthew 24:3). The same is true of these words of the Lord's—the last words of the same Gospel:

> Jesus said to the disciples, "As you teach, keep absolutely everything I have commanded you. And here, I myself am with you every day until the *close of the age.*" (Matthew 28:20)

The reason the Lord said he would be with the disciples until the close of the age is that his twelve disciples symbolize the same thing as the twelve tribes of Israel: everything involved in love and faith, and therefore everything involved in religion. See §§3354, 3488, 3858. For this symbolism of the twelve tribes, see §§3858, 3926, 3939, 4060. The church comes to a close when there is no longer any neighborly love in it and consequently no more faith, and this has been shown several times before.

Hardly any neighborly love or consequent faith remains in the current church, which is called Christian, so the close of its age is now at hand. This will be demonstrated later, by the Lord's divine mercy.

***

Genesis 35

1. And God said to Jacob, "Rise; go up to Bethel and stay there, and make there an altar to the God who appeared to you as you fled before Esau your brother."

2. And Jacob said to his household and to everyone who was with him, "Take away the foreigner's gods that are in your midst, and be purified, and change your clothes.

3. And let's rise and go up to Bethel, and I will make there an altar to the God answering me on the day of my distress—and he was with me on the way that I walked."

4. And they gave to Jacob all the foreigner's gods that were in their hand and the earrings that were in their ears, and Jacob hid them under the oak that was near Shechem.

5. And they set off. And the terror of God was on the cities that were around them, and [the inhabitants] did not pursue after the children of Jacob.

6. And Jacob came to Luz (which is in the land of Canaan)—that is, Bethel—he and the whole people that was with him.

7. And he built there an altar and called the place El-bethel, because there *gods* were revealed to him as he fled before his brother.

8. And Deborah, Rebekah's nursemaid, died and was buried below Bethel under the oak, and he called its name Allon-bacuth.

9. And God appeared to Jacob again as he came from Paddan-aram, and blessed him.

10. And God said to him, "Your name is Jacob. Your name will no longer be called Jacob; rather, Israel will be your name." And [God] called his name Israel.

11. And God said to him, "I am God Shaddai; be fruitful and multiply! A nation and a throng of nations will exist from you, and monarchs will come from your genitals.

12. And the land that I gave Abraham and Isaac, to you I will give it; and to your seed after you I will give the land."

13. And God went up from him in the place where he spoke with him.

14. And Jacob raised a pillar in the place where he spoke with him, a pillar of stone, and offered a drink offering on it and poured oil on it.

15. And Jacob called the name of the place where God spoke with him Bethel.

16. And they traveled from Bethel, and there was still a stretch of land to go to Ephrata, and Rachel gave birth and suffered hard things in her giving birth.

17. And it happened as she suffered hard things in her giving birth that the midwife said to her, "Don't be afraid, because this too is a son for you."

18. And it happened as her soul was departing that she was about to die, and she called his name Ben-oni. And his father called him Benjamin.

19. And Rachel died and was buried on the way to Ephrath, that is, Bethlehem.

20. And Jacob raised a pillar over her grave; it is the Pillar of Rachel's Grave to this day.

21. And Israel traveled and stretched his tent, from beyond the tower of Eder.

22. And it happened as Israel was dwelling in this land that Reuben went and lay with Bilhah, his father's concubine, and Israel heard. And Jacob's sons were twelve.

23. The sons of Leah: Jacob's firstborn, Reuben, and Simeon and Levi and Judah and Issachar and Zebulun.

24. The sons of Rachel: Joseph and Benjamin.

25. And the sons of Bilhah, Rachel's slave: Dan and Naphtali.

26. And the sons of Zilpah, Leah's slave: Gad and Asher. These were Jacob's sons, who were born to him in Paddan-aram.

27. And Jacob came to Isaac his father, to Mamre, Kiriath-arba (that is, Hebron), where Abraham and Isaac stayed as an immigrant.

28. And the days of Isaac were one hundred eighty years.

29. And Isaac breathed his last and died and was gathered to his peoples, old and full of days. And Esau and Jacob his sons buried him.

Summary

4536 THIS chapter's inner meaning is about the remainder of the Lord's earthly plane and how it was made divine. The inner depths of that plane, which became divine, are meant by Israel. Advancement to a more inward level, the level of rationality, is depicted by Benjamin's birth and then by the arrival of Jacob's sons to see Isaac.

Inner Meaning

4537 GENESIS 35:1, 2, 3, 4. *And God said to Jacob, "Rise; go up to Bethel and stay there, and make there an altar to the God who appeared to you as you fled before Esau your brother." And Jacob said to his household*

*and to everyone who was with him, "Take away the foreigner's gods that are
in your midst, and be purified, and change your clothes. And let's rise and
go up to Bethel, and I will make there an altar to the God answering me
on the day of my distress—and he was with me on the way that I walked."
And they gave to Jacob all the foreigner's gods that were in their hand and
the earrings that were in their ears, and Jacob hid them under the oak that
was near Shechem.*

God said to Jacob symbolizes a perception received from the Lord's
divine side by the earthly goodness that Jacob now stands for. *Rise, go
up to Bethel* means concerning his earthly divinity. *And stay there* symbolizes living a life. *And make there an altar to the God who appeared to
you* symbolizes something holy there. *As you fled before Esau your brother*
means when truth was given priority over goodness. *And Jacob said to his
household and to everyone who was with him* symbolizes a rearrangement
by earthly goodness, such as it now was. *Take away the foreigner's gods that
are in your midst* means that falsity would be rejected. *And be purified and
change your clothes* symbolizes a need to put on holiness. *And let's rise and
go up to Bethel* symbolizes earthly divinity. *And I will make there an altar
to the God* symbolizes the holiness on which deeper levels rest. *Answering
me on the day of my distress* means in a state of truth's priority over goodness. *And he was with me on the way that I walked* symbolizes the Lord's
divine providence. *And they gave to Jacob all the foreigner's gods that were in
their hand* means that he would reject everything false so far as he could.
And the earrings that were in their ears symbolizes [falsity] that had been
applied. *And Jacob hid them under the oak that was near Shechem* symbolizes eternal rejection, *the oak that was near Shechem* meaning what was
deceptive on the earthly plane.

God said to Jacob symbolizes a perception received from the Lord's
divine side by the earthly goodness that Jacob now stands for, as the following shows: In scriptural narrative, *saying* symbolizes perceiving, as discussed in §§1602, 1791, 1815, 1822, 1898, 1919, 2061, 2080, 2238, 2260,
2619, 2862, 3395, 3509. *God said*, then, means a perception received from
the Lord's divine side. And at this point, in the highest sense, *Jacob* represents the Lord's earthly goodness.

Earlier sections have shown what *Jacob* represents in the Word, and
since his representation has varied, I need to explain briefly. [2] In general, in the highest sense, Jacob represents the Lord's earthly divinity. Since
the Lord glorified his earthly level, though, this level was different in the
beginning from what it was during the process and at the end. As a result,
Jacob's representation has varied. At first he represented truth on the Lord's

4538

earthly level. During the process he represented truth-based goodness on the Lord's earthly level. At the end he represents goodness there.

The Lord's glorification advanced from truth to truth-based goodness and finally to goodness, as shown many times before. Because the process is now near its end, Jacob represents the Lord's earthly goodness. See previous demonstrations showing that in the highest sense Jacob represents the Lord's earthly divinity, at first in regard to truth (§§3305, 3509, 3525, 3546, 3576, 3599), but during the process, in regard to truth-based goodness (§§3659, 3669, 3677, 4234, 4273, 4337). Jacob now represents the Lord's earthly divinity in regard to goodness because the process is near its end, as noted.

[3] This process took place when the Lord made his earthly plane divine. A similar process also takes place when the Lord regenerates us. The Lord chose to make his humanity divine according to the same plan by which he remakes us. That is the reason for the repeated assertion that human rebirth is an image of the Lord's glorification (§§3138, 3212, 3296, 3490, 4402).

When the Lord is remaking us, he first teaches us religious truth. Without religious truth we do not know what the Lord is, what heaven is, what hell is, or even that they exist—not to mention countless things to be known *about* the Lord, his kingdom in heaven, and his kingdom on earth (the church), and about the identity and nature of their opposites in hell. [4] Until we know these things we cannot tell what goodness is.

By goodness I do not mean public and private goodness. We learn about this kind of goodness in the world, through laws and rules and through reflection on the ways of humankind. That is why nations outside the church also know about this kind of goodness. Instead, what I mean by goodness is spiritual goodness. In the Word this goodness is called charity, and in general it means willing and doing good to others not for any selfish reason but because we like to and want to. This goodness is spiritual goodness. The only way we can possibly arrive at this kind of goodness is through religious truth, taught to us by the Lord when we read or hear the Word.

[5] After we have been instructed in religious truth, the Lord gradually leads us to will what is true and to act on it because we will it. This truth is called truth-based goodness, because truth-based goodness is truth in our will and in our actions. It is called truth-based goodness because truth that was previously a matter of doctrine then becomes a

matter of life. Eventually, when we feel pleasure in willing and therefore doing good, it is no longer called truth-based goodness but goodness itself. Then we have been reborn. No longer do we will and do what is good at the inspiration of truth; instead we will and do what is true at the inspiration of goodness. Even the truth we then put into practice is essentially goodness, because it draws its essential nature from its origin, which is goodness.

These remarks clarify what it means to say that in the highest sense Jacob represents goodness on the Lord's earthly plane, and why it is that he does.

Jacob now represents this goodness because the inner meaning is dealing with further progress, or progress toward an inner level of the earthly plane—a level that Israel stands for (§4536). When the Lord is regenerating us, we cannot reach inner levels until the truth we know becomes goodness.

Rise, go up to Bethel means concerning his earthly divinity—a perception concerning it—as the following shows: *Rising* has a symbolism involving elevation, as mentioned in §§2401, 2785, 2912, 2927, 3171, 4103. In this case it means raising what is earthly to divinity. *Going up* means toward more inward levels, as discussed below. And *Bethel* symbolizes divinity on the earthly plane, or on the outermost level of the divine design, as noted in §4089. In the original language, Bethel means "house of God," and since the house of God is where one finds knowledge of goodness and truth, Bethel in its most directly related meaning symbolizes that knowledge, as shown in §1453.

4539

Inner levels rest on the outermost levels of the divine design and reach their end there. They coexist there and live in a single house, so to speak. Because of this, and because our earthly plane is our lowest plane, on which our inner levels rest, Bethel, the "house of God," generally symbolizes the earthly plane (§§3729, 4089). Specifically, it symbolizes what is good there, because a house in an inner sense means goodness (§§2233, 3720, 3729). Knowledge also resides on the earthly plane, or the outermost level of the divine design.

[2] *Going up* means toward inner levels because inner levels are the ones people refer to as higher (§2148). When the inner meaning has to do with advancement to inner levels, then, the text speaks of going up. For example, it speaks of going up from Egypt to the land of Canaan; within Canaan itself, of going up to the more central areas, and from all areas up to Jerusalem; and in Jerusalem, of going up to the House of God there.

Mention is made in Moses of going up from Egypt to Canaan:

> Pharaoh said to Joseph, "*Go up* and bury your father." And Joseph *went up*. And there *went up* with him all Pharaoh's servants, and there *went up* with him chariot and rider. (Genesis 50:6, 7, 8, 9)

In Judges:

> The angel of Jehovah *went up* from Gilgal to Bochim and said, "I have *caused* you *to come up* out of Egypt." (Judges 2:1)

Egypt, on an inner level, symbolizes secular knowledge, whose duty is to help us understand the workings of the Lord's kingdom. The land of Canaan symbolizes the Lord's kingdom. Since secular knowledge is lowlier (in other words, more outward) and what belongs to the Lord's kingdom is higher (in other words, more inward), the text speaks of going up from Egypt to Canaan. Conversely it speaks of going down from Canaan to Egypt, as in Genesis 42:2, 3; 43:4, 5, 15; and elsewhere.

[3] Mention is made in Joshua of going up from within Canaan itself to its more central areas:

> Joshua said, "*Go up* and scout out the land." And the men *went up* and scouted out Ai and returned to Joshua and said to him, "Don't have all the people *go up;* about two thousand men or about three thousand men shall *go up.*" So of the people, about three thousand men *went up.* (Joshua 7:2, 3, 4)

Since the land of Canaan symbolizes the Lord's kingdom, the parts farther from the outer limits symbolized its inner levels. That is why this passage speaks of going up.

Mention is likewise made of going from all surrounding areas up to Jerusalem, and in Jerusalem, up to the House of God, at 1 Kings 12:27, 28; 2 Kings 20:5, 8; Matthew 20:18; Mark 10:33; Luke 18:31; and many other places. Jerusalem was the heart of the land because it symbolized the Lord's spiritual kingdom, and the House of God was the heart of Jerusalem because it symbolized the Lord's heavenly kingdom and in the highest sense the Lord himself. So the text speaks of going up to these places.

This evidence makes clear the symbolism of *Rise, go up to Bethel,* and specifically of going up as advancement toward inner levels, the subject of the current chapter (§4536).

And stay there symbolizes living a life. This can be seen from the
symbolism of *staying* or settling as living a life (discussed at §§1293, 3384,
3613, 4451).

4540

And make there an altar to the God who appeared to you symbolizes
something holy there. This can be seen from the symbolism of an *altar*
as the main object representing the Lord (discussed at §§921, 2777, 2811,
4489). Because of this symbolism, *making an altar to God* symbolizes holiness in worship.

4541

As you fled before Esau your brother means when truth was given priority over goodness. This can be seen from the representation of *Esau*
as divine goodness in the Lord's earthly divinity (discussed in §§3322,
3494, 3504, 3576, 3599). The explanation of Jacob's fleeing before Esau
in Genesis 27 shows that it refers to a time when truth had priority over
goodness. The reason Jacob fled was that he had stolen Esau's birthright,
meaning that truth had promoted itself over goodness. At that point in
the story Jacob represents truth on the Lord's earthly plane, while Esau
represents goodness there. The reason truth put itself ahead of goodness
was that when we are being reborn, truth seems to come first; but once
we have been regenerated, goodness comes first, and truth second. (On
these matters, see §§3324, 3539, 3548, 3556, 3563, 3570, 3576, 3603, 3610,
3701, 4243, 4245, 4247, 4337.) This explains why *as you fled before Esau
your brother* means when truth was given priority over goodness.

4542

And Jacob said to his household and to everyone who was with him symbolizes a rearrangement by earthly goodness, such as it now was. This can
be seen from the symbolism of *saying to his household and to everyone who
was with him* as arranging, and from the representation of *Jacob* at this
point as earthly goodness (discussed above at §4538).

4543

The reason *saying to his household and to everyone who was with him*
means arranging is that the inner meaning of the next verses has to do
with the rearrangement of truth by goodness. When the spiritual goodness described above in §4538 starts to play the leading role in the earthly
mind, it arranges the truth there into an orderly pattern.

Take away the foreigner's gods that are in your midst means that falsity
would be rejected. This can be seen from the symbolism of *taking away*
as rejecting, and from that of a *foreigner's gods* as falsity. In the Word,
gods symbolize truth, and in a negative sense, falsity (§4402). *Foreigners*
was the term for people outside the church and consequently for people
under the sway of falsity and evil (§§2049, 2115). As a result, a foreigner's
gods mean falsity.

4544

4545   *And be purified and change your clothes* symbolizes a need to put on
holiness. This is indicated by the symbolism of being *purified,* or cleansed,
as becoming holy (dealt with below) and from that of *changing clothes* as
putting something on. Here it means putting on sacred truth, because on
an inner level of the Word, *clothes* symbolize truth.

Changing clothes was obviously a customary representation in the
church, but no one can tell what it represented without knowing that in
an inner sense clothes symbolize truth (see §2576). Because the theme of
the inner meaning here is the rejection of falsity and the rearrangement
of truth on the earthly level by the goodness there, the text mentions
Jacob's command that everyone change clothes.

[2] Other places in the Word can also demonstrate that changing clothes
was representative of putting on sacred truth. In Isaiah, for instance:

> Wake up! Wake up, Jerusalem! Put on your strength, Zion! *Put on your
> finest clothes,* Jerusalem, you holy city, because the uncircumcised and
> *unclean* will not continue to come into you any longer. (Isaiah 52:1)

Zion means a heavenly religion, and Jerusalem means a spiritual religion.
A heavenly religion is one that has goodness because it has love for the
Lord. A spiritual religion has truth because it has faith and charity. So
strength is mentioned in connection with Zion, and clothes in connection with Jerusalem, and [the text implies] that putting on these would
render them clean. [3] In Zechariah:

> Joshua was *dressed in defiled garments* and was standing in them before the
> angel. And [the angel] answered and said to those standing before him,
> saying, *"Take the defiled garments* off him." And to him he said, "Look! I
> have made your wickedness pass from upon you, *dressing you in ceremo-
> nial clothing."* (Zechariah 3:3, 4)

This passage shows that taking off clothes and being dressed in ceremonial clothing represented purification from falsity, because the passage says,
"I have made your wickedness pass from upon you." That is why people
had ceremonial clothing and called it "clothes for changing" (mentioned
here and there in the Word)—because they used such garments in creating representations.

[4] Since changing clothes had this representation, the part of Ezekiel
dealing in an inner sense with the new temple (which symbolizes a new
religion) says:

> When the priests go in, they shall not go out from the Holy Place to the
> outer court but shall there *put off their garments* in which they ministered

(because these are holiness) and *put on other garments* and approach the [areas] that are for the people. (Ezekiel 42:14)

And in the same author:

> When they go out to the outer court, to the people, they shall *strip off their garments* in which they are ministering and lay them aside in the holy rooms and *put on other garments* and consecrate the people while wearing *other garments.* (Ezekiel 44:19)

[5] Anyone can see that the new temple and the holy city and land of which the prophet speaks here and in the surrounding chapters does not mean a new temple, or a new city or new land. After all, he mentions sacrifices and rituals that were to be reinstated, when in reality they were going to be abolished. He also lists the tribes of Israel that would divide the land up among them into inheritances [Ezekiel 48], although they actually scattered and never returned. Clearly, then, the rituals mentioned there symbolize spiritual and heavenly aspects of religion. So does Aaron's change of clothing when he was ministering, as prescribed in Moses:

> When he is about to sacrifice the burnt offering, he shall *put on his vestment* [and] the linen shorts; the ash he shall put beside the altar. *Afterward he shall strip off his garments* and *put on other garments* and take the ash out to a clean place outside the camp, and in this way he shall sacrifice the burnt offering. (Leviticus 6:9–12)

[6] The idea that being cleansed means becoming holy can be seen from the required cleansings, such as washing one's flesh and clothes and being spattered with the water for removal [of sin]. Anyone who knows anything about the spiritual self can see that these acts make no one holy. What does wickedness and sin have to do with the clothes a person wears? Yet [the Word] says several times that after people cleansed themselves they would be holy.

It is plain, then, that the only sanctity in the Israelites' required rituals came from the fact that the rituals represented something sacred. Consequently they did not bestow any personal holiness on the people who did the representing. The holiness being represented, separately from the people representing it, was what affected the spirits with them and therefore the angels in heaven (§4307). [7] Heaven has to have communication with humankind—communication through the church—if the human race is to survive. Otherwise we would be like animals, lacking internal or external restraints, and therefore unfettered we would rush to destroy one other and assure our mutual extinction. And since at the time of the Israelites no communication was possible through any church, the Lord provided that it be achieved in a miraculous way through representations.

Many Scripture passages show that ritual washing and cleansing represented sanctification. When Jehovah came down onto Mount Sinai, for example, he said to Moses:

> *Consecrate* them today and tomorrow and have them *wash their clothes.* And have them be ready for the third day. (Exodus 19:10, 11)

In Ezekiel:

> I will *spatter clean water on you,* and you will be *cleansed* from all your *uncleannesses;* and from all your idols I will *cleanse you.* And I will give you a new heart, and a new spirit I will put in your midst. (Ezekiel 36:25, 26)

The spattering of clean water clearly represented purification of the heart, so the cleansing means sanctification.

4546 *And let's rise and go up to Bethel* symbolizes earthly divinity. This is established by remarks above at §4539, where the same words occur.

4547 *And I will make there an altar to the God* symbolizes the holiness on which inner levels rest. This can be seen from the symbolism of *making an altar to God* as holiness in worship (mentioned above in §4541). The reason for saying that deeper levels rest on it is that Jacob was going to make the altar in Bethel, which is what *there* means. Bethel symbolizes the earthly plane, on which inner levels rest; see above at §4539.

4548 *Answering me on the day of my distress* means in a state in which he was giving truth priority over goodness. This is established by the symbolism of a *day* as a state (discussed in §§23, 487, 488, 493, 893, 2788, 3462, 3785). The fact that the *day of my distress* symbolizes a state in which he was giving truth priority over goodness can be seen from the discussion above at §4542. The day of distress here involves the same meaning as the phrase there, "as you fled before Esau your brother."

4549 *And he was with me on the way that I walked* symbolizes the Lord's divine providence. This can be seen from the symbolism of *being with someone on the way that person walks,* when it applies to the Divine, or the Lord, as his divine providence. In its proper sense, to provide means to be right near a person and to guard him or her from evil.

And they gave to Jacob all the foreigner's gods that were in their hand **4550** means that he would reject everything false so far as he could, as the following shows: A *foreigner's gods* symbolize falsity, as noted in §4544. And *that were in their hand* means as far as possible. A *hand* symbolizes power (§§878, 3387), so something *in a hand* means within something's power, or its greatest potential.

They gave to Jacob means that goodness is what would reject falsity, because in this chapter *Jacob* represents earthly goodness (§4538).

And the earrings that were in their ears symbolizes [falsity] that had been **4551** applied. This is clear from the symbolism of *earrings* as tokens of obedience, which comes from the fact that *ears* symbolize obedience (§§2542, 3869). What results from obedience is a matter of actual application, because obeying something involves acting on it. What I am describing as applied is the falsity that was slated for rejection.

A few words need to be said about the rejection of falsity that had been applied as well, the current topic of the inner meaning. Until we arrive at goodness through rebirth from the Lord, and act on truth because goodness inspires us to do so, we have a great deal of falsity mixed in with our truth. Religious truth first leads us into [being reborn], and the only idea we have of that truth in our early years is one formed in childhood and youth. It stems from the external things that are part of the world and the sensory evidence of the body, so it cannot help being illusory and therefore false. This falsity becomes applied falsity because we base our actions on our beliefs. That is the kind of falsity meant here. It stays with us until we have been reborn—in other words, until we act on goodness—at which point goodness reorganizes all the truth we have absorbed so far. Or rather the Lord uses goodness to reorganize it. When he does, falsity is separated from truth and pushed aside.

[2] Although completely unaware of it, we are having falsity removed and rejected in this way from our earliest youth right up to the final stage of our life. It happens to all of us but especially to those who are being reborn. Something similar happens to people who are *not* being reborn, since once they grow up and their powers of judgment mature, they view their youthful judgments as foolish, laughable, and far behind them. The difference between the reborn and the unreborn is this: What the reborn view as far behind them is anything that fails to harmonize with the goodness urged by faith and charity. What the unreborn view that way is anything that fails to harmonize with the pleasures of the love

governing them. For the most part, then, the latter see truth as false, and falsity as true.

As for [what are called] earrings [here], there were actually two kinds. One kind was worn on the forehead above the nose, and the other was worn in the ears. The ones worn on the forehead above the nose were tokens of goodness and are called rings (see §3103). The ones worn in the ears were tokens of obedience and are earrings. The original language uses the same word for both.

4552   *And Jacob hid them under the oak that was near Shechem* symbolizes eternal rejection, as the following shows: *Hiding* symbolizes rejecting and burying something as if it were dead. *Under the oak* means forever. Because the oak is an extremely long-lived tree, to hide something under one symbolized permanence.

An oak also symbolized what was confused, and what was deceptive and false. The lowest plane of the earthly dimension, you see, is relatively confused and deceptive, so far as it draws its knowledge and pleasure from the physical senses and consequently from illusions. The specific symbolism of an oak is the lowest part of the earthly dimension, so in a positive sense it symbolizes what is true and good there, and in a negative sense, what is evil and false there.

[2] When falsity is removed from regenerate people, it is cast off to the bottom of their earthly dimension. It looks far removed, seen by their inner eye, once their powers of judgment have matured and they have gained insight; even more so when they have developed understanding and wisdom. In people who have been reborn, truth is located in the innermost part of their earthly level, near goodness, which is like a miniature sun there. Other truth branching off from it stands at a distance, according to the degree of kinship or family tie it has with goodness, so to speak. Misleading truth lies on the outskirts, and falsity is relegated to the outermost limits. These things stay with us forever, but when we allow the Lord to lead us, they adopt such an arrangement. The pattern is a heavenly one, because heaven itself is so arranged. When, on the other hand, we allow evil rather than the Lord to lead us, the arrangement is just the reverse. Evil together with falsity is then in the middle, truth is relegated to the outskirts, and genuine, divine truth is sent to the furthest limits. The pattern is hellish, because hell is so arranged. The outermost limits are the lowest part of the earthly dimension.

[3] Oaks mean falsity at the bottom of the earthly level, because in the ancient church, when outward worship was representative of the Lord's

kingdom, all trees of every kind symbolized something spiritual or heavenly. The olive tree and its oil symbolized attributes of heavenly love. The grapevine and its wine symbolized attributes of charity and of the resulting faith. Not to mention all the other trees, such as the cedar, fig, poplar, beech, and oak, whose symbolism has been shown in various explanations. That is why the Word so often mentions them, and also gardens, groves, and forests in general. The ancients held their worship in such places, under certain trees, but eventually this worship turned idolatrous. Jacob's descendants, among whom a representation of a religion was to be established, were prone to idolatry. They would have put idols in all those places. As a result they were barred from holding worship in gardens and groves under the trees; but trees still kept their symbolism. This now is why the trees mentioned in the Word each symbolize what they did in the ancient church, and not just the nobler trees, such as olives, grapevines, and cedars, but also poplars, beeches, and oaks.

[4] The positive symbolism of oaks as truth and goodness at the bottom of the earthly plane, and their negative symbolism as falsity and evil, can be seen from Scripture passages mentioning oaks, when those passages are taken in an inner sense. In Isaiah, for instance:

> Those who abandon Jehovah will be consumed, because they will be ashamed of the *oaks* for which you longed. And you will be like an *oak* dropping its leaves and like a *garden* that has no water. (Isaiah 1:28, 29, 30)

In the same author:

> The day of Jehovah Sabaoth will come over all the haughty and lowly and over all the *cedars* of Lebanon and over all the *oaks of Bashan*. (Isaiah 2:12, 13)

Anyone can see that the day of Jehovah will not come over cedars and oaks but over people symbolized by them. In the same author:

> Those who form a god cut *cedars* down for themselves and take *beech* and *oak* and secure these for themselves among the trees of the forest. (Isaiah 44:14)

[5] In Ezekiel:

> You will know that I am Jehovah when their victims of stabbing lie amid the idols around their altars on every high hill, on all the heads of the

mountains, and under *every green tree,* and under every *tangled oak,* in the place where they offered a restful smell to all their idols. (Ezekiel 6:13)

The ancients had also worshiped on hills and mountains because these symbolized heavenly love. However, when worship is offered by idolaters, as here, hills and mountains symbolize love for oneself and for worldly advantages (§§795, 796, 1430, 2722, 4210). The ancients had worshiped under trees because each species possessed a symbolism, as noted above. "Under a tangled oak" in this case means from falsity lying at the bottom of the earthly level, because this falsity is convoluted (§2831). In Hosea:

On the mountain heads they sacrifice, on the hills they burn incense, under *oak, poplar,* and *terebinth,* because its shade is good. Therefore your daughters are whoring, and your daughters-in-law are committing adultery. (Hosea 4:13)

Whoring means falsifying truth, and committing adultery means perverting what is good; see §§2466, 2729, 3399. In Zechariah:

Open your doors, Lebanon, and let fire consume the *cedars,* because the majestic ones have been ravaged. Wail, *oaks of Bashan,* because the forest of Bazir has come down. (Zechariah 11:1, 2)

4553   Genesis 35:5, 6, 7. *And they set off, and the terror of God was on the cities that were around them, and [the inhabitants] did not pursue after the children of Jacob. And Jacob came to Luz (which is in the land of Canaan)— that is, Bethel—he and the whole people that was with him. And he built there an altar and called the place El-bethel, because there gods were revealed to him as he fled before his brother.*

They set off symbolizes a continuation. *And the terror of God was on the cities that were around them, and they did not pursue after the children of Jacob* means that falsity and evil could not go near. *And Jacob came to Luz, which is in the land of Canaan,* symbolizes the earthly dimension in an earlier condition. *That is, Bethel* symbolizes earthly divinity. *He and the whole people that was with him* means with everything on that level. *And he built there an altar* means by being made holy. *And called the place El-bethel* symbolizes an earthly level that was holy. *Because there gods were revealed to him* symbolizes sacred truths. *As he fled before his brother* means after truth was given priority over goodness.

4554   *They set off* symbolizes a continuation. This can be seen from the symbolism of *setting off* as what came next (mentioned in §4375) and therefore a continuation—specifically, continuing progress toward inner levels.

And the terror of God was on the cities that were around them, and they did not pursue after the children of Jacob means that falsity and evil could not go near, as the following shows: The *terror of God* symbolizes protection, as discussed below. The *cities that were around them* symbolize falsity and evil. In a positive sense, cities mean truth in doctrine; in a negative sense, falsity in doctrine (§§402, 2449, 2943, 3216, 4478, 4492, 4493). These cities symbolize evil as well because their residents are also meant. In a positive sense, the residents of a city stand for what is good; in a negative sense, for what is evil (§§2268, 2451, 2712). And *not pursuing after them* symbolizes not being able to go near.

[2] The way things are done in the other world can illustrate that the *terror of God* means protection. The hells there can never go near heaven, nor can evil spirits go near any heavenly community, because they live in terror of God. Whenever evil spirits approach a community in heaven, they suddenly fall into distress and torment. The ones who have experienced this several times do not dare go near. This not-daring is what is meant in an inner sense by the terror of God. Not that God (the Lord) inflicts terror on them. Rather, because they are steeped in falsity and evil, they dwell in the opposites of truth and goodness. When they go near what is good and true, the falsity and evil themselves distress and torture them.

And Jacob came to Luz, which is in the land of Canaan, symbolizes the earthly dimension in an earlier condition. *That is, Bethel* symbolizes earthly divinity. This can be seen from the symbolism of *Luz* as the earthly dimension in an earlier condition—in other words, the earthly part that had been human. It had now become divine, as symbolized by *that is, Bethel.* For the symbolism of Bethel as earthly divinity, see §§4089, 4539.

Other places in the Word that mention Bethel also say, "Luz, that is, Bethel," and "Bethel once was Luz." In Joshua, for example:

> The border of the lot of the children of Benjamin went out between the children of Judah and the children of Joseph *to Luz (to the side of Luz* toward the south)—*that is, Bethel.* (Joshua 18:[11,] 13)

And in Judges:

> The house of Joseph went up to *Bethel* and scouted out *Bethel;* and the name of the city *once was Luz.* (Judges 1:23)

He and the whole people that was with him means with everything on that level, the earthly level. This can be seen from the representation of Jacob—*he*—as goodness on that level (discussed in §4538) and from the

4555

4556

4557

symbolism of a *people* as truth (discussed in §§1259, 1260, 2928, 3295, 3581). *The people that was with him,* then, means truth belonging to that goodness. Since everything on the earthly plane relates to goodness and truth, the phrase means with everything on that level.

4558   *And he built there an altar* means by being made holy. This is established by the symbolism of an *altar* as the main object representing the Lord and therefore as holiness in worship (mentioned at §4541). When associated with the Lord, an altar symbolizes his divine humanity and the holy influence coming from it (§2811). The chief object by which the Lord is represented in the church has as its highest meaning the Lord himself in his divine humanity. Whatever represents something, taken in its highest sense, *is* that thing.

The fact that the earthly level was made holy is symbolized by *he built there*—in Bethel—*an altar* because Bethel symbolizes earthly divinity; see just above in §4556.

4559   *And called the place El-bethel* symbolizes an earthly level that was holy. This is indicated by the symbolism of *Bethel* as earthly divinity (noted at §§4089, 4539, 4556), though when it is called *El-bethel* it does not mean earthly divinity but earthly holiness. When the Lord made his humanity divine, he first made it holy. The difference between making it divine and making it holy is that the Divine is Jehovah himself, while holiness is what comes from Jehovah. The former is divine reality; the latter is what emerges from it. When the Lord glorified himself, he turned even his humanity into the divine reality, or Jehovah (§§2156, 2329, 2921, 3023, 3035), but before that he made it holy. This is what happened during the glorification of the Lord's humanity.

For that reason Bethel is now called El-bethel, and the meaning of the prefix El is explained by the phrase "because there gods were revealed to him." In the original language, El means God. Here it is expressed as gods, in the plural, because in an inner sense gods mean holy truths (§4402). Later on it is referred to as Bethel, where the text says, "Jacob called the name of the place Bethel" (verse 15), adding "where God" in the singular "spoke with him." Bethel in the original language means "house of God," but El-bethel means "God of the house of God."

That is why El-bethel means earthly holiness and Bethel means earthly divinity.

4560   *Because there gods were revealed to him* symbolizes sacred truths. This can be seen from the symbolism of *gods* as sacred truths (discussed in

§4402). They are connected with the goodness that Jacob represents, as symbolized by *there gods were revealed to him.*

Obviously there is a secret in the fact that the place is called El-bethel despite being called Bethel earlier and later—in Genesis 28:19 and in verse 15 of the current chapter. There is also a secret in the fact that here, where it is called El-bethel, the text says "because there gods were revealed to him," in the plural, while later, in verse 15, it says "where God spoke with him," in the singular. Just as obviously, these secrets are knowable only from the inner meaning. There are many other secrets lying hidden in these words as well, but they cannot be revealed.

As he fled before his brother means after truth was given priority over goodness. This can be seen from the explanation above at §4542, where the same words occur.

4561

Genesis 35:8. *And Deborah, Rebekah's nursemaid, died and was buried below Bethel under the oak, and he called its name Allon-bacuth.*

4562

Deborah, Rebekah's nursemaid, died means that inherited evil was expelled. *And was buried below Bethel under the oak* symbolizes permanent rejection. *And he called its name Allon-bacuth* symbolizes the nature of the expelled earthly element.

Deborah, Rebekah's nursemaid, died means that inherited evil was expelled, as the following shows: *Dying* symbolizes an end, when something ceases to be what it was, as dealt with in §§494, 3253, 3259, 3276. Here it symbolizes expulsion, since the topic is inherited evil. And *Deborah, Rebekah's nursemaid,* represents inherited evil. In her role of nourishing and breastfeeding a baby, a nursemaid properly symbolizes the instilling of innocence through what is both heavenly and spiritual. (Milk means something heavenly-spiritual, §2184, and the baby it feeds means innocence, §§430, 1616, 2126, 2305, 2306.) In this case, though, Deborah, Rebekah's nursemaid, symbolizes what was acquired [by the Lord] from his mother and nourished from infancy onward. The fact that this was the evil the Lord inherited from his mother, which he fought against, can be seen from explanations of his maternal inheritance in §§1414, 1444, 1573. The fact that he expelled it, so as to cease being Mary's son in the end, can be seen from §§2159, 2574, 2649, 3036.

4563

[2] People recognize that we come by evil from both parents and that this evil is called inherited evil. We are born into it, but it does not come out in the open until we grow up and put our thoughts and therefore our wishes into practice. Meanwhile it lies hidden, especially in childhood. By

the Lord's mercy, we never incur guilt for inherited evil, only for actual evil (§§966, 2308), and inherited evil cannot become actual evil until we act from our own intellect and our own will. That is why little children are led by the Lord with the help of angels. Little ones accordingly seem to live in a state of innocence, but inherited evil still lurks in everything they do (§§2300, 2307, 2308). This evil serves to nourish them, but it resembles a nursemaid only till they come into their own judgment (§4063). If they then go through rebirth, the Lord leads them gradually to a stage of second childhood and eventually to heavenly wisdom. So he brings them into true childhood, or innocence, since this resides in wisdom (§§3183, 3505). The difference is that childhood innocence lies on the surface and has inherited evil inside, but wisdom's innocence lies inside and leaves actual and inherited evil on the surface.

This discussion and many previous remarks show that inherited evil more or less nourishes us from infancy up to our second childhood. That is why a nursemaid symbolizes inherited evil and also the instilling of innocence through what is both heavenly and spiritual.

[3] Since the inner meaning of the current chapter deals with the way goodness rearranged and reorganized truth on the Lord's earthly level and with his consequent advance toward more inward levels (§4536), it also talks about the expulsion of his inherited evil. This is the reason the current verse mentions Deborah, Rebekah's nurse, and her death and burial under the oak. Such an event would not have mattered enough to interrupt the thread of the story, if it had not involved this kind of meaning.

[4] The actual secret specifically symbolized by Rebekah's nurse cannot be disclosed yet. First the nature of the inflow from the rational plane into the earthly plane needs to be known. To be precise, goodness on the rational plane flows directly into the goodness of the earthly plane. It flows indirectly through rational-level truth into the truth-based goodness of the earthly plane. Rebekah stands for rational-level truth (§§3012, 3013, 3077), while Isaac stands for rational-level goodness (§§3012, 3194, 3210). Esau stands for goodness on the earthly plane produced by a direct inflow of rational-level goodness, or Isaac. Jacob stands for goodness (or truth-based goodness) on the earthly plane produced by an indirect inflow [of rational-level goodness] through rational-level truth, or Rebekah. For a discussion of this direct and indirect inflow, see §§3314, 3573. All this needs to be known first before the reader can see the secret, specific reason that Rebekah's nurse symbolizes and depicts inherited evil here, because it reveals what this evil was like.

And was buried below Bethel under the oak symbolizes permanent rejec- **4564**
tion. This can be seen from the symbolism of *being buried* as being rejected,
since what is buried is cast aside, and from the meaning of *under the oak*
as permanently (discussed above in §4552). *Below Bethel* means outside the
earthly dimension, because in an inner sense, anything described as below
or farther down than something is outside it (§2148). *Bethel* means earthly
divinity (§§4089, 4539).

[2] Here is the situation: Neither inherited nor actual evil in people
who are being reborn is rooted out so completely that it vanishes or ceases
to exist. It is merely separated, and the Lord arranges to have it cast to
the outer edges (§§4551, 4552). It stays with us, then, and stays with us
forever, but the Lord withholds us from evil and keeps us on a good path.
When that happens, it seems as though the evil has been rejected. We
appear to be purified of it, or to be justified, as they say.

All the angels in heaven confess that what they have on their own is
purely evil and therefore false, but what they have from the Lord is good
and therefore true. [3] Some individuals [in the other world] had formed
another view of the subject and had proved to themselves from their doctrines during life in the world that they were absolved of guilt, free of sin,
and holy. They are sent back into a state of evil, both actual and inherited,
and are kept in it until they see from personal experience that on their
own they are nothing but evil. They learn that the goodness they seemed
to themselves to possess was from the Lord and therefore belonged not to
them but to him. That is how the case stands with angels and therefore
with people who have been regenerated.

[4] It was otherwise with the Lord. He completely removed, expelled,
and discarded from himself all the evil he had inherited from his mother.
He did not inherit evil from his father, having been conceived of Jehovah;
only from his mother. This is the difference.

This is what it means to say that the Lord became righteousness, holiness itself, and divine.

And he called its name Allon-bacuth symbolizes the nature of the expelled **4565**
earthly element. This is established by the symbolism of *calling something's
name* as its quality (discussed in §§144, 145, 1754, 1896, 2009, 2724, 3006,
3421).

In the original language, *Allon-bacuth* means Oak of Weeping. The
place was called that because an oak means the lowest level of the earthly
plane, and [the Lord's] inherited evil was cast down to that level and
eventually outside it. For the meaning of an oak as the bottom of the

earthly plane and as permanence, see §4552. Weeping symbolizes a last goodbye, so it was customary to weep for the dead when they were being buried. People did this even though they knew that only the corpse was being discarded through burial and that the former inhabitants of what were now corpses were still alive in regard to their inner depths. This makes clear the quality symbolized by Allon-bacuth, or the Oak of Weeping.

4566   Genesis 35:9, 10, 11, 12, 13. *And God appeared to Jacob again as he came from Paddan-aram, and blessed him. And God said to him, "Your name is Jacob. Your name will no longer be called Jacob; rather, Israel will be your name"; and [God] called his name Israel. And God said to him, "I am God Shaddai; be fruitful and multiply! A nation and a throng of nations will exist from you, and monarchs will come from your genitals. And the land that I gave Abraham and Isaac, to you I will give it; and to your seed after you I will give the land." And God went up from him in the place where God spoke with him.*

God appeared to Jacob again as he came from Paddan-aram, and blessed him symbolizes an inner earthly perception. *And God said to him, "Your name is Jacob,"* symbolizes the nature of the Lord's outer earthly divinity. *Your name will no longer be called Jacob* means that it would no longer be merely external. *Rather, Israel will be your name* symbolizes the nature of his inner earthly level, or of the spiritual quality there, which is *Israel.* *And he called his name Israel* symbolizes his inner earthly level, or heavenly spirituality on his earthly level. *And God said to him* symbolizes a perception from his divine side. *I am God Shaddai* symbolizes a state of trial in the past and divine comfort in the present. *Be fruitful and multiply* symbolizes divine goodness and therefore truth. *A nation and a throng of nations will exist from you* symbolizes goodness and divine manifestations of goodness. *And monarchs will come from your genitals* symbolizes truth born from the divine marriage. *And the land that I gave Abraham and Isaac, to you I will give it* symbolizes the adoption of divine goodness on the earthly level. *And to your seed after you I will give the land* symbolizes the adoption of divine truth on the earthly level. *And God went up from him in the place where he spoke with him* symbolizes what was divine in that state.

4567   *God appeared to Jacob as he came from Paddan-aram, and blessed him* symbolizes an inner earthly perception. This can be seen from the symbolism of *God appeared* as an inner perception. Seeing means understanding and perceiving (see §§2150, 2807, 3764, 3863, 4403–4421), so when God is said to have been seen by the Lord, or to have appeared to him, it means a perception from his divine side, which is the same as an inner perception. The presence of this perception on an earthly plane is meant by God's appearing *to Jacob*, since Jacob represents the Lord's earthly plane, as shown many times.

Again as he came from Paddan-aram means after he had absorbed the knowledge of goodness and truth symbolized by Paddan-aram (discussed in §§3664, 3680, 4112). *He blessed him* symbolizes advancement toward inner levels of the earthly plane, and the union of goodness and truth on that plane. Every benefit we receive as a gift from the Divine is said to *bless* us (§§1420, 1422, 2846, 3017, 3406), especially the union of what is good and true (§§3504, 3514, 3530, 3565, 3584).

And God said to him, "Your name is Jacob," symbolizes the nature of the Lord's outer earthly divinity. This can be seen from the symbolism of a *name* as something's quality (discussed in §§144, 145, 1754, 1896, 2009, 2724, 3006, 3421) and from the representation of *Jacob* as the Lord's earthly divinity (discussed many times before). The reason for describing it as outer is that Israel means the Lord's inner earthly divinity, discussed just below.

4568

Your name will no longer be called Jacob means that it would no longer be merely external. This can be seen from the remarks just above and from those concerning Israel that immediately follow.

4569

Rather, Israel will be your name symbolizes the nature of his inner earthly level, or of the spiritual quality there, which is *Israel. And he called his name Israel* symbolizes his inner earthly level, or heavenly spirituality on his earthly level. This can be seen from the symbolism of a *name* as something's quality (mentioned just above in §4568) and from the symbolism of *Israel* as the inner depths of the Lord's earthly dimension.

4570

No one can tell why Jacob was called Israel without knowing what the inner earthly level and the outer earthly level are, and what heavenly spirituality on the earthly level is. Of course these things were explained before, where Jacob was named Israel by the angel, but since little if anything is known about them, I should explain again.

[2] In the human being there are two things that are perfectly distinct from each other: what is rational and what is earthly. Rationality constitutes the inner self, and earthliness the outer self, but both have their outer and inner parts. The outer part of the earthly level is made up of the physical senses and the impressions that flow in directly from the world through the senses. They keep us in touch with the worldly and bodily

realm. People intent only on this aspect of the earthly plane are described as sense-oriented because they rarely venture any further in their thinking. The inner part of the earthly level is made up of conclusions drawn from sense impressions through analysis and analogy, but it still draws and derives its character from the senses. So the earthly level communicates through our senses with the worldly and bodily realm; and through analysis and analogy it communicates with the rational plane, or the realm of the spiritual world. That is the nature of the earthly dimension.

There is also a middle part that communicates with both the outer and inner parts. Through the outer part it communicates with objects in the world of nature, while through the inner part it communicates with objects in the spiritual world. This part of the earthly level is what Jacob particularly represents, while the inner part of that level is what Israel represents.

The case is the same with the rational plane. It has an outer and an inner part and also a middle part. By the Lord's divine providence, this will be addressed where Joseph is discussed [§4585], since Joseph represents the outer part of the rational plane.

[3] Heavenly spirituality has been defined several times already [§§1001, 1824, 2184, 4286]. Heavenliness has to do with goodness, and spirituality with truth, so heavenly spirituality has to do with goodness that comes from truth.

Now because the Lord's church has an outer part and an inner part, and Jacob's descendants had to represent the church's inner depths through outward practices, Jacob could not be called Jacob any longer but Israel. See the evidence for this cited earlier, in §§4286, 4292.

It is also important to know that both the rational and earthly planes are described as heavenly and spiritual. They are described as heavenly when they receive what is good from the Lord, and spiritual when they receive what is true from him. The goodness that flows from the Lord into heaven is called heavenly, and the truth is called spiritual.

In the highest sense, the renaming of Jacob as Israel means that as the Lord made progress toward what was within, he made both the outer and inner parts of his earthly level divine. Whatever represents something, taken in its highest sense, *is* that thing.

4571 *And God said to him* symbolizes a perception from his divine side. This is established by the symbolism of *saying* in scriptural narrative as perceiving (discussed at §§1791, 1815, 1819, 1822, 1898, 1919, 2080, 2619, 2862, 3395, 3509). The fact that it came from his divine side is symbolized by *God said*. From conception the Lord had divinity within him. This divinity was his core being, because he was conceived by Jehovah, so his perceptions came from his divinity. The nature of his perceptions depended on the state of his human side's ability to receive them, though, because he gradually made the humanity in himself divine. Since he had divinity or God within him, then, *God said to him* obviously symbolizes a perception from his divine side.

I am God Shaddai symbolizes a state of trial in the past and divine comfort in the present. This can be seen from the symbolism of *God Shaddai* as trial followed by comfort. The ancients had referred to Jehovah (the Lord) as God Shaddai in regard to trials and the solace that follows them (see §§1992, 3667), which is why God Shaddai symbolizes a state of trial in the past and divine comfort in the present. The past is symbolized because Jacob formerly represented times of trial, especially when he wrestled the angel in Genesis 32:24–end and when he met Esau in Genesis 33. Present comfort is symbolized because trials are the means of uniting goodness and truth on the earthly plane. The union itself brings consolation because it is the end of the struggle, and everyone reaching the end is comforted in proportion to the hardships suffered along the way.

[2] To generalize, goodness is united with truth only through times of trial. This is because evil and falsity resist and rebel and make every possible attempt to block the union of goodness with truth and of truth with goodness. The struggle takes place between the spirits present with us—spirits dedicated to evil and falsity on one hand, and spirits dedicated to goodness and truth on the other. We perceive it as a crisis seemingly inside ourselves. When the spirits of goodness and truth overcome the spirits of evil and falsity and force them to withdraw, joy comes through heaven from the Lord to the spirits of goodness and truth. This joy we again seem to perceive inside ourselves, as a sense of comfort.

The joy and comfort are due not to the conquest but to the union of goodness and truth. Every bond between goodness and truth holds joy because such a bond is the heavenly marriage, which contains the divine marriage.

Be fruitful and multiply symbolizes divine goodness and therefore truth, as demonstrated by the association of *being fruitful* with goodness and of *multiplying* with truth (§§43, 55, 913, 983, 2846, 2847).

A nation and a throng of nations will exist from you symbolizes goodness and divine manifestations of goodness. This can be seen from the symbolism of a *nation* as the goodness in a religion (discussed in §§1259, 1260, 1362, 1416, 1849) and from that of a *throng of nations* as truth rising out of goodness—in other words, goodness manifested in a form. In the highest sense, which is about the Lord, it symbolizes divine truth rising out of divine goodness, or goodness manifested in a divine form.

[2] First, manifestations of goodness need to be defined; then the fact that a throng of nations symbolizes them needs to be discussed.

Truth that grows out of goodness is called goodness manifested in a form, because truth is simply goodness that has been given shape. No one who conceives of truth differently than this knows what truth is, and anyone who detaches truth from goodness knows even less about it. Truth does seem separate from goodness, as if it consisted of free-standing forms, but only to people lacking in goodness—that is, people whose thoughts and words are at odds with what they intend and therefore do. We were created to have an intellect and will that compose a single mind, which is what happens when our intellect is at one with our will—that is, when our thoughts and words match our intent and deeds. Then the contents of our intellect are forms manifesting our will. The contents of the intellect are what are called truths, because truth belongs to the intellect. The contents of the will are what are called goodness, because goodness belongs to the will. It follows, then, that regarded in itself, any product of the intellect is simply a product of the will given shape.

[3] The term *forms* savors of human philosophy, though, so I will illustrate with an example showing that truth is goodness manifested in a form. In public and private life there is such a thing as integrity and decency. Integrity is sincerely wishing others well in matters of public life, while decency is showing that integrity in words and actions. Decency regarded in itself, then, is nothing but integrity manifested in a form. Integrity is the source of decency, so when it displays itself in the decency of respectable speech and actions it is visible in every detail of that behavior. In fact, whatever is then expressed in words or demonstrated in action is clearly honorable. It is a form or image from which integrity beams. Integrity and decency are therefore unified as an essence and its form, or as what is essential and the shape it takes.

Those who sever integrity from decency, who wish ill to their companions but speak and behave well toward them, have no remaining trace of integrity in their speech or actions, no matter how hard they work to generate the appearance of it through decorum. All they have left is dishonor, and a clear-eyed observer calls it just that, because it is pretense, sham, and deceit.

[4] These comments show how matters stand with truth and good-ness, because truth is to one's spiritual life as decency is to one's public life, and goodness is to one's spiritual life as integrity is to one's public life. They show what truth is like when it is the manifestation of goodness, and what it is like when detached from goodness. When truth does not grow out of goodness, it grows out of something evil and is wickedness manifested in a form, however much it mimics forms of goodness.

The meaning of a *throng of nations* as forms of goodness can be seen from the symbolism of nations as goodness (discussed just above). A throng or assemblage of them consequently means a collection of them, and a col-lection of them is the same as a form, which is truth, as shown. Since truth is what is symbolized, and goodness is symbolized by a nation, the text says not only that a nation would exist from [Jacob] but also a throng of nations. Otherwise one or the other expression would have sufficed.

Besides, the Word speaks of throngs, assemblages, and multitudes in connection with truth. For this association in respect to a multitude, or multiplying, see §§43, 55, 913, 983, 2846, 2847.

And monarchs will come from your genitals symbolizes truth born from the divine marriage, as the following shows: *Monarchs* symbolize truth, as discussed in §§1672, 1728, 2015, 2069, 3009, 3670. And *genitals* symbol-ize facets of marriage love, as discussed in §§3021, 4277, 4280. So they symbolize facets of the heavenly marriage, and in the highest sense, of the divine marriage.

4575

Truth born from the divine marriage is truth radiating from the Lord's divine humanity, and it is called sacred truth. The Lord's divine human-ity, you see, is the divine marriage itself. The qualities radiating from it are holy and are called heavenly and spiritual. They create the heavenly marriage, which consists in truth united with goodness, and goodness united with truth. This marriage exists in heaven, in every inhabitant of heaven, and in every person in the church, as long as both goodness and truth are active in that person.

And the land that I gave Abraham and Isaac I will give to you symbol-izes the adoption of divine goodness, as the following shows: The *land* symbolizes goodness, because in an inner sense the land of Canaan—the land meant here—means the Lord's kingdom and therefore the church, which is the Lord's kingdom on earth (§§1607, 3481, 3705, 4447, 4517). Because it symbolizes these, it symbolizes goodness, since goodness is the very essence of the Lord's kingdom and the church. In the highest sense the land of Canaan means the Lord's divine goodness, because the

4576

goodness in the Lord's kingdom in the heavens and on earth comes from the Lord. *Abraham and Isaac* represent the Lord's divinity, Abraham representing divinity itself in him, and Isaac representing his divine humanity, specifically, his divine rationality. For Abraham's representation, see §§1989, [2010,] 2011, 3245, 3251, 3439, 3703, 4206, 4207. For Isaac's, §§1893, 2066, 2072, 2083, 2630, 2774, 3012, 3194, 3210, 4180. And *giving it*—the land—*to you* symbolizes its adoption by the earthly level. Jacob—*you*—represents the Lord's earthly divinity, as shown repeatedly.

This discussion shows that *the land that I gave Abraham and Isaac, to you I will give it* symbolizes the adoption of divine goodness.

4577 *And to your seed after you I will give the land* symbolizes the adoption of divine truth. This can be seen from the symbolism of *seed* as religious truth (discussed at §§1025, 1447, 1610, 1940), but on the highest level as divine truth (§3038), and from that of *giving the land* as adopting goodness (discussed just above in §4576). On the highest level, then, *giving the land to your seed* symbolizes the adoption of divine goodness by divine truth.

The reason it means adoption of divine truth is that until the Lord was glorified his humanity consisted in divine truth. That is why the Lord says he is the truth in John 14:6 and why he is called the woman's seed in Genesis 3:15. Once his human side had been glorified, though, he became divine goodness, and ever since then it is from the Lord as divine goodness that divine truth has radiated. This truth is the Spirit of Truth that the Lord promised to send, as recorded in John 14:16, 17; 15:26, 27; 16:13, 14, 15; see §3704. It is plain, then, that *to your seed after you* in the highest sense means that the Lord adopted divine truth and that divine truth radiates from the divine goodness in which he consists. That truth is also adopted by people devoted to goodness and therefore to truth.

4578 *And God went up from him in the place where he spoke with him* symbolizes what was divine in that state, as the following shows: *God's going up from him* symbolizes divinity, because *going up* involves elevation to inner levels, and in relation to the Lord, who is *God* here, it means elevation to divinity (§4539). And the *place where he spoke with him* symbolizes that state. A *place* means a state (see §§2625, 2837, 3356, 3387, 4321), so the place where he spoke with him means the state he was then in.

4579 Genesis 35:14, 15. *And Jacob raised a pillar in the place where he spoke with him, a pillar of stone, and offered a drink offering on it and poured oil on it. And Jacob called the name of the place where God spoke with him Bethel.*

Jacob raised a pillar in the place where he spoke with him, a pillar of stone, symbolizes the sacred power of truth in that divine state. *And offered a drink offering on it* symbolizes divine goodness-from-truth. *And poured oil on it* symbolizes divine goodness belonging to love. *And Jacob called the name of the place where God spoke with him Bethel* symbolizes earthly divinity and its state.

Jacob raised a pillar in the place where he spoke with him, a pillar of stone, symbolizes the sacred power of truth in that divine state. This can be seen from the symbolism of a *pillar* as the sacred power of truth (dealt with below) and from the meaning of *in the place where he spoke with him* as in that state (dealt with just above in §4578).

First I need to talk about the origin of putting up pillars, offering a drink offering on them, and pouring oil on them. [2] Pillars were erected in ancient times as a sign, as a witness, or for worship. The ones used for worship were anointed, which made them sacred, and people held their worship where these pillars stood, whether in temples, in groves, in forests under the trees, or somewhere else. The custom took its representation from a practice of the very earliest times. In those days stones were set up along the borders between the different nations' clans to keep them from crossing over to do each other evil. This is what Laban and Jacob did in Genesis 31:52. The ban on crossing over these stones to do evil was a "law of the nations" among them. These stones stood on the borders, so the earliest people—who habitually saw in every object on earth a corresponding spiritual or heavenly quality—would look at the stones as borders and think about truth on the outermost level of the divine design. Their descendants, who looked less to the spirit and heaven in these physical reminders, and more to the world, started to think of the stones with reverence simply because of the ancient respect for them. In the end, the descendants of the earliest people who lived just before the Flood no longer saw anything spiritual or heavenly in earthly and worldly objects. They began to consecrate the stones, pouring drink offerings over them and anointing them with oil. At that point the stones came to be called pillars and to be used for worship.

[3] The practice lingered after the Flood in the ancient church, which used representations. There was a difference, though, which was that the pillars served them as a means of achieving inward worship. Throughout their childhood the young would be taught by their parents what it was that these things represented. In the process they came to know the sacred objects and to be moved by their representation. That is why the ancients used pillars for worship in temples, groves, and forests, and on hills and mountains.

However, inward worship was obliterated along with the ancient church, and people started to consider the externals sacred and divine, worshiping them in an idolatrous manner. When this happened, they began to set up pillars for individual gods. Since Jacob's offspring were heavily inclined toward idolatry, they were forbidden to put up pillars, use groves, or even worship on mountains and heights. Instead, they were brought together to a single location—where the ark was, and later to Jerusalem, where the Temple was. Otherwise every clan would have had its own external objects and idols to worship, and the representation of a religion could not have been established with their nation.

See what was shown about pillars earlier, in §3727.

This information shows where pillars came from and what they symbolized. It also shows that sacred truth was what they represented when they were used in worship. That is why the text adds that it was a *pillar of stone,* because stone symbolizes truth on the outermost level of the divine design (§§1298, 3720, 3769, 3771, 3773, 3789, 3798).

Another important piece of information is that sacred power is especially an attribute of divine truth, because divine goodness exists in the Lord and divine truth emanates from it (§§3704, 4577) and is called the holy [influence of the spirit].

4581   *And offered a drink offering on it* symbolizes divine goodness-from-truth. This can be seen from the symbolism of a *drink offering* as divine goodness-from-truth, which will be discussed below, though first I need to define it. Goodness-from-truth is what I have elsewhere called good done out of faith, and it consists in love for one's neighbor, or charity.

There are two overarching categories of goodness. One is called good done out of faith; the other, good done out of love. Good done out of faith is symbolized by a drink offering, and good done out of love, by oil. People led toward goodness by the Lord along an inner path have a loving goodness, but people led along an outer path have a faith-inspired goodness. People in a heavenly religion, like angels in the third and inmost heaven, have a loving goodness, while people in a spiritual religion, like angels in the second or middle heaven, have a faith-inspired goodness. That is why the first kind is called heavenly goodness, while the second is called spiritual goodness. The difference is the same as that between wishing someone well out of goodwill and wishing someone well out of a good understanding. The latter—spiritual goodness, faith-inspired goodness, or goodness based on truth—is what a drink offering symbolizes.

The former—heavenly goodness, goodness based on love—is what oil means in an inner sense.

[2] This symbolism of oil and of drink offerings cannot be seen except from the inner meaning, admittedly, but anyone can see that they represented something holy. Without a holy representation, what would it be but idolatrous nonsense to offer a drink offering on a stone pillar and pour oil on it?

The same would be true during a coronation if the actions involved did not symbolize and imply something holy. Monarchs have a crown set on their head, their forehead and thumb are anointed with oil from a horn, a scepter is put in their hand, as are a sword and keys, they are robed in crimson, and then they take their seat on a silver throne. Afterward they ride in regal splendor, have nobles to wait on them at table, and so on. If these customs did not represent something holy and did not actually have holiness through correspondence with features of heaven and the church, they would be nothing more than child's play on a grand scale, or a theatrical production.

[3] In reality, all these rituals had their roots in earliest times, when rituals were sacred because they represented and corresponded with the holy attributes of heaven and therefore of the church. They are still held sacred today, not because people know what they represent or correspond to but because they interpret them the way they interpret other emblems in current use. If they knew what was represented by crowns, oil, horns, scepters, swords, keys, riding on a white horse, and being waited on at meals by nobles, if they knew what holy counterpart these things corresponded to, they would consider them with much greater reverence. They do not know, though, and astonishingly they do not want to know. That is how thoroughly the representation and symbolism in such items and throughout the Word has been erased from the modern mind.

[4] The symbolism of a drink offering as goodness-from-truth, or spiritual goodness, can be seen from the sacrifices in which drink offerings were used. Sacrificial animals came from either the herd or the flock and represented inward worship of the Lord (§§922, 923, 1823, 2180, 2805, 2807, 2830, 3519), and minhas and drink offerings were added to them. A minha, which consisted of flour mixed with oil, symbolized heavenly goodness—in other words, good done out of love. (Oil symbolized love for the Lord, and flour symbolized charity toward one's neighbor.) A drink offering, which consisted of wine, symbolized spiritual goodness—in other words, good

done out of faith. So these two, the minha and drink offering, had the same symbolism as the bread and wine of the Holy Supper.

[5] It can be seen in Moses that these were added to burnt offerings and sacrifices:

> You shall offer two lambs (offspring of a year) each day, a perpetual offering; one lamb you shall offer in the morning, and the other lamb you shall offer between the evenings. And a *tenth [of an ephah] of flour mixed with beaten oil,* a quarter of a hin, and a *drink offering of a quarter of a hin of wine* shall be for the first lamb. So also for the other lamb. (Exodus 29:38, 39, 40, 41)

In the same author:

> On the day on which you wave the sheaf of the harvest's first fruits, you shall offer a lamb, a sound one, an offspring of its [first] year, for a burnt offering to Jehovah, *of which the minha shall be two tenths [of an ephah] of flour mixed with oil,* and *its drink offering, wine,* a quarter of a hin. (Leviticus 23:12, 13, 18)

In the same author:

> On the day on which the days of their Naziriteship are fulfilled, they shall offer their gift to Jehovah: sacrifices, and a basket of unleavened loaves of flour, cakes mixed with oil, and wafers of unleavened bread anointed with oil, with *their minha* and *their drink offerings.* (Numbers 6:13, 14, 15, 17)

In the same author:

> On the burnt offering they shall offer a *minha of flour, a tenth [of an ephah] mixed with a quarter of a hin of oil,* [and] *wine for a drink offering,* a quarter of a hin. Other amounts on the burnt offering of a ram, and other amounts on that of an ox. (Numbers 15:3, 4, 5–11)

In the same author:

> For the perpetual burnt offering you shall offer a *drink offering,* a quarter of a hin for a lamb. *In the Holy Place, offer a drink offering of wine to Jehovah.* (Numbers 28:6, 7)

There is more in Numbers 28:7–end; 29:1–end on minhas and drink offerings in sacrifices of various kinds.

[6] This symbolism of minha and drink offering can also be seen from the fact that love and faith constitute all worship. In the Holy Supper, too, the bread (made of flour mixed with oil) and wine symbolize love and faith and therefore all worship, as discussed in §§1798, 2165, 2177, 2187, 2343, 3464, 3735, 3813, 4211, 4217.

[7] However, once people had fallen away from any genuine representation of worship for the Lord, turned to other gods, and offered drink offerings to them, the libations symbolized what is opposed to charity and faith—that is, the evils of materialism, and falsity. In Isaiah, for instance:

> You grew hot for your gods under every green tree. Even for them *you poured out a libation; you offered a minha.* (Isaiah 57:5, 6)

Growing hot for one's gods stands for hankering after falsity, since gods mean falsity (§§4402 at the end, 4544). "Under every green tree" means from a belief in all falsity (§§2722, 4552). Pouring out a libation to them and offering a minha stands for worship of falsity. In the same author:

> You are the ones who desert Jehovah, who forget my holy mountain, who set a table for Gad and fill a *drink offering* for Meni. (Isaiah 65:11)

In Jeremiah:

> The children gather wood, and the fathers light the fire, and the women knead dough to make cakes for the queen of the heavens, and to *offer a drink offering to other gods.* (Jeremiah 7:18)

[8] In the same author:

> Every word that has issued from our mouth we are determined to do, burning incense to the queen of the heavens and *offering her drink offerings* as we have done—we and our ancestors and our chieftains—in the cities of Judah and in the streets of Jerusalem. (Jeremiah 44:17, 18, 19)

The queen of the heavens stands for all falsities. In a positive sense the armies of the heavens mean true ideas, while in a negative sense they mean false ones, as do a king and queen. A queen, then, stands for all of them. Offering drink offerings to her means worshiping them. [9] In the same author:

> The Chaldeans will burn up the city and the houses on whose roofs people burned incense to Baal and *offered drink offerings to other gods.* (Jeremiah 32:29)

The Chaldeans stand for people devoted to a form of worship based on falsity. Burning up the city stands for destroying and devastating people committed to false doctrines. Burning incense to Baal on the roofs of houses stands for worshiping evil. Offering drink offerings to other gods stands for worshiping falsity. [10] In Hosea:

> They will not live in Jehovah's land, and Ephraim will return to Egypt, and in Assyria they will eat what is unclean; they will not *pour a libation of wine to Jehovah*. (Hosea 9:3, 4)

Not living in Jehovah's land stands for not having a goodness based on love. Ephraim's return to Egypt means that the church's intellectual activity will narrow down to factual and empirical knowledge. "In Assyria they will eat what is unclean" stands for the impure, profane products of skewed reasoning. "They will not pour a libation of wine to Jehovah" stands for the absence of worship that is based on truth. [11] In Moses:

> It will be said, "Where are their gods, the rock in which they trusted? Let the [gods] who have eaten the fat of the sacrifices, [who] have *drunk the wine of their drink offering*, get up and help them." (Deuteronomy 32:37, 38)

Gods stand for falsities, as above. "Who have eaten the fat of the sacrifices" means that they destroyed what was good in worship. "[Who] have drunk the wine of their drink offering" means that they destroyed what was true in worship.

In David, offerings of blood are also called libations:

> The troubles of [those] who hurried to another [god] will multiply. *May I never offer their drink offerings of blood!* May I never lift their names on my lips! (Psalms 16:4)

Here they symbolize profanation of truth, because in this sense blood means violence inflicted on charity (§§374, 1005), and profanation (§1003).

4582   *And poured oil on it* symbolizes divine goodness belonging to love. This can be seen from the symbolism (discussed in §§886, 3728) of *oil* as divine goodness belonging to love.

On an inner level, raising a pillar of stone, offering a drink offering on it, and pouring oil on it depict a process of advancement from truth on the outermost plane to truth and goodness on an inward plane and finally to a loving goodness. A pillar of stone is truth on the outermost level of the divine design (§4580); a drink offering is truth and goodness on an inward plane (§4581); and oil is a loving goodness. This is the process of advancement both that the Lord followed in making his humanity divine and that we follow when the Lord makes us heavenly through rebirth.

4583

And Jacob called the name of the place where God spoke with him Bethel symbolizes earthly divinity and its state. This is established by the symbolism of *calling something's name* as its quality (discussed in §§144, 145, 1754, 2009, 2724, 3006, 3421) and from that of Bethel as earthly divinity (discussed in §§4559, 4560). Its state is symbolized by *the place where God spoke with him,* as above in §4578.

4584

Genesis 35:16, 17, 18, 19, 20. *And they traveled from Bethel, and there was still a stretch of land to go to Ephrata, and Rachel gave birth and suffered hard things in her giving birth. And it happened as she suffered hard things in her giving birth that the midwife said to her, "Don't be afraid, because this too is a son for you." And it happened as her soul was departing that she was about to die, and she called his name Ben-oni. And his father called him Benjamin. And Rachel died and was buried on the way to Ephrath, that is, Bethlehem. And Jacob raised a pillar over her grave; it is the Pillar of Rachel's Grave to this day.*

They traveled from Bethel, and there was still a stretch of land to go to Ephrata means that heavenly spirituality would now exist (Joseph being spiritual heavenliness). *And Rachel gave birth and suffered hard things in her giving birth* symbolizes challenges to inner truth. *And it happened as she suffered hard things in her giving birth* means after those challenges. *That the midwife said to her, "Don't be afraid,"* symbolizes a perception received from the earthly level. *Because this too is a son for you* symbolizes spiritual truth. *And it happened as her soul was departing that she was about to die* symbolizes a state of trial. *And she called his name Ben-oni* symbolizes the nature of that state. *And his father called him Benjamin* symbolizes the nature of heavenly spirituality. *And Rachel died and was buried on the way to Ephrath* symbolizes the end of the previous desire for inner truth. *That is, Bethlehem* symbolizes its replacement by heavenly spirituality resurrected in a new form. *And Jacob raised a pillar over her grave* symbolizes the holy influence of the spiritual truth that would rise again on that level. *It is the Pillar of Rachel's Grave to this day* symbolizes a permanent state of holy influence.

4585

They traveled from Bethel, and there was still a stretch of land to go to Ephrata means that heavenly spirituality would now exist, as the following shows: *Traveling from Bethel* symbolizes divinity's continued advance from its earthly state. *Traveling* [or setting off] means a continuation (see §4554), and in the highest sense here it means divinity's continued advance, while *Bethel* means earthly divinity (§§4559, 4560). A *stretch of land to go* symbolizes a middle stage, as discussed below. And *Ephrata* symbolizes heavenly spirituality at a previous stage. This is discussed later, where Bethlehem is the focus [§4594]. Bethlehem means heavenly spirituality at a new stage, so verse 19 below says, "Ephrath, that is, Bethlehem."

[2] These verses are talking about progress toward deeper levels achieved by the Lord's divinity. When the Lord made his humanity divine, he advanced according to the same plan he follows when he makes us new through rebirth. He went from the outside in, and therefore from truth on the outermost level of the divine design to an inner kind of goodness, called spiritual goodness, and from this to heavenly goodness.

However, these ideas are inaccessible to the human intellect unless one knows what the outer and inner self are; that the inner self is distinct from the outer, even though they appear as one to us while we are living in our body; that the earthly dimension makes up the outer self, while rationality makes up the inner self; and what spirituality and heavenliness are.

[3] Such concepts have been explained several times before, it is true, but some people have not had any previous notion of them (or any ability to form a notion) because they have had no desire to know about subjects connected with eternal life. These people say, "What is the inner self? Can it be distinct from the outer self? What are the earthly and rational dimensions? Aren't they one and the same? And what are spirituality and heavenliness? This is a new distinction! We have heard of a spiritual plane, but we haven't heard that the heavenly plane is anything different." The fact of the matter is that some people have never before acquired any idea of these things because worldly and bodily cares monopolize their thinking, robbing them of any interest in other knowledge. Others consider it enough to know as much doctrine as the general population does. They see no value in exercising their mind any further, because "We can see this world but not the other. Maybe it exists; maybe not." People like this insulate themselves from such concepts, because they privately reject them at first glance.

[4] These are the ideas the Word holds in its inner meaning, though, and they cannot be explained without suitable terms. No terms more suitable exist than "earthly" for that which is on the outside and "rational" for what lies within, or "spiritual" for anything to do with truth and "heavenly" for anything to do with goodness. Consequently there is no alternative to the use of these words, because without a vocabulary suited to the

subject, nothing can be described. I need to say a few words, then, to give people who do want to know about it some notion of the heavenly spirituality represented by Benjamin and symbolized by Bethlehem.

The theme in the highest sense has been the glorification of the Lord's earthly level, and in a secondary sense, a person's rebirth on the earthly level. Previous remarks (§4286) have shown that Jacob represented the outward aspect of a person in the church, and Israel, the inward aspect. So Jacob represented the outer earthly part of such a person, and Israel, the inner earthly part. (The spiritual self arises out of the earthly level, and the heavenly self out of the rational level.) It has also been shown that the Lord's glorification moved from the outside in, just as human rebirth does, and that Jacob was renamed Israel in order to represent this.

[5] At present, though, the theme is further progress toward inner levels—or toward rationality, since rationality constitutes the inner self, as said just above. Something midway between the inner part of the earthly level and the outer part of the rational level is what is meant by the heavenly spirituality symbolized by Ephrata and Bethlehem and represented by Benjamin. This middle part draws some of its character from the inner part of the earthly level, or Israel, and some from the outer part of the rational level, which is Joseph. Anything that is intermediate draws on both sides. Otherwise it cannot serve as a middle ground. If we are to change from spiritual people into heavenly ones, we have to make our way through this intermediate area. It is impossible to climb higher without the middle step.

[6] The nature of the advance through this middle stage is depicted in an inner sense by Jacob's journey to Ephrata and the birth of Benjamin to Rachel there. Clearly, then, *they traveled from Bethel, and there was still a stretch of land to go to Ephrata* symbolizes the continuing advance of the Lord's divinity from its earthly state toward the heavenly spirituality symbolized by Ephrata and Bethlehem and represented by Benjamin.

Heavenly spirituality is this middle area that I am talking about. It is called spiritual on account of the spiritual self, which viewed in itself is the inner earthly self. It is called heavenly on account of the heavenly self, which viewed in itself is the rational self. Joseph stands for the outer rational self, so he is described as spiritual heavenliness growing out of rationality.

And Rachel gave birth and suffered hard things in her giving birth sym- **4586** bolizes challenges to inner truth, as the following shows: *Giving birth* symbolizes the emergence of spiritual qualities, which have to do with truth, and of heavenly qualities, which have to do with goodness. In an inner sense, giving birth has no other meaning than spiritual birthing and all it entails (see §§1145, 1255, 2584, 3860, 3868, 3905, 3915, 3919, 4070). *Rachel* represents a desire for inner truth, as discussed in §§3758, 3782, 3793, 3819. And *suffering hard things* means undergoing challenges. When hard things are said to be suffered in relation to truth and goodness, or to spiritual and heavenly qualities, that is all it can mean. No one can attain what is spiritual and heavenly except through struggle, since inner goodness and truth then fight with evil and falsity of both the inherited and applied kinds. This is because the Lord then anchors us in goodness and truth from within, and an assault is mounted by evil and falsity erupting from our heredity and clinging to us by practice. Or rather the spirits and demons with us who indulge in such evil and falsity mount an assault. This is the source of our trials. Trials are the means by which not only are evil and falsity cast out and banished when they are conquered but goodness and truth are strengthened. These are the experiences symbolized by *Rachel gave birth and suffered hard things in giving birth.*

4587   *And it happened as she suffered hard things in her giving birth* means after those challenges. This can be seen from the comments directly above in §4586 without further explanation.

4588   *That the midwife said to her, "Don't be afraid,"* symbolizes a perception received from the earthly level. This can be seen from the symbolism of *saying* in scriptural narrative as a perception (discussed in §§1791, 1815, 1819, 1822, 1898, 1919, 2080, 2619, 2862, 3395, 3509) and from that of a *midwife* as the earthly level. A midwife means the earthly level here because when we undergo inner challenges—that is, when our inner self undergoes challenges—the earthly level acts as a midwife. Unless the earthly level helps, no birth of inner truth ever takes place. The earthly level is what takes inner truth into its arms upon birth, since it gives truth the opportunity to make its way out. That is how the case stands with the offspring of spiritual birth; the earthly plane absolutely must be there to catch them. This is the reason that the first step in a person's regeneration is preparation of the earthly plane for reception; and the more receptive it grows, the greater the possibility for inner truth and goodness to be brought forth and multiply. It is also the reason we cannot receive religious truth and goodness in the next life (and therefore cannot be saved) if our earthly self has not been prepared to receive them during bodily life. Such is the meaning of the common saying that as a tree falls so it lies [Ecclesiastes 11:3], or as we die so we turn out. In the other life we keep our entire earthly memory (the entire memory of our earthly self), but we are not allowed to use it there (§§2469–2494). In that world, then, the earthly memory is like a platform for inner truth and goodness as they come down. If the platform is not able to accept goodness and truth flowing in from within, inner goodness and truth are snuffed out, corrupted, or rejected.

These considerations show that the earthly plane is like a midwife.

[2] This idea—that the earthly level resembles a midwife so far as it catches the baby when the inner self gives birth—can also be seen from the inner meaning of details in the story of the midwives who kept the sons of Hebrew women alive, in violation of Pharaoh's command. Here is how Moses tells it:

> The king of Egypt said to the *midwives* of the Hebrews, and he said, "*In midwifing* to the Hebrews, when you look on the [birthing] stools, if it is a son you shall kill him, and if it is a daughter, let her be kept alive." And the *midwives* feared God and did not do as the king of Egypt had spoken to them; they kept the sons alive. And the king of Egypt called the *midwives* and said to them, "Why have you done this thing and kept the sons alive?" And the *midwives* said to Pharaoh, "Because the Hebrew women are not like the Egyptian women, for they are lively; before the *midwife* comes to them they have given birth." And God dealt well with the *midwives,* and the people multiplied and became very numerous. And it happened, because the *midwives* feared God, that he made households for them. (Exodus 1:15–21)

The daughters and sons that the Hebrew women bore represent the goodness and truth of a new religion. The midwives represent the earthly level in the role it plays when receiving goodness and truth. The king of Egypt represents general secular knowledge (§§1164, 1165, 1186) that eradicates truth. This happens when it pries into matters of faith in a completely backward way, believing nothing unless sense experience and secular knowledge dictates it. The meaning of midwives as the acceptance of truth on the earthly level will be confirmed when the contents of that chapter come to be explained, by the Lord's divine mercy.

Because this too is a son for you symbolizes spiritual truth. This is established by the symbolism of a *son* as truth (discussed at §§489, 491, 533, 1147, 2623, 3373) and in this case as spiritual truth, since Benjamin is the son and he represents heavenly spirituality.

4589

And it happened as her soul was departing that she was about to die symbolizes a state of trial. This can be seen from the symbolism of a *soul's departing* and of *dying* as the final stage of trial, which is when the old self

4590

dies and the new self receives life. The symbolism is evident from previous remarks showing that "she suffered hard things in giving birth" means challenges to inner truth (§§4586, 4587) and from comments that follow at verse 19 on "Rachel died" [§4593].

4591   *And she called his name Ben-oni* symbolizes the nature of that state. This is established by the symbolism of *calling someone's name* as the quality of a thing (discussed many times before). The state described in the inner meaning here is one of trial, and its nature is what *Ben-oni* symbolizes. In the original language Ben-oni means "son of my sorrow" or "grief."

In ancient times, babies were given names symbolizing a state; see §§1946, 2643, 3422, 4298.

4592   *And his father called him Benjamin* symbolizes the nature of heavenly spirituality. This can be seen from the representation of *Benjamin* as heavenly spirituality. Heavenly spirituality was defined above at §4585 as the middle ground between spirituality and heavenliness, or between the spiritual and heavenly selves. In the original language, Benjamin means "son of my right hand," and the son of a person's right hand symbolizes spiritual truth developing out of heavenly goodness, along with the power that results. Goodness, you see, has its power through truth (§3563). A son means truth (§§489, 491, 533, 1147, 2623, 3373), and a hand means power (§§878, 3091, 3563), so a right hand means the highest power. This clarifies what sitting at God's right hand symbolizes: a state of power produced by the truth that comes of goodness (§3387). When ascribed to the Lord, it symbolizes omnipotence, and also divine truth radiating from the Lord's divine goodness, as in Psalms 110:1; Matthew 22:44; 26:63, 64; Mark 14:61, 62; 16:19; Luke 22:69. Since it means divine power, or omnipotence, the last of these passages says, "at the right hand of God's power" or "strength."

[2] From this it is plain what Benjamin symbolizes in a positive sense, which is spiritual truth growing out of the heavenly goodness that is Joseph. Both together, then, are the middle area that lies between the spiritual self and the heavenly self, as noted above at §4585. However, this goodness and this truth are different from the heavenly element represented by Judah and the spiritual element represented by Israel. The heavenly, Judah part is higher, or inward, and the spiritual, Israel part is lower, or outward, because (to repeat) Benjamin and Joseph are in between.

The only people who can form an idea of the goodness represented by Joseph and the truth represented by Benjamin are ones who are enlightened by light from heaven. Angels have a clear idea of it, because all their individual thoughts come from heavenly light shed by the Lord. By that light they see and perceive boundlessly more than a human could ever grasp, let alone express.

[3] Let me illustrate it this way: Everyone without exception is born earthly but has the potential to become either heavenly or spiritual. The Lord alone was born both spiritual and heavenly, and this being so, he was born in Bethlehem, on the border of the land of Benjamin. Bethlehem symbolizes heavenly spirituality, and Benjamin represents the same thing. The reason the Lord alone was born both spiritual and heavenly is that he had divinity within him. No one who is not in heaven's light can ever comprehend these things. People who are in the world's light and receive their insights from it barely know what truth and goodness are. Still less do they know what it means to climb by steps up to higher levels of truth and goodness. As a result they cannot know anything at all about the countless varieties of truth and goodness at each step, which to angels' eyes stand out in broad daylight, so to speak. This shows what angels' wisdom is like by comparison with ours.

[4] There are six names that come up over and over in prophetic passages about the church: Judah, Joseph, Benjamin, Ephraim, Israel, and Jacob. Anyone who does not know what facet of faith-inspired goodness and truth is meant by each of them in an inner sense can never see any of the divine secrets in those parts of the Word. And no one can know which of these facets is meant without knowing the identity of the heavenliness that is Judah, the spiritual heavenliness that is Joseph, the heavenly spirituality that is Benjamin, the intellectual side of religion that is Ephraim, the inner spirituality that is Israel, and the outer spirituality that is Jacob.

[5] Regarding Benjamin specifically, because he represents heavenly spirituality, and Joseph represents spiritual heavenliness, so both together represent a middle area between the heavenly and spiritual selves, and because they are tightly bound together, their bond is depicted by the following incidents in the Joseph story: Joseph told his brothers *they were to bring their youngest brother* if they did not want to die (Genesis 42:20). When they returned with Benjamin, and Joseph saw *Benjamin his brother,* he said, "Is this your youngest brother?" And he said, "*God be favorable to you, my son.*" *And Joseph hurried, because his inward parts were stirred toward his brother, and he sought to weep, so he went into his chamber and wept there* (Genesis 43:29, 30). He *multiplied Benjamin's share* above everyone's share *fivefold* (Genesis 43:34). After he revealed himself to his brothers, *he fell on the neck of Benjamin his brother and wept, and Benjamin*

wept on his neck (Genesis 45:14). He gave them all changes of clothes, *but to Benjamin, three hundred pieces of silver* and *five changes of clothes* (Genesis 45:22). [6] This shows that Joseph and Benjamin were tightly knit together, not because they had the same mother but because they represent the spiritual bond between the goodness that is Joseph and the truth that is Benjamin. As both mean the middle ground between the heavenly and spiritual selves, Joseph could not be united with his brothers or father except through Benjamin. Without an intermediary, there is no union. That is why Joseph did not reveal himself sooner.

[7] In other places in the Word as well—especially the prophetic parts—Benjamin symbolizes the spiritual truth that belongs to the church. For instance, in Moses' prophetic utterance concerning the children of Israel:

> *To Benjamin he said,* "[You are] Jehovah's beloved; [Jehovah] will dwell securely on him, covering him all day, and between his shoulders he will live." (Deuteronomy 33:12)

Jehovah's beloved means spiritual truth that comes from heavenly goodness. This goodness is being said to dwell securely with that truth, to cover it the whole day, and to live between its shoulders. Shoulders in an inner sense mean all power (§1085), and goodness gains all its power through truth (§3563). [8] In Jeremiah:

> Flee, *children of Benjamin,* from the middle of Jerusalem, and as you blow your horn, blow, and over the vineyard house raise an oracle; because evil looks out from the north, and great wreckage. (Jeremiah 6:1)

The children of Benjamin stand for spiritual truth produced by something heavenly. Jerusalem stands for a spiritual religion, as does the vineyard house, or Beth-kerem. Evil from the north means from humankind's empirical and therefore secular knowledge. In the same author:

> It will happen, if you keep the Sabbath day holy, that they will come in from the cities of Judah and from the environs of Jerusalem and *from the land of Benjamin* and from the plain and from the mountain and from the south bringing burnt offering and sacrifice and minha and frankincense and bringing a thanksgiving [sacrifice] to Jehovah's house. (Jeremiah 17:24, 26)

[9] And elsewhere in the same author:

> In the cities of the mountain, in the cities of the plain, in the cities of the south, and *in the land of Benjamin* and in the environs of Jerusalem

and in the cities of Judah, flocks again will cross over as directed by the
hands of the one counting them. (Jeremiah 33:13)

Here too the land of Benjamin stands for spiritual truth belonging to
the church. The cities of Judah, the environs of Jerusalem, the land of
Benjamin, the plain, the mountain, and the south symbolize everything
in the church from the first level to the last. [10] In Hosea:

> Blow, you horns in *Gibeah,* you trumpet in *Ramah!* Shout, *Beth-aven!*
> *[Look] behind you, Benjamin!* Ephraim will be as wastelands on the day
> of censure. (Hosea 5:8, 9)

Gibeah, Ramah, and Beth-aven stand for aspects of spiritual truth that is
produced by something heavenly, meant by Benjamin. Gibeah belonged
to Benjamin (Judges 19:14), as did Ramah (Joshua 18:25) and Beth-aven
(Joshua 18:12). Blowing the horn and trumpet and shouting stand for pro-
claiming that the church's intellectual ability (Ephraim) has been ravaged.
[11] In Obadiah:

> The house of Jacob will become a fire and the house of Joseph a flame; the
> house of Esau will serve as stubble, and southerners will inherit the moun-
> tain of Esau, and those on the plain [will inherit] the Philistines, and
> they will inherit the field of Ephraim and the field of Samaria, and
> *Benjamin* [will inherit] Gilead. (Obadiah verses 18, 19)

It is as obvious here as in other places that the names have symbolic meaning. After all, there is no understanding any of it unless one knows what is
symbolized by the house of Jacob, the house of Joseph, the house of Esau,
the mountain of Esau, the Philistines, the field of Ephraim, the field of
Samaria, Benjamin, and Gilead, and by southerners, a house, a plain, a
mountain, and a field. Furthermore, the events narrated here never came
to pass. On the other hand, people who know what each image involves
will discover secrets of heaven in the passage. Benjamin again means spirituality rising out of heavenliness. [12] The same holds true for this passage
from Zechariah:

> Jehovah will become monarch over the whole earth; on that day Jehovah
> will be one, and his name one. All around, the whole land will be like a
> plain, from Gibeah all the way to Rimmon, and it will dwell in its place
> from there, *the Gate of Benjamin,* to the place of the First Gate, to the
> Gate of the Corners and the Tower of Hananel, to the royal winepresses.
> (Zechariah 14:9, 10)

Likewise in David:

> Shepherd, turn an ear, you who lead Joseph like a flock, who sit upon the guardian beings, before Ephraim and *Benjamin* and Manasseh. Arouse your might and go save us! (Psalms 80:1, 2)

The same is true in Deborah and Barak's prophetic utterance:

> Jehovah will rule for me among the mighty, from Ephraim, whose root is in Amalek, *behind you, Benjamin, in your peoples;* from Machir, lawgivers will descend, and from Zebulun, those who draw the scepter of a scribe. (Judges 5:13, 14)

[13] In John:

> I heard the number of those sealed: one hundred forty-four thousand sealed from every tribe of Israel. From the *tribe of Zebulun,* twelve thousand sealed; from the *tribe of Joseph,* twelve thousand sealed; from the *tribe of Benjamin,* twelve thousand sealed. (Revelation 7:4, 8)

The tribes of Israel in this chapter symbolize people who have goodness and truth and are therefore in the Lord's kingdom. The tribes and the number twelve—or twelve thousand, which is the same thing—mean everything contained in love and faith, or in goodness and truth (§§577, 2089, 2129, 2130, 3272, 3858, 3913, 3926, 3939, 4060). These things are divided into four categories there, and the last category is the twelve thousand each sealed from Zebulun, Joseph, and Benjamin, because the tribe of Zebulun symbolizes the heavenly marriage (§§3960, 3961), which contains heaven and therefore contains everything. Joseph means spiritual heavenliness, or the goodness that comes of truth, and Benjamin means truth that comes of that goodness, or heavenly spirituality. This composes the marriage bond in heaven. That is why they are mentioned last.

[14] Since Benjamin was to represent heavenly spirituality in the church, or truth that comes of goodness, which lies between heavenly goodness and spiritual truth, Jerusalem fell as an inheritance to the children of Benjamin. Before the Temple was built there, you see, Jerusalem symbolized the church as a whole. To see that Jerusalem was allotted to Benjamin, read Joshua 18:28 and Judges 1:21.

4593   *And Rachel died and was buried on the way to Ephrath* symbolizes the end of the previous desire for inner truth, as the following shows: *Dying* means something's ceasing to be what it was, as discussed at §494, so it symbolizes an end. *Rachel* represents a desire for inner truth, as discussed at §§3758, 3782, 3793, 3819. Being *buried* symbolizes rejection of an earlier state and its revival in a new form, as discussed at §§2916, 2917, 3256. And *Ephrata* symbolizes heavenly spirituality at an earlier stage, as discussed at §4585. *Rachel died and was buried on the way to Ephrath,* then, plainly symbolizes the end of a previous state of desire for inner truth and its resurrection in a new form, which is Bethlehem, as discussed just below.

[2] In its true sense, "Rachel died and was buried on the way to Ephrath" means that [the Lord's] heredity was permanently expelled through his trials. This heredity was a merely human desire for inner truth, which a divine desire drove away. That is why the child's mother called him Ben-oni, son of my sorrow, while his father called him Benjamin, son of my right hand.

Human desire inherited from our mother contains a heredity in which there is evil, but divine desire contains nothing but goodness. Human desire holds personal and worldly glory as a goal for itself. The goal of divine desire, though, is to have glory for itself so as to give glory from itself in order to save the human race, according to the Lord's words in John:

> I pray for those whom you have given me, since everything of mine is yours and of yours is mine, *but I am glorified in them.* [I pray] that they may all be one; as you, Father, are in me, and I in you, that they too may be one in us. *I have given them the glory that you have given me,* so that they can be one as we are one—I in them and you in me. (John 17:9, 10, 21, 22, 23)

That is, Bethlehem symbolizes its replacement by heavenly spirituality resurrected in a new form. This can be seen from the symbolism of *Bethlehem* as heavenly spirituality in a new state. Ephrath means heavenly spirituality in an earlier state (§4585). "She was buried there" symbolizes its resurrection in a new form (§4593).

Rachel bore her second son, Benjamin, in Bethlehem, and died in giving birth; David was born in Bethlehem and anointed king there; and the Lord was born there. This involves a secret that has never yet been revealed. It could not be revealed to anyone who did not know what was symbolized by Ephrata and Bethlehem and what was represented by Benjamin and David. More importantly, it could not be revealed to anyone who did not know what heavenly spirituality was, since that is what was symbolized by these places and represented by these figures.

[2] The Lord was born there and nowhere else because he alone was born a spiritual-heavenly person. Everyone else is born earthly, with the

ability or potential to become either heavenly or spiritual through rebirth from the Lord. The Lord was born a spiritual-heavenly person so that he could make his humanity divine, progressing in order from the lowest level to the highest, reorganizing everything in the heavens and hells along the way. What is both spiritual and heavenly lies between the earthly, outer self and the rational, inner self (see above at §§4585, 4592). The earthly, outer plane consequently lay below that middle area, and the rational, inner plane lay above it.

[3] People who cannot grasp this will never understand why the Lord was born in Bethlehem, no matter how it is revealed. From earliest times Ephrath symbolized heavenly spirituality, so Bethlehem had the same symbolism later on. This, now, is the reason for the following words in David:

> He swore to Jehovah, he vowed to the Mighty One of Jacob: "If I enter the tent of my house, if I climb onto the couch of my bed, if I give sleep to my eyes, slumber to my eyelids, . . . ! Until I find a spot for Jehovah, dwelling places for the Mighty One of Jacob." *Look, we heard of him in Ephrata;* we found him in forest fields. We will enter his dwelling places; we will bow down at his footstool. (Psalms 132:2–7)

Obviously these words were spoken of the Lord. "We heard *of him*" and "we found *him*" is represented in the original language by the letter *h* at the ends of the words. The *h* is taken from the name of Jehovah. [4] And in Micah:

> You, *Ephratean Bethlehem*—it is a little thing for you to be among the thousands of Judah. [Yet] from you one will emerge for me who will be a ruler in Israel, and his emergence is from antiquity, from the days of old. (Micah 5:2; Matthew 2:6)

From these prophetic sayings the Jewish people knew that the Messiah or Christ would be born in Bethlehem, as is evident in Matthew:

> Herod, gathering all the high priests and scribes of the people, examined of them where the Christ [Messiah] was to be born. They told him, "In *Bethlehem* of Judea." (Matthew 2:4, 5)

And in John:

> The Jews said, "Doesn't Scripture say that from the seed of David and *from Bethlehem*—the city where David was—the Christ [Messiah] was to come?" (John 7:42)

He actually was born there, too; see Matthew 2:1; Luke 2:4, 5, 6, 7. Because of this, and because he was descended from David, the Lord was referred to as a new branch from the trunk of Jesse and as Jesse's root (Isaiah 11:1, 10). Jesse, David's father, was a native of Bethlehem. David was born and anointed king there (1 Samuel 16:1–14; 17:12), so Bethlehem was called the city of David (Luke 2:4, 11; John 7:42). David mainly represents the Lord's royal power, or divine truth (§1888).

And Jacob raised a pillar over her grave symbolizes the holy influence of the spiritual truth that would rise again on that level, as the following shows: A *pillar* symbolizes the holy influence of truth, as discussed in §4580, and in this case, the holy influence of spiritual truth from a heavenly origin, since that kind of truth is the current focus. And a *grave* symbolizes resurrection, as discussed in §§2916, 2917, 3256. **4595**

It is the Pillar of Rachel's Grave to this day symbolizes a permanent state of holy influence, as the following shows: A *pillar* symbolizes the holy influence of truth, and a *grave* symbolizes resurrection, as discussed just above. And *to this day* means without end, as discussed in §§2838, 3998. **4596**

Genesis 35:21, 22a. *And Israel traveled and stretched his tent, from beyond the tower of Eder. And it happened as Israel was dwelling in this land that Reuben went and lay with Bilhah, his father's concubine, and Israel heard.* **4597**

Israel traveled symbolizes the heavenly-spiritual dimension of the earthly plane at this point. *And stretched his tent, from beyond the tower of Eder* symbolizes the inner depths of this dimension. *And it happened as Israel was dwelling in this land* means while in this state. *That Reuben went and lay with Bilhah, his father's concubine,* symbolizes the profanation of goodness through detached faith. *And Israel heard* means that such faith was rejected.

Israel traveled symbolizes the heavenly-spiritual dimension of the earthly plane at this point, as the following shows: *Traveling* [or setting off] symbolizes developments, or a continuation, as noted in §§4375, 4554, and here it symbolizes movement toward more inward levels. *Israel* currently represents the heavenly-spiritual dimension of the earthly plane, as discussed in §4286. The heavenly-spiritual dimension of the earthly plane is the goodness that grows out of truth, or neighborly kindness acquired through religious truth, as I have already explained. **4598**

The world has little idea what progress inward is. It is not progress in secular knowledge. This progress frequently takes place without any advance toward inner depths, and often with movement in the opposite direction. It is not progress in mature judgment, which can also occur in one who abandons inner depth. Neither is it progress in the knowledge of inner truth, because knowledge makes no difference unless we are moved by it. Progress inward is advancement toward heaven and the Lord through a knowledge of truth grounded in the desire for that knowledge, and therefore through our desires.

[2] The nature of the headway we make in going inward is not visible to anyone in the world, but it is quite plain in the other life, where it consists in movement from a kind of fog into the light. People who restrict themselves to what is superficial live in comparative fog, and that is how angels see them; but people who go inward live in light and consequently in wisdom, since the light there is wisdom. Remarkably, the ones who live in fog cannot see that the people living in light are in the light, but the ones who live in light can see that the people living in fog are in a fog.

Since this passage is talking about progress the Lord's divinity made in going inward, Jacob is called Israel. Where the text is not about this progress, he is called Jacob. Take, for instance, the previous verse in this chapter (verse 20) or the final verse.

4599   *And stretched his tent, from beyond the tower of Eder* symbolizes the inner depths of this dimension, as the following shows: *Stretching a tent* symbolizes progress in holiness—in this case, progress in going inward. A *tent* symbolizes something holy; see §§414, 1102, 2145, 2152, 3312, 4391. *From beyond the tower* means in an inner direction, as discussed below. And *Eder* symbolizes the nature of the state—a state of progress in the deepening of holiness. This tower had the same symbolism since ancient times, but since it does not come up again in the Word, except in Joshua 15:21, the meaning cannot be proved by parallel passages, as it can with other names.

From beyond the tower means in an inner direction, because what lies within is described as high and tall—as a mountain, hill, tower, rooftop, and things like that. The reason is that inner depths look like heights to minds that take their ideas from the physical features of the world, through the outer senses (§2148).

[2] The symbolism of towers as inner depths can also be seen from other Scripture passages, such as this one in Isaiah:

> My beloved had a vineyard on a horn of the offspring of oil, which he surrounded and de-stoned; and he planted it with a choice grapevine *and built a tower in the middle of it.* (Isaiah 5:1, 2)

The vineyard stands for a spiritual religion; the choice grapevine, for spiritual goodness. "He built a tower in the middle of it" stands for the inner depths of truth. Likewise in a parable of the Lord's in Matthew:

> A person, a householder, planted a vineyard and set a hedge around it and dug a winepress in it and *built a tower* and rented it to some growers. (Matthew 21:33; Mark 12:1)

[3] In Ezekiel:

> The sons of Arvad and your army were on your walls all around, and the Gammadians were in *your towers;* their shields they hung on your walls all around. They perfected your beauty. (Ezekiel 27:11)

This is about Tyre, which symbolizes a knowledge of what is good and true, or people who have this knowledge. Gammadians in its towers stand for a knowledge of inner truth. [4] In Micah:

> Jehovah will reign over them on Mount Zion from now on forever; and you *tower of the flock,* you hill of Zion's daughter: to you it will come, and the former reign will return, the reign of Jerusalem's daughter. (Micah 4:7, 8)

This depicts the Lord's heavenly kingdom. Mount Zion portrays the core of that kingdom, or love for the Lord. The hill of Zion's daughter portrays an offshoot of that love, or mutual love, which is called charity for one's neighbor, from a spiritual point of view. The tower of the flock portrays inner truth springing from goodness, in that kingdom. From this comes the kingdom of heavenly spirituality, as symbolized by the reign of Jerusalem's daughter. In David:

> Mount Zion will be glad, Judah's daughters will rejoice, because of your judgments. Surround Zion and encircle it; *count its towers.* (Psalms 48:11, 12)

The towers stand for inner truth that defends what belongs to love and charity. [5] In Luke:

> Any who do not carry their cross and come after me cannot be my disciples. For *when you want to build a tower,* which of you does not first sit down and reckon the cost, whether you have what it takes to finish it? Or what king is there, proceeding to commit war with another king, [who] does not sit down first and deliberate whether he is strong

enough with ten thousand [soldiers] to meet the one who comes against him with twenty thousand? So any of you that do not renounce all your resources cannot be my disciples. (Luke 14:27, 28, 31, 33)

People who do not know the Word's inner meaning suppose that the Lord was merely speaking metaphorically here. They take the building of the tower and the making of war at face value, not knowing that all scriptural metaphors have symbolic and representative meaning. Building a tower means acquiring inner truth, and making war means using that truth in one's battles. The focus in this passage is on trials that people in the church undergo—people who are being called the Lord's disciples. The cross they carry symbolizes such trials. "You that do not renounce all your resources cannot be my disciples" means that it is not at all themselves and their own devices that bring them victory but the Lord. Viewed this way, the passage makes consistent sense, but if the statements about the tower and the war are taken as simple metaphors, without any inner meaning, it does not. This discussion makes plain how much light is available from the inner meaning.

[6] When people wallow in love for themselves and for worldly advantages, they use falsity in their battles and in proving the validity of their style of religion. This falsity is their inner plane, and it too is depicted by towers, in a negative sense, as in Isaiah:

> The loftiness of men will sink, and Jehovah Sabaoth will be exalted over all the proud and lofty and over all the haughty (and they will be brought down) and over all the cedars of Lebanon, tall and lifted up, and over all the oaks of Bashan, and over all the lofty mountains, and over all the tall hills, and *over every high tower,* and over every fortified wall. (Isaiah 2:11–18)

The cedars, oaks, mountains, hills, tower, and wall portray inner and outer aspects of the kinds of love mentioned above, the tower portraying inner falsity. So in this case too, tall things depict what lies within, though there is a difference. People devoted to what is evil and false consider themselves taller and higher than others, but people devoted to what is good and true consider themselves smaller and lowlier (Matthew 20:26, 27; Mark 10:43, 44). Goodness and truth are portrayed as high up because they are in heaven, closer to the Highest One, who is the Lord.

One more point: The Word speaks of towers in connection with truth but of mountains in connection with goodness.

And it happened as Israel was dwelling in this land means while in this
state—a state of goodness springing from truth—as the following shows:
Dwelling means living one's life, since it means almost the same as settling, with the difference that dwelling has to do with truth, but settling,
with goodness. For the symbolism of settling as existing and living and
therefore as a state, see §3384. The *land* symbolizes the church in regard
to goodness, as discussed at §§566, 662, 1066, 1068, 1262, 1413, 1607, 1733,
1850, 2117, 2118, 2571, 2928, 3355, 4447, 4535, and in this instance, in regard
to the goodness that springs from truth. A state of this goodness—Israel's
current state—is what is being symbolized.

4600

That Reuben went and lay with Bilhah, his father's concubine, symbolizes the profanation of goodness through detached faith. *And Israel heard*
means that such faith was rejected. This can be seen from the following:
Reuben represents doctrinal, intellectual faith, which is the first step in
the church, as mentioned in §§[3860,] 3861, 3866. Here he represents
such faith detached from neighborly love, as discussed below. *Lying with
Bilhah, his father's concubine* symbolizes profanation of what is good. Committing adultery means corrupting or adulterating goodness (§§2466, 2729,
3399), but lying with the concubine of one's father means profaning it. And
Israel heard means that such faith was rejected. Strictly speaking, "Israel
heard" means that the spiritual church knew and approved, because hearing
means listening favorably, and Israel symbolizes a spiritual religion. But the
true church does *not* approve, as later statements about Reuben will show.
Instead, the symbolism on an inner level is that this faith was rejected. The
text does not say what Jacob felt and thought in regard to this unspeakable
transgression, but his prophecy concerning Reuben makes clear his utter
loathing and abhorrence for the deed:

4601

> Reuben, my firstborn you are, my strength and the inception of my
> might, excelling in honor and excelling in power. Light as water, *do not
> excel! For you climbed onto your father's beds, then you profaned them; my
> pallet he climbed onto.* (Genesis 49:3, 4)

So does the fact that Reuben was deprived of the birthright on that account
(1 Chronicles 5:1). Clearly, then, "Israel heard" means that such a faith was
rejected. To see that the birthright symbolizes the faith of the church, see
§§352, 2435, 3325.

[2] Goodness is profaned by detached faith when people acknowledge
and believe in the church's truth and the goodness that goes with it and
yet live contrary to both. In people who separate matters of faith from

matters of neighborly love in their minds and therefore in their lives, evil unites with truth, and falsity unites with goodness. This union itself is what is called profanation. It is different for people who know about religious truth and goodness but do not believe it at heart. See previous discussions and explanations of profanation in §§301, 302, 303, 571, 582, 593, 1001, 1003, 1008, 1010, 1059, 1327, 1328, 2051, 2426, 3398, 3399, 3402, 3479, 3898, 4050, 4289. The profanation of goodness by detached faith was represented by Cain's murder of Abel, by the curse Ham's father put on him, and by the drowning of the Egyptians in the Red Sea (§3325). Now it is represented by Reuben (§§3325, 3870).

[3] To make it possible for people in the spiritual church to be saved, the Lord split their intellectual side from their volitional side in a miraculous way and planted in their intellectual side the power to receive a new will (§§863, 875, 895, 927, 928, 1023, 1043, 1044, 2256, 4328, 4493). As a consequence, when the intellect grasps and perceives what faith promotes as good and adopts it, but human will (that is, an evil will) continues to control and dominate, truth unites with evil, and goodness with falsity. This union is profanation and is meant by eating and drinking unworthily at the Holy Supper. The goodness symbolized by the body, and the truth symbolized by the blood, [cannot] be detached from people under these circumstances. What is united in such a way can never, ever be separated, so the very deepest hell awaits them. People who know about religious truth and goodness but do not believe it in their heart, on the other hand, cannot profane it, because their intellect does not accept and absorb it. This is the case with the majority today.

[4] The text deals with the rejection of such a faith here, because the next part treats of truth and goodness in their proper arrangement, and the part after that, of their union with the rational dimension, or the intellectual side. Jacob's sons, who are about to be named, mean truth and goodness in that arrangement, and Isaac means the rational dimension, or the intellectual side. The trip Jacob took with his sons to Isaac in an inner sense means the union with the intellectual side.

4602   Genesis 35:22b, 23, 24, 25, 26. *And Jacob's sons were twelve. The sons of Leah: Jacob's firstborn, Reuben, and Simeon and Levi and Judah and Issachar and Zebulun. The sons of Rachel: Joseph and Benjamin. And the sons of Bilhah, Rachel's slave: Dan and Naphtali. And the sons of Zilpah, Leah's slave: Gad and Asher. These were Jacob's sons, who were born to him in Paddan-aram.*

Jacob's sons were twelve symbolizes the current state of everything on the plane of earthly divinity. *The sons of Leah* symbolizes outer forms of divine goodness and truth in their order. *Jacob's firstborn, Reuben,* symbolizes good done out of faith. *And Simeon and Levi and Judah and Issachar and Zebulun* symbolizes their essential elements. *The sons of Rachel: Joseph and Benjamin,* symbolizes inner goodness and truth. *And the sons of Bilhah, Rachel's slave: Dan and Naphtali,* symbolizes secondary kinds serving the inner kinds. *And the sons of Zilpah, Leah's slave: Gad and Asher,* symbolizes those serving the outer kinds. *These were Jacob's sons, who were born to him in Paddan-aram,* symbolizes their origin and current state.

Jacob's sons were twelve symbolizes the current state of everything on the plane of earthly divinity. This can be seen from the representation of *Jacob* as earthly divinity (discussed many times before) and from the symbolism of *twelve* as everything. When applied to Jacob's sons or the tribes named for them, twelve symbolizes all varieties of truth and goodness, as discussed in §§2089, 2129, 2130, 3272, 3858, 3913, 3939.

4603

I have already spoken of the Lord's earthly level and the way he made the earthliness in himself divine, since this is what Jacob formerly represented. The text, however, is about to take up the union of his earthly divinity with his divine rationality. This union is represented by Jacob's trip to Isaac, because Isaac represents the Lord's divine rationality. That is why all Jacob's sons are listed once again. The Lord's earthly level had to be supplied with all the varieties of truth and goodness before it could fully unite with the rational level, because the earthly level serves as a storehouse for the rational level. Thus the list.

It is worth noticing that Jacob's sons are now named in a different order than before. Bilhah's and Zilpah's sons—Dan, Naphtali, Gad, and Asher—come last, even though they were born before Issachar, Zebulun, Joseph, and Benjamin. This is because the current theme is the arrangement of truth and goodness on the earthly level once it had been made divine. The state of the quality under discussion determines the order in which the sons are named; see §§3862, 3926, 3939.

The sons of Leah symbolizes outer forms of divine goodness and truth in their order. This is established by the representation of *Leah* as a desire for outer truth (discussed in §§3793, 3819). Her *sons* are the attributes represented by Reuben, Simeon, Levi, Judah, Issachar, and Zebulun, discussed below.

4604

Jacob's firstborn, Reuben, symbolizes good done out of faith. This is established by the symbolism of the firstborn as faith (discussed in §§352, 367, 2435, 3325); from the representation of *Jacob* as the goodness associated with earthly truth (discussed in §4538); and from that of *Reuben* as the nature of faith. In a positive sense Reuben symbolizes the truth

4605

associated with faith (§§[3860,] 3861, 3866), but now that the truth associated with faith has turned into goodness, he symbolizes good done out of faith. Faith regarded in itself actually is charity, so the truth associated with faith regarded in itself is good done out of faith, because faith cannot exist except as a result of charity, which is to say that truth cannot exist except as a result of goodness. When a person has been reborn, then, goodness is in first place, or is firstborn (see §§3325, 3494). That is why *Jacob's firstborn, Reuben,* symbolizes good done out of faith. It is similar elsewhere in Moses:

> *May Reuben live* and not die! And it will happen that his numbers will be few. (Deuteronomy 33:6)

Reuben means faith-inspired goodness in this passage because he comes first, and Judah, second. So in this prophecy of Moses' regarding Israel's sons, Reuben and Judah come in a different order than in Jacob's prophecy in Genesis 49. As noted above at the end of §4603, the order in which the sons are named depends on the state of the quality under discussion. [2] Likewise in John:

> I heard the number of those sealed: one hundred forty-four thousand sealed from every tribe. From the tribe of Judah, twelve thousand sealed; *from the tribe of Reuben,* twelve thousand sealed; from the tribe of Gad, twelve thousand sealed. (Revelation 7:4, 5)

Here Judah is mentioned first, Reuben second, and Gad third. These three constitute a first category. Since the passage is about the Lord's kingdom, Judah symbolizes heavenly goodness, the goodness of the third and inmost heaven; Reuben symbolizes spiritual goodness, which is the same as good done out of faith and is the goodness of the second or middle heaven; and Gad symbolizes earthly goodness, the goodness of the first heaven. The order is different in the prophecy of Deborah and Barak:

> Chieftains in Issachar were with Deborah; and Issachar (so [also] Barak) was sent into the valley on his feet. Among the divisions of *Reuben,* great statutes of the heart. Why do you live between two burdens to listen to the hissings of the droves? To the divisions of *Reuben,* great searchings of the heart. (Judges 5:15, [16])

Without knowing what Issachar, Deborah, Barak, and Reuben represent and what chieftains, a valley, a division, statutes of the heart, two burdens, and the hissings of the droves symbolize, no one can tell what these words mean. Reuben obviously means faith, in this passage.

And Simeon and Levi and Judah and Issachar and Zebulun symbolize **4606** their essential elements—the essential elements of divine goodness and truth in their outer forms. This can be seen from the individual representations. *Simeon* in the highest sense represents providence; in an inward sense, faith that belongs to the will; and on the surface, obedience. This is discussed at §§3869, 3870, 3871, 3872. *Levi* in the highest sense represents love and mercy; in an inward sense, charity, or spiritual love; and on the surface, union. This is discussed at §§3875, 3877. *Judah* in the highest sense represents the divinity of the Lord's love; in an inward sense, the Lord's heavenly kingdom; and on the surface, doctrine from the Word in a heavenly religion. This is discussed at §3881. *Issachar* in the highest sense represents divine goodness-from-truth and divine truth-from-goodness; in an inward sense, heavenly marriage love; and on the surface, mutual love. This is discussed at §§3956, 3957. And *Zebulun* in the highest sense represents the Lord's divinity itself and his divine humanity; in an inward sense, the heavenly marriage; and on the surface, marriage love. This is discussed at §§3960, 3961.

These are the essential elements of the Lord's divine goodness and truth in their outer forms. To explain all of them and their presence within that goodness and truth is something that can be done only by one who stands in heaven's light. In that light they reveal themselves the way answers revealed themselves in the Urim and Thummim—as flashes of light and fire and a consequent perception from the Lord. (The Urim and Thummim contained twelve precious stones, for the twelve tribes of Israel.)

The sons of Rachel: Joseph and Benjamin, symbolize inner goodness **4607** and truth. This can be seen from the representation of *Rachel* as a desire for inner truth (discussed at §§3758, 3782, 3793, 3819). The *sons of Rachel* therefore mean inner goodness and truth. The essential elements of these are represented by Joseph and Benjamin. *Joseph* in the highest sense represents spiritual divinity; in an inward sense, the spiritual kingdom; and on the surface, goodness in that kingdom. This is discussed at §3969. And *Benjamin* represents heavenly spirituality that is divine, as discussed at §§3969, 4592.

These are the elements of inner goodness and truth.

And the sons of Bilhah, Rachel's slave: Dan and Naphtali, symbolize **4608** secondary kinds serving the inner kinds. This can be seen from the representation of *Bilhah, Rachel's slave,* as a secondary desire serving as a means used by the desire for inner truth (discussed in §3849). A female *slave* is a middle ground serving to create a bond (§§3913, 3917, 3931). Her *sons* are those means. "Secondary goodness and truth" means goodness and truth that do not penetrate right away but develop out of the kind that does and are attached to it like domestic servants. They also serve as a go-between and support.

The essential elements of this goodness and truth are represented by Dan and Naphtali. *Dan* in the highest sense represents justice and mercy; in an inward sense, sacred faith; and on the surface, a good life (§§3921, 3923). And *Naphtali* in the highest sense represents autonomous power; in an inward sense, trials in which one wins; and on the surface, resistance put up by the earthly self (§§3927, 3928). These are the essential elements of the means that serve inner goodness and truth.

4609   *And the sons of Zilpah, Leah's slave: Gad and Asher,* symbolizes those serving the outer kinds. This can be seen from the representation of *Zilpah, Leah's slave,* as a secondary desire serving as a means used by the desire for outer truth (discussed in §3835). A female *slave* is a means serving to create a bond, as noted just above in §4608. Her *sons* are those means. Their essential elements are represented by Gad and Asher. *Gad* in the highest sense represents omnipotence and omniscience; in an inward sense, goodness inspired by faith; and on the surface, good deeds (§3934). *Asher* in the highest sense represents eternity; in an inward sense, the happiness of eternal life; and on the surface, pleasurable feelings (§§3938, 3939).

These are the attributes meant in the current list of Jacob's sons, but how they cohere, how one follows another, how one is contained in another—this cannot be seen in worldly light without the added illumination of heavenly light. What then becomes visible still cannot be put into words, though. Human language is based on ideas formed from objects of the world's light. These ideas are transcended by ideas originating in heaven's light—so much so that the latter cannot be expressed. They can only (and only in part) be thought about, by people granted the ability to draw their minds up out of sense impressions.

4610   *These were Jacob's sons, who were born to him in Paddan-aram,* symbolizes their origin and current state. This can be seen from the general and particular comments now made on Jacob's sons, namely, that as a group they symbolized everything involved in the Lord's earthly divinity (§4603). In fact, taken together those attributes now *are* Jacob. Their origin is symbolized by *born to him in Paddan-aram,* which means born from a knowledge of what is true and good, a knowledge symbolized by *Paddan-aram* (§§3664, 3680). Since all of them taken together now are Jacob, the text in the original language says "who was born to him," in the singular.

The next verses have to do with the bond between earthly divinity and divine rationality. This bond is represented by Jacob's trip to Isaac his father.

Genesis 35:27, 28, 29. *And Jacob came to Isaac his father, to Mamre, Kiriath-arba (that is, Hebron), where Abraham and Isaac stayed as an immigrant. And the days of Isaac were one hundred eighty years. And Isaac breathed his last and died and was gathered to his peoples, old and full of days. And Esau and Jacob his sons buried him.* 4611

Jacob came to Isaac his father means that divine rationality was what [earthly divinity] would now unite with. *To Mamre, Kiriath-arba* symbolizes its state. *That is, Hebron* symbolizes the state that would exist when they were united. *Where Abraham and Isaac stayed as an immigrant* symbolizes divine life in addition. *And the days of Isaac* symbolizes the state of divine rationality at this point. *Were one hundred eighty years* symbolizes the nature of that state. *And Isaac breathed his last and died* symbolizes its revival in earthly divinity. *And was gathered to his peoples* means that it now existed in the realm of earthly divinity. *Old and full of days* symbolizes new life. *And Esau and Jacob his sons buried him* means that it rose again in the goodness and the truth-based goodness of the earthly plane.

Jacob came to Isaac his father means that divine rationality was what [earthly divinity] would now unite with. This is established by the representation of *Jacob* as earthly divinity in the state described just above (§§4604–4610) and by the representation of *Isaac* as divine rationality (discussed in §§1893, 2066, 2072, 2083, 2630, 3012, 3194, 3210). Union is symbolized by the fact that Jacob *came to* Isaac. 4612

The theme from here to the end of the chapter is the union of the earthly and rational levels. This being so, the previous few verses told what the earthly level was like—that it had every kind of goodness and truth. Jacob's twelve sons symbolized the earthly level's nature because each of them represents some general category of truth or goodness, as shown.

[2] Regarding the union of earthliness and rationality that is the theme of the next few verses, it is important to know that the rational plane accepts truth and goodness more quickly and easily than the earthly plane does (§§3286, 3288, 3321, 3368, 3498, 3513). The rational plane is purer and more perfect than the earthly because it is more inward, or higher. Regarded in itself, rationality lives in heavenly light, to which it is suited. As a result, the rational plane accepts the objects of that light—truth and goodness, in other words, objects of understanding and wisdom—more quickly and

easily than the earthly plane does. The earthly dimension is coarser and less perfect because it is more external, or lower down. Regarded in itself, the earthly plane lives in the world's light, which contains no understanding or wisdom except so far as heavenly light coming by way of the rational plane mixes with it. This is exactly what the "inflow" that scholars talk about these days is.

[3] A word about the earthly level: Beginning in our childhood and youth, its character is formed by what flows in from the world through our outer senses. This inflowing material is the source of our intellect and the means by which we acquire it. At that stage, we enjoy the pleasures of self-love and materialism and are therefore subject to cravings rising out of both inherited and applied [evil]. The intellect we then acquire is full of such qualities. Anything that caters to our pleasures we view as good and true. As a result the contents of our earthly plane are arranged upside down and backward from the heavenly pattern. Under these conditions, the light of heaven does stream in through our rational mind, giving us the ability to think, reason, and speak, and to act appropriately and politely in outward appearance. Still, nothing enlightened, nothing that contributes to our eternal happiness, is present on the earthly level. The delights that reign supreme there resist it. The pleasures of self-love and materialism are intrinsically and diametrically opposed to the pleasures of love for our neighbor and consequently for the Lord. We might know about matters of light, or of heaven, but they cannot touch our heart except to the degree that they help us win high office or gain wealth—that is, to the degree that they favor our love for ourselves and worldly advantages.

[4] This discussion shows that the pattern on the earthly level is completely upside down and backward from the heavenly pattern. When heaven's light flows into the earthly dimension through the rational, then, it can only be deflected, smothered, or corrupted.

These remarks now explain why the earthly plane has to be reborn before it can unite with the rational plane. When the earthly plane has been reborn, qualities that flow in from the Lord by way of heaven and then by way of the rational plane to the earthly plane are accepted, because they harmonize. The earthly dimension is nothing but a storehouse for goodness and truth from the rational dimension, or rather from the Lord through the rational dimension.

The earthly dimension means the outer self, which is also called the earthly self. The rational dimension means the inner self.

I have presented these ideas first, to show the situation with the subjects that follow, because they will have to do with the union of the earthly and rational planes.

To Mamre, Kiriath-arba symbolizes its state. This can be seen from the symbolism of *Mamre* as the nature and extent of whatever it is connected with (discussed in §2970), and from the symbolism of *Kiriath-arba* as truth in the church (discussed in §2909) and therefore simply as truth. So *Mamre, Kiriath-arba* symbolizes the state of the earthly level in respect to truth, while Hebron symbolizes its state in respect to goodness, as below.

4613

That is, Hebron symbolizes the state that would exist when they were united. This is established by the symbolism of *Hebron* as the goodness taught by the church (discussed in §2909). In this case it symbolizes the divine goodness of the Lord's earthly divinity. Anything that symbolizes a facet of religion on an inner level symbolizes a facet of the Lord's divinity on the highest level, because everything that makes the church comes from the Lord.

4614

Here is why Hebron symbolizes the state that would exist when the rational and earthly planes were united: Isaac was living there, and he represents the Lord's divine rationality. Jacob came there, and he represents the Lord's earthly divinity. And his coming there symbolizes union (§4612).

The text says "Mamre, Kiriath-arba (that is, Hebron)," because goodness unites earthly divinity to the goodness on the rational plane. Isaac represents goodness in the Lord's divine rationality (§§3012, 3194, 3210), but Rebekah represents truth there (§§3012, 3013, 3077), and Rebekah is not mentioned.

Where Abraham and Isaac stayed as an immigrant symbolizes divine life in addition. This is established by the symbolism of *immigrating* as life (discussed in §§1463, 2025); from the representation of *Abraham* as the Lord's divinity itself (§§1989, [2010,] 2011, 3245, 3251, 3439, 3703, 4206, 4207); and from the representation of *Isaac* as his divine rationality (§§1893, 2066, 2072, 2083, 2630, 2774, 3012, 3194, 3210, 4180).

4615

The current passage is about the union of the Lord's earthly divinity with his divine rationality. So it names Abraham and Isaac and says that they stayed as immigrants there, to symbolize divine life in addition— that is, together with his earthly divinity, which is Jacob. And because divinity itself, divine rationality, and earthly divinity in the Lord are a single whole, it says "where Abraham and Isaac also stayed as an immigrant" in the singular, not "stayed as immigrants" in the plural.

4616 *And the days of Isaac* symbolizes the state of divine rationality at this point. This can be seen from the symbolism of *days* as states (discussed in §§23, 487, 488, 493, 893, 2788, 3462, 3785) and from the representation of *Isaac* as divine rationality (discussed just above at §4615).

4617 *Were one hundred eighty years* symbolizes the nature of that state. This is clear from the fact that all numbers in the Word symbolize something; see §§482, 487, 575, 647, 648, 755, 813, 1963, 1988, 2075, 2252, 3252, 4264, 4495. *One hundred eighty years,* then, symbolizes the nature of the topic, or the nature of the state under discussion. *One hundred* means a full state (see §2636). *Eighty* means times of trial (see §1963), and in this case, trials as a means. Other meanings are also involved, but they are unknowable, because a number takes its symbolism from the factors that produce it when they are multiplied together. This number, for instance, is the product of twelve and fifteen and also of other factors still smaller.

4618 *And Isaac breathed his last and died* symbolizes its revival in earthly divinity. This is clear from the symbolism of *breathing one's last and dying* as revival (discussed in §§3326, 3498, 3505). When the Word mentions a person's death, on an inner level it symbolizes the end of something for that person and a new form of it in someone else, so it symbolizes continuity. For example, when it says that the monarchs of Judah and Israel or the high priests died, the meaning in an inner sense is that a representative role ended for them but continued in someone else. The meaning, then, is revival. What is more, no one in the other world who is with us when we read these things takes them as a death of any kind. The inhabitants there have no idea what dying is. Instead, they perceive it as the continuation of something in another person. Besides, when we die the only part that dies is the physical part that was of service to us on earth. We continue the life of our spirit in a world where the body is no longer of any use.

[2] The reason *Isaac breathed his last and died* symbolizes a revival in the Lord's earthly divinity is that the rational plane has no life unless the earthly plane corresponds to it (§§3493, 3620, 3623). The situation resembles that of eyesight. Unless there is something outside for the eye to look at, it stops being able to see; and this is true for the other senses as well. The same happens if the objects the eye looks at are totally detrimental to it, because such sights kill the eye. The situation is also like the vein of a spring whose waters have no outlet, so that it stops up.

The case is similar with the rational plane. Unless its light is received on the earthly plane, it stops being able to see—facts on the earthly plane being the objects of rational sight. Rationality also loses its sight if these objects are detrimental to rational light—in other words, to an understanding of truth and a wisdom about what is good. Rational light cannot stream into anything damaging to it. So it is that the rational level in people devoted to evil and falsity is closed off. It opens no path for communication with heaven except through cracks, so to speak, which enable them to think, reason, and speak.

That is why the earthly level has to be prepared for reception if it is to unite with the rational level. This is accomplished through rebirth from the Lord. When they unite, rationality finds life on the earthly plane, because it sees its objects there, as mentioned—just as the sight of the eye finds life in the objects of the world.

[3] It is true that the rational plane has its own life separate from the life of the earthly plane, but rationality is still within what is earthly like a person in her or his house, or like the soul in its body.

The heavens work the same way. The third or inmost heaven does have life separately from the heavens below it, but its wisdom would vanish if not received by the second or middle heaven. Likewise if the second heaven's light and intelligence were not received by the first or outermost heaven, and if the same traits in this heaven were not received by our earthly minds; the intelligence of these heavens would equally disappear if the Lord did not provide for it to be received elsewhere. As a consequence the Lord formed the heavens in such a way that each heaven is to serve the heaven above it by receiving from it. In last place he formed humanity's earthly and sensory planes as the final container, because on these planes divinity arrives at the outermost level of the divine design and crosses over into the physical world.

Therefore if the outermost plane agrees or corresponds with the previous ones, the previous ones coexist on that plane. What comes last is a container for everything before it, and sequential levels exist simultaneously there.

These comments show what is meant by a revival in the Lord's earthly divinity.

And was gathered to his peoples means that it now existed in the realm of earthly divinity. This can be seen from *being gathered to one's peoples,* which in regard to representative roles means that there is nothing more about that person, as noted in §§3255, 3276. In this verse, then, it means that [divine rationality] existed in the realm of earthly divinity—a meaning that also follows from the discussion just above in §4618.

The ancients used to say when anyone died that the person had been gathered to his or her peoples. In the most direct sense they meant that the dead were now among their own in the other life. While we are alive in our body, the spirit of each of us lives in company with other spirits and angels, and we join those spirits after death (§§1277, 2379). That is what was meant by the peoples to whom one was gathered.

The Word's inner sense, though, is about goodness and truth in the church or in the Lord's kingdom. In that sense, being gathered to one's peoples means living amid particular truths and forms of goodness that agree or correspond. All the communities of heaven live amid truth and goodness, but [ties of] truth and goodness there resemble ties of blood and kinship on earth, in all kinds of variety (§§685, 917, 3815, 4121). One's peoples therefore mean true ideas held by compatible groups, or the groups that adopt those ideas. For the meaning of peoples as truth, see §§1259, 1260, 2928, 3295, 3581.

4620   *Old and full of days* symbolizes new life, as the following shows: *Old* symbolizes the shedding of an earlier state and the putting on of a new one, as dealt with in §§2198, 3016, 3254, 3492. Here it means new life, accordingly. And *full of days* symbolizes a full state.

4621   *And Esau and Jacob his sons buried him* means that it rose again in the goodness and the truth-based goodness of the earthly plane, as the following shows: Being *buried* symbolizes resurrection (as mentioned in §§2916, 2917) and a state of representation revived in another person (§3256). *Esau* represents goodness in the Lord's earthly divinity, as discussed in §§3302, 3576, 4241. And *Jacob* represents truth-based goodness in the Lord's earthly divinity, as discussed in §§4273, 4337, 4538. In light of this evidence and the statements above at §4618, *Esau and Jacob his sons buried him* clearly means that [divine rationality] rose again in the goodness and truth-based goodness of the earthly plane.

The reason being buried means rising again, in an inner sense, is that when the body has died, the soul rises again. When the Word mentions burial, then, angels do not think about the body that is cast off but the soul that rises again. They are immersed in spiritual thinking and therefore in matters relating to life. Everything in the physical world connected with death consequently symbolizes something in the spiritual world relating to life.

Correspondence with the Universal Human (Continued): Correspondence of Smells and the Nose

THE habitations of the blessed in the other life are varied and are built with such consummate art that they embody the essence of architecture, so to speak, or come directly from it. (Concerning these dwellings, see earlier descriptions from experience in §§1116, 1626, 1627, 1628, 1629, 1630.) Not only can they be seen by people in that life, they can also be touched. Everything there is suited to the sensory abilities of spirits and angels. None of it is accessible to the physical senses of a person on earth, only to the senses of those in that world. **4622**

I realize that many will find this unbelievable, but that is because they do not believe in anything they cannot see with their bodily eyes and feel with the flesh of their hands. That is why modern people whose inner depths are closed off know nothing about the features of the spiritual world or of heaven. They do say on the basis of the Word and their theology that heaven exists and that the angels there have joy and glory—and beyond this they know nothing. Yes, they wish they knew how things worked in the other world, but when told, they still do not believe it, because at heart they deny its existence. They form a desire to know about it only when doctrine sparks their curiosity, not when faith inspires pleasure in the knowledge. Also people without any faith deny it at heart. Believers, though, acquire ideas of heaven and its joy and glory from various sources, each from the area of her or his knowledge and expertise. The uneducated acquire an idea of it from physical sensation.

[2] Most people do not understand that spirits and angels have much keener sensation than people in the world—keener sight, hearing, smell, taste (or its equivalent), and touch, and especially keener pleasure in their emotions. If only they believed their inner essence was their spirit! If only they believed that the body with its senses and limbs was adapted just to needs in this world, while the spirit with its senses and organs was adapted to needs in the next world! Then, almost spontaneously, they would develop their own ideas about the state of their spirit after death. They would think

to themselves, "My spirit is the real me that thinks and has wishes, long-ings, and desires. So every sensation I experience in my body is actually felt by my spirit. My body feels it only through an inflow from my spirit." This they would prove to themselves in many ways. In the end they would find more pleasure in the faculties of their spirit than of their body.

[3] That describes how matters really stand, too. It is not the body but its spirit that sees, hears, smells, and feels. When the spirit is stripped of its body, then, it feels the sensations it had felt within the body, and feels them much more acutely. The physical apparatus, which is rela-tively dull, had blunted the sensations—all the more so because it had immersed them in what is earthly and worldly.

I can assert positively that spirits are much better at seeing than peo-ple in their bodies, and at hearing, smelling (which must come as a sur-prise), and particularly feeling, since they do see, hear, and touch each other. This is a conclusion that anyone who believes in life after death would reach by considering that life cannot exist without sensation and that qual-ity of life depends on quality of sensation. In fact, intellect is nothing but a subtle awareness of one's inner depths, and the higher levels of intellect are an awareness of spiritual matters. As a result, the capacities of the intellect and of its perceptions are called inner senses.

[4] About human sensation immediately after death: As soon as we die and our bodies grow cold, we are brought to life and to a state of full sen-sation. So complete are our senses that at first we have trouble realizing we are not still in our bodies. The sensations we have persuade us to think this way. But when we notice—especially in starting to talk with other spirits—that these senses are keener, we recognize that we are in the other world and that our body's death was a continuation of our spirit's life.

There have been two acquaintances of mine with whom I spoke on the day of their burial, and one of them was looking through my eyes at his coffin and bier. Since he still possessed all the senses he had enjoyed in the world, he talked with me about his funeral as I marched in the pro-cession. He also mentioned his body, saying, "They are welcome to throw it out, because I am still alive."

[5] It is important to know, however, that the inhabitants of the other world cannot see anything at all in this world through the eyes of any human. They could see through mine, though, because I am with them in the spirit and simultaneously with the inhabitants of this world as to my body. See §1880 as well.

It is also important to know that when I talked with inhabitants of the other world, I did not see them with my physical but with my spiritual eyes. Even so, I saw them as clearly as with my physical eyes, and sometimes more clearly, because the Lord in his divine mercy has opened the capacities of my spirit.

[6] Still, I realize that nothing I have said so far will be convincing to people immersed in bodily, earthly, and worldly concerns—or at least to the ones who make such concerns their ultimate goals. The only things they grasp are those that death puts an end to.

I also realize that my words will be unconvincing to people who have put a lot of thought and investigation into the soul without understanding that the soul is a person's spirit and that the spirit is the person's actual self that lives in the body. They have necessarily pictured the soul as something like thought, or like a flame, or like rarefied air, animating only the organic forms of the body, not the purer forms of the spirit within the body. So they have viewed it as something that decomposes with the body. This is especially true of those whose insights, artificially magnified by the persuasion that they are wiser than others, have hardened their thinking on the subject.

Yet it needs to be known that spirits have two kinds of sensory life: real and unreal. The distinction is that everything experienced by the inhabitants of heaven is real, while everything experienced by the inhabitants of hell is unreal.

Whatever comes from the Divine—the Lord—is real, because it comes from the ultimate reality and inherent life, but whatever comes from a spirit's sense of independent existence is unreal, because it does not come from ultimate reality and inherent life. People who respond to what is good and true have the Lord's life and therefore real life. The Lord is present in goodness and truth through their response to it. People who engage in evil and falsity because they respond to it, though, have the life of apparent autonomy and therefore life that is not real, because the Lord is not present in evil and falsity.

What is real is distinguished from what is not real in that what is real actually is the way it appears, and what is not real is not actually the way it appears.

[2] Hell's inhabitants have just as full a range of sensation [as heaven's] and are utterly convinced that things really, truly are just as they experience them. When they are examined by angels, though, the same things

look like apparitions and disappear from sight. The inhabitants themselves look monstrous rather than human.

I was given an opportunity to talk with them about it. "We believe these things are real, because we can see and touch them," some of them said, adding, "The senses don't lie."

"Those things are still unreal," I was allowed to answer. "They are unreal because you are intent on anything that is contrary or opposed to the divine nature, which means that you are intent on evil and falsity, no matter how real they seem to you. Besides, so far as you surrender to evil cravings and distorted convictions, your thoughts are nothing but hallucinations. To see anything from the viewpoint of hallucination is to see what is real as unreal, and what is unreal as real. If the Lord in his divine mercy did not grant you these sensations, you would have no sensory life. You would have no life at all, since sensation makes all life."

To relate all my experiences with them would fill a great many pages.

[3] People like this should therefore be careful not to let themselves be fooled when they go to the other world. Evil spirits know how to present various illusions to newcomers from the world. If the spirits fail to deceive the newcomers, they still try to use illusions to persuade them that nothing is real, everything is imaginary, even in heaven.

4624   Regarding the correspondence of the sense of smell and the nose with the universal human, the people who belong to that region are the ones with generalized perception, so that they can even be called perceptions. The sense, and therefore the organ, of smell corresponds to them. It is because of this that people whose conjectures strike close to the truth and who are quick to grasp things are described in everyday language as sniffing and catching a whiff, being keen-scented, and having a nose for something. After all, the inner resonance of the words of human language traces much of its origin to correspondence with the universal human, because as to our spirit we associate with spirits, and as to our body with people on earth.

4625   The number of communities that make up heaven in its entirety, or the universal human, is large, some communities being more broadly inclusive, some less. The more comprehensive ones are those to which entire limbs, organs, or viscera correspond. The less comprehensive ones are those to which the components and subcomponents of organs correspond.

Every community is an image of the whole, since any like-minded association is made up of so many images of itself. The more inclusive communities, being images of the universal human, include subgroups, which correspond in the same way.

Sometimes on being sent to a community, I talked with the members there belonging to the area of the lungs, heart, face, tongue, ears, and eyes, and with those belonging to the area of the nose. From these last I was allowed to learn what they are like—that they are embodiments of perception. They picked up on everything happening to the community in general. They did not pick up on particular events, however, as is done by those belonging to the area of the eyes, who have the type of perception that discerns and penetrates. I also was able to observe that the sensitivity of the [nasal spirits] varies in keeping with overall changes in the state of the community they belong to.

Whenever the Lord grants it, the presence of approaching spirits— **4626** even at a distance, while they are still hidden from sight—is perceived from a kind of spiritual aura that reveals the nature of their life, their desires, and their faith. From this aura, angelic spirits who excel in perception learn countless things about the state of the spirits' life and faith. This has been shown to me many times.

When the Lord pleases, these auras turn into scents, and the scent is plainly smelled. The reason they turn into scents is that a smell corresponds to a perception. A perception is essentially a spiritual smell, and that is where the phenomenon of odor comes from. See previous reports from experience on these subjects. *Auras:* §§1048, 1053, 1316, 1504–1519, 1695, 2401, 2489, 4464. *Perception:* §§483, 495, 503, 521, 536, 1383, 1384, 1388, 1391, 1397, 1398, 1504, 1640. *Resulting smells:* §§1514, 1517, 1518, 1519, 1631, 3577.

The [spirits] who relate to the inside of the nose have a fuller state of **4627** perception than those described above [§4625], who relate to the outside. Let me give the following account of them:

I once saw a sort of bathhouse, with long seats or benches, that was giving off heat. A matron showed up but soon disappeared into a darkish fog. I also heard some little children saying they did not want to be there.

Then I sensed several angel choruses, who were sent to me to ward off the efforts of certain evil spirits. Suddenly, little holes of various sizes opened up above my forehead, and through them shone a beautiful, warm-colored light. In the glow, through the holes, I could see some women in white. Then there appeared another set of holes in a different arrangement for the women inside to look through, and yet another set without the light gleaming through. Finally I saw a white light.

[2] I was told that this was where the [spirits] who make up the area of the inner nose had their homes. They were of the female sex. I was also told that in the world of spirits, openings like these represent the clear-eyed perception of the women there. In heaven, spiritual qualities are represented by physical features, or rather by features of the world of spirits that resemble physical ones.

Later I was allowed to talk with them, and they said that these representative openings allowed them an accurate view of what was happening below. When the holes open, they are pointed at the communities these women are working to observe. Since the holes had just then been trained on me, the women said they could perceive all my individual thoughts and all the thoughts of anyone near me. In addition, they said they not only perceived my thoughts but also saw the thoughts represented to them in various ways. Thoughts stemming from a desire for goodness were portrayed as tongues of flame to match [the desire], and those stemming from a desire for truth as shifting light patterns. They added that they saw certain angelic communities with me and saw the thoughts of those communities [portrayed] as different-colored items—the deep red found in embroidered hangings, and rainbow patterns on a dark background. From this they perceived that the communities were from the area of the eye.

[3] Then other spirits appeared, who were thrown out of there and scattered this way and that. The women described them as spirits who wormed their way in among them in order to perceive things and see what was going on below, but with treacherous intentions. This kind of eviction was seen to occur whenever angel choruses arrived—with whom I also conversed. They said the spirits who had been ousted related to mucus in the nose, and that they were dull, stupid, shameless, and therefore entirely lacking in inner perception.

The matron mentioned above whom I had seen symbolized traitors of this kind, and I was given an opportunity to talk with them as well. They were surprised to hear that some people have conscience; they had absolutely no idea what a conscience was. I described it as an inner sense of what is good and true and the distress one feels in doing anything to violate that awareness. They did not understand. Such are the spirits who correspond to mucus that makes trouble in the nostrils and is therefore expelled.

[4] Then I was shown the radiance in which the women who relate to the inside of the nose live. It was a radiance beautifully streaked with veins of golden flame and silver light. Passion for goodness is represented by the veins of golden flame, and passion for truth, by the veins of silver light.

I was also shown that there are holes for them opening off to the side, through which they see a blue sky with stars. I was told that they have so much light in their private rooms that the noonday light of the world cannot compare. Several other things I was told: The warmth around them is like that of spring and summer on earth. They have with them little children, several years old. And they do not like to stay when the traitors—the "mucuses"—arrive.

Countless representations of this kind appear in the world of spirits. These were representations of the types of perception possessed by the women corresponding to the sense of smell inside the nose.

To continue with the perception-filled auras that turn into scents: **4628** They have as plain a smell as scents on earth but do not reach the senses of a person whose inner depths are closed. They enter by an inner rather than an outer route.

These scents have two sources: a perception of goodness and a perception of evil. Those that come from a perception of goodness are lovely, like the scents given off by a garden of sweet-smelling flowers and by other fragrant objects, so pleasantly and in such great variety that it cannot be expressed. These are the smells that surround heaven's inhabitants.

The smells that come from a perception of evil, on the other hand, are most unpleasant. They stink and reek like fetid water, excrement, and corpses, and have the bad odor of rats and household pests. These are the stenches that surround hell's inhabitants.

Amazingly, the spirits living with these smells do not notice how bad they are. In fact, the stenches are delightful to them. When surrounded by them, they are in their element, pleased and delighted. However, when hell opens and the air wafting out reaches good spirits, they are seized with horror and distress, like people on earth happening upon a cloud of rotten odors like these.

To report on all my experiences with perception-filled auras converted **4629** into smells would take pages. See my earlier remarks on the subject at §§1514, 1517, 1518, 1519, 1631, 3577, to which I may add just the following:

I once perceived the shared thought of many spirits concerning the Lord and his human birth, and sensed that it consisted of nothing but objections. (Everything spirits think as a group and individually is clearly perceived by others.) Their aura smelled like fetid water and like garbage water.

4630   One invisible spirit was present above my head. I could tell the spirit was there by the stink, which was like the loathsome smell of [rotten] teeth. Later I picked up a stench like that of burnt horn or bone. Then a great horde of such spirits arrived, surging up from below not far from my back—a whole cloud of them. Since these too were invisible, I figured they were very subtle, but evil. However, I was told that where the atmosphere is spiritual, they are invisible, and where it is earthly, they are visible. These are the types who are so engrossed in the earthly level that they never think about anything spiritual and do not believe in hell or heaven yet use subtlety in their business dealings. They are called the "earthly unseen" and are sometimes revealed to others by their stench, as described above.

4631   Two or three times the smell of a corpse also wafted to me, and when I asked from whom it came, I was told that it came from a hell of the vilest thieves and assassins and of criminals who acted with gross deceit. Sometimes I smelled excrement and on asking where it came from was told it came from a hell of adulterers. When I smelled a smell that mixed dung with corpses, I was told it came from a hell of adulterers who were also abusive. And so on.

4632   Once I was thinking about the way the soul regulates the body and the way will turns into act. A latrinelike hell was slightly ajar, and I sensed that the only things the spirits there were thinking about were the way the soul regulates the anus and the way the will to move one's bowels turns into act. This made clear what kind of perceptions and therefore what kind of stench filled the aura surrounding them. The same thing happened when I was thinking about marriage love; the spirits in an adulterers' hell were mulling over nothing but sordid, adulterous crimes. When I considered honesty, deceitful spirits thought only about fraud.

4633   The remarks about perception and about smells above show that everyone's life and therefore everyone's desire lies open in the other world. Those people are badly mistaken who think no one there knows what kind of person they have been or what sort of life they live as a result, and who believe they can cover up their true state of mind as they did in the world. Not only are the things we know about ourselves obvious there, so are the things we do not know—the things we return to so often that they are eventually swallowed up in our core pleasures, dropping out of sight and out of mind. The purposes we genuinely aim at in our thoughts, words, and deeds (which become hidden to us for the same reason) are easy to perceive in heaven. Heaven lives in an atmosphere of purposes and has a perception of them.

There will be more about correspondence with the universal human  at the end of the next chapter, where the topic is the correspondence of hearing and the ears [§§4652–4660].

[CONTINUED IN VOLUME 7]

Biographical Note

E MANUEL SWEDENBORG (1688–1772) was born Emanuel Swedberg (or Svedberg) in Stockholm, Sweden, on January 29, 1688 (Julian calendar). He was the third of the nine children of Jesper Swedberg (1653–1735) and Sara Behm (1666–1696). At the age of eight he lost his mother. After the death of his only older brother ten days later, he became the oldest living son. In 1697 his father married Sara Bergia (1666–1720), who developed great affection for Emanuel and left him a significant inheritance. His father, a Lutheran clergyman, later became a celebrated and controversial bishop, whose diocese included the Swedish churches in Pennsylvania and in London, England.

After studying at the University of Uppsala (1699–1709), Emanuel journeyed to England, the Netherlands, France, and Germany (1710–1715) to study and work with leading scientists in western Europe. Upon his return he apprenticed as an engineer under the brilliant Swedish inventor Christopher Polhem (1661–1751). He gained favor with Sweden's King Charles XII (1682–1718), who gave him a salaried position as an overseer of Sweden's mining industry (1716–1747). Although Emanuel was engaged, he never married.

After the death of Charles XII, Emanuel was ennobled by Queen Ulrika Eleonora (1688–1741), and his last name was changed to Swedenborg (or Svedenborg). This change in status gave him a seat in the Swedish House of Nobles, where he remained an active participant in the Swedish government throughout his life.

A member of the Royal Swedish Academy of Sciences, he devoted himself to studies that culminated in a number of publications, most notably a comprehensive three-volume work on natural philosophy and metallurgy (1734) that brought him recognition across Europe as a scientist. After 1734 he redirected his research and publishing to a study of anatomy in search of the interface between the soul and body, making several significant discoveries in physiology.

From 1743 to 1745 he entered a transitional phase that resulted in a shift of his main focus from science to theology. Throughout the rest of his life he maintained that this shift was brought about by Jesus Christ, who appeared to him, called him to a new mission, and opened his perception to a permanent dual consciousness of this life and the life after death.

He devoted the last decades of his life to studying Scripture and publishing eighteen theological titles that draw on the Bible, reasoning, and his own spiritual experiences. These works present a Christian theology with unique perspectives on the nature of God, the spiritual world, the Bible, the human mind, and the path to salvation.

Swedenborg died in London on March 29, 1772 (Gregorian calendar), at the age of eighty-four.